DOMESDAY BOOK

Gloucestershire

History from the Sources

DOMESDAY BOOK

A Survey of the Counties of England

LIBER DE WINTONIA

Compiled by direction of

KING WILLIAM I

Winchester
1086

DOMESDAY BOOK

General editor

JOHN MORRIS

15

Gloucestershire

edited and translated by
John S. Moore

PHILLIMORE
Chichester
1982

1982

Published by

PHILLIMORE & CO. LTD.,
London and Chichester

Head Office: Shopwyke Hall,
Chichester, Sussex, England

ISBN 0 85033 320 2 (case)
ISBN 0 85033 321 0 (limp)

Printed in Great Britain by
Titus Wilson & Son Ltd.,
Kendal

GLOUCESTERSHIRE

Introduction

The Domesday Survey of Gloucestershire

Appendix
Notes on text and translation
Index of Persons
Index of Places
Maps and Map Keys
Systems of Reference
Technical Terms

History from the Sources
General Editor: John Morris

The series aims to publish history
written directly from the sources
for all interested readers, both
specialists and others. The first
priority is to publish important
texts which should be widely
available, but are not.

DOMESDAY BOOK

The contents, with the folio on which each county begins, are:

Domesday Book is termed *Liber de Wintonia* (The Book of Winchester) in column 332c

INTRODUCTION

The Domesday Survey

In 1066 Duke William of Normandy conquered England. He was crowned King, and most of the lands of the English nobility were soon granted to his followers. Domesday Book was compiled 20 years later. The Saxon Chronicle records that in 1085

> at Gloucester at midwinter ... the King had deep speech with his counsellors ... and sent men all over England to each shire ... to find out ... what or how much each landholder held ... in land and livestock, and what it was worth ... The returns were brought to him.[1]

William was thorough. One of his Counsellors reports that he also sent a second set of Commissioners 'to shires they did not know, where they were themselves unknown, to check their predecessors' survey, and report culprits to the King.'[2]

The information was collected at Winchester, corrected, abridged, chiefly by omission of livestock and the 1066 population, and fair-copied by one writer into a single volume. Norfolk, Suffolk and Essex were copied, by several writers, into a second volume, unabridged, which states that 'the Survey was made in 1086'. The surveys of Durham and Northumberland, and of several towns, including London, were not transcribed, and most of Cumberland and Westmorland, not yet in England, was not surveyed. The whole undertaking was completed at speed, in less than 12 months, though the fair-copying of the main volume may have taken a little longer. Both volumes are now preserved at the Public Record Office. Some versions of regional returns also survive. One of them, from Ely Abbey,[3] copies out the Commissioners' brief. They were to ask

> The name of the place. Who held it, before 1066, and now?
> How many *hides*?[4] How many ploughs, both those in lordship and the men's?
> How many villagers, cottagers and slaves, how many free men and Freemen?[5]
> How much woodland, meadow and pasture? How many mills and fishponds?
> How much has been added or taken away? What the total value was and is?
> How much each free man or Freeman had or has? All threefold, before 1066,
> when King William gave it, and now; and if more can be had than at present?

The Ely volume also describes the procedure. The Commissioners took evidence on oath 'from the Sheriff; from all the barons and their Frenchmen; and from the whole Hundred, the priests, the reeves and six villagers from each village'. It also names four Frenchmen and four Englishmen from each Hundred, who were sworn to verify the detail.

The King wanted to know what he had, and who held it. The Commissioners therefore listed lands in dispute, for Domesday Book was not only a tax-assessment. To the King's grandson, Bishop Henry of Winchester, its purpose was that every 'man should know his right and not usurp another's'; and because it was the final authoritative register of rightful possession 'the natives called it Domesday Book, by analogy

---

[1] Before he left England for the last time, late in 1086. [2] Robert Losinga, Bishop of Hereford 1079-1095 (see *E.H.R.* 22, 1907, 74). [3] *Inquisitio Eliensis*, first paragraph. [4] A land unit, reckoned as 120 acres. [5] *Quot Sochemani.*

from the Day of Judgement'; that was why it was carefully arranged by Counties, and by landholders within Counties, 'numbered consecutively ... for easy reference'.6

Domesday Book describes Old English society under new management, in minute statistical detail. Foreign lords had taken over, but little else had yet changed. The chief landholders and those who held from them are named, and the rest of the population was counted. Most of them lived in villages, whose houses might be clustered together, or dispersed among their fields. Villages were grouped in administrative districts called Hundreds, which formed regions within Shires, or Counties, which survive today with minor boundary changes; the recent deformation of some ancient county identities is here disregarded, as are various short-lived modern changes. The local assemblies, though overshadowed by lords great and small, gave men a voice, which the Commissioners heeded. Very many holdings were described by the Norman term *manerium* (manor), greatly varied in size and structure, from tiny farmsteads to vast holdings; and many lords exercised their own jurisdiction and other rights, termed *soca*, whose meaning still eludes exact definition.

The Survey was unmatched in Europe for many centuries, the product of a sophisticated and experienced English administration, fully exploited by the Conqueror's commanding energy. But its unique assemblage of facts and figures has been hard to study, because the text has not been easily available, and abounds in technicalities. Investigation has therefore been chiefly confined to specialists; many questions cannot be tackled adequately without a cheap text and uniform translation available to a wider range of students, including local historians.

Previous Editions

The text has been printed once, in 1783, in an edition by Abraham Farley, probably of 1250 copies, at Government expense, said to have been £38,000; its preparation took 16 years. It was set in a specially designed type, here reproduced photographically, which was destroyed by fire in 1808. In 1811 and 1816 the Records Commissioners added an introduction, indices, and associated texts, edited by Sir Henry Ellis; and in 1861-1863 the Ordnance Survey issued zincograph facsimiles of the whole. Texts of individual counties have appeared since 1673, separate translations in the Victoria County Histories and elsewhere.

This Edition

Farley's text is used, because of its excellence, and because any worthy alternative would prove astronomically expensive. His text has been checked against the facsimile, and discrepancies observed have been verified against the manuscript, by the kindness of Miss Daphne Gifford of the Public Record Office. Farley's few errors are indicated in the notes.

6*Dialogus de Scaccario* 1,16.

The editor is responsible for the translation and lay-out. It aims at what the compiler would have written if his language had been modern English; though no translation can be exact, for even a simple word like 'free' nowadays means freedom from different restrictions. Bishop Henry emphasized that his grandfather preferred 'ordinary words'; the nearest ordinary modern English is therefore chosen whenever possible. Words that are now obsolete, or have changed their meaning, are avoided, but measurements have to be transliterated, since their extent is often unknown or arguable, and varied regionally. The terse inventory form of the original has been retained, as have the ambiguities of the Latin.

Modern English commands two main devices unknown to 11th century Latin, standardised punctuation and paragraphs; in the Latin, *ibi* ('there are') often does duty for a modern full stop, *et* ('and') for a comma or semi-colon. The entries normally answer the Commissioners' questions, arranged in five main groups, (i) the place and its holder, its hides, ploughs and lordship; (ii) people; (iii) resources; (iv) value; and (v) additional notes. The groups are usually given as separate paragraphs.

King William numbered chapters 'for easy reference', and sections within chapters are commonly marked, usually by initial capitals, often edged in red. They are here numbered. Maps, indices and an explanation of technical terms are also given. Later, it is hoped to publish analytical and explanatory volumes, and associated texts.

The editor is deeply indebted to the advice of many scholars, too numerous to name, and especially to the Public Record Office, and to the publisher's patience. The draft translations are the work of a team; they have been co-ordinated and corrected by the editor, and each has been checked by several people. It is therefore hoped that mistakes may be fewer than in versions published by single fallible individuals. But it would be Utopian to hope that the translation is altogether free from error; the editor would like to be informed of mistakes observed.

The maps are the work of John Moore, Frank Thorn and Jim Hardy.

The preparation of this volume has been greatly assisted by a generous grant from the Leverhulme Trust Fund.

This support, originally given to the late Dr. J. R. Morris, has been kindly extended to his successors. At the time of Dr. Morris's death in June 1977, he had completed volumes 2, 3, 11, 12, 19, 23, 24. He had more or less finished the preparation of volumes 13, 14, 20, 28. These and subsequent volumes in the series were brought out under the supervision of John Dodgson and Alison Hawkins, who have endeavoured to follow, as far as possible, the editorial principles established by John Morris.

Conventions

★   refers to note on discrepancy between MS and Farley text

[ ]   enclose words omitted in the MS   ( )   enclose editorial explanation

TEMPORE Regis EDWARDI reddebat ciuitas de Glowe
ceſtre.xxxvi.liƀ numeratas.7 xii.ſextaria mellis ad men
ſurā ejuſd burgi.7 xxxvi.dicras ferri.7 c.uirgas ferreas
ductiles ad clauos nauiū regis.7 quaſdā alias minutas con
ſuetudines in aula 7 in camera regis.

Modo reddit ipſa ciuitas regi.lx.liƀ.de.xx.in ora.

7 De moneta⁰hr̄ rex.xx.liƀ.

In dn̄ica terra regis teñ Rogeri⁹de berchelai unā domū
7 unā piſcariā in ipſa uilla.7 eſt extra manū regis.

Hanc Balduiñ tenuit.T.R.E.

Osƀn eps teñ terrā 7 manſiones quas Edmarus tenuit
redd.x.ſolid cū alia conſuetudine.

Gaufrid de Manneuile teñ.vi.manſioñ.Hæ T.R.E.reddƀ
vi.ſolid 7 viii.denar cū alia cſuetud.

Wiłłs baderon.ii.manſioñ.de.xxx.denar.

Wiłłs ſcriba.i.manſioñ teñ de.li.denar.

Rogeri⁹de Laci.i.manſioñ de.xxvi.denar.

Osƀn ep̄s.i.manſioñ de.xli.denar.

Berner.i.manſioñ de.xiiii.denar.

Wiłłs caluus.i.manſioñ de.xii.denar.

Durand uicecom.ii.manſioñ de.xiiii.deñ.

Iſd Durand teñ.i.manſioñ de.xxvi.deñ.

7 adhuc unā manſioñ quæ nullā cſuetud redd.Γretinet.

Hadeuuiñ teñ.i.mans.quæ dat gablū.ſed aliā cſuetud
Gosƀt⁹.i.manſione.Dunning.i.mans.Widard.i.mans.

GLOUCESTERSHIRE

Before 1066 the City of GLOUCESTER paid £36 at face value,
12 sesters of honey at that Borough's measure, 36 dickers of
iron, 100 drawn iron rods for nails for the King's ships, and
certain other petty customary dues in the hall and the King's
chamber.

Now the City itself pays to the King £60 at 20 (pence) to
the *ora*. The King has £20 from the mint.

2   Roger of Berkeley holds 1 house in the King's lordship land,
and 1 fishery in that town; it is outside the King's hands.
Baldwin held this before 1066.

3   Bishop Osbern holds the land and residences which Edmer held.
He pays 10s with another customary due.

4   Geoffrey de Mandeville holds 6 residences; before 1066 these
paid 6s 8d with another customary due.
William (son of) Baderon 2 residences at 30d.
William the Scribe holds 1 residence at 51d.
Roger of Lacy 1 residence at 26d.
Bishop Osbern 1 residence at 41d.
Berner 1 residence at 14d.
William the Bald 1 residence at 12d.
Durand the Sheriff 2 residences at 14d.
Durand also holds 1 residence at 26d, and 1 residence more,
which pays no customary due.
Hadwin holds 1 residence which gives rent but keeps back
another customary due.
Gosbert 1 residence, Dunning 1 residence, Widard 1 residence.

Arnulf⁹ pb̄r . I . mans̄ . quæ redđ gablū . 7 aliā c̄suet̄ retin̄.
Om̄s istæ mansiones reddeb̄ regalē c̄suetud̄ . T.R.E.
Modo Rex . W . nichil inde hr̄ . nec Rotb̄t⁹ minister ej⁹.
Iste mansion̄ fuer̄ in firma regis . E . die qua fuit uiuus
7 mortuus . Modo ů sunt ablatæ de firma 7 c̄suetuđ regis.
T.R.E. erat dn̄iū regis in ciuitate totū hospitatū . ł uestitū.
Q̄do comes W . ad firmā recep̄: similit̄ uestitū fuit.
Sedecī dom⁹ erant ubi sedet castellū . quæ modo desunt.
7 in Burgo ciuitatis sunt wastatæ . XIIII . domus.

CASTELLV̄ de *ESTRIGHOIEL* fecit Wilł̄s comes.
7 ejus tēpore reddeb̄ . XL . soł tantū de nauib⁹ in siluā euntib⁹.
Tēpore ů Rogerij com̄ filij ej⁹ . reddiđ ipsa uilla XVI . lib̄.
7 medietatē habeb̄ Rad̄ de Limesi . Modo hr̄ rex inde . XII . lib̄.
Int̄ redditionē de carleion . 7 I . carucā quæ ibi . ē 7 VII . pis
carias in Waie 7 Huscha: exeunt . VII . lib̄ 7 X . soliđ.
In *WALES* sunt . III . Harduices . Lamecare 7 poteschiuet 7 Dinan.
In his sunt . VIII . car̄ . 7 XI . uiłłi dimidij . 7 XV . borđ . cū . VI . car̄.
ꝑ his . III . harduicis: uoleb̄ habere . C . soliđ Roḡ de jurei.
Sub Wasuuic p̄posito sunt XIII . uillæ . Sub Elmui . XIIII.
uillæ . Sub Bleio sunt . XIII . uillæ . Sub Idhel sun̄t . XIIII . uillæ.
☞ Hi reddun̄t . XLVII . sextaria mellis . 7 XL . porc̄ . 7 XL . I . uaccās.
7 XXVIII . soliđ ꝑ accipitrib; . Tot̄ hoc uał . IX . lib̄ 7 X . soł . 7 IIII . den̄.
De una Wasta t̄ra . redđ Walt̄ balistari⁹ . I . sext̄ meł . 7 I . porc̄.
Berdic joculator regis hr̄ . III . uillas . 7 ibi . V . car̄ . nil redđ.
Morin⁹ . I . uillā . Chenesis . I . Fili⁹ Wasuuic . I . Sessisbert . I.
Abrahā pb̄r . II . uillas . Hi hn̄t . VI . car̄ . 7 nichil reddunt.
Hos misit . W . comes ad c̄suetuđ Grifin regis . licentia regis . W.
☞ Sub eisđ p̄positis sun̄t . IIII . uillæ wastatæ ꝑ regē Caraduech.

Arnulf the priest 1 residence, which pays rent; he keeps back another customary due.

All these residences paid the royal customary dues before 1066; now King William has nothing from them, nor Robert his officer. These residences were in King Edward's revenue on the day he was alive and dead; but now they have been taken away from the King's revenue and customary dues.

Before 1066 the King's lordship in the City supplied all lodging or clothing; when Earl William acquired it in the revenue it supplied the clothing likewise.

Where the Castle is sited there were 16 houses which do not exist now, and 14 houses in the Borough of the City have been destroyed.

S

1 Earl William built the Castle of CHEPSTOW and in his time paid only 40s from the ships going into the woodland. In the time of his son, Earl Roger, this town paid £16 and Ralph of Limesy had half. Now the King has £12 from it.

2 £7 10s comes from the payments of Caerleon, from 1 plough which is there, and from 7 fisheries in the Wye and the Usk.

W

1 In WALES there are 3 dairy farms, Llanvair (Discoed), Portskewett and Dinham. In these there are 8 ploughs;
11 half-villagers and 15 smallholders with 6 ploughs.
Roger of Ivry wanted to have 100s for these 3 dairy farms.

2 Under Waswic the reeve there are 13 villages, under Elmwy 14 villages, under Bleio 13 villages, under Iudhaël 14 villages.

† These pay 47 sesters of honey, 40 pigs, 41 cows and 28s for hawks. The value of the whole of this is £9 10s 4d.

3 Walter the Gunner pays 1 sester of honey and 1 pig for one waste land.

4 Berdic the King's Jester has 3 villages; 5 ploughs there. He pays nothing.
Morin 1 village, Kenesis 1, Waswic's son 1, Sessisbert 1, Abraham the priest 2 villages. They have 6 ploughs. They pay nothing.
Earl William transferred these men to King Gruffydd's customary dues by King William's permission.

(misplaced line, written at the foot of col. 162 a and directed to its proper place by transposition signs)

† Under these reeves are 4 villages destroyed by King Caradoc.

/ In elemoſina regis.ē una uilla.quæ ꝑ anima ej

redđ æcclæ ad feſť Ŝ Martini . 11 . porč . 7 c . panes cũ ceruiſia.

/ Ad sčm Michaelē . ē . 1 . carucata træ . 7 ad sčm Deuuiñ

una carucata . Hæ non redđt ſeruitiũ niſi sčis.

/ Vn̉ Beluard de Caruen hť dimiđ car træ . 7 nichil redđ.

/ Sexaginta 7 v1 . porci exeuɴ́ de paſnag . 7 apꝑciant

xL.1111.ſoł.H̄ om̄a reddť.xL.liƀ 7 x11.ſoł.7 v111.den̉.

Dᵘⁱᶜᵉᶜᵒᵐ urand deđ ħ ead Wiłło de Ow . ꝑ . Lv . liƀ ad firm̄a.

/ Walteri baliſtari ten de rege . 11 . carucat træ . 7 ibi hť

111.caŕ.7 111.ſeruos 7 111.ancillas.Vał ħ xx.ſoł.

/ Girard hť . 11 . caruc træ . 7 ibi . 11 . caŕ . Vał . xx . ſoł.

/ Ouus ꝑpoſit regis . 11 . caruc træ . 7 ibi . 1111 . caŕ . Vał . xx . ſoł.

Ibi . ē in dñio regis . 1 . caruc træ quã tenuit dagoƀť.

/ Gozelin brito ten . v . caruc træ in caroen . 7 ibi ſunt

.11.caŕ cũ.11.Walenſiƀ.Vał.xx.ſoł.

/ Eꝑs c̄ſtantienſis ten de rege . v . caruc træ . 7 de eo un̉ hõ ej.

Ibi ſunt.11.caŕ in dñio.7 111.uillanoɼ.Vał.xL.ſoł.

/ Roger de Berchelai ten . 11 . car træ ad Strigoielg

7 ibi hť . v1 . borđ cũ . 1 . caŕ . Vał xx . ſoł.

/ Dᵘⁱᶜᵉᵉ urand ten de rege In caroen . 1 . trã Caldecote.

Ibi hť in dñio . 111 . caŕ . 7 xv . dimiđ uiłłos . 7 1111 . ſeruos.

7 unũ milite . Hi om̄s hñt . x11 . caŕ . Ibi moliñ de . x . ſoliđ.

Hoc totũ uał . v1 . liƀ.

/ Wiłłs de Ow . hť de Strigoielg . 1x . liƀ ꝑ c̄ſuetuđ

ut dicit . Sed Girard 7 alij hões dñt nil plus haƀe

5   In the King's alms there is 1 village which pays to the Church
at Martinmas for his soul's sake 2 pigs, 100 loaves with ale.

6   To St. Michael's belongs 1 carucate of land and to St. Dewy's
1 carucate. These do not pay service except to the Saints.

7   Belward of Caerwent has ½ carucate of land. He pays nothing.

8   From pasturage come 66 pigs; they are assessed at 44s.
All these pay £40 12s 8d.
Durand the Sheriff gave them to William of Eu for £55 at
a revenue.

9   Walter the Gunner holds 2 carucates of land from the King and
has 3 ploughs and
    3 male and 3 female slaves.
Value of them, 20s.

10   Gerard has 2 carucates of land; 2 ploughs there.
Value 20s.

11   Ows the King's reeve (has) 2 carucates of land; 4 ploughs there.
Value 20s.
In the King's lordship 1 carucate of land which Dagobert held.

12   Jocelyn the Breton holds 5 carucates of land in Caerwent.
2 ploughs there, with 2 Welshmen.
Value 20s.

13   The Bishop of Coutances holds 5 carucates of land from the King,
and a man of his from him. 2 ploughs in lordship;
    3 villagers.
Value 40s.

14   Roger of Berkeley holds 2 carucates of land at Chepstow and has
    6 smallholders with 1 plough.
Value 20s.

15   Durand the Sheriff holds 1 land from the King in Caerwent named
Caldicot. He has in lordship 3 ploughs and
    15 half-villagers, 4 slaves and 1 man-at-arms;
      they all have 12 ploughs.
    A mill at 10s.
The value of the whole of this £6.

16   William of Eu has £9 from Chepstow for customary dues, as he states.
But Gerard and the other men state that he has nothing more lawfully

illũ juste de . x . lib̃ . de c̃suetuđ Strigoielg . etiã si app̃ciaret̃
In Wales . hť isđ . W . in feudo . III . piscarias ⸋ . c . lib̃.
in Waie . reddt . LXX . soliđ . 7 in eođ feudo deđ Witts
com̃ Rađ de Limesi . L . carucatas t̃ræ sic̃ fit in Normannia.
Hoc testant̃ Hugo 7 alii lib̃atores qđ ita Rađ c̃cessit.
Modo dic̃ . W . de ow . ñ se hab̃e de hac t̃ra nisi . XXX.II . car̃.
Ibi sunt in dñio . VIII . car̃ . 7 hoẽs hñt . XVI . car̃ . Ibi . II°.
molini de . x . sol . Tot̃ ual . XII . lib̃ 7 x . sol.
⸋ Rog̃ de Laci ten̄ in feudo de Strigoielg tant̃ t̃ræ
hospitatæ cũ uno molino . qđ ual . XXXVI . soliđ.
⸋ Turstin⁹ fili⁹ Rolf hť int̃ Huschã 7 Waiã . XVII.
carucas . De his sunt in dñio . IIII . 7 dimiđ . aliæ sun̄t hõum.
Ibi . XI . borđ sunt . 7 molin⁹ de . VII . soliđ . Val . IX . lib̃ tot̃.
De hac t̃ra . v . caruc̃ 7 dimiđ . calũniant̃ p̃positi regis.
dicentes qđ eas Turst̃ sine dono ^as^ ĩsũpsit.
Isđ Turstin⁹ hť . VI . caruc̃ t̃ræ ult̃ Huschã . 7 ibi hoẽs ej⁹
hñt . IIII . car̃ . 7 molin̄ređ xv . sol . 7 dimiđ piscaria
de . x . sol . Tot̃ ual . LIIII . sol 7 VI . den̄.
⸋ Alured⁹ hispan̄ hť in feudo . II . carucat̃ t̃ræ . 7 ibi . II . car̃
in dñio . ⸋ Isđ . A . hť jn Wales . VII . uillas . quæ fuer̃
Witti comitis 7 Rog̃ filij ej⁹ in dñio . Hæ reddt . VI . mett
sextaria . 7 VI . porc̃ . 7 x . soliđ.

162 c

BVRGṼ de *WINCELCVBE* reddeb̃ T . R . E . VI . lib̃
de firma . De his habeb̃ Herald⁹ com̃ . III . den̄ . ciũ . idest . XL . sol.
Postea ređ . XX . lib̃ cũ toto Hunđ ej⁹ uillæ . Durand⁹
uicecom̃ apposuit . c . sol . 7 Roger⁹ de Jurei . LX . soliđ.
Modo adjunctis . III . hunđ . ređ . XXVIII . lib̃ de xx^ti^ . in Ora.

from the £10 of the customary dues of Chepstow, even if it were assessed at £100.

In Wales William also has 3 fisheries in the Wye in (his) Holding; they pay 70s.

In the same Holding Earl William gave to Ralph of Limesy 50 carucates of land as is done in Normandy. Hugh and the others who transferred (the land) testified that he granted it to Ralph in this way. Now William of Eu states that he has only 32 carucates of this land. In lordship 8 ploughs. The men have 16 ploughs.

2 mills at 10s.

The value of the whole £12 10s.

17   Roger of Lacy holds in the Chepstow Holding as much populated land with 1 mill as is worth 36s.

18   Thurstan son of Rolf has 17 ploughs between the Usk and the Wye; of these 4½ are in lordship, and the others are the men's.

11 smallholders.

A mill at 7s.

The value of the whole £9.

The King's reeves claim 5½ carucates of this land, saying that Thurstan took them without a gift.

Thurstan also has 6 carucates of land beyond the Usk. His men have 4 ploughs.

A mill which pays 15s; ½ fishery at 10s.

The value of the whole 54s 6d.

19   Alfred of 'Spain' has 2 carucates of land in the Holding.

2 ploughs in lordship.

Alfred also has 7 villages in Wales, which were Earl William's and his son Roger's in lordship.

These pay 6 sesters of honey, 6 pigs and 10s.

B

1   The Borough of WINCHCOMBE paid £6 in revenue before 1066.   162 c
Of this Earl Harold had the third penny, that is, 40s. Later it paid £20, with the whole of the Hundred of this town. Durand the Sheriff added 100s, and Roger of Ivry 60s. Now, with the three adjoining Hundreds, it pays £28 at 20 (pence) to the *ora*.

.I. REX WILLELMVS.

.II. Archieps Eboracenfis.

.III Eps de Wireceftre.

.IIII. Eps de Hereforde.

.V. Eps de Execeftre.

.VI. Eps de S Laudo.

.VII. Æccla de Bade.

.VIII Abbatia de Glaftingbie.

.IX. Abbatia de Malmesbie.

.X. Abbatia de Glouuceftre.

.XI. Abbatia de Wincelcube.

.XII. Abbatia de Euefham.

.XIII Abbatia de Abendone.

.XIIII Abbatia de Perfore.

.XV. Abbatia de Couentreu.

.XVI. Abbatia de Cormelies.

.XVII Abbatia de Lire.

.XVI. Abbatia de Eglefham.

.XIX Abbatia de Weftmonaft.

.XX. Æccla S Dionifij parifij.

.XXI Æccla de Lanheig.

.XXII Æccla S Ebrulfi.

.XXIII Æccla S kinitat cadomens.

.XXII. Æccla de Troarz.

.XXV. Eccla de Cireceftre.

.XXVI Renbaldus pbr.

.XXVI. Comes Rogerius.

.XXVI. Comes Hugo.

.XXIX Comes Moritonienfis.

.XXX Giflebtus maminoth. eps Lifiaefis.

.XXXI. Willelmus de Ow.

.XXXII. Wills filius Baderon.

.XXXII. Wills camerarius.

.XXXII. Wills goizenboded.

.XXXV. Wills filius Widon.

.XXXVI. Wills froiffeleuu.

.XXXVII. Wills filius Norman.

.XXXVI. Wills Leuric.

.XXXIX. Rogerius de Laci.

.XL. Rogerius de Belmont.

.XLI. Rogerius de Juri.

.XLII. Rogerius de Berchelai.

.XLIII. Radulfus frater ej.

.XLIIII. Radulfus Pagenel.

.XLV. Radulfus de Todeni.

.XLVI. Robtus de Todeni.

.XLVII. Robtus Difpenfator.

.XLVIII Robertus de Oilgi.

.XLIX. Ricardus Legatus.

.L. Osbernus Gifard.

.LI. Goisfrid orleteile.

.LII. Giflebt fili Turold.

.LIII. Durand uicecomes.

.LIIII. Drogo filius ponz.

.LV. Walteri filius ponz.

.LVI. Walterius filius Rog.

.LVII. Walterius Diacon.

.LVIII. Walterius baliftari.

.LIX. Henric d Ferieres.

.LX. Ernulf de Hefding.

.LXI. Heraldus fili Rad.

.LXII. Hugo de Grentemaifn.

.LXIII. Hugo Lafne.

.LXII. Milo crifpin.

.LXV. Vrfo de Abetot.

.LXVI. Hafcoit mufard.

.LXVII. Turftin fili Rolf.

.LXVII Ansfrid de Cormel.

.LXIX Hunfrid camerari.

.LXX. Hunfrid de Medehalle.

.LXXI. Hunfrid coquus.

.LXXII. Sigar de Cioches.

.LXXII Maci de Mauritanie.

.LXXII. Gozelin brito.

.LXXV. Rogeri fili Radulfi.

.LXXVI. Vxor Geri.

.LXXVII Balduinus.

.LXXVII Elfi 7 alij taini regis.

162 c

LIST OF LANDHOLDERS IN GLOUCESTERSHIRE

1 King William	39 Roger of Lacy
2 The Archbishop of York	40 Roger of Beaumont
3 The Bishop of Worcester	41 Roger of Ivry
4 The Bishop of Hereford	42 Roger of Berkeley
5 The Bishop of Exeter	43 Ralph his brother
6 The Bishop of St. Lô	44 Ralph Pagnell
7 Bath Church	45 Ralph of Tosny
8 Glastonbury Abbey	46 Robert of Tosny
9 Malmesbury Abbey	47 Robert the Bursar
10 Gloucester Abbey	48 Robert d'Oilly
11 Winchcombe Abbey	49 Richard the Commissioner
12 Evesham Abbey	50 Osbern Giffard
13 Abingdon Abbey	51 Geoffrey Orlateile
14 Pershore Abbey	52 Gilbert son of Thorold
15 Coventry Abbey	53 Durand the Sheriff
16 Cormeilles Abbey	54 Drogo son of Poyntz
17 Lyre Abbey	55 Walter son of Poyntz
18 Eynsham Abbey	56 Walter son of Roger
19 Westminster Abbey	57 Walter the Deacon
20 St. Denis' Church, Paris	58 Walter the Gunner
21 Lambeth Church	59 Henry of Ferrers
22 St. Evroul's Church	60 Arnulf of Hesdin
23 Holy Trinity Church, Caen	61 Harold son of Ralph
24 Troarn Church	62 Hugh of Grandmesnil
25 Cirencester Church	63 Hugh Donkey
26 Reinbald the Priest	64 Miles Crispin
27 Earl Roger	65 Urso of Abetot
28 Earl Hugh	66 Hascoit Musard
29 The Count of Mortain	67 Thurstan son of Rolf
30 Gilbert Maminot, Bishop of Lisieux	68 Ansfrid of Cormeilles
31 William of Eu	69 Humphrey the Chamberlain
32 William son of Baderon	70 Humphrey of Maidenhill
33 William the Chamberlain	71 Humphrey Cook
34 William Goizenboded	72 Sigar of Chocques
35 William son of Guy	73 Matthew of Mortagne
36 William Breakwolf	74 Jocelyn the Breton
37 William son of Norman	75 Roger son of Ralph
38 William Leofric	76 Gerwy's wife
	77 Baldwin
	78 Alfsi and others of the King's Thanes

TERRA REGIS.

Rex Edward tenuit *CHINTENEHA*. Ibi erant . VIII . hidæ 7 dim.
Ad æcclā ptin . I . hiđ 7 dim . Reinbald teñ eam.

In dñio . erant . III . car . 7 xx . uilli 7 x . borđ 7 VII . ſerui . cū . XVIII .
car . Prōri . II . car . Ibi . II . molini de . XI . ſol 7 VIII . denar.
Huic ⋒ accreuit p̃poſit regis . W . duos borđ 7 IIII . uillos
7 III . molinos . Hoᵹ . II . ſunt regis . tcius p̃poſiti . 7 I . car plus . ē ibi.
T.R.E . redđƀ . IX . liƀ 7 v . ſol . 7 ter mille panes canibᵹ.
Modo redđ . xx . liƀ . 7 xx . uaccas . 7 xx . porc . 7 XVI . ſol ꝓ panib.

In *BERTVNE* habuit rex . E . nouē hiđ . De his eraǥ . VII . in dñio.
7 ibi . III . car . 7 XIIII . uilli 7 x . borđ cū . IX . car . Ibi . VII . ſerui.
De hoc ⋒ teñ II . libi hões . II . hiđ . 7 hñt ibi . IX . car . Ipſi ſe
ñ poſſunt | trā ſeparare a Manerio . Ibi moliñ de . IIII . ſoliđ.
P̃poſit . W . regis accreuit . VIII . borđ 7 II . molinos . 7 I . carucā.
T.R.E . reddeƀ . IX . liƀ . 7 v . ſoliđ . 7 ter mille panes canibᵹ.
Modo redđ . xx . liƀ . xx . uaccas . xx . porc . 7 ꝓ panib . XVI . ſol.

⌐ De hoc ⋒ preſtitit Ældred archieƥs . I . mēbrū *BREWERE*.
Ibi ſunt . III . uirg træ . 7 III . hões . Milo criſpin tenet.

⌐ Alter mēbrū nōe *OPTVNE* preſtitit Aluui uicecom . Ibi
una hida træ . 7 ibi ſunt . IIII . hões . Hunfrid teñ.

⌐ Terciū mēbrū nōe *MERWEN* preſtitit iſđ Aluui . Ibi ſunt
III . uirg træ . Nigell medicus tenet.

IN *DVDESTAN HVND* habuit q̃đā taiñ Edmær . III . maner.
Herſefel . 7 Athelai 7 Sanher . Iſte hō poterat dare 7 uende trā
ſuā cui uoluiſſet . ꝓ . II . hiđ ſe defdƀ h̄ tra . In dñio erant
VIII . car . 7 IIII . uilli 7 IIII . borđ . 7 xxx . ſerui . cū . v . car.
Ibi p̃tū ſufficienᵹS carucis.

In *HERSECOME* teneƀ Wiflet . III . uirg træ . libas ſīc 7 Edmer.
Ibi habeƀ . II . car . 7 II . borđ . 7 v . ſeruos . 7 prata carrucis.

[In CHELTENHAM Hundred]
1 King Edward held CHELTENHAM. There were 8½ hides. 1½ hides
belong to the Church; Reinbald holds them. In lordship there
were 3 ploughs;
> 20 villagers, 10 smallholders and 7 slaves with 18 ploughs;
> > the priests, 2 ploughs.
> 2 mills at 11s 8d.
> King William's reeve added to this manor 2 smallholders, 4
> villagers and 3 mills; two of them are the King's, the third
> the reeve's; 1 more plough there.
> Before 1066 it paid £9 5s, and 3000 loaves for dogs; now it
> pays £20, 20 cows, 20 pigs and 16s for bread.

[In DUDSTONE Hundred]
2 In '(Kings) BARTON' King Edward had 9 hides; 7 of them were
in lordship; 3 ploughs there;
> 14 villagers and 10 smallholders with 9 ploughs. 7 slaves.
> > 2 free men hold 2 hides of this manor and have 9 ploughs; they
> > cannot separate themselves nor their land from the manor.
> A mill at 4s.
> King William's reeve added 8 smallholders, 2 mills and 1 plough.
> Before 1066 it paid £9 5s, and 3000 loaves for dogs; now it pays
> £20, 20 cows, 20 pigs and 16s for bread.
> Archbishop Aldred leased one member of this manor, BRAWN.
> 3 virgates of land; 3 men. Miles Crispin holds it.
> Alwin the Sheriff leased another member named UPTON
> (St. Leonards). 1 hide of land; 4 men. Humphrey holds it.
> Alwin also leased a third member named MURRELLS (End).
> 3 virgates of land. Nigel the doctor holds it.

In DUDSTONE Hundred
3 A thane, Edmer, had 3 manors, HARESFIELD, (Down) HATHERLEY
and SANDHURST. This man could give or sell his land to whom he
would. This land answered for 2 hides. In lordship there were 8
ploughs;
> 4 villagers, 4 smallholders and 30 slaves with 5 ploughs.
> Meadow sufficient for the ploughs.

4 In HARESCOMBE Wiflet held 3 virgates of land, free, like Edmer.
He has 2 ploughs and
> 2 smallholders and 5 slaves.
> Meadows for the ploughs.

In Bʀᴏsᴛᴏʀᴘ tenuit Aluric . ɪɪɪ . uirǵ trǽ.

hic habeƀ ɪɪ . car̊ . 7 uñ uiƚƚm . ɪɪɪ . borđ . ɪɪɪɪ . feruos.

Has . ᴠ . tras abſtulit Herald poſt morte̅ regis . ᴇ.

Has eafđ Rog̊ de Jurei pofuit ad firma̅ ꝑ. xʟᴠɪ . liƀ . 7 xɪɪɪ . fot.

In eođ HVNĐ juxta ciuitate̅ habuit Vluuard dimiđ hiđa̅.

de rege . ᴇ . đeta̅ . 7 ibi . ɪɪ . car̊ 7 ɪɪɪɪ . ferui.

Hanc deđ . ᴡ . com̅ cuiđa̅ coquo fuo . Vluuard eni̅ vtlag fact . e̅.

In Cɪʀᴇᴄᴇsᴛʀᴇ HĐ habuit rex . ᴇ . ᴠ̃ . hiđ trǽ.

Ibi in dñio . ᴠ . car̊ . 7 xxxɪ . uiƚƚm cu̅ . x . car̊ . Ibi . xɪɪɪ . ferui.

7 x . borđ 7 ɪɪɪ . molini de . xxx . foliđ . 7 Prata . 7 ɪɪ . filuas de . ʟ . fot.

7 ibi . ɪɪ . liƀi hōes . ɪɪ . car̊ hn̅tes . Lana̅ ouiu̅ regina habeƀ.

ᴛ.ʀ.ᴇ . reddeƀ hoc M̅ . ɪɪɪ . modios frum̅ti 7 dimiđ . 7 braifi . ɪɪɪ . mođ.

7 meƚƚ . ᴠɪ . fextar̊ 7 dimiđ . 7 ɪx . liƀ . 7 ᴠ . fot . 7 ter mille pan̅ canib̅.

Modo redđ . xx . liƀ . 7 ᴠ . fot . xx . uaccas . xx . porc̊ . 7 ꝑ pan̅ . xᴠɪ . fot.

7 De nouo foro . xx . fot . quoꝫ h̅ꞇ S Mᴀʀɪᴀ tciu̅ den̅.

In Cireceſtre uñ liƀ hō teneƀ . ɪɪ . hiđ trǽ . 7 reddeƀ . xx . fot in

firma . 7 p tota̅ Anglia̅ uicecomiti feruitiu̅ faciebat.

Wiƚƚs com̅ hanc tra̅ mifit ext firma̅ . 7 cuiđa̅ fuo hōi deđ ea̅.

In SᴠɪɴHᴇᴠᴇ HĐ . erant ᴛ.ʀ.ᴇ . ad firma̅ . xxxᴠɪ . hidǽ in

ʙᴇᴛᴠɴᴇ . cu̅ . ɪɪ . me̅bris Wapelei 7 Wintreborne.

In dñio erant . ᴠ . car̊ . 7 xʟɪ . uiƚƚs . 7 xxɪx . borđ . cu̅ . xʟᴠ . car̊.

Ibi . xᴠɪɪɪ . ferui . cu̅ . ɪ . molino.

Hoc M̅ ᴛ.ʀ.ᴇ . reddeƀ firma̅ uni̅ noctis . 7 m̊ fimilit facit.

In SᴀʟᴇMᴀɴᴇsʙᴇʀɪᴇ HĐ tenuit . ᴇ . rex Sᴄʟᴏsᴛʀᴇ.

Ibi erant . ᴠɪɪ . hidǽ . 7 In dñio . ɪɪɪ . car̊ . 7 ɪx . uiƚƚi 7 xɪ . borđ

cu̅ . ᴠɪɪɪ . car̊ . Ibi . ᴠɪɪ . ferui . 7 ɪɪ . molini de una marka arg̅ti.

Prata de . x . fot . 7 de una ex his hiđ . x . foliđ . 7 canibꝫ . ᴠ . foliđ.

163 a

De hoc M̅ reddeƀ qđ uoleƀ uicecom̅ ᴛ.ʀ.ᴇ . Idō nefciun̅ apꝓciari.

Modo uicecom̅ Accreu̅ ibi . ɪ . car̊ . 7 ᴠ . borđ cu̅ . ɪ . car̊.

Redđ nc̅ de M̅ ipfo 7 de hund . xxᴠɪɪ . liƀ . ad numeru̅.

5   In BROOKTHORPE Aelfric held 3 virgates of land. He had 2 ploughs and
    1 villager, 3 smallholders and 4 slaves.

Earl Harold took away these five lands after King Edward's death.
Roger of Ivry placed them in the revenue at £46 13s 4d.

6   In the same Hundred near the City Wulfward held ½ hide from
King Edward, exempt. 2 ploughs there; 4 slaves.
    Earl William gave it to a cook of his, for Wulfward was made
an outlaw.

In CIRENCESTER Hundred
7   King Edward had 5 hides of land. In lordship 5 ploughs;
    31 villagers with 10 ploughs. 13 slaves; 10 smallholders.
    3 mills at 30s; meadows and 2 woods at 5s.
    2 free men who have 2 ploughs. The Queen had the sheep's wool.
Before 1066 this manor paid 3½ measures of wheat, 3 measures of
malt, 6½ sesters of honey, £9 5s, and 3000 loaves for dogs; now it
pays £20 5s, 20 cows, 20 pigs and 16s for bread. From the new
market 20s, of which St. Mary('s Church) has the third penny.

8   In CIRENCESTER a free man held 2 hides of land and paid 20s in
revenue, and served the Sheriff through the whole of England.
Earl William put this land out of the revenue and gave it to one
of his men.

In SWINEHEAD Hundred
9   Before 1066 there were in the revenue 36 hides in BITTON, with
its two members, WAPLEY and WINTERBOURNE. In lordship there
were 5 ploughs;
    41 villagers and 29 smallholders with 45 ploughs.
    18 slaves with 1 mill.
Before 1066 this manor paid one night's revenue; now it does
likewise.

In SALMONSBURY Hundred
10 King Edward held (Lower) SLAUGHTER. There were 7 hides.
In lordship 3 ploughs;
    9 villagers and 11 smallholders with 8 ploughs.
    7 slaves; 2 mills at 1 mark of silver; meadows at 10s.
    From one of these hides 10s, and 5s for dogs.
Before 1066 the Sheriff paid from this manor what he wished,   163 a
therefore they do not know what it is assessed at; now the
Sheriff has added 1 plough and 5 smallholders with 1 plough.
He now pays from this manor and the Hundred £27 at face value.

In *WESBERIE*.xxx.hidæ.Ibi habeƀ.E.rex.v.car̄
in dn̄io.7 xxxii.uiłłos 7 xv.borƌ cū xxviii.car̄.
Ibi.i.feruus.

Hoc Ꝏ reddeƀ unā noɗē de firma.T.R.E.Similiꝉ T.R.W:
p̄.iiii.annos.Poftea ablatæ funt de ifto Ꝏ.vi.hidæ
In chire.7 in Cliftone.x.hidæ.In Noent 7 Chingeftune.
viii.hiƌ.In Ladeuent.i.hiƌ.

Has tras ten m̄ abƀ de Cormelijs.7 Osƀn̄ 7 Witłs.f.Ricardi.
7 tam̄ de remanenti inuen̄ uicecom̄ totā firmam.

Dn̄t auꞇ hões de comitatu qƌ Sapina jacuit in Wef
berie ad firmā regis.E.

In *CHEFTESIHAT* hƌ tenuit.E.rex *LANGEBERGE*.
cū uno mēbro nōe *MENE*.In utroꝗ erant.viii.hidæ.
In dn̄io.iii.car̄.7 x.uitti 7 iiii.borƌ cū.vi.car̄.7 molin̄
de.v.foł.7 vi.ferui.Pratū de.x.foł.

T.R.E.reddeƀ uicecom̄ de hoc Ꝏ qƌ exibat ad firmā.
Modo redƌ.xv.liƀ.cū.ii.hunƌ quos ibi uicec̄ appofuit.

In *BLITESLAV* hƌ tenuit.E.rex *AVRE*.Ibi.v.hidæ.
7 in dn̄io.i.car̄.7 xii.uitti 7 viii.borƌ cū.xiiii.car̄.Ibi
un̄ feruus.7 molin̄ de.xxx.denar̄.7 falina de.xxx.fūmis.
falis.7 Æccła cū.i.uirǥ træ.

Hoc Ꝏ reddeƀ dimiƌ firmā noɗis.T.R.E 7 m̄ fimiliꝉ facit.
De eoƌ Ꝏ jacet waftata dimiƌ hida.7 idō n̄ redƌ nifi
.xii.liƀ.Vicecom̄ tam̄ redƌ totā firmā.

Extra Ꝏ funt.iii.mēbra quæ fēp in eo fueꝛ.7 effe debeꝗ
ut teftant̄ hões de comitatu.Id eft Peritone.Etefłau.Blitefłau.
In his funt.vii.hidæ.7 in dn̄io.i.car̄.7 xx.uitti 7 iii.borƌ
cū.xiii.car̄.7 ii.ferui.7 pifcaria.

Peritone.ē.in feudo Witłi comitis.Etelau.ten̄ Roǥ de berchelai.
Blitefłau ten̄ Witłs fili baderon.Aluui uicecom̄ mifit ħ exꞇ firm̄.

[In WESTBURY Hundred]

11 In WESTBURY (on Severn) 30 hides. King Edward had 5 ploughs in lordship, and
  32 villagers and 15 smallholders with 28 ploughs. 1 slave.
Before 1066 this manor paid one night's revenue; likewise for 4 years after 1066.
  Later 6 hides in KYRE were taken from this manor; and in CLIFTON (on Teme) 10 hides; in NEWENT and KINGSTONE 8 hides; in EDVIN (Loach) 1 hide. The Abbot of Cormeilles, Osbern and William sons of Richard, now hold these lands; however the Sheriff finds the whole revenue from the remainder. The men of the County state, however, that the fir-wood lay in Westbury in King Edward's revenue.

In KIFTSGATE Hundred

12 King Edward held (Upper) CLOPTON with a member named MEON. There were 8 hides in each. In lordship 3 ploughs;
  10 villagers and 4 smallholders with 6 ploughs.
  A mill at 5s; 6 slaves; meadow at 10s.
Before 1066 the Sheriff paid to the revenue what came from this manor; now, with the two Hundreds which the Sheriff has placed there, it pays £15.

In BLEDISLOE Hundred

13 King Edward held AWRE. 5 hides. In lordship 1 plough;
  12 villagers and 8 smallholders with 14 ploughs.
  1 slave; a mill at 30d; a salt-house at 30 packloads of salt;
    a church with 1 virgate of land.
Before 1066 this manor paid half a night's revenue; now it does likewise. Of this manor ½ hide lies waste and therefore it pays nothing but £12. The Sheriff, however, pays the whole revenue.
  Outside the manor there are three members which were always and should be in it, as the men of the County testify; they are PURTON, ETLOE and BLEDISLOE. 7 hides in them. In lordship 1 plough;
  20 villagers and 3 smallholders with 13 ploughs; 2 slaves.
  A fishery.
PURTON is in Earl William's Holding. Roger of Berkeley holds ETLOE. William son of Baderon holds BLEDISLOE. Alwin the Sheriff placed them out of the revenue.

In *LANGELEI*| tenuit Herald ᴴᵛᴺᴰ' *ALWESTAN*. Ibi erant. x. hidæ.

In dñio . ɪ . car.7 xxiii . uilli 7 v . borð cū . xxii . car.7 ii . ſerui.

Ibi ꝑpoſit accreuit . ii .car.7 v .ſeruos . Redð . xii . liƀ ad penſū.

IN BERCHELAI habuit. E.rex.v.hið.7 in dñio.v.car.

7 xx . uilli 7 v . borð cū . xi . car.7 ix . ſerui.7 ii . molini

de . xii . ſolið . Ibi . x . radcheniſtres . hñtes . vii . hið.7 vii . car.

Ibi uñ forū in quó maneƱ . xvii . hões.7 reddt censū in firma.

Hæ *BEREW* ptiñ ad *BERCHELAI*.

In Hilla . iiii . hide . In Almintune . iiii . hidæ . In Hinetune

iiii . hidæ . In Camma . vi . hidæ.7 aliæ xi . hidæ . In Goſintune

iiii . hidæ . In Derſilege . iii . hidæ . In Couelege . iiii . hidæ.

In Euuelege . ii . hidæ . In Nimdesfelle . iii . hidæ . In Vutune

xv . hidæ 7 dimið v . In Simondeſhale dimið hida.

In Chingeſcote . iiii . hidæ 7 dimið . In Beureſtane . x . hidæ.

In Oſleuuorde dimið hida . In Almodeſberie . ii . hidæ.

In Horefelle . viii . hidæ . In Weſtone . vii . hidæ 7 una v.

In Eldbertone . v . hide . In Cromale . ii . hidæ . In Erlingehā

ix . hidæ . In Eſceleuuorde . iii . hidæ.

Hæc ſuꝑdicta mēbra oīa ptinent ad Berchelai.

Int totū.

In his.T.R.E.in dñio . xlix . car 7 dimið.7 cc.xl.ii . uilli.

7 cxl.ii . borð . cū . c.xxvi . car . Ibi . cxx.vii . ſerui.

Ibi . xix . liƀi hões Radcheniſt . hñtes . xlviii . car . cū ſuis hōiƀ.

Ibi xxii . coliƀti.7 xv . ancillæ.

Ibi . viii . molini de . l.vii . ſol 7 vi . denar.

163 b

In iſto cō tenuer . ii . frs T.R.E. in *CROMHAL* . v . hidas.

hñtes in dñio . ii . car .7 vi . uill.7 v . borð hñtes . vi . car.

Hi . ii . frs cū tra ſua ſe poteraƱ uertere quo uolebaƱ.

Tc Valeƀ . iiii . liƀ . m . iii . liƀ . Hos . W . com cōmdauit

ꝑpoſito de berchelai ; ut eoᷓ habet ſeruitiū . ſic dic Roger.

In LANGLEY Hundred

14 Earl Harold held ALVESTON. There were 10 hides. In lordship
1 plough;
  23 villagers and 5 smallholders with 22 ploughs; 2 slaves.
  The reeve added 2 ploughs and 5 slaves.
It pays £12 by weight.

[In BERKELEY Hundred]

15 King Edward had 5 hides in BERKELEY. In lordship 5 ploughs;
  20 villagers and 5 smallholders with 11 ploughs; 9 slaves.
  2 mills at 12s.
  10 riding men who have 7 hides and 7 ploughs.
  A market in which 17 men live and pay dues to the revenue.

These outliers belong to BERKELEY:
  in HILL 4 hides; in ALKINGTON 4 hides; in HINTON 4 hides;
in CAM 6 hides and another 11 hides; in GOSSINGTON 4 hides;
in DURSLEY 3 hides; in COALEY 4 hides; in ULEY 2 hides; in
NYMPSFIELD 3 hides; in WOTTON (under Edge) 15 hides and
½ virgate; in SYMONDS HALL ½ hide; in KINGSCOTE 4½ hides;
in BEVERSTONE 10 hides; in OZLEWORTH ½ hide; in
ALMONDSBURY 2 hides; in HORFIELD 8 hides; in KINGSWESTON
7 hides and 1 virgate; in ELBERTON 5 hides; in CROMHALL
('Abbots') 2 hides; in ARLINGHAM 9 hides; in ASHLEWORTH
3 hides.
All these said members belong to BERKELEY. In total there
were in them before 1066 49½ ploughs in lordship;
  242 villagers and 142 smallholders with 126 ploughs.
    127 slaves. 19 free men, riding men, who have 48 ploughs
    with their men. 22 freedmen and 15 female slaves.
  8 mills at 57s 6d.

16 In this manor two brothers held 5 hides before 1066 in   163 b
CROMHALL ('Lygon'); they have 2 ploughs in lordship;
  6 villagers and 5 smallholders who have 6 ploughs.
  These two brothers could turn with their land where they
  would.
The value was then £4; now £3.
  Earl William assigned these men to the reeve of Berkeley,
so that he might have their service, as Roger states.

De hoc M̄ cū oīibʒ ad eū ꝑtinentibʒ . redd̄ Rogeri⁹
ad firmā . CLXX . liƀ . arſas 7 penſatas.

★ Ipſe Rogeri⁹ hŧ de tra huj⁹ M̄ in Heſlinbruge . I . hid̄.
Ad Claenhangare . I . hid̄ . Ad hirſlege . I . hid̄ . Ad Neueton
VII . hid̄ . Ibi ſunt in dn̄io . X . car̄ . 7 XIII . uiŧŧi 7 XXI . bord̄.
cū . XXII . car̄ . Ibi . XVI . ſerui . 7 Moliñ de . V . ſolid̄.
Toŧ . T.R.E . ualƀ . IX . liƀ . Modo . XI . liƀ 7 X . ſolid̄.
Iſd̄ Rogeri⁹ ten tr̄a Bernardi pƀri . V . hid̄ . Ibi hŧ . III . car̄.
7 II . uiŧŧos . 7 VI . bord̄ . cū . V . car̄ . Val 7 ualuit . LX . ſol.
In NESSE ſunt . V . hidæ ꝑtinent ad Berchelai . q̄s
W . cōm miſit ext ad faciendū uñ caſtellulū . h Roger⁹
In EDREDESTANE hd̄ tenuit Eddid regina ∫ calūniaŧ.
MERESFELDE . Ibi . XIIII . hidæ . In dn̄io . V . car̄ . 7 XXXVI.
uiŧŧi 7 XIII . bord̄ cū . XXX . car̄ . Ibi . XVIII . ſerui.
Pƀr hŧ unā ex his hid̄.
T.R.E . reddƀ . XXXV . liƀ . Modo . XLVII . liƀ.
In BERTVNE apud BRISTOV erant . VI . hid̄ . In dn̄io
III . car̄ . 7 XXII . uiŧŧi 7 XXV . bord̄ cū . XX.V . car̄ . Ibi . IX.
ſerui . 7 XVIII . coliƀti . hñtes . XIIII . car̄ . Ibi . II . molini
de . XX . ſolid̄ . Q̄do Roger⁹ receꝑ hoc M̄ de rege ꞓ inueñ
ibi . II . hid̄ 7 II . car̄ . in dn̄io . 7 XVII . uiŧŧi 7 XXIIII . bord̄
cū . XXI . car̄ . Ibi . IIII . ſeruos . 7 XIII . coliƀtos cū . III . car̄.
In uno mēbro ejd̄ M̄ Manegodeſfelle . VI . boucs in dn̄io.
De ead̄ tr̄a . ten æccŧa de Briſtou . III . hid̄ . 7 I . car̄ habeŧ ibi.
Vñ Radcheniſt ten . I . hid̄ . 7 hŧ . I . car̄ . 7 IIII . bord̄ cū . I . car̄.
Hoc M̄ 7 BRISTOV reddŧ regi . C 7 X . mark̄ argenti.
Burgenſes dn̄t qd̄ eꝑs . G . hŧ XXXIII . mark̄ argenti
7 unā mark̄ auri . ꝑter firmā regis.
In BRADELEI hd̄ . habuʼt Balduin⁹ . f . Heɪluini M̄
uñ in quo erant . X . hidæ . Hoc M̄ tenuit eꝑs baioꞓſis.
m̊ eſt in manu regis & geldat . Ibi ſunt in dn̄io . II . car̄.

From this manor with all that belongs to it Roger pays to the revenue £170 assayed and weighed.

17 Roger himself has of this manor's land 2 hides in SLIMBRIDGE, 1 hide at CLINGRE, 1 hide at HURST, 7 hides at NEWINGTON (Bagpath). In lordship 10 ploughs;
13 villagers and 21 smallholders with 22 ploughs.
16 slaves; a mill at 5s.
The value of the whole before 1066 £9; now £11 10s.

18 Roger also holds the land of Bernard the priest. 5 hides.
He has 3 ploughs and
2 villagers and 6 smallholders with 5 ploughs.
The value is and was 60s.

19 In SHARPNESS 5 hides which belong to Berkeley, which Earl William placed outside to build a small castle. Roger claims them.

In EDDERSTONE Hundred
20 Queen Edith held MARSHFIELD. 14 hides. In lordship 5 ploughs;
36 villagers and 13 smallholders with 30 ploughs. 18 slaves.
A priest has one of these hides.
Before 1066 it paid £35; now £47.

[In SWINEHEAD Hundred]
21 In 'BARTON (Regis)' at Bristol there were 6 hides. In lordship 3 ploughs;
22 villagers and 25 smallholders with 25 ploughs. 9 slaves and
18 freedmen who have 14 ploughs.
2 mills at 27s.
When Roger acquired this manor from the King he found there 2 hides and 2 ploughs in lordship;
17 villagers and 24 smallholders with 21 ploughs. 4 slaves
and 13 freedmen with 3 ploughs.
In MANGOTSFIELD, a member of this manor, 6 oxen in lordship.
Bristol Church holds 3 hides of the same land; 1 plough is recorded there.
1 riding man holds 1 hide and has 1 plough. 4 smallholders
with 1 plough.
This manor and BRISTOL pay 110 marks of silver to the King; the burgesses state that Bishop G(eoffrey) has 33 marks of silver and 1 mark of gold besides the King's revenue.

In BRADLEY Hundred
22 Baldwin son of Herlwin had a manor in which there were 10 hides.
The Bishop of Bayeux held this manor; now it is in the King's hands and pays tax. In lordship 2 ploughs;

7 vii . uilli 7 v . borđ cū . vi . car̃ . Ibi . v . ferui . 7 ii . molini

de . xx . foliđ . Ibi pƀr . T.R.E . ualƀ . xii . liƀ . Modo.́ vi . liƀ.

In CIRECESTRE hđ habuit Elmar HVNLAFESED.

in quo erant . iii . hidæ 7 dim̃ . Eƥs baioc̄fis tenuit . M̊ eſt

in manu regis . In dñio . ē . i . car̃ . 7 iiii . uilli 7 iiii . borđ

cū . iii . car̃.   Valuit . iiii . liƀ . m̊ . L . fot.

In TEODECHESBERIE fuer̃ T.R.E . quat̃ xx . 7 xv . hidæ.

Ex his funt in dñio . xLv . 7 erant quiete ab omĩ fer

uitio regali 7 geldo . ƥter feruitiũ ipfius dr̄i cuj erat m̃.

In capite m̃ erant in dñio . xii . car̃ . 7 L . int̃ feruos

7 ancillas . 7 xvi . borđ circa aulã manebant . 7 ii . mo

lini de . xx . foliđ . 7 una pifcaria . 7 una falina aƥ Wichã

ƥtin ad m̃.

Aƥ Sudwichã . iii . hiđ . In Trotintune . vi . hidæ . In Fiten

tone . vi . hide . In Pamintonie . viii . hidæ . In Natone . iii . hidæ . 7 dim̃.

In Waltone . iii . hidæ.   In Eſtone . vi . hidæ.

Ibi eraƞ́ uilli . xxi . 7 ix . Radcheniſt . hn̄tes . xxvi . car̃.

7 v . coliƀti 7 uñ borđ cū . v . car̃ . Hi Radcheniſt

arabaƞ́ 7 herciabant ad curiã dñi.

In Glouueceſtre erant . viii . burg̃fes . redđtes . v . foliđ

7 iiii . deñ 7 feruientes ad curiã.

In tota Teodechefberie funt . cxx . ac̃ ƥti . 7 filua . una

leuga 7 dimiđ long̃ . 7 tantđ lat̃.

Aƥ Teodekefberie funt m̊ . xiii . burg̃fes redđtes . xx . fot

ƥ anñ . Mercatũ qđ regina c̄ſtituit ibi . redđ . xi . foliđ

7 viii . denar̃ . Ibi . ē una car̃ plus . 7 xxii . int̃ feruos

7 ancillas . Vna pifcaria 7 una falina aƥ Wichã

Ibi . iii . Radcheniſt̃ . T.R.E . ƥtineƀ . Vñ eoꝛ tenebat

jn Eſtone . vi . hiđ . Modo teñ Girard . Alt̃ tenebat

jn Waltone . iii . hiđ . Modo teñ Radulf̃ . Terci teneƀ

jn Fitentone . ii . hiđ . Modo teñ Bernard.

7 villagers and 5 smallholders with 6 ploughs.
5 slaves; 2 mills at 20s. A priest.
Value before 1066 £12; now £6.

In CIRENCESTER Hundred

23   Aelmer had HULLASEY, in which there were 3½ hides. The Bishop of
Bayeux held it; now it is in the King's hands. In lordship 1 plough;
    4 villagers and 4 smallholders with 3 ploughs.
The value was £4; now 50s.

[In TEWKESBURY Hundred]

24   In TEWKESBURY before 1066 there were 95 hides. 45 of them are
in lordship; they were exempt from all royal service, apart from
the service of the lord himself whose manor it was. In the head
of the manor there were in lordship 12 ploughs; 50 slaves, male
and female.
    16 smallholders lived around the hall.
    2 mills at 20s; a fishery; a salt-house at Droitwich which belongs
      to this manor.
At SOUTHWICK 3 hides; in TREDINGTON 6 hides; in FIDDINGTON 6 hides;
in PAMINGTON 8 hides; in NATTON 3½ hides; in WALTON (Cardiff) 3
hides; in ASTON (on Carrant) 6 hides.
    There were 21 villagers and 9 riding men who had 26 ploughs;
    5 freedmen and 1 smallholder with 5 ploughs. These riding
    men ploughed and harrowed at the lord's court.
    In Gloucester there were 8 burgesses who paid 5s 4d and
    served at the court.
    In the whole of Tewkesbury, meadow, 120 acres; woodland
    1½ leagues long and as wide.
    At Tewkesbury there are now 13 burgesses who pay 20s a year; 163 c
    a market which the Queen set up there which pays 11s 8d. 1
    more plough; 22 slaves, male and female.
    A fishery; a salt-house at Droitwich.
    3 riding men belonged there before 1066; one of them held 6
    hides in ASTON (on Carrant); Gerard now holds them;
    another held 3 hides in WALTON (Cardiff); Ralph now holds
    them; the third held 2 hides in FIDDINGTON ; Bernard now
    holds them.

In his.xi.hid ſunt.x.caŕ in dñio.7 iiii.uiłłi 7 i.borđ
7 ix.ſerui.cū una caŕ.Ibi.xviii.ăc p̄ti.

Toť T.R.E.ualƀ.x.liƀ.Modo tantđ.

Ap̄ OXENDONE.T.R.E.erat Aula.7 v.hidæ p̄tiñtes
ad Teodekesƀie.Ibi ſunt.v.caŕ in dñio.7 v.uiłłi
7 ii.radcheniłł hñtes vii.caŕ.7 inť ſeruos 7 anciłł.

xii.Ibi xxiiii.ăc p̄ti.Ap̄ Wicecōbe.iii.burḡſes
redđ.xl.deñ.   Toť hoc uał 7 ualuit.viii.liƀ.

Hæc Subſcripta ťra p̄tiñ æcclæ de Teodekeſberie.

✠ IN STANWEGE.ſunt.vii.hidœ.p̄tiñ æcclæ.

Ibi.ii.caŕ in dñio.7 viii.uiłłi 7 ii.borđ cū.viii.
caŕ.Ibi monaſter.7 inť ſeruos 7 ancillas.v.7 ap̄ Wichā
una ſalina.7 viii.ăc p̄ti.Silua.iii.q̄ɀ łḡ.7 una lať.
T.R.E.ualƀ.viii.iiƀ.Modo.vii.liƀ.

x IN TATINTONE.iiii.hidœ.Ibi ſunt.ii.caŕ.7 xi.uiłłi
7 uñ Radchen cū.ii.caŕ.7 iii.borđ.7 ix.ſerui.
Valeƀ.vi.liƀ.Modo.c.ſoł.

x IN LIMENTONE.iii.hidœ.Ibi ſunt.ii.caŕ.7 viii.uiłłi
cū.iiii.caŕ.7 vi.ſerui.7 uñ borđ.
Valuit.lx.ſoł.modo.xl.ſoliđ.

x IN WASEBORNE.iii.hidœ.Ibi ſunt.ii.caŕ.7 vi.uiłłi
cū.iii.caŕ.7 i.borđ.7 ix.ſerui cū anciłł.
Valuit 7 uał.lx.ſoliđ.

x IN FITENTONE.ii.hidæ.Ibi uñ uiłłs 7 ii.coliƀti cū.ii.
caŕ.Vał 7 ualuit.x.ſoł.Vna ex his hiđ q̄eta ťra fuit.

x IN ÆTONE.i.hida.q̄etæ ťræ.7 ibi.i.caŕ.Vał.x.ſoł.

x IN STANLEGE.iiii.hidæ 7 dimiđ.Ibi.ē.i.caŕ.7 iiii.
uiłłi cū.ii.caŕ.7 iii.borđ 7 v.ſerui.Ħ ťra q̄eta fuit.
Valuit.iiii.liƀ.Modo.xl.ſoliđ.

Tota ťra p̄tiñ æcclæ geldaƀ p̄.xx.hiđ.T.R.E.

In these 11 hides are 10 ploughs in lordship;
  4 villagers, 1 smallholder and 9 slaves with 1 plough.
  Meadow, 18 acres.
The value of the whole before 1066 £10; now as much.

25 At OXENTON there was a hall before 1066 and 5 hides which belonged to Tewkesbury. 5 ploughs in lordship;
  5 villagers and 2 riding men who have 7 ploughs; 12 slaves, male and female.
  Meadow, 24 acres.
  At Winchcombe 3 burgesses who pay 40d.
The value of the whole is and was £8.

26 THE LAND MENTIONED BELOW BELONGS TO TEWKESBURY CHURCH.

†27 In STANWAY 7 hides which belong to the Church. 2 ploughs in lordship;
  8 villagers and 2 smallholders with 8 ploughs.
  A monastery; 5 slaves, male and female.
  A salt-house at Droitwich; meadow, 8 acres; woodland 3 furlongs long and 1 wide.
Value before 1066 £8; now £7.

+28 In TADDINGTON 4 hides. 2 ploughs there.
  11 villagers and 1 riding man with 2 ploughs; 3 smallholders and 9 slaves.
The value was £6; now 100s.

+29 In (Lower) LEMINGTON 3 hides. 2 ploughs there.
  8 villagers with 4 ploughs; 6 slaves and 1 smallholder.
The value was 60s; now 40s.

+30 In (Great) WASHBOURNE 3 hides. 2 ploughs there.
  6 villagers with 3 ploughs; 1 smallholder and 9 male slaves with a female slave.
The value was and is 60s.

+31 In FIDDINGTON 2 hides.
  1 villager and 2 freedmen with 2 ploughs.
The value is and was 10s.
  One of these hides was exempt land.

+32 In NATTON 1 hide of exempt land. 1 plough there.
Value 10s.

+33 In STANLEY (Pontlarge) 4½ hides. 1 plough there.
  4 villagers with 2 ploughs; 3 smallholders and 5 slaves.
  This land was exempt.
The value was £4; now 40s.

The whole of the land which belongs to the Church paid tax for 20 hides before 1066.

In eod $\widetilde{\text{co}}$ de Teodekefberie ptineƀ.IIII.hidæ fine
dñio quæ funt in Hanlege.Ibi T.R.E.erant in dñio
.II.cař.7 inť uiƚƚos 7 borƌ.XL.7 inť feruos 7 ancillas
VIII.7 moliñ de XVI.deñ.Silua in qua.ē Haia.
H̄ tra fuit.W.comitis.m̄.ē ad firmā regis in Hereford.
T.R.E.ualuit.XV.liƀ.modo.X.liƀ.
In Fortemeltone.IX.hidæ.ptineƀ huic $\widetilde{\text{co}}$.Ibi.II.cař.
in dñio.7 XX.inť uiƚƚos 7 borƌ.7 VI.inť feruos 7 anciƚƚ.
Ibi filua.Valuit.X.liƀ.T.R.E.m̄.VIII.liƀ.
Has.II.tras tenuit W.com̄.7 geldƀ ꝓpť Tedekesƀie.
In Senendone.X.hidæ ptiñ eiƌ $\widetilde{\text{co}}$.Ibi funt.IIII.
cař.7 VIII.uiƚƚi 7 IIII.borƌ.7 V.radcheniƚt cū.VIII.cař.
Ibi.XII.ferui.7 moliñ de.III.foƚ.H̄ tra gelƌ ꝑ.VII.hiƌ.
T.R.E.ualƀ.XX.liƀ.modo:'VIII.liƀ.In Manu regis.ē.
Roƀt de olgi teñ ad firmā.
In CLIFORT.VII.hidæ ptiñ eiƌ $\widetilde{\text{co}}$.Ibi.III.cař in dñio.
7 XIIII.uiƚƚi cū.V.cař.7 moliñ de.XII.foƚ.7 II.ac̄ pti.
Ibi erant inť feruos 7 Anciƚƚ.XIII.7 æccƚa 7 pƀr cū.I.cař.
Valƀ.VIII.liƀ.Modo.VI.liƀ.Hanc trā deƌ regina
Rogerio de Bufli.7 geldƀ ꝑ.IIII.hiƌ in Tedechefberie.
Quať XX.7 XV.hidas quæ ptiñ ad Tedechefberie q̃nq̃
ginta hidæ fuꝑ memoratæ facieƀ ꝙetas 7 libas ab om̄i
geldo 7 regali feruitio.

163 d

Maneriū iftud Tedekefberie cū erat toť fimul T.R.E.ualƀ.c.liƀ.
Qdo Radulf recep:'XII.liƀ.ꝙa deftrucť 7 c̄fusū erat.Modo
apꝑciať.XL.liƀ.Tam̄ Radulf redƌ.L.liƀ.
Hoc $\widetilde{\text{co}}$ tenuit Briƌtric fili Algar.T.R.E.7 has fubfcriptas
tras alioꝣ teinoꝣ ipfo tꝓr in fua poteftate habuit.

4 Also in the manor of TEWKESBURY there belonged 4 hides not
in lordship; they are in HANLEY (Castle). Before 1066 2 ploughs
in lordship;
    40 villagers and smallholders; 8 slaves, male and female.
    A mill at 16d; woodland in which there is a hedged enclosure.
This land was Earl William's; now it is in the King's revenue
in Hereford.
Value before 1066 £15; now £10.

5 In FORTHAMPTON 9 hides belonged to this manor. 2 ploughs in
lordship;
    20 villagers and smallholders; 6 slaves, male and female.
    Woodland.
Value before 1066 £10; now £8.

Earl William held these two lands; they paid tax with Tewkesbury.

6 In SHENINGTON 10 hides belonged to this manor. 4 ploughs there.
    8 villagers, 4 smallholders and 5 riding men with 8 ploughs.
    12 slaves; a mill at 3s.
This land paid tax for 7 hides.
Value before 1066 £20; now £8.
It is in the King's hands. Robert d'Oilly holds it at a revenue.

7 In CLIFFORD (Chambers) 7 hides belonged to this manor. 3 ploughs
in lordship;
    14 villagers with 5 ploughs.
    A mill at 12s; meadow, 2 acres. There were 13 slaves, male and
      female; a church and a priest with 1 plough.
The value was £8; now £6.
The Queen gave this land to Roger of Bully; it paid tax for 4
hides in Tewkesbury.

8 The above mentioned 50 (exempt) hides caused (all) the 95 hides
which belong to Tewkesbury to be exempt and free from all tax
and royal service.
The value of this manor of TEWKESBURY before 1066, when it   163 d
was complete, was £100; when Ralph acquired it, £12, because
it was destroyed and dismembered; now it is assessed at £40;
however Ralph pays £50.

9 Brictric son of Algar held this manor before 1066. He had the lands
written below of other thanes completely in his power at that time.

In ESSETONE tenuit un tein̄. IIII. hiđ. 7 Ꝏ erat.

Modo ten̄ Girard. 7 ibi h̄t. I. car̄. 7 II. uiłłos cū. I. car̄.

Vał 7 ualuit. XL. foliđ.

In CHENEMERTONE tenuit. Let. VIII. hiđ. 7 Ꝏ erat. Modo

★ ten̄ Girard. 7 ibi h̄t. III. car̄. 7 XIIII. uiłł cū. IVI car̄. Ibi. VIII.

ferui. 7 III. molini de. XV. foliđ. Valuit. VIII. liƀ. Modo. VI. liƀ.

Ad hoc Ꝏ adjacent. III. hidæ in Botintone. Iſđ Girard ten̄.

7 ibi h̄t. II. car̄. 7 IIII. uiłł cū. III. car̄. 7 ibi. III. ferui. 7 molin̄

de. VIII. foliđ. 7 VIII. ac̄ p̄ti.   Vał 7 ualuit. XL. fol.

In WENECOTE tenuit un̄ tein̄. III. hiđ. Regina deđ hanc

trā Rainaldo capellano. Ibi funt. III. uiłłi. cū dimiđ car̄.

Valuit. XL. foliđ.

In ALDRITONE tenuit Dūning. VI. hiđ 7 dimiđ. 7 In Dricle

done. IIII. hiđ 7 dim̄. 7 In Hundeuuic. I. hiđ tenuit. I. tein̄.

Has ten̄ tras Hunfrid de rege. 7 ibi h̄t. IIII. car̄ in dn̄io.

7 V. uiłłi 7. VIII. borđ cū. III. car̄. 7 un̄ Radcheniſt cū. I. car̄.

7 in Wicecōbe un̄ burḡſis. 7 ibi hn̄tur. XII. ac̄ p̄ti.

Toꝋ T.R.E. ualƀ. XI. liƀ. Modo. VI. liƀ.

In TVNINGE teneƀ. IIII. uiłłi. II. hiđ. 7 un̄ tein̄ dimiđ hiđ.

Ibi funt. IIII. car̄. 7 III. ac̄ p̄ti. Regina deđ hanc trā Joħi camer̄.

Vał 7 ualuit. XXXV. foliđ.

In STOCHES tenuer̄ Hermer 7 Aluuin̄. III. hiđ. una V̄ min̄.

Modo ten̄ Bernard de rege. 7 h̄t ibi. I. car̄ in dn̄io. 7 IIII. ac̄s

p̄ti. Valuit. LX. foliđ. Modo. XL. foliđ.

Qui T.R.E. has tras tenebaꝺ. 7 fe 7 tras fuas fub Briđtrici

poteſtate fūmifer̄.   IN LANGELEI HD̄.

BRICTRIC fili Algar tenuit TVRNEBERIE. Ibi. T.R.E. erant

XI. hidæ. 7 IIII. car̄ in dn̄io. 7 XLII. uiłłi. 7 XVIII. radcheniſtre

cū. XXI. car̄. 7 XXIIII. borđ. 7 XV. ferui. 7 IIII. coliƀti. Ibi. II. mo

In ASHTON (under Hill) a thane held 4 hides; it was a manor. Now Gerard holds it; he has 1 plough and
  2 villagers with 1 plough.
The value is and was 40s.

In KEMERTON Let held 8 hides; it was a manor. Now Gerard holds it; he has 3 ploughs;
  14 villagers with 6 ploughs.
  8 slaves; 3 mills at 15s.
The value was £8; now £6.
  3 hides in BODDINGTON are attached to this manor; Gerard also holds them; he has 2 ploughs;
  4 villagers with 3 ploughs.
  3 slaves; a mill at 8s; meadow, 8 acres.
The value is and was 40s.

In WINCOT a thane held 3 hides. The Queen gave this land to Reginald the chaplain.
  3 villagers with ½ plough.
The value was 40s.

In ALDERTON Dunning held 6½ hides, and in DIXTON 4½ hides. In 'HENTAGE' a thane held 1 hide. Humphrey holds these lands from the King; he has 4 ploughs in lordship;
  5 villagers and 8 smallholders with 3 ploughs; a riding man
    with 1 plough; a burgess in Winchcombe.
  Meadow, 12 acres recorded there.
The value of the whole before 1066 £11; now £6.

In TWYNING 4 villagers held 2 hides and 1 thane ½ hide.
  4 ploughs there.
  Meadow, 3 acres.
  The Queen gave this land to John the Chamberlain.
The value is and was 35s.

In STOKE (Orchard) Hermer and Alwin held 3 hides, less 1 virgate. Now Bernard holds it from the King; he has 1 plough in lordship and
  meadow, 4 acres.
The value was 60s; now 40s.

The holders of these lands before 1066 put themselves and their lands in Brictric's power.

In LANGLEY Hundred

Brictric son of Algar held THORNBURY. Before 1066 there were 11 hides. 4 ploughs in lordship;
  42 villagers and 18 riding men with 21 ploughs; 24 smallholders,
    15 slaves and 4 freedmen.

lini de . vi . folid 7 iiii . den . Silua de . i . lev̇ lḡ . 7 una laṫ.

Ibi forū de . xx . folid . Modo accreuit p̄pofit molīn ibi de . viii . deṅ.

Hoc M̄ fuit reginæ Mathildis . Hunfrid redd̄ de eo . l . liƀ ad numer̄.

In hoc M̄ eſt uñ p̄tū de . xl . folid̄ . 7 ad Wiche . xl . fexṫ falis.

uel . xx . deṅ . 7 piſcaria de Glouueceſtre de . l . 7 viii . denar̄.

Iſd Briĉtric tenuit SOPEBERIE . IN EDERESTAN HVND̄.

Ibi T.R.E . erant . x . hidæ . 7 iiii . caṙ in dñio . 7 xii . uiłłi cū . v .

caṙ . 7 iiii . bord̄ 7 xviii . ſerui . 7 uñ parcus . 7 molīn de . v . foṫ.

Modo creuit p̄pofit . i . molīn de . xl . denar̄ . Ibi filua

de una leuua lḡ . 7 una laṫ.

Hunfrid redd̄ de hoc M̄ . xvi . liƀ 7 x . folid̄.

Ad hoc M̄ ptiñ una v̇ in Wiche . quæ reddeƀ . xxv . fexṫ

falis . Vrfus uicecoṁ ita uaſtauit hōes . qd̄ ṁ redde n̄ poſſuƞ̇ fal.

Iſd Briĉtric tenuit AVENINGE . Ibi IN LANGETREV HD̄.

T.R.E . erant . x . hidæ . 7 in dñio . viii . caṙ . 7 xxiiii . uiłłi . 7 v .

bord̄ 7 xxx . ſerui . cū . xvi . caṙ . Ibi . iiii . molini de . xix . foṫ

7 ii . deṅ . Modo creuit p̄pofit uñ molīn de . xl . denar̄ . Ibi

filua . ii . leuuis lḡ . 7 dimid̄ leuua laṫ . Ibi . ē aira accipitris . Vł . xx . vii . [lib.]

Iſd Briĉtric tenuit FAREFORDE . IN BRISTOLDESBERG HD̄.

Ibi T.R.E . erant . xxi . hidȧ . 7 lvi . uiłłos 7 ix . bord̄ cū . xxx . caṙ.

Ibi pƀr qui teneƀ unā v̇ træ de dñio . 7 iii . molini de . xxxii .

folid̄ . 7 vi . deṅ . In dñio non ſunt nifi . xiii . hidæ 7 una v̇.

Hoc M̄ tenuit Mathild̄ regina . Hunfrid redd̄ . xxxviii . liƀ.

7 x . foṫ ad numerū . ⌐De tra huj̇ M̄ ded̄ regina . iiii . hid̄

Johi camerario . Ibi ſunt . ii . caṙ . 7 ix . uiłłi 7 iiii . bord̄ cū . iiii . caṙ.

Ibi . xiiii . ſerui . Redd̄ . ix . liƀ de firma.

164 a

Ipſa regina ded̄ Balduino . iii . hid̄ 7 iii . uirġ de ead̄ tra.

7 ibi ht̄ . ii . caṙ . 7 v . feruos . 7 uñ liberū hōem hñtem . i . caṙ.

7 ii . bord̄ . Vał . iiii . liƀ.

⌐Qui has . ii . tras tenuer̄ T.R.E . n̄ poteraƞ̇ recedė a capite M̄.

2 mills at 6s 4d; woodland at 1 league long and 1 wide.
  A market at 20s. Now the reeve has added a mill at 8d.
  This manor was Queen Matilda's.
Humphrey pays £50 from it at face value.
  In this manor a meadow at 40s and at Droitwich 40 sesters of salt or 20d; a fishery in Gloucester at 58d.

In EDDERSTONE Hundred

8   Brictric also held (Old) SODBURY. Before 1066 there were 10 hides. 4 ploughs in lordship;
  12 villagers with 5 ploughs; 4 smallholders and 18 slaves.
  A park; a mill at 5s. Now the reeve has added 1 mill at 40d.
    Woodland at 1 league long and 1 wide.
Humphrey pays £16 10s from this manor.
  1 virgate in Droitwich belongs to this manor; it paid 25 sesters of salt. Urso the Sheriff so oppressed the men that now they cannot pay the salt.

In LONGTREE Hundred

9   Brictric also held AVENING. Before 1066 there were 10 hides.
  In lordship 8 ploughs;
  24 villagers, 5 smallholders and 30 slaves with 16 ploughs.
  4 mills at 19s 2d. Now the reeve has added a mill at 40d.
    Woodland 2 leagues long and ½ league wide. A hawk's eyrie.
Value £27.

In BRIGHTWELLS BARROW Hundred

0   Brictric also held FAIRFORD. Before 1066 there were 21 hides.
  56 villagers and 9 smallholders with 30 ploughs. A priest who held 1 virgate of land of the lordship.
  3 mills at 32s 6d.
  In lordship nothing but 13 hides and 1 virgate.
  Queen Matilda held this manor.
Humphrey pays £38 10s at face value.
  The Queen gave 4 hides of this manor's land to John the Chamberlain. 2 ploughs there.
  9 villagers and 4 smallholders with 4 ploughs. 14 slaves.
It pays £9 in revenue.

1   The Queen herself gave 3 hides and 3 virgates of this land   164 a
to Baldwin. He has 2 ploughs and 5 slaves and
  1 free man who has 1 plough; 2 smallholders.
  Value £4.

2   The holders of these two lands before 1066 could not withdraw from the head of the manor.

Rex.E.tenuit *DIMOCH*.Ibi erant.xx.hidæ.7 ii.car

in dñio.7 xl.ii.uilli.7 x.borđ.7 xi.colibti hñtes.xli.

car.Ibi pbr tenens.xii.acras.7 iiii.Radcheniſtre

cũ.iiii.car.Ibi filua.iii.leuu lg.7 una lat.

De hoc ⓜ reddeb uicecom qđ uoleb T.R.E.

Rex.W.tenuit in dñio ſuo.iiii.annis.Poſtea habuit

eũ com.W.7 Rogeri fili ej.Hões de comitatu neſciuɴ

quomodo.Modo redđ xxi.lib.   *In Bliteslav hd.*

Herald tenuit *NEST*.Ibi erant.v.hidæ.7 in dñio.i.car.

7 x.uilli 7 ii.borđ cũ.ix.car.T.R.E.non fuit ad firmã.

Comes û.W.adjunx illũ.ii.alijs ⓜ.ſcilicet pontune

7 peritune.In his erant.ix.hidæ.7 ii.car in dñio.7 xv.

uilli 7 ii.borđ 7 ii.ſerui.cũ.ix.car.Ibi.i.piſcaria.

Modo creuit ppoſit in pontune.i.car.Peritune.ē in

calũnia ad firmã regis.Inť toť redđ.xi.lib.

In *LINDENEE* fecit com.W.uñ ⓜ de.iiii.tris quas

ab earũ dñis accepit.De dñio epi de hereford.iii.hiđ.

De dñico uiđtu monacho₂ de pſore.vi.hiđ.ubi eraɴ

vi.uilli cũ.iiii.car.De duob₂ teinis accep.iii.hiđ 7 dim.

Ibi ſunt in dñio.iii.car.7 viii.borđ.7 moliñ de.xl.den.

Silua.i.leuua lg.7 dimiđ lat.Inť toť redđ.vii.lib.

In *TEDENEHÁ HVND* habuit abb de *BADE* uñ Man

nõe *TEDENEHÁ*.Ibi habebant.xxx.hidæ.Harũ.x.eraɴ

in dñio.Ibi erant.xxxviii.uilli hñtes.xxxviii.car.7 x.borđ.

In Sauerna.xi.piſcariæ|dñio.7 xlii.piſcariæ uillano₂.

In Waia.i.piſcaria.7 uillano₂.ii.piſcariæ 7 dimidia.

Roger comes creuit in Waia.ii.piſcarias.Ibi.ē filua

.ii.leuu lg.7 dimiđ leuua lat.7 xii.borđ plus ſunt.

In BOTLOE Hundred

King Edward held DYMOCK. There were 20 hides. 2 ploughs
in lordship;
    42 villagers, 10 smallholders and 11 freedmen who have
       41 ploughs. A priest who holds 12 acres. 4 riding men
       with 4 ploughs.
    Woodland 3 leagues long and 1 wide.
Before 1066 the Sheriff paid what he wished from this manor.
King William held it in his lordship for 4 years. Later Earl
William and his son Roger had it; the men of the County do
not know how. Now it pays £21.

In BLEDISLOE Hundred

Earl Harold held NASS. There were 5 hides. In lordship 1 plough;
    10 villagers and 2 smallholders with 9 ploughs.
Before 1066 it was not in the revenue. Earl William joined it to
two other manors, namely Poulton and Purton. In them there
were 9 hides. 2 ploughs in lordship;
    15 villagers, 2 smallholders and 2 slaves with 9 ploughs.
    A fishery. Now the reeve has added 1 plough in Poulton.
    Purton is claimed for the King's revenue.
In total they pay £11.

[In LYDNEY Hundred]

In LYDNEY Earl William made a manor from 4 lands which he
received from their lords. From the Bishop of Hereford's
lordship 3 hides. From the household supplies of the monks
of Pershore 6 hides, where there were 6 villagers with 4 ploughs.
From two thanes he received 3½ hides. In lordship 3 ploughs;
    8 smallholders.
    A mill at 40d; woodland 1 league long and ½ wide.
In total it pays £7.

In TIDENHAM Hundred

The Abbot of Bath had a manor named TIDENHAM. 30 hides were
recorded; 10 of them were in lordship.
    There were 38 villagers who had 38 ploughs; 10 smallholders.
    In the Severn 11 fisheries in lordship and 42 villagers' fisheries.
    In the Wye 1 fishery and 2½ villagers' fisheries. Earl Roger
    added 2 fisheries in the Wye. Woodland 2 leagues long and
    ½ league wide.
    There are 12 more smallholders.

W.com ded de hac t̃ra fr̃i fuo.O.epo unā v t̃ræ cū.i.
uitto.7 Walterio de Laci ded.ii.pifcar in Sauerna.
7 dimid in Waia.cū uno uitio.Rad de Limefi ded
ii.pifcar in Waia cū uno uitto.Abbatiæ de Lira
ded dimid hid t̃ræ 7 æcctam ⊙ cū decima.
Hoc ⊙ n̄ reddeb censū.T.R.E.nifi uictū monachis.
Stigand Archieps teneb illū.q̃do com.W.accep eū.
Modo redd.xxv.lib.de.xx.in ora.7 albas.
Ibi.ē m̃ molin̄ de.xl.denarijs. *IN RESPIET HVND.*
Wlward tenuit *CEDEORDE*.Ibi.xv.hidæ int filuā 7 pla
num 7 pratū.7 vii.car in dñio T.R.E.7 xvi.uitti 7 iii.bord
cū.vi.car.7 iii.molini de.xiiii.folid 7 ii.denar.7 thelo
neū fat qd uenieb ad aulā.Ibi creuit uicecom.viii.
uittos.7 iii.bord hn̄tes.iiii.car. *IN BEGEBERIE HD.*
Chenvichelle tein regis.E.tenuit *ALVREDINTVNE*.
Ibi erant.v.hidæ.7 iiii.car in dñio.7 xii.uitti
7 un bord cū.vi.car.7 xvi.int feruos 7 ancillas.
7 ii.molini de.xx.folid.Silua.i.leuua lḡ.7 dim lat.
Hoʒ ii.Manerioʒ p̃pofiti qd uoleb reddeb T.R.E.
Modo reddt.xl.lib alboʒ nūmoʒ de.xx.in ora.
Rog com tenuit. *IN TETBOLDESTANE HD.*
Rotlesc Hufcarle.R.E.tenuit.*BECEFORD*.Ibi erañ
xi.hidæ.7 iii.car in dñio.7 xxxiiii.uitti 7 xvii.bord
164 b
hn̄tes.xxx.car.Ibi.xii.ferui.7 iiii.ancillæ.
De hoc ⊙ ded.W.com.iii.hid Ansfrido de Cormeliis.
in quibʒ erant.xii.uitti cū.v.car.
Tvrbertvs tein Heraldi tenuit *ESTONE*.Ibi funt
viii.hidæ 7 iiii.car in dñio.7 x.uitti 7 iiii.bord
cū.vi.car.Ibi.viii.ferui.7.iii.Ancillæ.

Of this land Earl William gave to his brother Bishop Osbern
1 virgate of land, with 1 villager. He gave to Walter of Lacy
2 fisheries in the Severn and half in the Wye, with 1 villager.
He gave to Ralph of Limesy 2 fisheries in the Wye, with 1
villager. He gave to the Abbey of Lyre ½ hide of land and
the manor's church with the tithes.
This manor did not pay dues before 1066 except for the monks'
supplies. Archbishop Stigand was holding it when Earl William
received it.   Now it pays £25, blanched, at 20(pence) to the *ora*.
There is a mill there now at 40d.

In RAPSGATE Hundred
Wulfward held CHEDWORTH.   15 hides in both woodland and open
land and meadow. 7 ploughs in lordship before 1066;
16 villagers and 3 smallholders with 6 ploughs.
3 mills at 14s 2d; a toll on salt which came to the hall.
The Sheriff added 8 villagers and 3 smallholders who have
4 ploughs.

In BIBURY Hundred
Cynwy Chelle, a thane of King Edward's, held ARLINGTON. There
were 5 hides. In lordship 4 ploughs;
12 villagers and 1 smallholder with 6 ploughs; 16 slaves, male
and female.
2 mills at 20s; woodland 1 league long and ½ wide.
The reeves of these two manors paid what they wished before 1066;
now they pay £40 of blanched money at 20(pence) to the *ora*.
Earl Roger held them.

In TIBBLESTONE Hundred
Rotlesc, a guard of King Edward's, held BECKFORD. There were 11
hides. 3 ploughs in lordship;
34 villagers and 17 smallholders who have 30 ploughs.   164 b
12 male and 4 female slaves.
Earl William gave 3 hides of this manor to Ansfrid of Cormeilles,
in which there were 12 villagers with 5 ploughs.

Thorbert, a thane of Earl Harold's, held ASHTON (under Hill).
8 hides. In lordship 4 ploughs;
10 villagers and 4 smallholders with 6 ploughs. 8 male and
3 female slaves.

De his. ii . uillis fec̄ com̄ . W . uñ m̄.7 ñ eraꝫ ad firmā

donec Rog̃ de Jurei miſit ad . xxx . liƀ firmæ.

Decimā u̅ 7 æcctas cu̅ . ii . uittis 7 iii . virg̃ tre . ded̄

ipſe com̄ abbatiæ de Cormeliis.

Hȭes de comitatu inꝗſiti dixer̄ ſe nunꝗ uidiſſe

breuē regis qui hanc trā diceret datā . ēe . comiti . W .

W̲LGAR teign̄ regis . E . tenuit IN LANGENEI HD̄

T̲OCHINTVNE . Ibi fuer . viii . hidæ . 7 v . car̄ in dñio.

7 xx . uitti 7 xii . borđ 7 x . ſerui . cu̅ xx . car̄.

Hoc m̄ ñ redđ firmā T . R . E . ſed inde iuueƀ cuꝰ erat.

Com̄ . W . tenuit in dñio . 7 ibi creuit p̄poſit . i . car̄.

7 moliñ de . viii . denar̄.

Modo redđ . xxiiii . liƀ . candidoꝫ nu̅moꝫ de x̄x̄ . in ora.

E̲DRIC Lang tein̄ Heraldi tenuit IN DODESTAN HD̄

HECHANESTEDE . Ibi erant . v . hidæ 7 in dñio . iii . car̄.

7 vi . uitti 7 viii . borđ cu̅ . vi . car̄ . Ibi . vi . ſerui.

7 dimiđ piſcaria . Hoc m̄ cep̄ . W . com̄ in dñio . 7 non

fuit ad firmā . Sed m̄ uicecom̄ poſuit eu̅ ad . lx . ſot . nu̅o.

G̲VEDA mat Heraldi tenuit VDECESTRE . IN LANGETREV HD̄ .

Goduin emit ab Azor 7 ded̄ ſuæ uxori . ut inde iuueret donec

ad Berchelai maneret . Noleƀ eñi de ipſo m̄ aliꝗd comedere.

ꝓ deſtructione abbatiæ . Hanc trā ten̄ Eduuarđ in firma

de Wiltefcire . injuſte ut dicit comitat . ꝗa non ꝑtin̄ ad aliꝗ

firmā . De quo m̄ nemo Legatis regis redđ ratiōe . nec

aliꝗs eoꝫ uenit ad hanc deſcriptiōe . H̄ trā redđ . vii . liƀ.

B̲RICTRIC tenuit . iii . hiđ in MODIETE . IN TVIFERDE HD̄ .

7 geldaƀ . In dñio h̄t rex ibi . ii . piſcarias . Roger̄ de Laci

h̄t unā piſcar̄ . cu̅ dimiđ hida . Aƀƀ de Malmeſberiā h̄t

unā piſcar̄ cu̅ dimiđ hida . 7 hoc dono regis ſic dicunt.

Witts de Ow . h̄t . ii . hiđ . 7 ipſas . iiii . piſcarias calu̅niat̄.

Hæ piſcariæ ſuꝗ in Waia . 7 reddeƀ . iiii . liƀ.

Earl William made one manor out of these two villages.
They were not in the revenue until Roger of Ivry set them at a
revenue of £30. The Earl himself gave the tithes and churches
with the two villagers and 3 virgates of land to the Abbey of
Cormeilles.

The men of the County when questioned stated that they had
never seen the King's writ which said that this land had been given
to Earl William.

In LANGLEY Hundred

1 Wulfgar, a thane of King Edward's, held TOCKINGTON. There were
8 hides. 5 ploughs in lordship;
20 villagers, 12 smallholders and 10 slaves with 20 ploughs.
This manor did not pay revenue before 1066 but its owner lived
off it. Earl William held it in lordship. The reeve added 1 plough
and a mill at 8d. Now it pays £24 of white money at 20(pence)
to the *ora*.

In DUDSTONE Hundred

2 Edric Lang, a thane of Earl Harold's, held HEMPSTED. There were
5 hides. In lordship 3 ploughs;
6 villagers and 8 smallholders with 6 ploughs.
6 slaves; ½ fishery.
Earl William took this manor into (his) lordship and it was not in
the revenue; but now the Sheriff has placed it (there) at 60s at
face value.

In LONGTREE Hundred

3 Gytha, Earl Harold's mother, held WOODCHESTER. Earl Godwin
bought it from Azor and gave it to his wife, so that she could
live off it while she lived at Berkeley. For she did not wish to
consume anything from that manor because of the Abbey's
destruction. Edward holds this land in the revenue of Wiltshire,
wrongfully as the County states because it does not belong to
any revenue. Nobody has rendered account of this manor to the
King's Commissioners, nor has any of them come to this survey.
This land pays £7.

In TWYFORD Hundred

4 Brictric held 3 hides in MADGETT; they paid tax. In lordship the
King has 2 fisheries. Roger of Lacy has 1 fishery with ½ hide.
The Abbot of Malmesbury has 1 fishery with ½ hide; this is by
the King's gift, so they state. William of Eu has 2 hides and claims
these 4 fisheries. These fisheries are in the Wye.
They paid £4.

Ednod tenuit *OMENEL*.T.R.E.Ibi.xv.hidæ geld.

De his pdonauit rex.E.Ednodo.v.hid.ut dicit scira.

7 postea reddid de.x.hid hoc ꝳ.In dñio.iiii.car.

7 pbr 7 xix.uiłłi 7 iii.bord cū.x.car.Ibi.xii.serui.

Hoc ꝳ fuit epi baioc͞sis.7 uałb.xx.łib.Modo redd

xxvi.łib in firma regis.   *IN BERNITONE HD.*

Tovi Widenesci huscarle heraldi.tenuit *BERNITONE.*

Ibi.iiii.hidæ.In dñio suꝗ.ii.car.7 x.uiłłi 7 v.bord cū.v.

car.Ibi.iiii.serui.7 molin de.v.solid.

Vał 7 ualuit.vii.łib.Elsi de ferendone ten in firma regis.

Eilmer tenuit in *BERNITONE*.iiii.hid ꝓ ꝳ.T.R.E.

In dñio.ē.i.car.7 vii.uiłłi 7 iii.bord cū.iiii.car.

Ibi.vi.serui.7 molin de.v.soł.Valuit.c.solid.m͞.lx.solid.

Goduin de Stantone ten in firma regis.

164 c

II. Sᴛɪɢᴀɴᴅ TERRA THOME ARCHIEPI.

Stigand archieps tenuit *CIRCESDVNE*.Ibi erant

xv.hidæ 7 dimid.7 ii.car in dñio.7 xviii.uiłłi 7 v.bord

7 vii.Radchenist.cū xxx̨car.Ibi Silua dimid leuua

lg.7 iii.q̨z lat.Tc uałeb.xiii.łib.Modo.xii.łib.

Isd Stig tenuit *HOCHILICOTE*.Ibi erant.iiii.hidæ.

7 in dñio.ii.car.7 xi.uiłłi 7 v.bord cū.xi.car.

Ibi.ē molin de.xxxii.den.7 silua.i.leuua lg.7 dim

lat.Tc 7 m uał.iiii.łib.

Isd Stig tenuit *NORTVNE*.Ibi erant.v.hidæ 7 dim.

7 in dñio.ii.car.7 xv.uiłłi cū.xv.car.7 iiii.serui.

7 molin de.xxxii.den.Tc 7 m uał.iiii.łib.

Hos.iii.Man ten m Thomas archieps.

Nortune ten Walchelin de eo.nepos epi de Winton.

In GARSDON Hundred

5 Ednoth held (Down) AMPNEY before 1066. 15 hides which pay tax.
King Edward remitted 5 hides of these for Ednoth, as the County
states, and later this manor paid for 10 hides. In lordship 4 ploughs;
    a priest, 19 villagers and 3 smallholders with 10 ploughs.
       12 slaves.
    This manor was the Bishop of Bayeux's.
The value was £20; now it pays £26 in the King's revenue.

In BARRINGTON Hundred

6 Tovi Widenesci, a guard of Earl Harold's, held (Great) BARRINGTON.
4 hides. In lordship 2 ploughs;
    10 villagers and 5 smallholders with 5 ploughs.
    4 slaves; a mill at 5s.
The value is and was £7.
    Alfsi of Faringdon holds it in the King's revenue.

7 Aelmer held 4 hides in (Great) BARRINGTON as a manor before 1066.
In lordship 1 plough;
    7 villagers and 3 smallholders with 4 ploughs.
    6 slaves; a mill at 5s.
The value was 100s; now 60s.
    Godwin of Stanton holds it in the King's revenue.

2   LAND OF ARCHBISHOP THOMAS   164 c

[In DUDSTONE Hundred]

1 Archbishop Stigand held CHURCHDOWN. There were 15½ hides.
In lordship 2 ploughs;
    18 villagers, 5 smallholders and 7 riding men with 30 ploughs.
    Woodland ½ league long and 3 furlongs wide.
Value then £13; now £12.

2 Stigand also held HUCCLECOTE. There were 4 hides.
In lordship 2 ploughs;
    11 villagers and 5 smallholders with 11 ploughs.
    A mill at 32d; woodland 1 league long and ½ wide.
Value then and now £4.

3 Stigand also held (Bishops) NORTON. There were 5½ hides.
In lordship 2 ploughs;
    15 villagers with 15 ploughs; 4 slaves.
    A mill at 32d.
Value then and now £4.

Archbishop Thomas now holds these three manors. Walkelin, the
Bishop of Winchester's nephew, holds (Bishops) Norton from him.

Eldred archieps ten *Otintvne*. *In Salmanesberie hd.*

7 cū *Berew* Condicote. Ibi erant. x. hide. 7 ii. car in

dnio. 7 xvi. uitti 7 ii. Radchenist. 7 iiii. bord cū. xiiii. car.

H̄ tra nunq̄ geldau. T.R.E. Valb. vi. lib. m̄. x. lib. Thomas

archieps ten. Scs Petrus de Glouuecestre habuit

in dnio. donec|. W. in Angliā uenit. *In Ciltehā hd.*

Stigand Archieps tenuit *Svindone*. Ibi erant

iii. hidæ. 7 ii. car in dnio. 7 vii. uitti 7 ii. bord. 7 hn̄t

vii. car. Ibi sunt. iiii. serui. Tc̄ ualb. iii. lib. m̄. iiii. lib

7 x. solid. Hoc m̄ ten Thomas Arch. de tra S̄ Osuualdi.

7 geldat. *In Wacrescvbe hd.*

Gvndvlf tenuit 7 ten in *Scipetvne*. un̄ m̄ de una

hida. 7 geld. 7 ibi. i. car in dnio. 7 Val. viii. solid.

De Thoma arch ten.

Pin tenuit. i. m̄ de. i. hida in *Hagepine*. 7 geld.

Ansger ten de Thoma Arch. 7 h̄t. i. car in dnio.

Valuit. xx. sot. Modo. x. solid. *In Bradelege hd.*

Scs Petrus de Glouuec tenuit *Lecce*. 7 Eldred archieps

tenuit cū abbatia. Ibi erant. xxiiii. hidæ. In dnio sunt

. iiii. car. 7 xxxiii. uitti 7 xvi. bord cū. xxx. car. Ibi sūs

iiii. serui. 7 ii. molini de. vii. solid 7 iiii. den.

Ad hoc m̄ adjacet Stanunelle. Ibi sunt. ii. car in dnio.

7 v. uitti cū. v. car. 7 molin de. xl. den. 7 iiii. serui.

7 ii. ancillæ. 7 in Culberlege. ē una hida p̄in huic m̄.

★ De hac tra huj m̄ ten Walt fili pontu un̄ m̄ de. xii. hid.

q̄ jacuit in eod m̄ T.R.E. Ibi sunt. ii. car in dnio ap̄ Tor

mentone. 7 xxv. uitti cū. xii. car. 7 iiii. serui.

Tot m̄ T.R.E. ualb. xviii. lib. Thomas arch misit ad firmā

p̄ xxvii. lib. Hida de Culberlege. p̄ciat. xx. solid.

Q̄d Walt ten. ual. xiiii. lib. Thomas arch caluniat

In SALMONSBURY Hundred

4   Archbishop Aldred held ODDINGTON, with an outlier CONDICOTE.
There were 10 hides. In lordship 2 ploughs;
    16 villagers, 2 riding men and 4 smallholders with 14 ploughs.
    Before 1066 this land never paid tax.
The value was £6; now £10.
    Archbishop Thomas holds it. St. Peter's of Gloucester had it
in lordship until King William came to England.

In CHELTENHAM Hundred

5   Archbishop Stigand held SWINDON. There were 3 hides.
In lordship 2 ploughs.
    7 villagers and 2 smallholders; they have 7 ploughs. 4 slaves.
Value then £3; now £4 10s.
    Archbishop Thomas holds this manor from the land of
St. Oswald's (Church), and pays tax.

In WATTLESCOMB Hundred

6   Gundulf held and holds a manor of 1 hide in SHIPTON (Solers)
and pays tax. In lordship 1 plough.
Value 8s.
    He holds from Archbishop Thomas.

7   Pin held a manor of 1 hide in HAMPEN and paid tax. Ansger holds
from Archbishop Thomas. He has 1 plough in lordship.
The value was 20s; now 10s.

In BRADLEY Hundred

8   St. Peter's of Gloucester held NORTHLEACH. Archbishop Aldred
held it with the Abbey. There were 24 hides. In lordship 4 ploughs;
    33 villagers and 16 smallholders with 30 ploughs.
    4 slaves; 2 mills at 7s 4d.
STOWELL is attached to this manor. In lordship 2 ploughs;
    5 villagers with 5 ploughs.
    A mill at 40d; 4 male and 2 female slaves.
In (Upper) COBERLEY 1 hide which belongs to this manor.
Walter son of Poyntz holds a manor of 12 hides of this manor's
land; it lay in this manor before 1066. In lordship 2 ploughs at
FARMINGTON;
    25 villagers with 12 ploughs; 4 slaves.
Value of the whole manor before 1066 £18; Archbishop Thomas
put it at a revenue of £27; the hide of (Upper) Coberley is assessed
at 20s; value of what Walter holds £14. Archbishop Thomas claims it.

Stigand archieps̄ tenuit *CVNTVNE*. Ibi erant. ıx. hidæ.
Ibi funt. ıı. car̄ 7 v. ac̄ p̄ti. 7 xxıı. uiłłi 7 v. bord̄ cū. xı.
car̄. Ibi. v. ſerui. 7 molin̄ de. v. ſolid̄.
T.R.E. ualb̄. ıx. lib̄. Modo. vıı. lib̄. Thomas arcħ tenet.
Vn̄ hō Roḡ de Jurei ten̄ un̄ ꝏ de. ııı. hid̄ p̄tin̄ huic ꝏ.
Hoc ipſe arcħ calūniat̄.   IN WITESTAN HD̄.

Eldred Archieps̄ tenuit *STANEDIS*. De dn̄io S̄ Petri
de Glouuecestre fuit. Ibi erant. xv. hidæ. T.R.E. In dn̄io
funt. ııı. car̄. 7 ıx. uiłłi 7 xıııı. bord̄ cū. xvı. car̄. 7 vıı.
Radcheniſt hn̄tes. xvıı. car̄. Ibi. vııı. ſerui. 7 dım piſcaria.
Silua dım̄ leuua l̄g. 7 una q̄ƶ lat̄.
Tot ꝏ T.R.E. ualb̄. xvı. lib̄. Modo. xıı. lib̄. Thomas arcħ
ten̄. 7 ſimilit̄ geldat̄.
De hac t̄ra huj̄ ꝏ ten̄ abb̄ de Glouuec̄. ı. hid̄. 7 jure deb̄ tene.

164 d

Hugo ten̄ unā hid̄ injuſte. Durand̄ ten̄. ııı. hid̄. q̄s. W. com̄
ded̄ fri ej Rogerio. Has calūniat̄ arcħ Thomas.
Sc̄s Oswald de Glouuec̄ tenuit *WIDIFORDE*. IN BERNITON HD̄.
Ibi T.R.E. erant. ıı. hidæ. 7 ıı. car̄ in dn̄io. 7 ıııı. uiłłi 7 ııı : bord̄
cū. ıı. car̄. Ibi. ıııı. ſerui. 7 vııı. ac̄ p̄ti. 7 molin̄ de. x. ſolid̄.
T.R.E. ualb̄. xl. ſot. m̄. lx. ſot. Rannulf ten̄ de eod̄ ſc̄o.
Qualis tc̄ fuit. talis. ē modo.   IN RESPIGETE HD̄
Sc̄s Oswald tenuit in *CERNEI*. un̄ ꝏ de. ıııı. hid̄. T.R.E.
Iſd Sc̄s ten̄ adhuc. 7 ħt. ıı. car̄ in dn̄io. 7 vı. uiłł 7 ıı. bord̄
cū. v. car̄. Ibi. ı. ſeru. 7 molin̄ de. vıı. ſot. 7 ıı. ac̄ p̄ti.
Tc̄ ualuit. c. ſot. Modo. ıııı. lib̄. IN LANGEBRIGE HD̄.
Vlchetel tenuit *LESSEDVNE*. ꝏ de. ıı. hid̄. Modo ten̄
Roḡ de Thoma Arcħ. ħ tra geld̄. In dn̄io. ē una car̄. 7 v. uiłłi
7 ıı. bord̄ cū. ııı. car̄. Ibi. ııı. ſerui. 7 xx. ac̄ p̄ti. Valuit xl. ſot. M. xxx.

9   Archbishop Stigand held COMPTON (Abdale). There were 9 hides.
2 ploughs there.
  Meadow, 5 acres.
  22 villagers and 5 smallholders with 11 ploughs.
  5 slaves; a mill at 5s.
Value before 1066 £9; now £7.
  Archbishop Thomas holds it. A man of Roger of Ivry's holds
a manor of 3 hides which belongs to this manor. The Archbishop
claims this himself.

In WHITSTONE Hundred
10   Archbishop Aldred held STANDISH. It was of the lordship of
St. Peter's of Gloucester. Before 1066 there were 15 hides.
In lordship 3 ploughs;
  9 villagers and 14 smallholders with 16 ploughs; 7 riding men
    who have 17 ploughs.
  8 slaves; ½ fishery; woodland ½ league long and 1 furlong wide.
Value of the whole manor before 1066 £16; now £12.
  Archbishop Thomas holds it and likewise pays tax.
  The Abbot of Gloucester holds 1 hide of this manor's land and
rightly ought to hold it. Earl Hugh holds 1 hide wrongfully.   164 d
Durand the Sheriff holds 3 hides which Earl William gave to his
brother Roger. Archbishop Thomas claims these lands.

In BARRINGTON Hundred
11   St. Oswald's of Gloucester held WIDFORD. Before 1066 there were
2 hides. In lordship 2 ploughs;
  4 villagers and 3 smallholders with 2 ploughs.
  4 slaves; meadow, 8 acres; a mill at 10s.
Value before 1066, 40s; now 60s.
  Ranulf holds it from St. (Oswald's). It is as it was then.

In RAPSGATE Hundred
12   St. Oswald's held a manor of 4 hides in (North) CERNEY before 1066.
St. Oswald's still holds it and has 2 ploughs in lordship;
  6 villagers and 2 smallholders with 5 ploughs.
  1 slave; a mill at 7s; meadow, 2 acres.
Value then 100s; now £4.

In LONGBRIDGE Hundred
13   Ulfketel held LASSINGTON, a manor of 2 hides. Now Roger holds it
from Archbishop Thomas. This land pays tax. In lordship 1 plough;
  5 villagers and 2 smallholders with 3 ploughs.
  3 slaves; meadow, 20 acres.
The value was 40s; now 30s.

S̄ca Terra Æcclæ de Wirecestre. *In Bernintrev Hd̄.*

Ŝca maria de Wireceſtre tenuit 7 ten̄ *HVESBERIE.*

Ibi fueř 7 ſunt.L.hidæ.In dn̄io ſunt.II.caŕ.7 VIII.uiłłi 7 VI.
borđ cū.VIII.caŕ.Ibi.IIII.ſerui 7 una Ancilla.

Ad hoc m̄ ptin̄ h̄ mēbra.Henberie.Redeuuiche.Stoche.

Giete.In his ſunt.IX.caŕ in dn̄io.7 XXVII.uiłłi 7 XXII.
borđ.cū.XXVI.caŕ.Ibi.XX.ſerui 7 II.ancillæ.7 XX.colibti
cū.X.caŕ.7 molin̄ de.XX.den̄.

Ad m̄ ptin̄.VI.Radcheniſt hn̄tes.VIII.hiđ.7 VIII.caŕ.

Ñ poterant a m̄ ſeparari.7 In Briſtou.II.dom̄ reddeƀ.XVI.den̄.

De hac tra huj̄ m̄ ten̄ Turſtin̄ fili Rolf.V.hiđ In Auſtre
cliue 7 Giſłeƀt fili Turold.III.hiđ 7 dimiđ jn Contone.
7 Conſtantin̄.V.hiđ jn Icetune.In his tris ſunt.V.caŕ
in dn̄io.7 XVI.uiłłi 7 XII.borđ cū.XII.caŕ.Ibi.XI.ſerui.

De eađ tra huj̄ m̄ ten̄ Osƀn̄ gifard.V.hiđ.7 nullū ſeruitiū facit.

Toť m̄ cū mēbris ſuis.T.R.E.ualƀ XXIIII.liƀ.

Modo dn̄iū Ŝ Mariæ.uał.XXIX.liƀ 7 XIIII.ſoł.7 VI.den̄.

Qđ hoēs ten̄.IX.liƀ. *In Respigete Hd̄.*

Ipſa æccła tenuit *COLESBORNE.*7 Suein de ea.Ñ poterat
recedere.Ibi.VIII.hidæ gelđ.Walteri.f.Roḡ ten̄ de æccła.

In dn̄io.ē una caŕ.7 XVIII.uiłłi 7 II.borđ cū.V.caŕ.Ibi.II.
ſerui.7 III.ač p̄ti.7 II.molini de.VII.ſoliđ.7 VI.denaŕ.

Tc ualuit.VIII.liƀ.Modo.IIII.liƀ.

Ipſa æccła ten̄ *AICOTE.*7 Ailric de ea.In Begeberie jacet.

Ibi una hida.In dn̄io ſunt.II.caŕ.7 II.uiłłi 7 IIII.borđ cū
II.caŕ.Ibi.II.ſerui.7 VIII.ač p̄ti.7 molin̄ de.LXIIII.den̄.

Valuit.XX.ſoł.Modo.XXX.ſoliđ.Ordric ten̄ de ep̄o.

Ipſa æccła tenuit *BECHEBERIE. In Becheberie Hvnd̄.*

Ibi.XXI.hida.In dn̄io ſunt.IIII.caŕ.7 XIX.uiłłi 7 II.borđ
cū.XI.caŕ.Ibi.III.Radcheniſt hn̄tes.IIII.hiđ 7 IIII.caŕ.
7 pƀr hn̄s.III.hiđ.7 cū ſuis.IIII.caŕ.Ibi.XI.int ſeruos
7 ancillas.7 II.molini de.XVII.ſoliđ.7 X.ač p̄ti.

LAND OF THE CHURCH OF WORCESTER

In BRENTRY Hundred

1   St. Mary's of Worcester held and holds WESTBURY (on Trym).
There were and are 50 hides. In lordship 2 ploughs;
    8 villagers and 6 smallholders with 8 ploughs. 4 male slaves,
    1 female.

These members belong to this manor: HENBURY, REDWICK,
STOKE (Bishop), YATE. In them are 9 ploughs in lordship;
    27 villagers and 22 smallholders with 26 ploughs. 20 male and
    2 female slaves and 20 freedmen with 10 ploughs.
A mill at 20d.
To this manor belong 6 riding men who have 8 hides and 8 ploughs;
they could not be separated from the manor.
    In Bristol 2 houses paid 16d.
Of this manor's land Thurstan son of Rolf holds 5 hides in AUST,
Gilbert son of Thorold 3½ hides in COMPTON (Greenfield);
Constantine 5 hides in ITCHINGTON. In these lands 5 ploughs in
lordship;
    16 villagers and 12 smallholders with 12 ploughs. 11 slaves.
Osbern Giffard holds 5 hides also of this manor's land and does
no service.

Value of the whole manor with its members before 1066 £24; value
now of St. Mary's lordship £29 14s 6d; of what the men hold £9.

In RAPSGATE Hundred

2   The Church held (Great) COLESBOURNE itself, and Swein from it.
He could not withdraw. 8 hides which pay tax. Walter son of
Roger holds from the Church. In lordship 1 plough;
    18 villagers and 2 smallholders with 5 ploughs.
    2 slaves; meadow, 3 acres; 2 mills at 7s 6d.
Value then £8; now £4.

3   The Church held EYCOT itself, and Alric from it. It lies in Bibury.
(lands). 1 hide. In lordship 2 ploughs;
    2 villagers and 4 smallholders with 2 ploughs.
    2 slaves; meadow, 8 acres; a mill at 64d.
The value was 20s; now 30s.
Ordric holds it from the Bishop.

In BIBURY Hundred

4   The Church held BIBURY itself. 21 hides. In lordship 4 ploughs;
    19 villagers and 2 smallholders with 11 ploughs. 3 riding men
        who have 4 hides and 4 ploughs; a priest who has 3 hides and,
        with his men, 4 ploughs.
    11 slaves, male and female; 2 mills at 17s; meadow, 10 acres.

De ead tra huj M ten Durand de epo. uñ M de. III. hid
7 unā v iñ Bernesleis 7 Eudo. VII. uirgat ibid p M.
In his funt. v. car in dñio. 7 XII. uilli cū. VI. car. Ibi. XII.
ferui. Tot M. T.R.E. ualuit. XVIII. lib. 7 m fimilit.
Vlftan eps teñ. 7 geldat.   IN WACRESCVBE HD.
Ipfa æccla teñ WIDINDVNE. Ibi. XXX. hidæ. Tres ex his
nunq geldauer. In dñio funt. II. car. 7 XVI. uilli 7 VIII.

165 a

bord cū. VII. car. Ibi. VI. ferui. 7 x. ac pti. Silua. I. leuua lg
7 dim lat. 7 In Contone. e una car. 7 II. uilli 7 II. bord cū. I. car.
7 II. ferui. 7 molin de. V. folid.
In eod M. funt. IIII. Radchenift hñtes. II. hid 7 III. uirg. 7 hñt
II. car. 7 pbr hñs dimid hid 7 I. car. In Glouuec. IIII. burgfes
redd VII. den 7 obolū.
De hac tra huj M ten de epo Moriñ. III. hid in Fufcote.
Anfchitil. II. hid in Colefburne 7 Willecote. Robt. IIII. hid
7 dimid. in Dodefuuelle 7 Peclefurde. Scheliñ. v. hid in Nate
graue. Drogo. x. hid in Eftone.
In his tris funt. XVI. car in dñio. 7 LI. uills. 7 VII. bord
cū XXVIII. car. Ibi. XLI. feruus. 7 III. molini de. XIII. folid.
7 IIII. denar. In Wicelcūbe. I. burgfis redd. III. folid.
In quibdā locis ptū 7 filua. fed ñ multa.
Tot M T,R.E. ualb. XXXVIII. lib. Modo: XXXIII. lib. int oms.
Vlftan eps teñ hoc M   IN TEDBOLDESTAN HD.
Ipfa æccla tenuit CLIVE. Ibi. XXX. hidæ. In dñio funt
III. car. 7 XVI. uilli 7 XIX. bord cū. XVI. car. Ibi: VIII. ferui.
7 un afrus. Ibi pbr ht. I. hid 7 II. car. 7 uñ Radchenift hñs
unā hid 7 II. car. Ibi filua paruula.

Also of this manor's land Durand holds from the Bishop a manor of 3 hides and 1 virgate in BARNSLEY, and Eudo 7·virgates there also, as a manor. In them are 5 ploughs in lordship;
12 villagers with 6 ploughs. 12 slaves.
Value of the whole manor before 1066 £18; now the same.
Bishop Wulfstan holds it and pays tax.

In WATTLESCOMB Hundred
5 The Church holds WITHINGTON itself. 30 hides. 3 of them have never paid tax. In lordship 2 ploughs;
16 villagers and 8

The following entry is added at the top of col. 165 a with no transposition signs.

In WITLEY Hundred
6 The Church itself holds 2 hides in CONDICOTE, and Osbern from   165 a
the Bishop. The value is and was 40s.

(3,5 continued)
(16 villagers and 8) smallholders with 7 ploughs.
6 slaves; meadow, 10 acres; woodland 1 league long and ½ wide.
In (Cassey) COMPTON 1 plough;
2 villagers and 2 smallholders with 1 plough. 2 slaves.
A mill at 5s.
Also in this manor 4 riding men who have 2 hides and 3 virgates; they have 2 ploughs; a priest who has ½ hide and 1 plough.
In Gloucester 4 burgesses who pay 7½d.
Of this manor's land Morin holds from the Bishop 3 hides in FOXCOTE, Ansketel 2 hides in (Little) COLESBOURNE and HILCOT, Robert 4½ hides in DOWDESWELL and PEGGLESWORTH, Azelin 5 hides in NOTGROVE, Drogo 10 hides in ASTON (Blank). In these lands are 16 ploughs in lordship;
51 villagers and 7 smallholders with 28 ploughs.
41 slaves. 3 mills at 13s 4d; in Winchcombe 1 burgess who pays
3s; meadow and woodland in certain places but not much.
Value of the whole manor before 1066 £38; now £33 between them.
Bishop Wulfstan holds this manor.

In TIBBLESTONE Hundred
7 The Church held (Bishops) CLEEVE itself. 30 hides. In lordship 3 ploughs;
16 villagers and 19 smallholders with 16 ploughs. 8 slaves;
1 draught animal. A priest has 1 hide and 2 ploughs;
1 riding man who has 1 hide and 2 ploughs.
A very small wood.

De hac t̃ra ej̃d m̃ ten de æcc̃la Durand `uicec'`. vi. hiđ in Surhā.

Radulf. iiii. hiđ. in Sapletone. Turſtin. f. Rolf. vi. hiđ in

Godrinton. In his t̃ris ſunt iñ dñio. viii. cař. 7 xxii. uiłłi

7 vii. borđ cū. xiii. cař. Ibi. xx ſeꝛui. 7 iii. afri. 7 moliñ de. xii.

deñ. 7 aliqtū p̃ti. ꝼDe eađ t̃ra ten Bernarđ 7 Raynalđ

vii. hiđ in *Stoches*. 7 ſeruitiū S̃ Marie nolunt facere.

Tot m̃ T.R.E ualuit. .vi. xxx. liƀ. Modo. xxvi. liƀ. int̃ om̃s.

Hoc m̃ ten Vlſtan eps.

.IIII. **E**ps de HEREFORD tenuit PRESTEBERIE. Ibi. xxx. hidæ.

TERRA ÆCCLÆ DE HEREFORD. *IN CLITEHĀ HVNĎ*.

In dñio ſunt. iii. cař. 7 xviii. uiłłi 7 v. borđ cū. ix. cař.

Ibi p̃br 7 uñ Radchenilt cū. ii. cař. 7 in Wicelcube. i. bur

genſis redđ. xviii. deñ. 7 int̃ ſeruos 7 ancillas. xi. Ibi. xx.

ãc p̃ti. 7 Silua de una leuua lḡ. 7 dimiđ lat.

Ad hoc m̃ adjacet una uilla *SEVENHĀTONE* ext̃ iſt *HVNĎ*.

Ibi ſunt. xx. hidæ de ſup̃diĉtis. xxx. hiđ.

7 ibi ſunt. ii. cař. 7 xxi. uiłłi cū. xi. cař. Ibi. iii. liƀi h̃oes

h̃ntes. vii. cař cū ſuis h̃oibȝ.

De his. xx. hiđ ten Durand de ep̃o. iii. hiđ.

Tot m̃ T.R.E. ualuit xii. liƀ. Modo: xvi. liƀ.

Hoc m̃ ten Rotƀt ep̃s ej̃d urbis.

.V. **E**ps de EXECESTRE ten *ALDELANDE*. Aluui tenuit

TERRA EP̃I OSBERNI. *IN SINESHOVEDES HĎ*.

h̃o Heraldi `com̃`. 7 poterat ire quo uolebat. Ibi. ii. hidæ. una gelđ

alia non. In dñio ſunt. ii. cař. 7 uñ uiłłs 7 vi. borđ cū. i. cař.

Ibi. ii. ſerui. 7 x. ãc p̃ti. Tc ualuit. iiii. liƀ. m̃. xx. ſot.

Iſđ eps ten *TIDRENTVNE*. Aluui *IN BACHESTANES HĎ*.

tenuit T.R.E. Ibi. v. hidæ. 7 ii. cař ſunt iñ dñio. 7 uñ

uiłłs 7 v. borđ. 7 ii. ſerui. 7 xx. ãc p̃ti. Silua dimiđ leuua

in lḡ 7 lat. Valuit. c. ſoliđ. modo: xl. ſot.

Of this manor's land Durand the Sheriff holds from the Church
6 hides in SOUTHAM, Ralph 4 hides in 'SAPPERTON'. Thurstan
son of Rolf 6 hides in GOTHERINGTON. In these lands 8 ploughs
in lordship;
>   22 villagers and 7 smallholders with 13 ploughs. 20 slaves.
>   3 draught animals; a mill at 12d; some meadow.
>   Bernard and Reginald hold 7 hides of this land in STOKE (Orchard).
They refuse to do service to St. Mary's.
Value of the whole manor before 1066 £36; now £26 between them.
Bishop Wulstan holds this manor.

4   **LAND OF THE CHURCH OF HEREFORD**

In CHELTENHAM Hundred
1   The Bishop of Hereford held PRESTBURY. 30 hides. In lordship 3
ploughs;
>   18 villagers and 5 smallholders with 9 ploughs. A priest and a
>   riding man with 2 ploughs; in Winchcombe 1 burgess who
>   pays 18d; 11 slaves, male and female.
>   Meadow, 20 acres; woodland at 1 league long and ½ wide.
SEVENHAMPTON, a village outside that Hundred, is attached to this
manor. 20 hides of the said 30 hides there. 2 ploughs there;
>   21 villagers with 11 ploughs. 3 free men who have 7 ploughs
>   with their men.
Durand holds 3 hides of these 20 hides from the Bishop.
Value of the whole manor before 1066 £12; now £16.
Robert, Bishop of this town, holds this manor.

5   **LAND OF BISHOP OSBERN**

In SWINEHEAD Hundred
1   The Bishop of Exeter holds OLDLAND. Alfwy, a man of Earl Harold's,
held it and could go where he would. 2 hides; 1 which pays tax,
the other not. In lordship 2 ploughs;
>   1 villager and 6 smallholders with 1 plough.
>   2 slaves; meadow, 10 acres.
Value then £4; now 20s.

In BAGSTONE Hundred
2   The Bishop also holds TYTHERINGTON. Alfwy held it before 1066.
5 hides. In lordship 2 ploughs;
>   1 villager, 5 smallholders and 2 slaves.
>   Meadow, 20 acres; woodland ½ league in length and width.
The value was 100s; now 40s.

VI. **E**TERRA EPI CONSTANTIENS. *IN BACHESTANES HD*

PS de S *LAVDO* ten *ACTVNE*.7 Ilger de eo.Ibi.II.

hidæ.7 in dnio.ē.I.car.7 IIII.uiłłi 7 v.borđ.7 I.feru.7 II.

Ancillæ.cū.I.car 7 dimiđ.Ibi dimiđ moliñ de.xvi.den.

7 x.ac pti.7 una q̃ꝝ filuæ.Vał 7 ualuit.xL.foliđ. ꝼHD.

Ebbi tenuit hoc ᴔ hō Briĉtric.F.Algar.*IN SINESHOVEDES*

Iſđ eꝑs teñ *HANBROC*.7 Ofulf de eo.Algar tenuit de rege.E.

165 b

Tra.ē.v.car.

7 poterat ire quó uoleƀ.Ibi.II.hide.In dñio funt

II.car.7 II.uiłłi cū.II.car.7 II.fcrui.7.vI.ac pti.

Valuit.c.foł.Modo.Lx.foliđ.

Iſđ eꝑs teñ uñ Maner de una hida 7 Goifmer de eo.

In iſta hida qdo arat non funt nifi.LxIIII.ac træ.

Ibi.ē in dñio.I.car.Valuit.xx.foł.M.xvi.foliđ.

Iſđ eꝑs teñ *ESTOCH* 7 Tetbalđ de eo.Eldrēd tenuit

de Heraldo.7 poterat ire quó uoleƀ.Ibi.II.hide.

una gelđ.alia non.In dñio.ē una car.7 II.uiłłi

7 I.borđ cū.I.car.Ibi.vI.ferui.7 v.ac pti.

Valuit.xL.foliđ.Modo.xx.foliđ. *IN PVLCRECERCE HD.*

Iſđ eꝑs teñ *DIDINTONE*.7 Roƀt de eo.Aluuarđ

tenuit teiñ regis.E.Ibi.v.hidæ gelđ.In dñio

funt.III.car.7 xIIII.uiłłi 7 vIII.borđ.cū.vIII.car.

Ibi.x.ferui.7 II.molini de.x.foł.7 x.den.7 II.hões

de.v.foliđ.7 xII.ac pti.Silua dimiđ leuua łg.

7 dim łat. Vał 7 ualuit.vIII.liƀ.

Iſđ eꝑs teñ *WAPELIE*.7 Aldred de eo.Iſđ tenuit T.R.E.Ibi

una hida.7 in dñio.I.car.7.II.ferui.Vał 7 ualuit.xx.foliđ.

Iſđ eꝑs teñ *LEGA*.7 Roƀtus de eo.Algar *IN LETBERGE HD*

tenuit T.R.E.Ibi.I.hida gelđ.7 II.car in dñio.7 III.borđ

7 II.ferui.cū.I.car.Vał 7 ualuit.xx.foliđ. *IN LANGELEI HD.*

Iſđ eꝑs teñ *HERDICOTE*.7 Roƀt de eo.Cuulf tenuit T.R.E.

165 a, b

LAND OF THE BISHOP OF COUTANCES

In BAGSTONE Hundred

1 The Bishop of St. Lô holds 'ACTON (Ilger)' and Ilger from him.
2½ hides. In lordship 1 plough;
4 villagers, 5 smallholders, 1 male and 2 female slaves
with 1½ ploughs.
½ mill at 16d; meadow, 10 acres; woodland, 1 furlong.
The value is and was 40s.
Ebbi, a man of Brictric son of Algar, held this manor.

The Bishop also holds

in SWINEHEAD Hundred

2 HAMBROOK. Oswulf holds from him. Algar held it from King Edward
and could go where he would. 2 hides. Land for 5 ploughs.   165 b
In lordship 2 ploughs;
2 villagers with 2 ploughs; 2 slaves.
Meadow, 6 acres.
The value was 100s; now 60s.

3 a manor of 1 hide. Gosmer holds from him. When it is ploughed,
there are only 64 acres of land in that hide. In lordship 1 plough.
The value was 20s; now 16s.

4 (Harry) STOKE. Theobald holds from him. Aldred held it from
Earl Harold and could go where he would. 2 hides; 1 which pays
tax, the other not. In lordship 1 plough;
2 villagers and 1 smallholder with 1 plough.
6 slaves; meadow, 5 acres.
The value was 40s; now 20s.

in PUCKLECHURCH Hundred

5 DOYNTON. Robert holds from him. Alfward, a thane of King Edward's,
held it. 5 hides which pay tax. In lordship 3 ploughs;
14 villagers and 8 smallholders with 8 ploughs.
10 slaves; 2 mills at 10s 10d; 2 men at 5s; meadow, 12 acres;
woodland ½ league long and ½ wide.
The value is and was £8.

6 WAPLEY ('Rectory'). Aldred holds from him. He also held it before
1066. In lordship 1 plough; 2 slaves.
The value is and was 20s.

in LEDBURY Hundred

7 'LEE'. Robert holds from him. Algar held it before 1066. 1 hide
which pays tax. In lordship 2 ploughs;
3 smallholders and 2 slaves with 1 plough.
The value is and was 20s.

in LANGLEY Hundred

8 (Gaunts) EARTHCOTT. Robert holds from him. Cuthwulf held it

Ibi.ii.hidæ gelđ.7 ii.cař funt in dñio.7 ii.borđ.7 iiii.ſerui.7 iiii.uiłłi.
7 x.ac̃ p̃ti.7 ſilua   Val 7 ualuit.xl.ſol.
Ipſe eps̃ ten̊ DODINTONE.7 Roger de eo.Vlnod IN EDREDESTAN HĎ.
tenuit.T.R.E.Ibi.i.hida 7 dim̃.7 tcia pars đim hidæ.In
dñio.ē.i.cař.7 iiii.uiłłi 7 un̊ borđ cũ.i.cař.Ibi.iii.ſerui.
Val 7 ualuit.xxx.ſoliđ.

VII ◦TERRA ÆCCLÆ DE BADE. IN LANGELEI HĎ.

S̃cs PETRVS de BADA tenuit ALVESTONE.Ibi.v.hidæ.Tres geldaℵ
Ex his.7.ii.n̄ gelđ,c̃ceſſu.E.7 W.regũ.In dñio funt.ii.cař.
7 ix.uiłłi 7 vi.borđ 7 pbr̃ 7 un̊ Radchen̊.cũ.x.cař.
Ibi.vii.ſerui.7 p̃ta 7 ſilua ad m̃ ſuſtinenđ.Valuit.c.ſol
modo:̃iiii.lib̃.Ipſa æccła ten̊ adhuc. IN PVLCRECERCE HĎ.
Ipſa æccła ten̊ ESCETONE.Ibi.v.hidæ.Harũ.ii.funt a geldo
quietæ.c̃ceſſu.E.7 W.regũ.Tres û gelđ.In dñio.ē una cař.
7 iii.uiłłi 7 iii.borđ 7 un̊ Radchen̊.Int̃ oms̃.iii.cař.Ibi.i.colib̃t.
7 molin̄ de.l.denař.7 vi.ac̃ p̃ti.Val 7 ualuit.iiii.lib̃.

.VIII. ◦TERRA ÆCCLÆ GLASTINGBER.IN PVLCRECERCE HVNĎ.

S̃cA MARIA de GLASTINGEBERIE ten̊ PVLCRECERCE.
Ibi.xx.hidæ.In dñio funt.vi.cař.7 xxiii.uiłłi 7 viii.borđ.
cũ.xviii.cař.Ibi.x.ſerui.7 vi.hões redđt c.maſſas ferri
.x.min.7 in Glouueceſtre.i.burg̃ſis redđ.v.den̊.7 ii.colib̃ti
redđ.xxxiiii.den̊.7 iii.francig̃ ſunt ibi.7 ii.molini de.c.den̊.
Ibi.lx.ac̃ p̃ti.7 ſilua dimiđ leuua lg̃.7 dimiđ lat̃.
Valuit.xx.lib̃.modo:̃xxx.lib̃.

.IX ◦TERRA ÆCCLÆ MALMESBER. IN LANGELEI HVNĎ.

S̃cA MARIA de MALMESBERIE ten̊ LITELTONE.Ibi.v.hidæ
Harũ.ii.7 dimiđ gelđ.aliæ ſunt q̃etæ.In dñio ſunt.ii.cař.7 xiii.
uiłłi 7 ii.borđ cũ.viii.cař.Ibi æccła 7 pbr̃.7 xxx.ac̃ prati.
Valuit.lx.ſoliđ.Modo:̃c.ſoliđ.

before 1066. 2 hides which pay tax. In lordship 2 ploughs;
2 smallholders, 4 slaves and 4 villagers.
Meadow, 10 acres; woodland ...
The value is and was 40s.

In EDDERSTONE Hundred

9   The Bishop holds DODINGTON himself, and Roger from him.
Wulfnoth held it before 1066. 1½ hides and the third part
of ½ hide. In lordship 1 plough;
4 villagers and 1 smallholder with 1 plough. 3 slaves.
The value is and was 30s.

7   LAND OF THE CHURCH OF BATH

In LANGLEY Hundred

1   St. Peter's of Bath held OLVESTON. 5 hides; 3 of them pay tax
and 2 do not, by the assent of Kings Edward and William. In
lordship 2 ploughs;
9 villagers, 6 smallholders, a priest and 1 riding man with
10 ploughs.
7 slaves; meadows and woodland to maintain the manor.
The value was 100s; now £4.
The Church itself still holds it.

In PUCKLECHURCH Hundred

2   The Church holds (Cold) ASHTON itself. 5 hides; 2 of them are
exempt from tax by the assent of Kings Edward and William,
but 3 pay tax. In lordship 1 plough;
3 villagers, 3 smallholders and 1 riding man; 3 ploughs between
them.
1 freedman; a mill at 50d; meadow, 6 acres.
The value is and was £4.

8   LAND OF GLASTONBURY CHURCH

In PUCKLECHURCH Hundred

1   St. Mary's of Glastonbury holds PUCKLECHURCH. 20 hides.
In lordship 6 ploughs;
23 villagers and 8 smallholders with 18 ploughs. 10 slaves;
6 men pay 100 lumps of iron, less 10; in Gloucester 1 burgess
who pays 5d; 2 freedmen who pay 34d; 3 Frenchmen there.
2 mills at 100d. Meadow, 60 acres; woodland ½ league long
and ½ wide.
The value was £20; now £30.

9   LAND OF MALMESBURY CHURCH

In LANGLEY Hundred

1   St. Mary's of Malmesbury holds LITTLETON (on Severn). 5 hides;
2½ of them pay tax, the others are exempt. In lordship 2 ploughs;
13 villagers and 2 smallholders with 8 ploughs.
A church and a priest; meadow, 30 acres.
The value was 60s; now 100s.

X. **S**TERRA ꝫ PETRI·DE GLOWEC̄. *In Dvdestanes hd̄.*

C̄s Petrvꝭ De Glowecestre tenuit T.R.E. C̄O
Bertvne cū mēbris adjacentibꜩ Berneuude.

Tuffelege. Mereuuent. Ibi. xxii. hidæ. una v̊ min.

Ibi ſunt in dn̄io. ix. car̄.7 xlii. uiłłi 7 xxi. bord.

cū. xlv. car̄. Ibi. xii. ſerui.7 moliñ de. v. ſolid.

7 c.xx. ac̄ p̄ti.7 ſilua. v. q̄ꜩ lḡ.7 iii. lat.

Valuit. viii. liƀ. Modo. xxiiii. liƀ.

Hoc C̄O q̄etū fuit sēp a geldo.7 ab om̄i regali ſeruitio.

Ipſa ead æccła tenuit Frowecestre. *In Blacelavves hd̄.*

Ibi. v. hidæ. In dn̄io ſunt. iiii. car̄.7 viii. uiłłi 7 vii.

bord cū. vii. car̄. Ibi. iii. ſerui.7 x. ac̄ p̄ti.7 Silua

iii. q̄ꜩ lḡ.7 ii. q̄ꜩ lat. Valuit. iii. liƀ. modo. viii. liƀ.

Ipſa æccła ten Boxewelle. *In Griboldestowes hd̄.*

Ibi. v. hidæ. In dn̄io ſunt. ii. car̄.7 xii. uiłłi 7 i. Rad

cheniſt hn̄tes. xii. car̄. Ibi. viii. ſerui.7 moliñ de. v. ſoł.

Valuit. lxx. ſoł. modo. c. ſoł. *In Brictvvoldesberg hd̄.*

Ipſa æccła ten Cvlne. Ibi. iiii. hidæ. In dn̄io ſunt

iii. car̄.7 xi. uiłłi 7 vii. bord cū. xii. car̄. Ibi. iiii. ſerui.

Valuit. vi. liƀ. modo. viii. liƀ. Dụo molini reddeƀ

xxv. ſolid. *In Begebriges hd̄.*

Ipſa æccła ten Aldesorde. Ibi. xi. hidæ. In dn̄io

ſunt. iii. car̄.7 xxi. uiłłs 7 v. bord 7 ii. francig cū. xv.

car̄. Ibi. vi. ſerui. Valuit. c. ſoł. Modo. viii. liƀ.

Ipſa æccła ten Bochelande. *In Wideles hvnd.*

Ibi. x. hidæ. In dn̄io ſunt. iii. car̄.7 xxii. uiłłi 7 vi.

bord. cū. xii. car̄. Ibi. viii. ſerui.7 x. ac̄ p̄ti.

Valuit. iii. liƀ. modo. ix. liƀ. *In Tetboldestanes hd̄.*

Ipſa æccła ten Hinetvne. Ibi. xv. hidæ. In dn̄io

ſunt. ii. car̄.7 xxx. uiłłi 7 vii. bord cū. xvi. car̄.

In DUDSTONE Hundred

1   St. Peter's of Gloucester held the manor of '(Abbots) BARTON'
with the attached members, BARNWOOD, TUFFLEY and 'MORWENTS
(End)' before 1066. 22 hides, less 1 virgate. In lordship 9 ploughs;
    42 villagers and 21 smallholders with 45 ploughs.
    12 slaves; a mill at 5s; meadow, 120 acres; woodland 5 furlongs
     long and 3 wide.
The value was £8; now £24.
    This manor was always exempt from tax and from all royal
service.

In BLACKLOW Hundred

2   The Church also held FROCESTER itself. 5 hides. In lordship
4 ploughs;
    8 villagers and 7 smallholders with 7 ploughs.
    3 slaves; meadow, 10 acres; woodland 3 furlongs long
     and 2 furlongs wide.
The value was £3; now £8.

The Church itself holds

in GRUMBALDS ASH Hundred

3   BOXWELL. 5 hides. In lordship 2 ploughs;
    12 villagers and 1 riding man who have 12 ploughs.
    8 slaves; a mill at 5s.
The value was 70s; now 100s.

in BRIGHTWELLS BARROW Hundred

4   COLN (St. Aldwyns). 4 hides. In lordship 3 ploughs;
    11 villagers and 7 smallholders with 12 ploughs. 4 slaves.
The value was £6; now £8.
    2 mills paid 25s.

in BIBURY Hundred

5   ALDSWORTH. 11 hides. In lordship 3 ploughs;
    21 villagers, 5 smallholders and 2 Frenchmen with 15 ploughs.
    6 slaves.
The value was 100s; now £8.

in WITLEY Hundred

6   BUCKLAND. 10 hides. In lordship 3 ploughs;
    22 villagers and 6 smallholders with 12 ploughs.
    8 slaves; meadow, 10 acres.
The value was £3; now £9.

in TIBBLESTONE Hundred

7   HINTON (on the Green). 15 hides. In lordship 2 ploughs;
    30 villagers and 7 smallholders with 16 ploughs.

Ibi . xi . ſerui .7 uñ francigena.

Valuit . iii . liƀ . Modo:́ x . liƀ . Hoc ꝏ quietũ . ē a geldo

7 ab oī̃ forenſi ſeruitio . p̃ter æccłæ. *In* Tolangebriges HD́.

r Ipſa æccła teñ Hamme . Ibi . vii . hidæ . In dñio ſunt . iii.

car .7 xxii . uiłłi 7 iiii . borđ cũ . vii . car ̓. Ibi . viii . ſerui.

7 xxx . ac̃ p̃ti . Silua q̃ ꝏ ſufficit . Valuit . xl . ſoł . m̃ . iiii . liƀ.

Ipſa æccła teñ Prestetvne . Ibi . ii . hidæ . In dñio ſuꝓ

.ii . car ̓.7 viii . uiłłi 7 iiii . borđ cũ . viii . car ̓. Ibi . iiii . ſerui.

Valuit . xxx . ſoł . Modo:́ iiii . liƀ. *In* Botelewes HD́.

Ipſa æccła teñ Ledene . Ibi . iiii . hidæ . In dñio ſunt . ii . car ̓.

7 viii . uiłłi 7 uñ borđ cũ . viii . car ̓. Ibi . iiii . ſerui .7 moliñ

de . iiii . ſoliđ .7 x . ac̃ p̃ti . Silua . ii . leuũ lḡ .7 ii . q̃ɀ lat̃.

Vix uał xxx . ſoł. *In* Westberies HD́.

Ipſa æccła teñ Hame .7 Mortvne . Int̃ ſiluā 7 plañ . v . hiđ.

In dñio ſunt . ii . car ̓.7 vii . uiłłi 7 ii . borđ cũ . vi . car ̓.

Silua . i . leuũ lḡ .7 una lat̃. Ibi habuit æccła uenationē

ſuā ꝑ . iii . haias . T.R.E .7 tp̃r . W . Valuit . xx . ſoł . m̃ . xl . ſoł.

In Omenie teñ fr̃ Reinbaldi . ii . hiđ. *In* Gersdvnes HD́.

Ibi . ii . car ̓.7 v . uiłłi cũ . iii . car ̓.7 iiii . ſerui .7 xxiiii . ac̃ p̃ti.

7 moliñ de . v . ſoł . Valuit . xl . ſoł . Modo:́ uix . xx . ſoł.

Uxor Walterij de Laci c̃ceſſu regis . W . *In* Cirecestre HD́.

deđ s̃co Petro ꝑ Anima uiri ſui Dvntesborne . Man ̓

de . v . hiđ . In dñio . iii . car ̓.7 viii . uiłłi cũ . v . car ̓. Ibi

xvi . ſerui .7 moliñ de . ii . ſoliđ. Vał . iiii . liƀ.

165 d

T.R.E . habeƀ ſc̃s Petrus in Glouueceſtre de ſuis burgenſibɀ

xix . ſoliđ 7 ́ v . deñ .7 xvi . ſalmons . Modo hƚ totiđ ſalmons

7 l . ſoł . Ibi . ē moliñ de . xii . ſoł .7 iiii . piſcariæ ađ uic̃tũ monachoɀ.

11 slaves; 1 Frenchman.
The value was £3; now £10.
This manor is exempt from tax and from all outside service
except to the Church.

in LONGBRIDGE Hundred
8   HIGHNAM. 7 hides. In lordship 3 ploughs;
    22 villagers and 4 smallholders with 7 ploughs.
    8 slaves; meadow, 30 acres; woodland sufficient
      for the manor.
The value was 40s; now £4.

9   PRESTON. 2 hides. In lordship 2 ploughs;
    8 villagers and 4 smallholders with 8 ploughs. 4 slaves.
The value was 30s; now £4.

in BOTLOE Hundred
10   UPLEADON. 4 hides. In lordship 2 ploughs;
    8 villagers and 1 smallholder with 8 ploughs.
    4 slaves; a mill at 4s; meadow, 10 acres; woodland 2 leagues
      long and 2 furlongs wide.
Value scarcely 30s.

in WESTBURY Hundred
11   CHURCHAM and 'MORTON'. 5 hides in both woodland and open land.
  In lordship 2 ploughs;
    7 villagers and 2 smallholders with 6 ploughs.
    Woodland 1 league long and 1 wide. The Church had its
      hunting here in 3 hedged enclosures before and after 1066.
The value was 20s; now 40s.

In GARSDON Hundred
12   In AMPNEY (St. Peter) Reinbald's brother holds 2 hides.
  2 ploughs there.
    5 villagers with 3 ploughs; 4 slaves.
    Meadow, 24 acres; a mill at 5s.
The value was 40s; now scarcely 20s.

In CIRENCESTER Hundred
13   Walter of Lacy's wife gave DUNTISBOURNE (Abbots), a manor of
  5 hides, to St. Peter's for her husband's soul, with King William's
  assent. In lordship 3 ploughs;
    8 villagers with 5 ploughs.
    16 slaves; a mill at 2s.
Value £4.

14   Before 1066 St. Peter's had 19s 5d and 16 salmon from its   165 d
  burgesses in GLOUCESTER; now it has as many salmon and 50s.
    A mill at 12s; 4 fisheries for the monks' supplies.

Eccla S Marie de Wincelcvbe ten Scirebvrne.

TERRA ÆCCLÆ DE WINCELCVBE *In Salemones Hd.*

Ibi.xxx.hidæ.Ex his.x.funt liberæ.ad curiā ptiń.

Ibi funt in dñio.v.caŕ.7 xL.uilti 7 vii.borđ cū.xxii.caŕ.

Ibi.xii.ferui.7 iiii.molini de.xL.fol.7 xxx.āc p̃ti.

T.R.E.ualb.xx.lib.m̃.xiiii.lib.

Ipfa æccta teń *Bladintvn*.Ibi.vii.hidæ.In dñio funt.ii.caŕ.

7 viii.uilti 7 iiii.borđ cū.v.caŕ.7 viii.ferui.7 ii.Ancillæ.Ibi

moliñ de.v.fol.7 xxx.āc p̃ti. Valuit.iiii.lib.Modo.iii.lib.

Ipfa æccta teń *Tveninge*.Ibi.iii.hidæ gelđ. *In Gretestanes Hd.*

In dñio funt.ii.caŕ.7 xxiiii.uilti 7 viii.borđ cū.xxvii.caŕ.

Ibi.viii.ferui 7 ii.Ancillæ.7 xL.āc p̃ti.Silua.ii.q̃ʒ lg̃.7 i.lat̃.

Valuit.viii.lib.Modo.vii.lib.

Ipfa æccta teń *Freolintvne*.Ibi.ẽ una hida.7 in dñio.iiii.

caŕ.7 vi.ferui.7 ii.ancillæ.H̃ tra liba fuit 7 q̃eta ab om̃i geldo

7 regali feruitio. Valuit.xL.fol.M̃.L.foliđ.

Ipfa æccta teń *Aldritone*.7 q̃dā miles de abbe.Ibi.ii.hidæ

7 dimiđ.In dñio funt.ii.caŕ.7 uñ uilts cū una caŕ.7 adhuc.iii.

poffunt.ẽẽ.Ibi.iiii.ferui.Vat 7 ualuit.xxx.fol.

Ipfa æccta teń *Niwetone*.7 ii.milites de abbe.Ibi.iii.hidæ 7 dim̃.

In dñio funt.iii.caŕ.7 iii.ferui.7 ii.uilti cū.i.caŕ.7 adhuc.vi.ibi

poffeɴ.ẽẽ.Vat 7 ualuit.xL.foliđ.

Ipfa æccta teń *Stantone*.Ibi.iii.hidæ.In dñio funt.ii.caŕ.

7 xiiii.uilti cū.vii.caŕ.Ibi.iii.borđ 7 vi.ferui.7 vi.āc p̃ti.

Silua una leuua lg̃.7 dimiđ lat̃.Vat 7 ualuit.iii.lib.

Ipfa æccta teń *Cerletone*.Ibi.ii.hidæ liberæ 7 quietæ.

In dñio.ẽ.i.caŕ.7 iiii.uilti 7 ii.borđ cū.iiii.caŕ.Ibi.vi.ferui.

7 moliñ de.xx.deń.7 ii.āc p̃ti.Vat 7 ualuit.xx.foliđ.

Ipfa æccta teń *Snawesille*.Ibi.vii.hidæ *In Holefordes Hd.*

geldantes.In dñio funt.iii.caŕ.7 xii.uilti ⁊ ii.borđ cū.vi.caŕ.

Ibi.vi.ferui. Vat 7 ualuit.c.foliđ.

LAND OF THE CHURCH OF WINCHCOMBE

In SALMONSBURY Hundred

St. Mary's Church of Winchcombe holds SHERBORNE. 30 hides; 10 of them are free; they belong to the court. In lordship 5 ploughs;
>   40 villagers and 7 smallholders with 22 ploughs.
>   12 slaves; 4 mills at 40s; meadow, 30 acres.

Value before 1066 £20; now £14.

The Church itself holds

BLEDINGTON. 7 hides. In lordship 2 ploughs;
>   8 villagers and 4 smallholders with 5 ploughs;
>>   8 male and 2 female slaves.

>   A mill at 5s; meadow, 30 acres.

The value was £4; now £3.

in GRESTON Hundred

TWYNING. 3 hides which pay tax. In lordship 2 ploughs;
>   24 villagers and 8 smallholders with 27 ploughs.
>   8 male and 2 female slaves; meadow, 40 acres;
>>   woodland 2 furlongs long and 1 wide.

The value was £8; now £7.

FRAMPTON. 1 hide. In lordship 4 ploughs; 6 male and 2 female slaves. This land was free and exempt from all tax and royal service. The value was 40s; now 50s.

ALDERTON. A man-at-arms holds from the Abbot. 2½ hides. In lordship 2 ploughs;
>   1 villager with 1 plough; a further 3 possible. 4 slaves.

The value is and was 30s.

NAUNTON. 2 men-at-arms hold from the Abbot. 3½ hides. In lordship 3 ploughs; 3 slaves;
>   2 villagers with 1 plough; a further 6 would be possible.

The value is and was 40s.

STANTON. 3 hides. In lordship 2 ploughs;
>   14 villagers with 7 ploughs. 3 smallholders and 6 slaves.
>   Meadow, 6 acres; woodland 1 league long and ½ wide.

The value is and was £3.

CHARLTON (Abbots). 2 hides, free and exempt. In lordship 1 plough;
>   4 villagers and 2 smallholders with 4 ploughs.
>   6 slaves; a mill at 20d; meadow, 2 acres.

The value is and was 20s.

in HOLFORD Hundred

SNOWSHILL. 7 hides which pay tax. In lordship 3 ploughs;
>   12 villagers and 2 smallholders with 6 ploughs. 6 slaves.

The value is and was 100s.

Ipfa æccła teñ *HENIBERGE*.Ibi.x.hidæ fuꝧ.Harū.ii.in

dñio.7 ad feruitiū.viii.In dñio funt.v.car.7 xv.uiłłi cū.v.

car.Ibi.ix.ferui 7 iii.ancillæ.Valuit.vi.lib.Modo.viii.lib.

Ipfa æccła teñ *EDELMINTONE*.Ibi.iii.hidæ 7 dimidia.

In dñio funt.ii.car.7 xiii.uiłłi cū.vi.car.Ibi.iiii.ferui.

7 ii.ancillæ.Valuit.iiii.lib.Modo.iii.lib.

Ipfa æccła teñ *HIDICOTE*.Ibi.ii.hidæ liberæ.In dñio.ē.i.car.

cū.i.feruo.Vał 7 ualuit.xl.folid.

T.R.E.defdb fe ħ æccła iu GLOWECESTREfcẏre p.lx.hid.

ELSI de ferendone teñ de ipfa abbatia.iii.hid 7 dimid In *WENRIC*.

Bolle tenuit 7 abbatiæ dedit.ꝗ cū ifta tra poterat ire quo uoleb.

In dñio fuñꝧ.v.car.7 i.uiłł 7 vii.bord cū.i.car.7 x.ferui.7 moliñ 7 dimid ☞

.XII. TERRA Ⓢ MARIÆ DE EVESHĀ. *IN SALEMONES HVND.*

Eccła Ⓢ MARIÆ De EVESHAM teñ *MALGERESBERIÆ*.

ad Eduuardeſtou.Ibi T.R.E.eraꝧ.viii.hidæ.7 nona hida

jacet ad æcclam Ⓢ Edwardi.Rex Adelredus ꝗetā dedit ibi.

In dñio funt.iii.car.7 xii.uiłłi.7 un lib hō 7 pbr inť fe hñtes

vii.car.Ibi.vi.ferui.7 moliñ de.viii.folid.pti aliꝗtū.

T.R.E.ualb.c.folid.Modo.vii.lib.

Ipfa æccła teñ *TEDESTROP*.Ibi.vii.hidæ.In dñio funt.ii.

car.7 x.uiłłi 7 ii.bord cū.iii.car.Ibi.iiii.ferui.7 un miles

cū.ii.car.Ibi parū pti. Valuit.iiii.lib.Modo.c.folid.

Ipfa æccła teñ *BORTVNE*.Ibi.x.hidæ.In dñio funt.vi.

car.7 xvi.uiłłi 7.viii.bord.7 ii.libi hōes cū.vii.car.

165 c, d

☞de xii.folid 7 vi.deñ. Vał totū.viii.lib.Vluric tenuit de hac tra.

ii.hid ᵱ.ꝏ.7 Toui.v.uirg ᵱ ꝏ.7 Leuuin.i.virg ᵱ ꝏ.

Hoc ꝏ qué teñ Elfi de abbe.injufte jacuit in Salemonefberie ħd.

poftꝗ Bolle mortuus fuit.Modo jacet in Bernitoné ħd.judicio hōūm

ejdé hund.

in CHELTHORN Hundred
(Cow) HONEYBOURNE. 10 hides; 2 of them in lordship; 8 liable for service. In lordship 5 ploughs;
15 villagers with 5 ploughs. 9 male and 3 female slaves.
The value was £6; now £8.

ADMINGTON. 3½ hides. In lordship 2 ploughs;
13 villagers with 6 ploughs. 4 male and 2 female slaves.
The value was £4; now £3.

HIDCOTE (Boyce). 2 hides, free. In lordship 1 plough, with 1 slave.
The value is and was 40s.

Before 1066 this Church answered for 60 hides in Gloucestershire.

[In BARRINGTON Hundred]
Alfsi of Faringdon holds 3½ hides from the Abbey itself in WINDRUSH.
Bolle held it and gave it to the Abbey; he could go with that land where he would. In lordship 5 ploughs;
1 villager and 7 smallholders with 1 plough; 10 slaves.
1½ mills   †

Continued at foot of page after 12,3, written across both columns and directed to its proper place by transposition signs.

LAND OF ST. MARY'S OF EVESHAM

In SALMONSBURY Hundred
St. Mary's Church of Evesham holds MAUGERSBURY near STOW (on the Wold). Before 1066 there were 8 hides and a ninth hide lies near St. Edward's Church. King Aethelred gave it, exempt.
In lordship 3 ploughs;
12 villagers, 1 free man and a priest, who between them have
7 ploughs.
6 slaves; a mill at 8s; some meadow.
Value before 1066, 100s; now £7.

The Church itself holds ADLESTROP. 7 hides. In lordship 2 ploughs;
10 villagers and 2 smallholders with 3 ploughs.
4 slaves; a man-at-arms with 2 ploughs. A little meadow.
The value was £4; now 100s.

The Church itself holds BOURTON (on the Water). 10 hides.
In lordship 6 ploughs;
16 villagers, 8 smallholders and 2 free men with 7 ploughs.
† *(11,14 continued)*
(1½ mills) at 12s 6d.
In total, value £8.
Wulfric held 2 hides of this land as a manor, Tovi 5 virgates as a manor, and Leofwin 1 virgate as a manor.
This manor, which Alfsi holds from the Abbot, wrongfully lay in Salmonsbury Hundred after Bolle died; now it lies in Barrington by the judgement of the men of that Hundred.

Ibi p̄br cū dim̄ car. Valuit.viii.lib̄.Modo.'xii.lib̄.

Ibi / xiii. / ſerui

Ipſa æccła ten̄ *BRADEWELLE* .Ibi.x.hidæ.Ibi.vi.car.in dn̄io. 7 xxv.uiłłi 7 viii.borđ 7 un̄ lib̄ hō 7 p̄br.Int̄ om̄s hn̄t.xii.car.

In Glouuec̄.iiii.burgſes.7 in Wicelcōbe un̄.Redđt.xxvii.den̄. Valuit tot̄.viii.lib̄.Modo.'xii.lib̄. *IN WIDELEI HVND.*

Ipſa æccła ten̄ *SVVELLE*.Ibi.iii.hidæ.7 ix.uiłłi 7 ii.borđ. 7 p̄br.Int̄ om̄s.iiii.car.Ibi.vi.ſerui.Valuit.iiii.lib̄.M̊.v.lib̄.

In dn̄io ſunt.iii.car.Ibi.iii.molin̄.xx.ſoł.

Ipſa æccła ten̄ *WILLERSEI*.Ibi.viii.hidæ.i.ad Wiquennā. Ibi.iii.car in dn̄io.7 xvi.uiłłos.7 iiii.borđ.7 p̄br.cū.vi.car. Ibi.ii.ſerui.7 parū prati.Valuit.iiii.lib̄.Modo.c.ſoliđ.

Ipſa æccła ten̄ *WESTVNE*.Ibi.iii.hidæ.7 una libera.In dn̄io ſunt.ii.car.7 v.uiłłi.7 p̄br cū.ii.car.Valuit.xx.ſoł.m̄.xl.ſoł.

Ipſa æccła ten̄ *STOCH*.Ibi.ii.hidæ.In dn̄io.ē una car.7 vii. uiłłi.7 ii.borđ cū.ii.car.Ibi.i.ſeru̇.Vał 7 ualuit.xl.ſoliđ.

Ipſa æccła ten̄ *HEDECOTE*.Ibi.iii.hidæ.In dn̄io.ē una car. 7 ii.ſerui.7 uxores.iiii.uiłło_ꝛ nup̃ defunctoꝛ hn̄t.i.car. Vał 7 ualuit.xx.ſoliđ.

Has.ii.uillas ht̄ abb̄.ii̇ᵗ.militib_ꝛ ſuis cōmendatas.

In Ferdingo de *WICELCŌBE*.habuit S̄ MARIA de EVESHĀ lvi.hidas.T.R.E.

.XIII. E TERRA S̄ MARIE DE ABENDONE. *IN GRETESTAN HD.* cclA S̄ MARIÆ de ABENDVNE ten̄ *DVBENTONE*.Ibi vii.hidæ 7 dim̄.In dn̄io ſunt.iiii.car.7 xiii.uiłłi 7 viii.borđ cū.viii.car.Ibi.vi.ſerui.7 molin̄ de.vi.ſoliđ.

T.R.E.uałb̄.xii.lib̄.modo.ix.lib̄.Hoc ꝳ gelđab̄ T.R.E.

(12,3 continued)

A priest with ½ plough.
The value was £8; now £12.

The Church itself holds

4   BROADWELL. 10 hides. In lordship 6 ploughs;
25 villagers, 8 smallholders, 1 free man and a priest; between
them they have 12 ploughs. 13 slaves. In Gloucester 4
burgesses, in Winchcombe 1; they pay 27d.
The value of the whole was £8; now £12.

in WITLEY Hundred

5   (Upper) SWELL. 3 hides.
9 villagers, 2 smallholders and a priest; between them 4 ploughs.
6 slaves.
The value was £4; now £5.
In lordship 3 ploughs; 3 mills there, 20s.

6   WILLERSEY. 8 hides; 1 at WICKHAMFORD. In lordship 3 ploughs;
16 villagers, 4 smallholders and a priest with 6 ploughs.
2 slaves; a little meadow.
The value was £4; now 100s.

7   WESTON ('Cantilupe'). 3 hides; 1 free. In lordship 2 ploughs;
5 villagers and a priest with 2 ploughs.
The value was 20s; now 40s.

8   (Lark) STOKE. 2 hides. In lordship 1 plough;
7 villagers and 2 smallholders with 2 ploughs. 1 slave.
The value is and was 40s.

9   HIDCOTE (Bartrim). 3 hides. In lordship 1 plough; 2 slaves.
The wives of 4 villagers lately dead have 1 plough.
The value is and was 20s.
The Abbot has these two villages, assigned to two of his men-at-arms.

10 In the Quarter of Winchcombe St. Mary's of Evesham had 56 hides
before 1066.

13   **LAND OF ST. MARY'S OF ABINGDON**

In GRESTON Hundred

1   St. Mary's Church of Abingdon holds DUMBLETON.   7½ hides.
In lordship 4 ploughs;
13 villagers and 8 smallholders with 8 ploughs.
6 slaves; a mill at 6s.
Value before 1066 £12; now £9.
This manor paid tax before 1066.

.XIIII. ᴇTERRA SC̃Æ MARIÆ DE PSORE. *In Respigete Hvnd.*

Eccĺa S̃ mariæ de persore ten̋ *Kvlege*. Ibi. v. hidæ
geld. In dñio funt. ii. car̋.7 xiiii. uiłłi 7 uñ borð cū. vii. car̋.
Ibi. v. ſerui.7 moliñ de. ʟ. den̋.7 vi. ac̃ p̃ti.7 ſilua. iii. q̃z
lg̃.7 una lat̋. Vaɫ. c. ſoliđ. *In Griboldestov*

Ipſa æccła ten̋ *Havochesberie*. Ibi. xvii. hidæ. In dñio
v. car̋.7 xviii. uiłłi 7 xxv. borð. cū. xv. car̋. Ibi. ii. ſerui.
7 vii. colibti. Ibi. iii. molini de. xix. ſoɫ.7 ii. den̋.7 x. ac̃ p̃ti.
Silua de. ii. leuu lg̃.7 una lat̋. Valuit. xvi. liɓ. m̃. x. liɓ.

.XV. ᴇTERRA S̃ MARIÆ DE COVENTREV *In Celfleode Hvnd*

Eccła S̃ mariæ de Coventrev. ten̋ *Merestone*. Ibi
x. hidæ. In dñio funt. iii. car̋.7 xv. uiłłi.7 iii. borð cū. xii. car̋.
Ibi. vi. ſerui.7 p̃tū de. x. ſoɫ. Valuit. viii. liɓ. Modo: c. ſoliđ.

.XVI. ᴇTERRA S̃ MARIÆ DE CORMELIJS. *In Boteslav Hđ.*

Eccła S̃. mariæ de Cormelies ten̋ *Noent*. Rex. E.
tenuit. Ibi. vi. hidæ ñ geldauer̋. Rog̃ com̃ deđ huic æccłæ
.p anima patris ſui. c̄ceſſu regis. W. In dñio funt. iii. car̋.

★ 7 ix. uiłłi 7 ix. borð cū. xii. car̋. p̃poſit⁹ hñs. i. uiłłm 7 dim̋.
7 v. borð. Int om̃s hñt. v. car̋.7 moliñ de. xx. den̋. Ibi. ii. ſerui.
7 ii. molini de. vi. ſoɫ 7 viii. den̋. De ſilua: xxx. den̋.

ᒋDe hac tra ten̋ Durand de abɓe. i. hiđ.7 ibi hɫ. i. car̋.7 v. borð.
7 ii. ſeruos. cū. ii. car̋. Ibi. ii. haiæ. quas hɫ ſaiſitas rex.
Totū m̃ T.R.E. ualɓ. iiii. liɓ. m̃: c. ſoɫ. Hida Durandi: xii. ſoɫ.

ᒋDe tra huj⁹ m̃ ten̋ Wiłłs fili⁹ Baderon unā v̋ p uim.

XVII. ᴇTERRA SC̃Æ MARIÆ DE LIRE. *In Respiget Hvnd.*

Eccła S̃ mariæ de Lire. ten̋ *Tantesborne*. Ibi. i. hida
7 una v̋. In dñio. ē una car̋.7 ii. borð. Vaɫ 7 ualuit. xx. ſoliđ.
Hanc tr̃a deđ ipſi æcctæ Roger⁹ de Laci. Edmer tenuit. T.R.E.

LAND OF ST. MARY'S OF PERSHORE

In RAPSGATE Hundred
St. Mary's Church of Pershore holds COWLEY. 5 hides which pay tax.
In lordship 2 ploughs;
  14 villagers and 1 smallholder with 7 ploughs.
  5 slaves; a mill at 50d; meadow, 6 acres; woodland 3 furlongs
    long and 1 wide.
Value 100s.

In GRUMBALDS ASH [Hundred]
The Church holds HAWKESBURY itself. 17 hides. In lordship 5 ploughs;
  18 villagers and 25 smallholders with 15 ploughs.
  2 slaves and 7 freedmen.
  3 mills at 19s 2d; meadow, 10 acres; woodland at 2 leagues long
    and 1 wide.
The value was £16; now £10.

LAND OF ST. MARY'S OF COVENTRY

In CHELTHORN Hundred
St. Mary's Church of Coventry holds (Long) MARSTON. 10 hides.
In lordship 3 ploughs;
  15 villagers and 3 smallholders with 12 ploughs.
  6 slaves; meadow at 10s.
The value was £8; now 100s.

LAND OF ST. MARY'S OF CORMEILLES

In BOTLOE Hundred
St. Mary's Church of Cormeilles holds NEWENT. King Edward
held it. 6 hides did not pay tax. Earl Roger gave it to this Church
for his father's soul, with King William's assent. In lordship 3 ploughs;
  9 villagers and 9 smallholders with 12 ploughs; a reeve who has
    1½ villagers and 5 smallholders; between them they have 5
    ploughs and a mill at 20d.
  2 slaves; 2 mills at 6s 8d; from the woodland 30d.
Durand holds 1 hide of this land from the Abbot. He has 1 plough
and
  5 smallholders and 2 slaves with 2 ploughs.
  2 hedged enclosures of which the King has taken possession.
Value of the whole manor before 1066 £4; now 100s; of Durand's
hide, 12s.
  William son of Baderon holds 1 virgate of this manor's land by force.

LAND OF ST. MARY'S OF LYRE

In RAPSGATE Hundred
St. Mary's Church of Lyre holds DUNTISBOURNE (Leer). 1 hide and
1 virgate. In lordship 1 plough;
  2 smallholders.
The value is and was 20s.
  Roger of Lacy gave this land to this Church. Edmer held it
before 1066.

.XVIII. ${}_{\text{E}}$TERRA ÆCCLÆ DE EGLESHÃ. *In Celfledetorn hð.*

Eccia de Eglesha ten *Mvceltvde*. Ibi. xiiii. hidæ

In dñio funt. v. cař. 7 xx. uiłłi 7 vii. borđ cũ. x. cař.

Ibi. viii. ſerui. 7 ii. ancillæ. 7 xxiiii. menſuræ ſalis de Wich.

Val 7 ualuit. x. liƀ.   Ead æccia tenuit. T.R.E.

.XIX. ${}_{\text{E}}$TERRA S PETRI WESTMON. *In Derhest hvnđ.*

Eccia S petri Westmonast. ten *Derheste*. Ibi

funt. lix. hidæ.

In capite ᛗ erant T.R.E. v. hidæ. Ibi funt. iii. cař. 7 xx.

uiłłi 7 viii. borđ cũ. x. cař. Ibi. vi. ſerui. 7 lx. ãc p̃ti.

Silua. ii. leuu lḡ. 7 dimiđ leuu lat. Val 7 ualuit. x. liƀ

Ad hoc ᛗ p̃tin hæ Berew Herdeuuic. Bortune. Teodehã.

Sudtune. Int tot. xxv. hiđ. Ibi in dñio funt. xiii. cař.

7 xlv. uiłłi. 7 xxvii. borđ. cũ. xxi. cař. Ibi. xxx.vii. ſerui.

7 iiii. molini de. xx. ſoliđ. 7 xx. ãc p̃ti.

Silua. i. leuu lḡ. 7 dim lat. 7 Brocæ. iii. q̃ɀ lḡ. 7 i. lat.

⌐De tra huj ᛗ teneƀ Radchen ideſt liƀi hões. T.R.E.

qui tam oms ad op̃ dñi arabaɴ 7 herciabaɴ. falcabaɴ 7 metebaɴ.

⌐Ad Almundeſtan. Brictric. i. hidã.   Reinbald ten.

⌐Ad Telinge Godric. ii. hiđ. Ad Wicfeld Eduui. i. hiđ.

Ad Toteham Eduui. i. hiđ. H̃ ten Walteri pontheri.

⌐Ad Botingtune. ii. hiđ. Ad Bortune. ii. hiđ. Has tenuit

Wluui. Ad Chinemertune dim hiđ. Leuuin tenuit.

Girard tenet iſtas tras. ~~Ibid dimiđ hiđ. Baldeuuin ten.~~

⌐Ad Giuingtune Eluui. i. hiđ 7 unã v. Ad Tereige Leuuin

dimiđ hiđ. Ad Trinleie Edric. ii. virg 7 dimiđ.

H̃ ten Wiłłs filius Baderon.

⌐Ad Trinleie Edric. ii. uirg 7 dimiđ. Ad Chinemertune

Eluuin dimiđ hiđ.   H̃ ten Balduin aƀƀ.

8   **LAND OF THE CHURCH OF EYNSHAM**   166 b

In CHELTHORN Hundred

1   The Church of Eynsham holds MICKLETON. 14 hides. In lordship
5 ploughs;
    20 villagers and 7 smallholders with 10 ploughs.
    8 male and 2 female slaves; 24 measures of salt from Droitwich.
The value is and was £10.
The Church also held it before 1066.

9   **LAND OF ST. PETER'S OF WESTMINSTER**

In DEERHURST Hundred

1   St. Peter's Church of Westminster holds DEERHURST. 59 hides.
Before 1066 5 hides in the head of the manor. 3 ploughs there.
    20 villagers and 8 smallholders with 10 ploughs.
    6 slaves; meadow, 60 acres; woodland 2 leagues long and
      ½ league wide.
The value is and was £10.

2   These outliers belong to this manor:
    HARDWICKE, 5 hides; BOURTON (on the Hill), 8 hides; TODENHAM,
7 hides; SUTTON (under Brailes), 5 hides; in total 25 hides. In
lordship 13 ploughs;
    45 villagers and 27 smallholders with 21 ploughs.
    37 slaves; 4 mills at 20s; meadow, 20 acres; woodland 1 league
      long and ½ wide; water-meadows 3 furlongs long and 1 wide.
Riding men, that is, free men, held of this manor's land before 1066,
who all, however, ploughed, harrowed, scythed and reaped for the
lord's work.
    At ELMSTONE Brictric (held) 1 hide; Reinbald holds it.
    At 'ELLINGS' Godric (held) 2 hides; at WIGHTFIELD Edwy 1 hide;
at TODENHAM Edwy 1 hide; Walter Ponther holds them.
    At HAYDEN 2 hides.; at BOURTON (on the Hill) 2 hides; Wulfwy
held them. At KEMERTON ½ hide; Leofwin held it. Gerard holds
these lands. *There also Abbot Baldwin holds ½ hide.*
    At EVINGTON Alfwy (held) 1 hide and 1 virgate; at ORIDGE (Street)
Leofwin ½ hide; at RYE Edric 2½ virgates; William son of Baderon
holds them.
    At RYE Edric (held) 2½ virgates; at KEMERTON Alwin ½ hide;
Abbot Baldwin holds them.

Ad Hasfelde Briċtric . I . hiđ 7 dimiđ . Turſtin⁹ . f . rolf ten⁷.

Ad Leminingtune Auti . III . hiđ . Giſleƀt⁹ . f . Turoldi ten⁷.

Ad Mortune Elfriđ⁹ dimiđ hiđ . Idem ipſe tenet.

In his tris⁷|in dn̄io . XI . car⁷ 7 dimiđ . 7 XIIII . uiłti.

7 XXVII . borđ . cū . VII . car⁷ . Ibi . XIIII . ſerui . 7 xx̄ . ac p̃ti.

Præter hæc ten⁷ Girard⁹ camerari⁹ jn Chenemertune

VIII . hiđ . 7 in Botingtune . III . hiđ . quæ sēp geldaueꝛ

7 ſeruitia alia feceꝛ in derheſte hunđ . Sed poſtquā

Girard⁹ habuit . nec gelđ nec ſeruitiū reddidit.

Totū M̄ T.R.E. dabat de firma . XL.I . liƀ 7 VIII.

ſextaria mellis ad menſurā regis . Modo ual̄ . XL . liƀ.

De his p̃tin⁷ ad dn̄icū M̄ . XXVI . liƀ . 7 ad hões . XIIII . liƀ.

.XX. TERRA SC̄I DẎONISIJ PARISIJ.

Eccła S̄ DẎONISIJ ten̄ has uillas in DERHEST HD̄.

Hochinton . V . hiđ . Staruenton . III . hiđ . Colne

7 Caldecot . V . hiđ . Contone . XII . hiđ . Præſton . X . hiđ.

Welleford . XV . hiđ . In his tris⁷ ſuꝗ in dn̄io . XV . car⁷.

7 LXXV . uiłti . 7 XII . borđ . cū . XXXIX . car⁷ . Ibi . XXXVIII.

ſerui . 7 IIII . molini de . XL . ſoliđ . 7 XXXVI . ac p̃ti.

Silua . II . leuū 7 dim⁷ lg⁷ . 7 una leuua 7 II . q̃ꝗ lat⁷.

De hac tra⁷ ſup̃diċta ten⁷ . V . libi hões . IIII . hiđ 7 dimiđ.

Ad eunđ M̄ p̃tin⁷ . II . hidæ 7 dimiđ ult̄ Sauerne.

In Olſendone . V . hidæ . In Lalege . I . hida . In Valton . I . hida.

In Caneberton dimiđ hida . In his tris⁷ ſunt in dn̄io . V . car⁷.

7 V . uiłti 7 XVIII . borđ cū . IX . car⁷ . Ibi manet . I . liƀ hō.

Ibi . XXXVIII . ac p̃ti ; Silua dim⁷ leuua lg⁷ . 7 II . q̃ꝗ lat⁷.

Ad hoc M̄ p̃tin̄ xxx . burg̃ſes in Glouuec⁷ . redđ xv . ſol

7 VIII . den̄ . 7 In Wicelcōbe . II . burg̃ſes . redđ . X . denaꝛ.

T.R.E. tot̄ M̄ ualeƀ . XXVI . liƀ 7 x . ſoliđ . Modo: xxx . liƀ.

At HASFIELD Brictric (held) 1½ hides; Thurstan son of Rolf holds them.

At ('Upper') LEMINGTON Auti (held) 3 hides; Gilbert son of Thorold holds them.

At MORETON (in Marsh) Alfrith (held) ½ hide; he also holds it himself.

In these lands in lordship 11½ ploughs;
14 villagers and 27 smallholders with 7 ploughs.
14 slaves; meadow, 20 acres.

Besides these (lands) Gerard the Chamberlain holds 8 hides in KEMERTON and 3 hides in BODDINGTON which have always paid tax and rendered other services in Deerhurst Hundred. But after Gerard had them, they rendered neither tax nor service.

Before 1066 the whole manor gave in revenue £41 and 8 sesters of honey by the King's measure; value now £40, of which £26 belongs to the lord's manor and £14 to the men.

LAND OF ST. DENIS', PARIS

In DEERHURST Hundred

The Church of St. Denis holds these villages:
UCKINGTON, 5 hides; STAVERTON, 3 hides; COLN (St. Dennis) and CALCOT, 5 hides; (Little) COMPTON, 12 hides; PRESTON (on Stour), 10 hides; WELFORD (on Avon), 15 hides.

In these lands in lordship 15 ploughs;
75 villagers and 12 smallholders with 39 ploughs.
38 slaves; 4 mills at 40s; meadow, 36 acres; woodland 2½ leagues long and 1 league and 2 furlongs wide.

Of the above land 5 free men hold 4½ hides.
2½ hides beyond the Severn also belong to the manor.
In WOOLSTONE, 5 hides; in LEIGH, 1 hide; in (Deerhurst) WALTON, 1 hide; in KEMERTON, ½ hide.

In these lands in lordship 5 ploughs;
5 villagers and 18 smallholders with 9 ploughs. 1 free man lives there.

Meadow, 38 acres; woodland ½ league long and 2 furlongs wide.

30 burgesses in Gloucester belong to this manor who pay 15s 8d; in Winchcombe 2 burgesses who pay 10d.

Value of the whole manor before 1066 £26 10s; now £30.

XXI. TERRA ÆCCLÆ DE LANHEIE. *IN CELFLEDETORN HD.*

Eccła S᷑ Mariæ de LANHEIE. ten᷑ ESTVNE. Goda
comitiſſa tenuit. T.R.E. Ibi. iiii. hidæ. In dñio ſunt. iii.
car᷑.7 vi. uilli.7 un miles cū. iii. car᷑ 7 dim᷑. Ibi. vi. ſerui.
7 iii. ancillæ.　　　　　　Valuit. c. ſoł. m̃. iiii. liƀ.

.XXII. TERRA SCI EBRVLFI.　　*IN HOLEFORD HD.*

Eccła S᷑ EBRVLFI ten᷑ de rege RAWELLE. Wluuard
tenuit. T.R.E. Ibi. x. hidæ. In dñio ſunt. iiii. car᷑.
7 xvi. uilli 7 ii. borđ cū. vi. car᷑. Ibi. iii. ſeruꝭ.
Vał 7 ualuit. x. liƀ. Hoc m̄ nunq̄ geldauit.

.XXIII. TERRA ÆCCLÆ MONIALIV DE CADOM *IN CIRECESTRE H.*

Eccła Monialiū de CADOMO ten᷑ de rege PENNE
BERIE. Ibi. iii. hidæ. In dñio ſunt. iii. car᷑.7 viii. uilli
7 un faber cū. iii. car᷑. Ibi. ix. ſerui.7 molin᷑ de xl. den᷑.
Vał 7 ualuit. iiii. liƀ.　　*IN LANGETREV HD.*

Ipſa æccła ten᷑ HANTONE. Goda comitiſſa tenuit. T.R.E.
Ibi. viii. hidæ. In dñio ſunt. v. car᷑.7 xxxii. uilli 7 x. borđ
cū. xxiiii. car᷑. Ibi pƀr 7 x. ſerui.7 viii. molini de. xlv. ſoł.
7 xx. ac̄ p̃ti. Silua. ii. leuū lḡ.7 dimiđ leuū lat᷑.
Valet. xxviii. liƀ.

.XXIIII. TERRA ÆCCLÆ DE TROARZ.　*IN LANGETREW HD.*

Eccła S᷑ MARTINI de ꝛOARZ ten᷑ HORSELEI. dono
regis. W. Goda tenuit ſoror. R.E. Ibi. x. hidæ. In
dñio ſunt. iiii. car᷑.7 vi. uilli 7 v. borđ. cū. vi. car᷑.
7 un Radcheniſt.7 in Glouueceſtre｜de. vi. den᷑. Ibi una domus
molin᷑ de. l. denar᷑.　Valuit. xii. liƀ. Modo. xiiii. liƀ.

.XXVII. TERRA ROGERIJ COMITIS. *IN GERSDONES HD*

Comes ROGERIVS ten᷑ HANTONE.7 Turold de eo nepos Wigot☞

LAND OF THE CHURCH OF LAMBETH 166 c

1

In CHELTHORN Hundred

St. Mary's Church of Lambeth holds ASTON (Subedge). Countess Goda held it before 1066. 4 hides. In lordship 3 ploughs;
6 villagers and 1 man-at-arms with 3½ ploughs. 6 male and 3 female slaves.
The value was 100s; now £4.

LAND OF ST. EVROUL'S

2

In HOLFORD Hundred

The Church of St. Evroul holds ROEL from the King. Wulfward held it before 1066. 10 hides. In lordship 4 ploughs;
16 villagers and 2 smallholders with 6 ploughs. 3 slaves.
The value is and was £10.
This manor has never paid tax.

LAND OF THE NUNS' CHURCH OF CAEN

3

In CIRENCESTER Hundred

The nuns' Church of the Holy Trinity at Caen holds PINBURY from the King. 3 hides. In lordship 3 ploughs;
8 villagers and 1 smith with 3 ploughs.
9 slaves; a mill at 40d.
The value is and was £4.

In LONGTREE Hundred

2

The Church holds MINCHINHAMPTON itself. Countess Goda held it before 1066. 8 hides. In lordship 5 ploughs;
32 villagers and 10 smallholders with 24 ploughs. A priest and 10 slaves.
8 mills at 45s; meadow, 20 acres; woodland 2 leagues long and ½ league wide.
Value £28.

LAND OF THE CHURCH OF TROARN

4

In LONGTREE Hundred

1

St. Martin's Church of Troarn holds HORSLEY by King William's gift. Goda, King Edward's sister, held it. 10 hides. In lordship 4 ploughs;
6 villagers and 5 smallholders with 6 ploughs; 1 riding man.
In Gloucester a house at 6d. A mill at 50d.
The value was £12; now £14.

† *(Chs. 25 and 26 are entered after ch. 29 at the bottom of col. 166c and top of col. 166d, directed to their proper place by transposition signs.)*

LAND OF EARL ROGER

27

In GARSDON Hundred

1

Earl Roger holds (Meysey) HAMPTON, and Thorold, Wigot's nephew, from him. Ψ

(Continued at the foot of col. 166c, within 26,1, directed to its proper place by transposition signs.)

.XXVI. ^{II.} **C**TERRA HVGONIS COMITIS. *IN BISELEIE HVND.*

COMES HVGO ten *BISELEGE*.7 Roḃt de eo. Ibi. VIII.
hidæ. In dnĩo funt. IIII. car.7 xx. viłłi 7 xxvIII.borđ
cũ. xx. car. Ibi. VI. ſerui.7 IIII. Ancillæ. Ibi. II. pḃri 7 VIII.
Radcheniſt hntes. x. car.7 alii. xxIII. hões redđtes
xL.IIII. ſoliđ.7 II. ſextar mełł. Ibi. v. molini de xvI.
ſolid.7 Silua de. xx. ſoliđ.7 In Glouuec. xI. burgſes

☭
In Langeŧev HĐ. redđtes. Lxvi. den.   Valuit. xxIIII. liḃ. Modo: xx. liḃ.

Iᵈ cõm ten Westone **I**biđ ten ipſe comes. I. hiđ ad *TROHĀ*. Leuenod te
Elnod tenuit T.R.E.
Iḃí. III. hidæ gełđ.   nuit de rege. E.7 poterat ire quo uoleḃ. H tra gelđ.
In ipſò Hđ tenuit   Ibi funt. IIII.borđ cũ. I.car.7 IIII.ač pti. Vał. xx. ſoł.
Leuuin . I . hiđ.   **I**biđ ten ipſe cõm dimiđ łiđ ; quã Rog de Laci ca
lũniat ađ Egeiſuurde. teſte comitatu. Vał. x. ſoł.7 gelđ.
Ipſe comes ten *CAPEDENE*.Harold cõm IN *WITELAI HĐ.*
tenuit. Ibi. xv. hidæ. geldant. In dnĩo. VI. car.7 L.uiłłi
7 VIII.borđ. cũ. xxI. car. Ibi. xII. ſerui.7 II. molini
de. VI. ſoliđ 7 II.denar. Ibi. III. Ancillæ.
Valuit. xxx. liḃ. modo. xx. liḃ.   IN *LANGETREVV HĐ.*

☭ **I**pſe cõm ten. II. ĈĐ de. IIII.hiđ geldant.7 II. hões ej
de eo. Elnod 7 Leuuin tenuer. T.R.E. Non fuit q̃ reſpon
deret de his tris. ſed p hões comitat appciant. VIII. liḃ.

.XXIX. **C**TERRA COMITIS MORITON. IN *WITELAI HĐ.*

COMES MoritoN ten *LANGEBERGE*. Toui tenuit
T.R.E. Ibi. II. hide. In dnĩo funt. II. car.7 III. uiłłi 7 un
borđ cũ. I. car.7 IIII. ſerui. Valuit. IIII. liḃ. m̃. xL.ſoł.7 gelđ.

LAND OF EARL HUGH

In BISLEY Hundred

1   Earl Hugh holds BISLEY, and Robert from him. 8 hides.
In lordship 4 ploughs;
    20 villagers and 28 smallholders with 20 ploughs. 6 male
      and 4 female slaves. 2 priests and 8 riding men who
      have 10 ploughs; another 23 men who pay 44s and 2
      sesters of honey.
    5 mills at 16s; woodland at 20s.
    In Gloucester 11 burgesses who pay 66d.
The value was £24; now £20.

(28,5-6 in margin, directed to their proper place by transposition signs.)

⊕In LONGTREE Hundred

5   The Earl also holds WESTONBIRT. Alnoth held it before 1066.
3 hides which pay tax.

6   In this Hundred Leofwin held 1 hide.

2   There also the Earl holds 1 hide at THROUGHAM himself. Leofnoth
held it from King Edward and could go where he would. This land
pays tax.
    4 smallholders with 1 plough.
    Meadow, 4 acres.
Value 20s.

3   There also the Earl himself holds at EDGEWORTH ½ hide which Roger
of Lacy claims, as the County testifies.
Value 10s. It pays tax.

In WITLEY Hundred

4   The Earl holds (Chipping) CAMPDEN himself. Earl Harold held it.
15 hides which pay tax. In lordship 6 ploughs;
    50 villagers and 8 smallholders with 21 ploughs.
    12 slaves; 2 mills at 6s 2d. 3 female slaves.
The value was £30; now £20.

⊕ *(28,5-6 entered in margin; see above after 28,1)*

In LONGTREE Hundred

7   The Earl himself holds two manors of 4 hides which pay tax, and
two of his men from him. Alnoth and Leowin held before 1066.
There was no one to make a return for these lands, but they are
assessed by the men of the County at £8.

29   # LAND OF THE COUNT OF MORTAIN

In WITLEY Hundred

1   The Count of Mortain holds LONGBOROUGH. Tovi held it before 1066.
2 hides. In lordship 2 ploughs;
    3 villagers and 1 smallholder with 1 plough. 4 slaves.
The value was £4; now 40s. It pays tax.

☞ .XXV. ᴇTERRA ÆCCLE DE CIRECESTRE. *IN CIRECESKE HD.*

ᴇccᴌᴀ de CIRECESTRE teñ de rege . 11 . hiđ in elemo
fina . 7 de rege . E . tenuit đetas ab omĩ c̄ſuetudine
Ibi ſunt . vi . ac̄ p̃ti.   Vaɫ 7 ualuit hoc . xʟ . ſoɫ.

166 c, d ᴛERRA RENBALDI PRBI. *IN GERSDONES HD.*

☞ Leuenot tenuit.Ibi.v.hidæ.In dñio.E.ɪ.car̄.7 ɪɪɪɪ.uilli 7 ɪɪ.borđ 7 pᵬr 7 dᴠo alij hōēs.
Inꞇ om̄s hñt.ɪɪ.car̄ 7 dimiđ.Ibi.vɪ.ſerui.Valuit.vɪɪɪ.liᵬ.Modo:´ɪɪɪ.liᵬ.

166 d

.XXVI. ᴚEINBALD teñ *OMENIE* de rege . Godric tenuit . ᴛ.R.E.Ibi
ɪɪɪɪ.hidæ 7 una v̄ . In dñio.ɪɪ.car̄.7 vɪɪɪ.uilli 7 ɪ.borđ
cū.vɪ.car̄ 7 pᵬro.Ibi.vɪɪɪ.ſerui.7 ɪɪ.molini de.x.ſoliđ.
7 xx.ac̄ pᵗi.   Vaɫ 7 ualuit.c.ſoliđ.

Iſđ Reinbald teñ *DRIFELLE*.Elaf tenuit de comite Toſti.
Ibi.vɪɪ.hidæ.In dñio.ɪɪɪɪ.car̄.7 vɪ.uilli 7 ɪɪ.borđ 7 pᵬr cū.vɪ
car̄.Ibi.xv.ſerui.7 moliñ de.v.ſoliđ.7 xx.ac̄ pᵗi.

Vaɫ 7 ualuit.vɪɪɪ.liᵬ.   *IN CIRECESTRE HD.*

Iſđ Rainbald teñ in *NORTCOTE*.ɪ.hiđ.Godric tenuit ᴛ.R.E.
In dñio.ē una car̄.7 ɪɪ.uilli 7 ɪɪ.borđ cū.ɪɪ.car̄.Ibi.vɪ.ſerui.
Vaɫ.xʟ.ſoliđ.Hic tain poterat ire quo uolebat.

Iſđ Rainᵬ teñ *PRESTETVNE*.Elaf tenuit ᴛ.R.E.Ibi.vɪɪɪ.hidæ
gelđ pᵗer dñiū.In dñio ſunt.ɪɪɪɪ.car̄.7 vɪɪ.uilli 7 vɪ.borđ.
cū.vɪ.car̄.Ibi.ɪx.ſerui.7 xɪɪ.ac̄ pᵗi.Vaɫ 7 ualuit.vɪɪɪ.liᵬ.
Ipſe Elaf poterat ire quo uoleᵬ.

(Chs. 25 and 26 are entered at the foot of col. 166 c and the top of col. 166 d, directed to their proper place by transposition signs.)

†25   LAND OF THE CHURCH OF CIRENCESTER

In CIRENCESTER Hundred

1   The Church of Cirencester holds 2 hides from the King in alms, and held them from King Edward exempt from all customary dues.
Meadow, 6 acres.
The value of it is and was 40s.

[26]   LAND OF REINBALD THE PRIEST

In GARSDON Hundred

(27,1 continued, directed to its proper place by transposition signs.)

27,1   Ψ Leofnoth held it. 5 hides. In lordship 1 plough;
4 villagers, 2 smallholders, 1 priest and 2 other men; between them they have 2½ ploughs. 6 slaves.
The value was £8; now £3.

†26   *(Ch. 26 continued)*

1   Reinbald holds AMPNEY (St. Mary) from the King. Godric held   166 d
it before 1066. 4 hides and 1 virgate. In lordship 2 ploughs;
8 villagers and 1 smallholder with 6 ploughs and 1 priest.
8 slaves; 2 mills at 10s; meadow, 20 acres.
The value is and was 100s.

2   Reinbald also holds DRIFFIELD. Elaf held it from Earl Tosti.
7 hides. In lordship 4 ploughs;
8 villagers, 2 smallholders and a priest with 5 ploughs.
15 slaves; a mill at 5s; meadow, 20 acres.
The value is and was £8.

In CIRENCESTER Hundred

3   Reinbald also holds in NORCOTE 1 hide. Godric held it before
1066. In lordship 1 plough;
2 villagers and 2 smallholders with 2 ploughs. 6 slaves.
Value 40s.
This thane could go where he would.

4   Reinbald also holds PRESTON. Elaf held it before 1066. 8 hides
which pay tax besides the lordship (land). In lordship 4 ploughs;
7 villagers and 6 smallholders with 6 ploughs.
9 slaves; meadow, 12 acres.
The value is and was £8.
Elaf himself could go where he would.

HTERRA GISLEBERTI EPI LISIACSIS. *IN LANGETREW HD.*

Hvgo maminot.ten REDMERTONE de Gislebto epo Lisiacsi.
7 ipse de rege.Ibi.ii.hidæ.In dnio sunt.ii.car.7 i.uills 7 ii.
bord 7 pbr cu.i.car.Ibi.ii.serui.Valuit.iiii.lib.Modo.iii.lib.
Leuuin tenuit de rege.E.

Isd Hugo ten de ipso epo LESSEBERGE.Leuuin tenuit.Ibi.v.
hidæ.In dnio.e una car.7 v.uilti 7 pbr cu.ii.car.Ibi.vii.serui.
Valuit.x.lib.Modo.L.solid.   *IN GRIBOLDESTOV HD.*
Isd Hugo ten SOPEBERIE de eod epo.Aluuard tenuit T.R.E.
Ibi.v.hidæ geld.In dnio sunt.ii.car.7 iiii.uilti 7 ii.bord cu.ii.car.
Ibi.iiii.serui.7 xx.ac pti.Siluæ aliqtulu.Valuit.viii.lib.modo.
iiii.lib.

WTERRA WILLELMI DE OW. *IN BLACHELEW HD.*

Wills de OW ten STANHVS.Toui tenuit T.R.E.Ibi erant
vii.hid.Ibi sunt in dnio.ii.car.7 xxi.uills 7 ix.bord cu.xx.car.
Ibi.iiii.serui.7 ii.molini de.xvii.solid 7 vi.denar.Ibi.ii.arpenz
uineæ.Val 7 ualuit.viii.lib.Hoc M geldat. *IN LEDENEI HVND.*
Isd Wills ten ALVREDESTONE.Bondi tenuit.T.R.E.Ibi.iii.hidæ
geldant.Nil ibi.e in dnio.sed.v.uilti 7 iii.bord hnt.iii.car.Ibi
piscaria de.xii.den.7 x.ac pti.Silua dimid leuua lg.7 dimid lat.
Valuit.xx.solid.modo.xxx.sol.Henric de fererijs caluniat.eo qd
Bondi tenuerit.Willi antecessor tenuit.Rad de Limesi.

Isd W.ten ibid.ii.hid geld.7 ibi sunt.ii.uilti cu.ii.car.Vlnod
tenuit.Val 7 ualuit.x.solid.

Isd.W.tenuit WIGHEIETE.7 Rad de Limesi ante eu.Alestan
tenuit T.R.E.Nc est jussu regis in foresta sua.Ibi erant.vi.hidæ.
7 geldb.7 ualeb.Lx.solid.Modo n est nisi piscaria de.x.solid.

30 **LAND OF GILBERT BISHOP OF LISIEUX**

In LONGTREE Hundred

1 Hugh Maminot holds RODMARTON from Gilbert, Bishop of Lisieux, and he from the King. 2 hides. In lordship 2 ploughs;
1 villager, 2 smallholders and a priest with 1 plough. 2 slaves.
The value was £4; now £3.
Leofwin held it from King Edward.

2 Hugh also holds LASBOROUGH from the Bishop himself. Leofwin held it. 5 hides. In lordship 1 plough;
5 villagers and a priest with 2 ploughs. 7 slaves.
The value was £10; now 50s.

In GRUMBALDS ASH Hundred

3 Hugh also holds (Little) SODBURY from the Bishop. Alfward held it before 1066. 5 hides which pay tax. In lordship 2 ploughs;
4 villagers and 2 smallholders with 2 ploughs.
4 slaves; meadow, 20 acres; a small amount of woodland.
The value was £8; now £4.

31 **LAND OF WILLIAM OF EU**

In BLACKLOW Hundred

1 William of Eu holds STONEHOUSE. Tovi held it before 1066.
There were 7 hides. In lordship 2 ploughs;
21 villagers and 9 smallholders with 20 ploughs.
4 slaves; 2 mills at 17s 6d. Vineyard, 2 *arpents*.
The value is and was £8.
This manor pays tax.

In LYDNEY Hundred

2 William also holds 'ALVERSTON'. Bondi held it before 1066.
3 hides which pay tax. Nothing in lordship, but
5 villagers and 3 smallholders have 3 ploughs.
A fishery at 12d; meadow, 10 acres; woodland ½ league
long and ½ wide.
The value was 20s; now 30s.
Henry of Ferrers claims it because Bondi held it, but Ralph of Limesy held it as William's predecessor.

3 William also holds 2 hides there which pay tax.
2 villagers with 2 ploughs.
Wulfnoth held it.
The value is and was 10s.

4 William also held WYEGATE, and Ralph of Limesy before him.
Alstan held it before 1066. Now it is, by the King's order, in his Forest. There were 6 hides; they paid tax.
The value was 60s; now there is only a fishery at 10s.

Iſd.W.ten ODELAVESTON.Brictric.F.algari IN TVVIFERDE HD.

tenuit.Ibi.II.hidæ.Nil ibi.e in dnĩo.niſi.v.uiłłi cũ.v.car.Ibi

una piſcaria in Sauerna de.v.ſolid.7 molin de.XL.denar.

Vał 7 ualuit xx.ſolid.H̃ tra geld.

Iſd W.ten in TIDEHA unã v 7 dimid geldant.Stigand Arcħ tenuit

Ibi.I.uiłłs cũ.I.car 7 II.piſcariæ.Vał 7 ualuit.x.ſoł.

Iſd.W.ten DVNTESBORNE.Aleſtan tenuit T.R.E. IN CIRECESTRE HD.

Ibi.v.hidæ 7 dim̃ geld.In dnĩo ſunt.II.car.7 VI.uiłłi 7 IIII.bord

cũ.v.car 7 dimid.Ibi.VII.ſerui.7 molin de.VIII.ſolid.

Hoc Ꝏ ten Radulf de Wiłło 7 geld.ſed ipſe geld retin de.III.hid.

Vn francig ten dimid hid de ipſa tra.7 ibi ht.I.car cũ ſuis hõibȝ.

Tot T.R.E.ualeb.x.lib.modo.VIII.lib.

Iſd.W.ten in TORNENTONE.I.hid.7 Herbt de eo.Leuric tenuit

T.R.E.7 potuit ire quo uoluit.In dnĩo.e una car.7 IIII.ſerui.

Valuit.XL.ſolid.modo:'xx.ſoł. IN LANGETREV HVND.

Iſd.W.ten SCIPTONE.ſic Rad de Limeſi teneb.Wlui tenuit T.R.E.

Ibi.II.hidæ.In dnĩo ſunt.II.car.7 II.bord 7 VIII.ſerui.Vał 7 ualuit

XL.ſoł.Ipſe Wluui poterat ire quo uellet.Hugo ten de Wiłło.

Iſd.W.ten CVLCORTORNE.7 Herbt de eo.Scireuold tenuit

T.R.E.Ibi.III.uirg 7 v.acræ.In dnĩo.e una car 7 III.ſerui.

Vał 7 ualuit.xxxv.ſoł.Hanc tra tenuit Rad de Limeſi.ſed n̄ fuit Aleſtani.

Iſd.W.ten BEIEWRDE.Aleſtan tenuit IN DVDESTANES HD.

Ibi.VIII.hidæ.In dnĩo ſunt.VI.car.7 xx.uiłłi 7 XIIII.bord

cũ.XXIIII.car.Ibi.XVII.ſerui.7 molin de XII.denar.Silua.II.leuu

lg 7 una lat.Valuit.xv.lib.Modo:'XIII.lib. IN SALEMANES

Iſd.W.ten SVELLE.Erneſi tenuit T.R.E. [BERIE HD.

Ibi.III.hidæ geld.Valuit.XL.ſoł.modo.x.ſoł.

William also holds
in TWYFORD Hundred

5   WOOLASTON. Brictric son of Algar held it. 2 hides. Nothing in lordship, but
> 5 villagers with 5 ploughs.
> A fishery in the Severn at 5s; a mill at 40d.

The value is and was 20s.
This land pays tax.

6   in TIDENHAM 1½ virgates which pay tax. Archbishop Stigand held it.
> 1 villager with 1 plough.
> 2 fisheries.

The value is and was 10s.

in CIRENCESTER Hundred

7   'DUNTISBOURNE'. Alstan held it before 1066. 5½ hides which pay tax. In lordship 2 ploughs;
> 6 villagers and 4 smallholders with 5½ ploughs.
> 7 slaves; a mill at 8s.

Ralph holds this manor from William and pays tax, but he keeps back the tax on 3 hides.
A Frenchman holds ½ hide of this land and has 1 plough with his men.
The value of the whole before 1066 £10; now £8.

8   in TARLTON 1 hide. Herbert holds from him. Leofric held it before 1066 and could go where he would. In lordship 1 plough; 4 slaves.
The value was 40s; now 20s.

in LONGTREE Hundred

9   SHIPTON ('Dovel'), as Ralph of Limesy held it. Wulfwy held it   167 a
before 1066. 2 hides. In lordship 2 ploughs;
> 2 smallholders and 8 slaves.

The value is and was 40s.
This Wulfwy could go where he would.
Hugh holds it from William.

10   CULKERTON. Herbert holds from him. Sheerwold held it before 1066. 3 virgates and 5 acres. In lordship 1 plough; 3 slaves.
The value is and was 35s.
Ralph of Limesy held this land but it was not Alstan's.

in DUDSTONE Hundred

11   BADGEWORTH. Alstan held it. 8 hides. In lordship 6 ploughs;
> 20 villagers and 14 smallholders with 24 ploughs.
> 17 slaves; a mill at 12d; woodland 2 leagues long and 1 wide.

The value was £15; now £13.

in SALMONSBURY Hundred

12   (Lower) SWELL. Erneis held it before 1066. 3 hides which pay tax.
The value was 40s; now 10s.

XXXII. **W**TERRA WILLI FILIJ BADERON. *IN CIRECESTRE HD.*

Wills filius BADERON ten.ɪɪ.hid in *CIRECESTRE*.7 Hugo ten
de eo.In dñio.e una car.7 un uills 7 dimid.7 ɪɪɪɪ.bord cu.ɪ.car.
Ibi.ɪɪ.ſerui.Valuit.c.ſolid.modo ʟxx.ſolid.Aluui tenuit hanc tra.

★ **I**ſd Wills ten *DVNTESBORNE*.Chetel Aluric tenuer.7 poteraȵ
ire q̊ uolebaȵ.Ibi.ɪɪɪ.hidæ 7 dimid.In dñio.ɪ.car 7 dimid eſt.
7 un uills 7 ɪɪ.bord cu.ɪ.car.Ibi.ɪ.ſeru.Valuit.x.lib.m.ʟxx.ſol.

Iſd.W.ten in *SVDITONE*.ɪ.hid.Oſuuid tenuit.T.R.E.7 potuit
ire quo uoluit.In dñio.e.ɪ.car.7 ɪɪɪɪ.ſerui Val 7 ualuit xxɪɪɪɪ.ſol.

Iſd.W.ten *WESTONE*.Bricſi tenuit T.R.E. *IN LANGETREV HD.*
Ibi.ɪɪɪ.hidæ.In dñio ſunt.ɪɪ.car.7 ɪɪ.uilli 7 ɪɪɪ.bord cu.ɪɪ.car.
Ibi.ɪɪɪɪ.ſerui.7 vɪ.ac p̃ti.Valuit.vɪ.lib.modo.ɪɪɪ.lib.

Iſd.W.ten *TEBRISTON*| Vlfelm tenuit de rege.E. *IN BOTELAV*
7 poterat ire quo uellet.In dñio ſunt.ɪɪɪ.car.7 x.uilli ʄHVND
7 vɪɪɪ.bord cu.vɪɪɪ.car.Ibi.ɪɪɪɪ.ſerui.7 Silua.ɪɪɪ.leuu lg.
7 una lat.Valuit.vɪ.lib.7 x.ſol.Modo:́c.ſolid.

Iſd.W.ten *HVNTELEI*.Aluuin tenuit de Ældred archiepo.
7 poterat ire quo uoleb.Ibi.ɪɪ.hidæ.In dñio.e una car.7 ɪɪɪɪ.
uilli 7 vɪ.bord cu.ɪɪɪ.car.Ibi.ɪ.ſeru.Silua.ɪɪ.leuu lg.7 ɪ.lat.
Valuit.xʟ.ſolid.Modo:́xxx.ſolid. *IN WESTBERIE HVND.*

Iſd.W.ten *HOPE*.Forne 7 Vlfeg——tenuer de rege.E. ⊹
Ibi.v.hidæ geld.7 poteraȵ ipſi teini ire quo uoleb.In dñio ſuȵ
.ɪɪ.car.7 xɪɪ.uilli 7 un bord cu.xɪɪ.car.Ibi.ɪɪɪ.ſerui.7 moliñ
de.xvɪɪ.denar.Valuit.vɪɪɪ.lib.modo.c.ſol.   ʄſol.

Iſd.W.ten *STAVRE*.Vlfeg tenuit T.R.E.Valuit.x.ſol.m.v.
Ibi.e una hida 7 ñ geldat.

LAND OF WILLIAM SON OF BADERON

In CIRENCESTER Hundred

1 William son of Baderon holds 2 hides in CIRENCESTER.
Hugh holds from him. In lordship 1 plough;
1½ villagers and 4 smallholders with 1 plough. 2 slaves.
The value was 100s; now 70s.
Alfwy held this land.

William also holds

2 'DUNTISBOURNE'. Ketel and Aelfric held it and could go where
they would. 3½ hides. In lordship 1½ ploughs;
1 villager and 2 smallholders with 1 plough. 1 slave.
The value was £10; now 70s.

3 in SIDDINGTON (House) 1 hide. Oswith held it before 1066 and
could go where he would. In lordship 1 plough; 4 slaves.
The value is and was 24s.

in LONGTREE Hundred

4 'WESTON (Dovel)'. Brictsi held it before 1066. 3 hides.
In lordship 2 ploughs;
2 villagers and 3 smallholders with 2 ploughs.
4 slaves; meadow, 6 acres.
The value was £6; now £3.

in BOTLOE Hundred

5 TIBBERTON. 5 hides. Wulfhelm held it from King Edward and
could go where he would. In lordship 3 ploughs;
10 villagers and 8 smallholders with 8 ploughs.
4 slaves; woodland 3 leagues long and 1 wide.
The value was £6 10s; now 100s.

6 HUNTLEY. Alwin held it from Archbishop Aldred and could go
where he would. 2 hides. In lordship 1 plough;
4 villagers and 6 smallholders with 3 ploughs.
1 slave; woodland 2 leagues long and 1 wide.
The value was 40s; now 30s.

in WESTBURY Hundred

7 LONGHOPE. Forne and Wulfheah held it from King Edward;
these thanes could go where they would. 5 hides which pay
tax. In lordship 2 ploughs;
12 villagers and 1 smallholder with 12 ploughs.
3 slaves; a mill at 17d.
The value was £8; now 100s.

8 STEARS. Wulfheah held it before 1066.
The value was 10s; now 5s.
1 hide; it does not pay tax.

Ísd.W.ten.ii.uirg 7 dimid.7 ibi ht.i.uittm 7 i.bord.Ante
ceffor ej Wihanoc tenuit.fed comitat affirmat hanc trā
eē.de dñica firma regis in Weftberie.Vat.iii.fot.
Ísd.W.ten NEVNEHAM.Ibi.i.hida.7 iii.uitti 7 iii.bord.
reddtes.xx.fot.h tra ñ geldat.Silua ibi.ii.q̃ʒ lg.7 una lat.
Ísd.W.ten LEDENEI.Alfer tenuit IN LEDENEI HVND.
T.R.E.Ibi.vi.hidæ geld.In dñio funt.ii.car.7 iii.uitti.7 v.
bord cū.ii.car.Ibi.iii.ferui.7 molin de.v.fot.7 xx.ac pti
7 in Waie dimid pifcar.Silua.i.leuu lg.7 dimid lat.
Valuit.iiii.lib.Modo:́xl.folid.
Ísd.W.tenuit HIWOLDESTONE.Vlfeg tenuit T.R.E.
Ibi.iii.hidæ.H tra juffu regis.ē in forefta.Valb xxx.fot.

☞

.XXXIII. TERRA WILLELMI CAMERARIJ. IN WITELAI HD.
Witts camerari ten WENECOTE.Wenric tenuit.T.R.E.
Ibi.iii.hidæ.In dñio funt.iii.car.7 ii.uitti 7 ii.bord cū.i.car.
Ibi.iiii.ferui.Vat 7 ualuit.iiii.lib.Hoc M̃ geldat.
☞ Ísd.W.ten HAGENEPENE.7 Goisfrid de eo.Eduui IN WACRESCVBE HD.
tenuit.Ibi.v.hidæ In dñio funt.ii.car.7 vi.uitti cū.iii.car.Ibi
iiii.ferui.H tra geldat.   Valuit.c.fot.Modo:́lx.fot.

167 b
.XXXII. WTERRA WILLI GOIZENBODED. IN CEOLFLEDE HD.
Witts Goizinboded.ten PEBEWORDE de rege.
Vluiet 7 Vluuard tenuer T.R.E.p̄.ii.M̃.
Ibi.vi.hidæ 7 una v.In dñio.ē una car.7 i.bord
7 un feruus.   Valuit.vii.lib.m̃.iiii.lib
Ísd Witts ten WENITONE.Vn tain   ⌈7 x.fot.
tenuit T.R.E.Ibi.v.hidæ.In dñio funt.ii.car.7 ii.
uitti 7 un francig ten.i.hid 7 dimid.cū.i.car.

167 a, b

9   2½ virgates. He has
       1 villager and 1 smallholder.
       His predecessor, Wihenoc, held it, but the County affirms that
       this land is of the King's lordship revenue in WESTBURY (on Severn).
       Value 3s.

10   NEWNHAM. 1 hide.
       3 villagers and 3 smallholders who pay 20s.
       This land does not pay tax.
       Woodland there 2 furlongs long and 1 wide.

       in LYDNEY Hundred
11   '(Little) LYDNEY'. Alfhere held it before 1066. 6 hides which pay tax.
       In lordship 2 ploughs;
       3 villagers and 5 smallholders with 2 ploughs.
       3 slaves; a mill at 5s; meadow, 20 acres; ½ fishery in the Wye;
          woodland 1 league long and ½ wide.
       The value was £4; now 40s.

12   William also held HEWELSFIELD. Wulfheah held it before 1066.
       3 hides. This land is, by the King's order, in the Forest.
       The value was 30s.

†   *(32,13 is written at the foot of col. 167 a)*

33   LAND OF WILLIAM THE CHAMBERLAIN

       In WITLEY Hundred
1   William the Chamberlain holds WINCOT. Wynric held it before 1066.
       3 hides. In lordship 3 ploughs;
       2 villagers and 2 smallholders with 1 plough. 4 slaves.
       The value is and was £4.
       This manor pays tax.

†   *(Misplaced entry, directed to its proper place by transposition signs.)*
       In WATTLESCOMB Hundred
32,13 William also holds (Lower) HAMPEN, and Geoffrey from him.
       Edwy held it. 5 hides. In lordship 2 ploughs;
       6 villagers with 3 ploughs. 4 slaves.
       This land pays tax.
       The value was 100s; now 60s.

34   LAND OF WILLIAM GOIZENBODED   167 b

       In CHELTHORN Hundred
1   William Goizenboded holds PEBWORTH from the King. Wulfgeat
       and Wulfward held it before 1066 as two manors. 6 hides and
       1 virgate. In lordship 1 plough;
       1 smallholder and 1 slave.
       The value was £7; now £4 10s.

       William also holds
2   ULLINGTON. A thane held it before 1066. 5 hides. In lordship
       2 ploughs.
       2 villagers and 1 Frenchman hold 1½ hides with 1 plough.

Hoc Ꝏ misit Algar in pebeuuorde . Valuit . c . sol.

Isd . W . ten CLOPTVNE . Hufcarle tenuit ⌐ m̃ XL . sol.

T.R.E.Ibi . x . hidæ . In dñio . III . car . 7 XII . uilli 7 IIII.

bord 7 un Radchenist cũ . IX . car . In Wicelcōbe

Valuit . VIII . lib . Modo. c . solid. ⌐ un burgsis.

Isd Wills ten BRISTENTVNE . IN WITELAI HĎ.

Brismar tenuit . Ibi . x . hidæ . In dñio . IIII . car.

7 XVIII . uilli 7 IIII . bord cũ . XIIII . car . Ibi . VIII . serui

7 III . Ancillæ . 7 II . molini de . xv . solid. ⌐ HVND.

Valuit . XII . lib . Modo . VII . lib. IN SALESMANESBERIE

Isd . W . ten CALLICOTE . 7 Rannulf de eo . Aluuin

tenuit . T.R.E . Ibi . III . hidæ geld . In dñio . III . car.

7 VIII . int seruos 7 ancillas . Valuit . LX . sol . M̊ . XL . sol.

Isd . W . ten AILEWRDE . Aluuin tenuit . T . R . E . Ibi

una hida geld . In dñio . I . car . 7 II . serui . Valuit . VI . sol.

Isd . W . ten FERNECOTE . IN HOLEFORD HĎ . ⌐ m̃ . III . sol.

Aluuin tenuit . Ibi . III . hidæ . geld . In dñio . II . car.

7 IIII . uilli cũ . IIII . car . 7 XIII . int seruos 7 Ancillas.

Goisfrid ten de Willo. Valuit . x . lib . m̃ . III . lib.

★ Isd . W . ten GETINGE . Rex . E . tenuit . 7 accomo

dauit eũ Aluuino uicecomiti suo ut in uita sua habet.

non tam dono dedit ut comitat testat . Mortuo ũ

Aluuino. rex . W . ded Ricardo cuidã juueni uxore

ej 7 trã . Nc Wills succeffor Ricardi ita ten hanc trã.

Ibi . x . hidæ . Harũ . IX . geldant . In dñio sunt . IIII.

car . 7 IIII . uilli 7 III . francig . 7 II . Radchenist . 7 pbr

cũ . II . bord . int oms hnt . v . car . Int seruos 7 an

cillas . XI . 7 II . molini de . XIIII . solid Ibi . v . sa

linæ reddt . xx . sũmas salis . In Wicelcōbe . II . bur

genses reddt . XI . sol 7 IIII . denar.

Valuit . XVI . lib . Modo. VI . lib.

Earl Algar placed this manor in Pebworth.
The value was 100s; now 40s.

3 (Lower) CLOPTON. Huscarl held it before 1066. 10 hides.
In lordship 3 ploughs;
12 villagers, 4 smallholders and 1 riding man with 9 ploughs.
In Winchcombe 1 burgess.
The value was £8; now 100s.

in WITLEY Hundred

4 EBRINGTON. Brictmer held it. 10 hides. In lordship 4 ploughs;
18 villagers and 4 smallholders with 14 ploughs.
8 male and 3 female slaves; 2 mills at 15s.
The value was £12; now £7.

in SALMONSBURY Hundred

5 'CALDICOTT'. Ranulf holds from him. Alwin held it. 3 hides which
pay tax. In lordship 3 ploughs; 8 slaves, male and female.
The value was 60s; now 40s.

6 AYLWORTH. Alwin held it before 1066. 1 hide which pays tax.
In lordship 1 plough; 2 slaves.
The value was 6s; now 3s.

in HOLFORD Hundred

7 FARMCOTE. Alwin held it. 3 hides which pay tax. In lordship
2 ploughs;
4 villagers with 4 ploughs; 13 slaves, male and female.
Geoffrey holds it from William.
The value was £10; now £3.

8 GUITING (Power). King Edward held it and leased it to Alwin his
Sheriff so that he might have it for his lifetime; however he did
not give it as a gift, as the County testifies.
On Alwin's death King William gave his wife and land to Richard,
a young man. Now William, Richard's successor, holds this land
thus. 10 hides; 9 of them pay tax. In lordship 4 ploughs;
4 villagers, 3 Frenchmen, 2 riding men and a priest with
2 smallholders; between them they have 5 ploughs.
11 slaves, male and female.
2 mills at 14s. 5 salt-houses pay 20 packloads of salt.
In Winchcombe 2 burgesses pay 11s 4d.
The value was £16; now £6.

Iſd.W.teñ Cᴀᴛᴇꜱʟᴀᴛ.Aluuiñ tenuit.Ibi.ii.hidæ
gelð.In dñio.ii.caɍ.7 iiii.ſerui.7 moliñ de.v.ſoliđ.
Valuit.xʟ.ſoliđ.modo.x.ſoliđ. Iɴ Bᴏᴛᴇʟᴀᴠ ʜᴆ.
Iſd.W.teñ Tᴇᴛɪɴᴛᴏɴ.Aluuiñ tenuit.Ibi.vi.hidæ.
In dñio.ē una caɍ.7 ix.uiłłi 7 vii.borđ cū.ix.caɍ.
Valuit.vi.liƀ.Modo.iii.liƀ. Iɴ Bᴇʀɴɪɴᴛᴏɴᴇ ʜᴆ.
Iſd.W.teñ.ii.hiđ in Bᴇʀɴɪɴᴛᴏɴᴇ.7 Radulf de eo.
Aluuiñ tenuit T.R.E.In dñio.ē.i.caɍ.7 uñ ſeruus.
7 moliñ de.xʟ.deñ.7 vi.aċ p̃ti.Vał 7 ualuit.xʟ.ſoł.
Iſd.W.teñ dimiđ hiđ træ.7 dimiđ piſcariā Iɴ Wᴇꜱᴛʙᴇʀɪᴇ ʜᴆ.
Aluuiñ uicecoñ tenuit.7 uxori ſuæ dedit.H̄ tañ
fueɍ de firma regis in Weſtberie. Iɴ Gʀᴇᴛᴇꜱᴛᴀɴ ʜᴆ.
Iſd W.teñ in Dᴠɴʙᴇɴᴛᴠɴᴇ.i.hiđ.Sauuiñ tenuit.T.R.E.
7 potuit ire quo uoluit.Valuit.xx.ſoliđ.modo.xii.ſoliđ.

.XXXV. Wᴛᴇʀʀᴀ Wɪʟ̃ʟɪ Fɪʟɪᴊ Wɪᴅᴏɴ. Iɴ Gʀɪ̄ʙᴏʟᴅᴇꜱᴛᴏᴠ ʜ̄
Wiłłs fili Widonis teñ de rege Dɪʀʜᴀᴍ.Aluric
tenuit.T.R.Æ.Ibi.vii.hidæ gelđ.In dñio.ē una caɍ.7 xiii.
uiłłi 7 xiii.borđ cū.ii.caɍ.Ibi.viii.int̃ ſeruos 7 Ancillas.
7 iii.molini de.xv.ſoliđ.7 vi.aċ p̃ti.Valuit.xii.liƀ.
Modo.viii.liƀ.
Iſd Wiłłs tenuit.iii.hiđ|quibᷦ Durand uicecoñ ſaiſierat
S Mᴀʀɪᴀ̄ de perſore juſſu regis.quas.W.coñ dederat
Turſtino filio Rolf cū hoc m̃.

.XXXVI. Wᴛᴇʀʀᴀ Wɪʟ̃ʟɪ Fʀᴏɪꜱꜱᴇʟᴇᴡ.Iɴ Dᴠᴅᴇꜱᴛᴀɴ ʜᴆ.
Wiłłs Froiſſeleuu.teñ de rege Vʟᴇᴛᴏɴᴇ.
Godric tenuit.Ibi.ii.hidæ.In dñio ſunt.ii.caɍ.
7 iiii.borđ 7 iiii.ſerui.Valuit.xxx.ſoł.M̊.ʟx.ſoł.

9   CASTLETT. Alwin held it. 2 hides which pay tax. In lordship
2 ploughs; 4 slaves.
   A mill at 5s.
The value was 40s; now 10s.

in BOTLOE Hundred

0   TAYNTON. Alwin held it. 6 hides. In lordship 1 plough;
   9 villagers and 7 smallholders with 9 ploughs.
The value was £6; now £3.

in BARRINGTON Hundred

1   in (Little) BARRINGTON 2 hides. Ralph holds from him. Alwin
held them before 1066. In lordship 1 plough; 1 slave.
   A mill at 40d; meadow, 6 acres.
The value is and was 40s.

in WESTBURY Hundred

2   ½ hide of land and ½ fishery. Alwin the Sheriff held it and gave
it to his wife. However this was (part) of the King's revenue in
WESTBURY (on Severn).

in GRESTON Hundred

3   in DUMBLETON 1 hide. Saewin held it before 1066 and could go
where he would.
The value was 20s; now 12s.

5   **LAND OF WILLIAM SON OF GUY**

In GRUMBALDS ASH Hundred

1   William son of Guy holds DYRHAM from the King. Aelfric held it
before 1066. 7 hides which pay tax. In lordship 1 plough;
   13 villagers and 13 smallholders with 2 ploughs.
   8 slaves, male and female; 3 mills at 15s; meadow, 6 acres.
The value was £12; now £8.

2   William also held 3 hides of this manor. Durand the Sheriff had
put St. Mary's of Pershore in possession of them at the King's
order; Earl William had given them to Thurstan son of Rolf with
this manor.

6   **LAND OF WILLIAM BREAKWOLF**   167 c

In DUDSTONE Hundred

1   William Breakwolf holds WOTTON from the King. Godric
held it. 2 hides. In lordship 2 ploughs;
   4 smallholders and 4 slaves.
The value was 30s; now 60s.

Ifđ.W.ten In CONNICOTE dim̃ hiđ.gelđ. Ibi erat

.I.car 7 IIII.ſerui.Valuit.xx.ſoł.Modo:ˊIII.ſoliđ.

Brictric tenuit.T.R.E.   IN GRETESTAN HĐ.

Iſđ.W.ten in LITENTVNE.I.hidã.Godric tenuit

In dñio ſunt.II.car.7 II.borđ.7 III.ſerui.7 molĩ

de.IIII.ſoliđ.Valuit.xL.ſoł.Modo:ˊxxx.ſoł.7 geld.

.XXXVII. **TERRA WILLI FILIJ NORMAN** IN LANGEBRIGE HĐ.

Wilłs filius Norman ten MORCOTE.Vlfegh

tenuit.T.R.E.Ibi.I.hida.In dñio.ẽ una car.cũ.II.

borđ.Valuit VIII.ſoł.modo:ˊx.ſoł.H̃|ᴺᵒⁿ tra gelđ.

Iſđ Wilłs ten BICANOFRE.Mor IN WESTBERIE HĐ.

ganau tenuit T.R.E.Ibi dimiđ hida.In dñio.ẽ dim̃

car cũ.VI.borđ.Valuit.v.ſoł.modo.x.ſoł.

Iſđ.W.ten in DENE.II hiđ.7 II.virg træ.7 dimiđ.

Has tenuer.III.teini.Godric Elric 7 Ernui.T.R.E.

In dñio ſunt.III.car.Ibi.xxxVIII.borđ hñtes

.VII.car 7 dimiđ.7 tres ex eis redđt.VIII.ſoliđ.

Valuit.xxxIII.ſoł.modo.xLIIII.ſoliđ.

Has tras c̃ceſſit rex.E.qetas á geldo.p̃ foreſta cuſtođ.

Iſđ.W.ten TATINTON.Vlgar IN BOTELAV HĐ.

tenuit de rege.E.H̃ tra liba eſt.

Ibi ſunt.VI.borđ.cũ.I.car.Vał 7 ualuit.xx.ſoliđ.

Ibiđ una v træ jacet ad foreſtã.7 redđ xII.den.

Iſđ.W.ten.I.hiđ 7 dimiđ v træ IN BLIDESLAWE HĐ.

Siuuarđ 7 Winſtan tenuer In dñio ſunt.II.car.

7 xvII.borđ cũ.v.car.Valuit.xv.ſoł.M:ˊxxx.ſoł.

In WITLEY Hundred

William also holds in CONDICOTE ½ hide which pays tax. There was 1 plough. 4 slaves.
The value was 20s; now 3s.
Brictric held it before 1066.

In GRESTON Hundred

3 William also holds 1 hide in 'LITTLETON'. Godric held it.
In lordship 2 ploughs;
2 smallholders and 3 slaves.
A mill at 4s.
The value was 40s; now 30s.
It pays tax.

LAND OF WILLIAM SON OF NORMAN

37

In LONGBRIDGE Hundred

1 William son of Norman holds MOORCROFT. Wulfheah held it before 1066. 1 hide. In lordship 1 plough, with
2 smallholders.
The value was 8s; now 10s.
This land does not pay tax.

William also holds

in WESTBURY Hundred

2 (English) BICKNOR. Morganwy held it before 1066. ½ hide.
In lordship ½ plough, with
6 smallholders.
The value was 5s; now 10s.

3 in MITCHELDEAN 2 hides and 2½ virgates of land. Three thanes, Godric, Alric and Ernwy, held them before 1066. In lordship 3 ploughs.
38 smallholders who have 7½ ploughs; 3 of them pay 8s.
The value was 33s; now 44s.
King Edward assigned these lands exempt from tax in return for guarding the Forest.

in BOTLOE Hundred

4 (Little) TAYNTON. Wulfgar held it from King Edward. This land is free.
6 smallholders with 1 plough.
The value is and was 20s.
1 virgate of land also lies in the Forest there and pays 12d.

in BLEDISLOE Hundred

5 1 hide and ½ virgate of land. Siward and Winstan held them.
In lordship 2 ploughs;
17 smallholders with 5 ploughs.
The value was 15s; now 30s.

.XXXVIII. **W**TERRA WILLI LEVRIC. *IN CILTEHA HD.*

Wills Leuric ten de rege *LECHANTONE*. Ofgot
tenuit T.R.E. Ibi. III. hidæ geld. In dnio funt. II. car.
7 II. uilli 7 VIII. bord cu. I. car. Ibi. IIII. ferui. Silua
una q̃ʒ lg̃.7 una lat. Val 7 ualuit XL. fol.

Ifd. W. ten *HEILE*. Ofgot *IN GRETESTAN HD.*
tenuit. T.R.E. Ibi. XI. hidæ. In dnio funt. III. car. 7 IX.
uilli 7 XI. bord cu. VIII. car. Ibi erãy. XII. ferui. quos
Wills liberos fecit. Ibi molin de. X. folid. Silua una
leuua lg̃.7 dimid lat. Valuit. XII. lib. M̊. VIII. lib.
Hoc ⊙ geldat. *IN WACRESCUBE HD.*

Ifd. W. ten *WITETVNE*. Ofgot tenuit. Ibi. III. hidæ
7 geld. In dnio funt. II. car. 7 VI. uilli 7 uñ Radchen
7 IIII. bord cu. IIII. car. Ibi molin de. X. fol. Silua
una leuua lg̃.7 dimid lat. Valuit. c. fol. m̊. LX. fol.

Ifd. W. ten in *SCIPETVNE*. III. hid. unã v min.
7 geld. Goisfrid ten de eo. Ofgot tenuit. In dnio funt
II. car. 7 prbr 7 I. uills. 7 IIII. ferui. fine car.
Valuit XL. fol. Modo: XX. fol. *IN BRADELEG HD.*

Ifd. W. ten *TVRGHEDENE*. 7 Goisfrid de eo. Ofgot
tenuit. Ibi. v. hidæ 7 una v 7 dimid. In dnio nichil.
Ibi funt. II. uilli 7 III. bord cu. I. car. H̊ tra geld.
Valuit. IIII. lib. Modo. X. fol.

167 d
.IX.
.XXX **R** TERRA ROGERIJ DE LACI. *IN BOTELAV HVND.*

ROGERIVS de Laci ten de rege *CHENEPELEI*. Edric 7 Le
uric tenuer T.R.E. p.II.⊙.7 poterant ire quo uolebãy.
Ibi. III. hidæ. In dnio funt. III. car. 7 X. uilli 7 VII. bord
cu. XII. car. Ibi. VII. ferui. Valuit. IIII. lib. modo: c. fol.

Ifd Rog ten *HORSENEHAL*. Turchil tenuit de Heraldo.
7 poterat ire quo uoleb. Ibi. III. hidæ. In dnio funt. II. car.

LAND OF WILLIAM LEOFRIC

In CHELTENHAM Hundred

William Leofric holds LECKHAMPTON from the King. Osgot held it
before 1066. 3 hides which pay tax. In lordship 2 ploughs;
  2 villagers and 8 smallholders with 1 plough.
  4 slaves; woodland 1 furlong long and 1 wide.
The value is and was 40s.

William also holds

in GRESTON Hundred

HAILES. Osgot held it before 1066. 11 hides. In lordship 3 ploughs;
  9 villagers and 11 smallholders with 8 ploughs.
    There were 12 slaves whom William freed.
  A mill at 10s; woodland 1 league long and ½ wide.
The value was £12; now £8.
This manor pays tax.

in WATTLESCOMB Hundred

WHITTINGTON. Osgot held it. 3 hides; they pay tax. In lordship
2 ploughs;
  6 villagers, 1 riding man and 4 smallholders with 4 ploughs.
  A mill at 10s; woodland 1 league long and ½ wide.
The value was 100s; now 60s.

in SHIPTON (Oliffe) 3 hides, less 1 virgate; they pay tax. Geoffrey
holds from him. Osgot held it. In lordship 2 ploughs;
  a priest, 1 villager and 4 slaves without a plough.
The value was 40s; now 20s.

in BRADLEY Hundred

(Lower) TURKDEAN. Geoffrey holds from him. Osgot held it.
5 hides and 1½ virgates. Nothing in lordship.
  2 villagers and 3 smallholders with 1 plough.
  This land pays tax.
The value was £4; now 10s.

LAND OF ROGER OF LACY   167 d

In BOTLOE Hundred

Roger of Lacy holds KEMPLEY from the King. Edric and Leofric
held it before 1066 as two manors and could go where they would.
3 hides. In lordship 3 ploughs;
  10 villagers and 7 smallholders with 12 ploughs. 7 slaves.
The value was £4; now 100s.

Roger also holds

OXENHALL. Thorkell held it from Earl Harold and could go where
he would. 3 hides. In lordship 2 ploughs;

7 v.uilli 7 iii.bord cu.v.car.Ibi.ii.ferui.7 In Glouuecest

iii.burgſes.de xv.den.   Val 7 ualuit.xl.folid.

Iſd Rog ten CRASOWEL.7 Odo de eo.Vlfel tenuit T.R.E.

7 poterat ire quo uellet.Ibi.i.hida 7 una v.In dnio.e una car.

7 iii.uilli 7 un bord cu.iii.car.Val 7 ualuit.xx.folid.

Iſd Rog ten ICCVBE.7 Radulf de eo.Haldene IN SALEMANESBERIE HD.

tenuit.Ibi.ii.hide.In dnio funt.ii.car.7 ii.uilli 7 ii.bord cu.i.car.

Ibi.iiii.ferui.7 iii.ancillæ.Val 7 ualuit.xl.fol.H tra geld.

Iſd Rog ten RISEDVNE.7 Hugo de eo.Ibi.viii.hidæ geldtes.

Aluuard 7 Afchil 7 Æluuard 7 Vluui tenuer p.iiii.M.In dnio fuɴ

vii.car.7 iiii.uilli cu.ii.car.Ibi.xii.ferui 7 ii.ancillæ.Ibi molin

de.x.folid.Val 7 ualuit.vii.lib 7 x.lib. IN HOLEFORD HD.

Iſd Rog ten GETINGE.Ibi.x.hidæ geld pter dniu qd n geld.

Brictric tenuit tein regis.E.In dnio funt.v.car.7 xxv.uilli

7 pbr 7 vii.radchen cu xviii.car.Ibi.xviii.int feruos 7 an

cillas.7 iii.molini de xxiiii.folid.7 falina de.xx.fol.7 xii.fumas

falis.7 in Wincelcube.iii.burgſes de xxxii.den.7 In Glouuec

ii.burgſes de.x.den.De filua 7 paftura.xl.gallinas.

Val 7 ualuit.x.lib.   IN RESPIGETE HD.

Iſd Rog ten TANTESBORNE.7 Giflebt de eo.Keneuuard tenuit.

tein regis.E.7 poterat ire q uoleb.Ibi.ii.hidæ.In dnio.e.i.car.

7 ii.uilli 7 ii.bord cu.i.car 7 dim.Ibi.ii.ferui.Val xl.fol.7 ualuit.

Iſd Rog ten WICHE.Ibi una hida geld. IN BISELEGE HVND.

Erneſi tenuit.In dnio.e.i.car.7 xxxv.uilli 7 xvi.bord 7 pbr

7 iii.Radchen Int oms hnt.lii.car.Ibi.xi.ferui.7 iiii.molini

de.xxiiii.fol.Silua.v.leuu lg.7 ii.lat.

5 villagers and 3 smallholders with 5 ploughs. 2 slaves.
    In Gloucester 3 burgesses at 15d.
The value is and was 40s.

CARSWALL. Odo holds from him. Wulfhelm held it before 1066
and could go where he would. 1 hide and 1 virgate. In lordship
1 plough;
    3 villagers and 1 smallholder with 3 ploughs.
The value is and was 20s.

in SALMONSBURY Hundred
ICOMB ('Place'). Ralph holds from him. Haldane held it. 2 hides.
In lordship 2 ploughs;
    2 villagers and 2 smallholders with 1 plough.
    4 male and 3 female slaves.
The value is and was 40s.
    This land pays tax.

(Wick) RISSINGTON. Hugh holds from him. 8 hides which pay
tax. Alfward, Askell, Alfward and Wulfwy held it as four manors.
In lordship 7 ploughs;
    4 villagers with 2 ploughs. 12 male and 2 female slaves.
    A mill at 10s.
The value is and was £7 10[s].

in HOLFORD Hundred
(Temple) GUITING. 10 hides which pay tax, besides the lordship
(land) which does not pay tax. Brictric, a thane of King Edward's,
held it. In lordship 5 ploughs;
    25 villagers, a priest and 7 riding men with 18 ploughs.
    18 slaves, male and female; 3 mills at 24s; a salt-house at 20s
        and 12 packloads of salt; in Winchcombe 3 burgesses at 32d;
        in Gloucester 2 burgesses at 10d; from the woodland and
        pasture 40 hens.
The value is and was £10.

in RAPSGATE Hundred
DUNTISBOURNE (Abbots). Gilbert holds from him. Kenward,
a thane of King Edward's, held it and could go where he would.
2 hides. In lordship 1 plough;
    2 villagers and 2 smallholders with 1½ ploughs. 2 slaves.
The value is and was 40s.

in BISLEY Hundred
PAINSWICK. 1 hide which pays tax. Erneis held it. In lordship
1 plough;
    35 villagers, 16 smallholders, a priest and 3 riding men;
        between them they have 52 ploughs.
    11 slaves; 4 mills at 24s; woodland 5 leagues long and 2 wide.

Valuit xx.lib.m̃ xxiiii.lib.Ipſe tein̾ poterat ire quo uoleƀ.

In hac t̾ra ten̾ S̃ Maria de Cireceſtre.1.uiłłm.7 part̃ ſiluæ.

Hoc c̄ceſſit ei.W.rex.Vał.x.ſoł.

Iſd Rog̾ ten̾ Egesworde.Ibi.1.hida 7 dim̾.geld.Eluuin̾ tenuit.
In dñio ſunt.iiii.car̃.7 iiii.uiłłi 7 iii.bord.cū.ii.car̃.Ibi.ii.libi
hões cū.ii.car̃.Ibi.xv.ſerui.7 molin̄ de xxx.den̾.7 ii.ac̃ p̃ti.
Silua.1.leuua lg̃ 7 dimid̾ lat̾.Vał 7 ualuit.vi.liƀ.

Iſd Rog̾ ten̾ dimid̾ hidā cū.1.piſcaria in Waie.7 ibi.1.uiłłs cū
una car̃.H̃ t̾ra uocat̾ modiete.Vał 7 ualuit.xx.ſoł.Brictric

Iſd Rog̾ ten̾ dim̾ hidā in Tedeha̅.Stigand tenuit. Ƒtenuit.
Ibi.1.uiłłs cū.1.car̃.7 iiii.piſcariæ 7 dimid̾.Vał 7 ualuit.xx.ſoł.

Iſd Rog̾ ten̾ Qvenintone.Ibi.viii.hidæ.In Brictwoldesberg hd̃.
Tres libi hões tenuer̃.Dodo 7 alt dodo 7 Æluuold̾.p.iii.c̃õ.7 poteraſ
ire quó uoleƀ.7 geld.In dñio ſunt.iii.car̃.7 xx.uiłłi 7 vii.bord
7 pƀr 7 p̃poſit.Int oms hñt.xii.car̃.7 ii.radchen̾ cū.1.car̃.Ibi
.xii.ſerui.7 ii.molini de.xx.ſoł.7 x.ac̃ p̃ti.In Glouuec̾.1.burgſis
redd.iiii.ſoccos.7 faƀ.1.redd.ii.ſoł.Valuit.viii.liƀ.modo.x.liƀ.

Iſd Rog̾ ten̾ Lecce.7 Wiłłs de eo.Ibi.v.hide.Alduin̾ tenuit.T.R.E.
In dñio ſunt.ii.car̃.7 xii.uiłłi 7 i.bord cū.v.car̃.Ibi.v.ſerui.
7 viii.ac̃ p̃ti.Vał 7 ualuit.vi.liƀ.

Iſd Rog̾ ten̾ Hetrope.7 Wiłłs de eo.Ibi.ii.hidæ.Dūning tenuit.
T.R.E.In dñio ſunt.ii.car̃.7 iii.uiłłi 7 iii.bord cū.i.car̃.Ibi.vi.
ſerui.Vał 7 ualuit.c.̾ſoł.   In Bernintone hd̃.

Iſd Rog̾ ten̾ Wenric.7 Radulf̾ de eo.Ibi.ii.hidæ.Wluric te
nuit T.R.E.In dñio.ẽ.i.car̃.7 iii.uiłłi 7.ii.bord cū.i.car̃.Ibi.v.
ſerui.7 molin̄ de.v.ſoł.7 x.ac̃ p̃ti.Valuit.c.ſoł.Modo.iiii.liƀ.

The value was £20; now £24.

This thane could go where he would.

On this land St. Mary's of Cirencester holds 1 villager and part of the woodland. King William assigned this to it. Value 10s.

EDGEWORTH. 1½ hides which pay tax. Alwin held it. In lordship 4 ploughs;

4 villagers and 3 smallholders with 2 ploughs. 2 free men with 2 ploughs.

15 slaves; a mill at 30d; meadow, 2 acres; woodland 1 league long and ½ wide.

The value is and was £6.

[in TWYFORD Hundred]

½ hide with 1 fishery in the Wye.

1 villager with 1 plough.

This land is called MADGETT.

The value is and was 20s.

Brictric held it.

in TIDENHAM ½ hide. Archbishop Stigand held it.

1 villager with 1 plough.

4½ fisheries.

The value is and was 20s.

in BRIGHTWELLS BARROW Hundred

QUENINGTON. 8 hides. Three free men, Doda, another Doda and Alfwold, held it as 3 manors and could go where they would. It pays tax. In lordship 3 ploughs;

20 villagers, 7 smallholders, a priest and a reeve; between them they have 12 ploughs; 2 riding men with 1 plough.

12 slaves; 2 mills at 20s; meadow, 10 acres.

In Gloucester 1 burgess who pays 4 ploughshares; 1 smith who pays 2s.

The value was £8; now £10.

EASTLEACH (Turville). William holds from him. 5 hides. Aldwin held it before 1066. In lordship 2 ploughs;

12 villagers and 1 smallholder with 5 ploughs.

5 slaves; meadow, 8 acres.

The value is and was £6.

HATHEROP. William holds from him. 2 hides. Dunning held it before 1066. In lordship 2 ploughs;

3 villagers and 3 smallholders with 1 plough. 6 slaves.

The value is and was 100s.

in BARRINGTON Hundred

WINDRUSH. Ralph holds from him. 2 hides. Wulfric held it before 1066. In lordship 1 plough;

3 villagers and 2 smallholders with 1 plough.

5 slaves; a mill at 5s; meadow, 10 acres.

The value was 100s; now £4.

Iſd Rog̓ teñ ibid unã hid 7 unã v̓.7 Hugo de eo. Godric tenuit

teiñ.R.E. In dñio.e̅.i.car̅.7 ii.bord 7 uñ ſeru.7 moliñ de.iii.

ſolid.7 viii.ac̓ p̓ti.Val 7 ualuit.xxiiii.ſol. IN CIRECESTRE HD̃.

Iſd Rog̓ teñ STRATONE.Ibi.v.hidæ. geld.preter dominium. Edmund tenuit T.R.E.

In dñio ſunt.iii.car̅.7 xvi.uilli 7 vii.bord cũ pbro hñtes.ix.car̅.

Ibi.v.ſerui.7 ii.molini de.xx.ſolid. Valuit.viii.lib̃.M̊.vi.lib̃.

Iſd Rog̓ teñ SVINTONE.7 mat ej teñ de ſua dote.Ibi.vi.hidæ

Godric̓ 7 Leuuiñ tenuer̅ ꝑ.ii.ꝏ.In dñio ſunt.iii.car̅.7 ix.

uilli.7 vi.bord 7 pbr cũ.vii.car̅.Ibi.ii.ſerui.7 molinũ

de.x.ſol.Valuit.viii.lib̃.Modo:̓ix.lib̃.

Iſd Rog̓ teñ ACHELIE.Ibi.i.hida 7 dimid.Leuuiñ tenuit.

Modo teñ Girard de Rog̓.In dñio ſunt.ii.car̅.7 ii.uilli cũ

pbro hñtes.ii.car̅ 7 dimid.Ibi.ix.ſerui. Valuit.iiii.lib̃.m̊

Iſd Rog̓ 7 mat ej teñ SCLOSTRE. IN SALESMANES BERIE HVND'. ₤iii.lib̃.

Ibi.iii.hide.Offa 7 Leuuiñ tenuer̅ ꝑ.ii.ꝏ.7 poterant ire

quo uoleb̃. In dñio ſunt.iiii.car̅.7 iiii.bord 7 viii.ſerui.7 mo

liñ de.xii.ſolid. Val 7 ualuit.vi.lib̃.De his.iii.hid

geldab̃.i.hida ſingul annis ꝑ.x.ſolid ad opus regis.

Iſd Rog̓ teñ WERMETVN.Walt.f.ercold de eo. IN GRETESTAN HD̃.

Ibi.v.hide.geld.Eduui tenuit.In dñio ſunt.ii.car̅.7 vi.uilli cũ.ii.

car̅.Ibi.ii.ſerui.7 moliñ de.viii.ſolid.7 x.ac̓ p̓ti.Valuit.c.ſol.m̊.

iiii.lib̃

.XL. TERRA ROGERIJ DE BELMONT. IN CEOLFLEDE HVND̓.

R̲OGERIVS de Belmont teñ DORSINTVNE 7 Rob̓t de eo.

Ibi.x.hidæ.Saxi tenuit. In dñio.iii.car̅.7 viii.uilli cũ.v.car̅.

7 vi.ſerui.   Valuit.viii.lib̃.modo.c.ſolid.

Roger also holds there 1 hide and 1 virgate, and Hugh from him. 168 a
Godric, a thane of King Edward's, held it. In lordship 1 plough;
2 smallholders and 1 slave.
A mill at 3s; meadow, 8 acres.
The value is and was 24s.

Roger also holds

in CIRENCESTER Hundred

STRATTON. 5 hides which pay tax besides the lordship (land).
Edmund held it before 1066. In lordship 3 ploughs;
16 villagers, 7 smallholders with a priest who have 9 ploughs.
5 slaves; 2 mills at 20s.
The value was £8; now £6.

SIDDINGTON, and his mother holds it as her dowry. 6 hides.
Godric and Leofwin held it as two manors. In lordship 3 ploughs;
9 villagers, 6 smallholders and a priest with 7 ploughs.
2 slaves; a mill at 10s.
The value was £8; now £9.

OAKLEY. 1½ hides. Leofwin held it. Now Gerard holds from Roger.
In lordship 2 ploughs;
2 villagers with a priest who have 2½ ploughs. 9 slaves.
The value was £4; now £3.

In SALMONSBURY Hundred

Roger and his mother also hold (Upper) SLAUGHTER. 3 hides.
Offa and Leofwin held it as two manors and could go where
they would. In lordship 4 ploughs;
4 smallholders and 8 slaves.
A mill at 12s.
The value is and was £6.
Of these 3 hides 1 hide paid tax each year at 10s for the King's use.

In GRESTON Hundred

Roger also holds WORMINGTON. Walter son of Arcold holds from him.
5 hides which pay tax. Edwy held it. In lordship 2 ploughs;
6 villagers with 2 ploughs.
2 slaves; a mill at 8s; meadow, 10 acres.
The value was 100s; now £4.

LAND OF ROGER OF BEAUMONT

In CHELTHORN Hundred

Roger of Beaumont holds DORSINGTON, and Robert from him.
10 hides. Saxi held them. In lordship 3 ploughs;
8 villagers with 5 ploughs; 6 slaves.
The value was £8; now 100s.

.XLI R TERRA ROGERIJ DE IVERI. *IN BRADELEGE HD.*

ROGERIVS de IVREI ten HANTONE. Ibi.x.hidæ. Eldred arcħ tenuit. Rex. E. deđ ei. II. hiđ q̃etas ex his. x. ut dicunt.

In dñio funt. III. caſ.7 x. uiłłi cũ pƀro 7.I. borđ cũ. v. caſ.

Ibi. xI. ſerui.7 In Wincelcũbe. x. burgſes reddt. LXV. denaſ.

Valuit. vIII. liƀ. Modo. vI. liƀ. *IN LANGETREWES HD.*

Iſđ Rog̃ ten̄ TETEBERIE. Ibi. xxIII. hidæ geld. Siuuard tenuit T. R. E. In dñio ſunt. vIII. caſ.7 xxxII. uiłłi 7 II. borđ 7 II. radchen cũ pƀro. int oms hñtes. xIIII. caſ. Ibi. xIx. ſerui. 7 molin̄ de. xv. den̄.7 paſtura de. x. ſoliđ.7 x. ãc p̃ti.

Iſđ Rog̃ ten̄ VPTONE. Ibi. II. hidæ 7 una v̄ gelđ. Aluricus tenuit de rege. E. In dñio ſunt. II. caſ.7 v. uiłłi 7 III. borđ cũ. III. caſ. Ibi. vIII. ſerui.

Hec duo M̃ T.R.E. ualƀ. xxxIII. liƀ. Modo ſuꝗ̃ ad firmã ᵱ. L. liƀ.

Aluric tenuit.
Iſđ Rog̃ ten̄ CVLCORTORNE.7 Anſchitil de eo. Ibi. I. hida 7 dim̄.

In dñio. II. caſ.7 IIII. ſerui. Valuit. xx. ſoł. Modoː xxx. ſoliđ.

Iſđ Rog̃ ten̄ HASEDENE. Ibi. III. hidæ 7 III. virg̃ geld. Elnoc tenuit. T.R.E. In dñio ſunt. IIII. caſ.7 vII. dimidij uiłłi 7 I. borđ cũ. III. caſ.7 xvII. ſerui.7 dimiđ molin̄ de. xxx. denaſ.7 xv. ãc p̃ti. Hoc M̃ tenuit q̃đã hō Rog̃ de ep̃o baioc̃ſi. ᵱ. xvI. liƀ.

Poſtea deđ ep̃s eiđ Rogerio cũ firma.

.XLII R TERRA ROGERIJ DE BERCHELAI. *IN RESPIGETE HVND.*

ROGERIVS de Berchelai ten̄ COBERLEIE. Ibi. x. hidæ. Dena tenuit tein̄ regis. E. In dñio ſunt. II. caſ.7 xIx. uiłłi 7 IIII. borđ cũ. v. caſ. Ibi. IIII. ſerui.7 v. ãc p̃ti. Silua. III. q̃ꝗ̃ lg̃.7 II. lat̃.

Valuit. vII. liƀ. Modo. vIII. liƀ. *IN HEDREDESTAN HD.*

Iſđ Rog̃ ten̄ DODINTONE. Ibi. III. hidæ.7 ii. partes dimiđ hidæ. Aluuin̄ tenuit T.R.E. In dñio. ē. I. caſ.7 vII. uiłłi 7 IIII. borđ cũ. IIII. caſ. Ibi. IIII. ſerui.7 x. ãc p̃ti. Val 7 ualuit. III. liƀ.

LAND OF ROGER OF IVRY

In BRADLEY Hundred

Roger of Ivry holds HAMPNETT. 10 hides. Archbishop Aldred held it; King Edward gave him 2 hides of these 10 exempt, as they state. In lordship 3 ploughs;
> 10 villagers with a priest and 1 smallholder with 5 ploughs.
>> 11 slaves; in Winchcombe 10 burgesses pay 65d.

The value was £8; now £6.

In LONGTREE Hundred

Roger also holds TETBURY. 23 hides which pay tax. Siward held it before 1066. In lordship 8 ploughs;
> 32 villagers, 2 smallholders and 2 riding men with a priest,
> who between them have 14 ploughs.
>> 19 slaves; a mill at 15d; pasture at 10s; meadow, 10 acres.

Roger also holds (Tetbury) UPTON. 2 hides and 1 virgate which pay tax. Aelfric held from King Edward. In lordship 2 ploughs;
> 5 villagers and 3 smallholders with 3 ploughs. 8 slaves.

Value of these two manors before 1066 £33; now they are at a revenue of £50.

Roger also holds CULKERTON, and Ansketel from him. Aelfric held it. 1½ hides. In lordship 2 ploughs; 4 slaves.

The value was 20s; now 30s.

Roger also holds HAZLETON. 3 hides and 3 virgates which pay tax. Alnoth held it before 1066. In lordship 4 ploughs;
> 7 half-villagers and 1 smallholder with 3 ploughs; 17 slaves.
>> ½ mill at 30d; meadow, 15 acres.

A certain Roger held this manor from the Bishop of Bayeux for £16; later the Bishop gave it to this Roger with the revenue.

LAND OF ROGER OF BERKELEY

In RAPSGATE Hundred

Roger of Berkeley holds COBERLEY. 10 hides. Dena, a thane of King Edward's, held it. In lordship 2 ploughs;
> 19 villagers and 4 smallholders with 5 ploughs.
>> 4 slaves; meadow, 5 acres; woodland 3 furlongs long and 2 wide.

The value was £7; now £8.

In EDDERSTONE Hundred

Roger also holds DODINGTON. 3 hides and 2 parts of ½ hide. Alwin held it before 1066. In lordship 1 plough;
> 7 villagers and 4 smallholders with 4 ploughs.
>> 4 slaves; meadow, 10 acres.

The value is and was £3.

Iſd Rog ten̄ SISTONE. Anne tenuit. IN PVLCRECERCE HD̄.

Ibi. v. hidæ geld. In dn̄io ſunt. II. car̄. 7 VIII. uilti 7 x. bord̄

cū. IIII. car̄. Ibi. IIII. ſerui. 7 VIII. ac̄ p̄ti. Val 7 ualuit. c. ſolid.

.XLIII. **R** TERRA RADVLFI DE BERCHELAI *IN PVLCHECERGE HD̄*:
ADVLFVS fr̄ ipſius Rogerij ten̄ de rege WAPELIE.

Ibi. I. hida. Godric tenuit. In dn̄io. ē una car̄. 7 IIII. ſerui:

Val 7 ualuit. xx. ſolid. IN BLACELEW HD̄:

Iſd Rad ten̄ STANLEGE. Ibi. IIII. hidæ 7 dim̄. Godric

7 Wiſnod tenuer̄ p̄. II. CO. In dn̄io ſunt. II. car̄. 7 VI. uilti

7 XIIII. bord̄ cū XII. car̄. Ibi. v. ſerui. 7 x. ac̄ p̄ti.

Valuit 7 ual. c. ſolid.

.XLII. **R** TERRA RADVLFI PAGENEL. IN CIRECESTRE HD̄.
ADVLFVS pagenel ten̄ TORENTVNE. 7 Radulf de eo.

Ibi. IIII. hidæ 7 dimid̄ geld̄. Merleſuen tenuit. In dn̄io

ſunt. III. car̄. 7 x. uilti 7 I. bord̄ cū. III. car̄. Ibi. x. ſerui.

⋆ Valuit. x. lib. modo. c. ſolid. *IN LANGETREWES HD̄* Teneb Rog de Jurei

page
unā v træ 7 dimid de Rad
quā utriq; dereliqruṅ.

.XLV. **R** TERRA RADVLFI DE TODENI. *IN WITELAI HVND̄.*
ADVLFVS de Todeni ten̄ CHEVRINGAVRDE. 7 Rogeri

de eo. Ibi. x. hidæ. Briſmar tenuit. In dn̄io. III. car̄.

7 XIII. uilti 7 un̄ Radchen cū. vi. car̄. 7 IX. int ſeruos

7 ancillas. Valuit. VIII. lib. Modo. vi. lib. *IN SALEMANESBERIE*

Iſd Radulf ten̄ ICVBE. 7 Rog de eo. Ibi. x. hidæ. geldantes. Γ HVND̄:

In dn̄io. III. car̄. 7 XII. uilti 7 II. bord̄ cū. VII. car̄. Ibi

VIII. ſerui. Val 7 ualuit. vi. lib. IN BOTELAV HD̄.

Iſd Rad ten̄ BRVNMEBERGE. Ibi. v. hide. Herald com̄ tenuit

In dn̄io. ē. I. car̄. 7 XI. uilti 7 VIII. bord̄ cū. XIIII. car̄. Ibi

In PUCKLECHURCH Hundred

Roger also holds SISTON. Anna held it. 5 hides which pay tax.
In lordship 2 ploughs;
    8 villagers and 10 smallholders with 4 ploughs.
    4 slaves; meadow, 8 acres.
The value is and was 100s.

LAND OF RALPH OF BERKELEY   168 b

In PUCKLECHURCH Hundred

Ralph, brother of the same Roger, holds WAPLEY from the King.
1 hide. Godric held it. In lordship 1 plough; 4 slaves.
The value is and was 20s.

In BLACKLOW Hundred

Ralph also holds (Leonard) STANLEY. 4½ hides. Godric and
Wisnoth held it as two manors. In lordship 2 ploughs;
    6 villagers and 14 smallholders with 12 ploughs.
    5 slaves; meadow, 10 acres.
The value was and is 100s.

LAND OF RALPH PAGNELL

In CIRENCESTER Hundred

Ralph Pagnell holds TARLTON, and Ralph from him. 4½ hides which
pay tax. Merleswein held it. In lordship 3 ploughs;
    10 villagers and 1 smallholder with 3 ploughs. 10 slaves.
The value was £10; now 100s.

In LONGTREE Hundred

Roger of Ivry held from Ralph Pagnell 1½ virgates of land which
they both abandoned.

LAND OF RALPH OF TOSNY

In WITLEY Hundred

Ralph of Tosny holds CHARINGWORTH, and Roger from him.
10 hides. Brictmer held it. In lordship 3 ploughs;
    13 villagers and 1 riding man with 6 ploughs; 9 slaves, male
      and female.
The value was £8; now £6.

Ralph also holds

in SALMONSBURY Hundred

'COMBE (Baskerville)'. Roger holds from him. 10 hides which pay
tax. In lordship 3 ploughs;
    12 villagers and 2 smallholders with 7 ploughs. 8 slaves.
The value is and was £6.

in BOTLOE Hundred

BROMSBERROW. 5 hides. Earl Harold held it. In lordship 1 plough;
    11 villagers and 8 smallholders with 14 ploughs.

un feruus.Silua.ii.leuu lg̅.7 una lat̅.

Valuit.viii.lib̅.Modo.c.folid̅. IN GERSDONES HD̅.

Ist Radulf ten HAREHILLE.7 Roger de eo.Ibi.v.hidæ.

Elric 7 Aluuin 7 Vluric tenuer̅ ꝑ.iii.ꞔ.

Ist Radulf ten OMENIE 7 CERNEI.7 Roger de eo.

Ibi.iiii.hidæ.Quattuor teini tenuer̅ ꝑ.iiii.ꞔ.7 poteraꞩ
ire quó uoleb̅.In dn̅io.x.car̅.7 i.uitts 7 i.bord̅.Ibi
xxi.feru.7 molin̅ de.v.fot.7 xxx.ac̅ ꝑti.

Valeb̅.x.lib̅.Modo.vi.lib̅. IN SALEMANESBERIE HD̅.

Ist Rad̅ ten SVELLE.7 Drogo de eo.Ernefi tenuit.

Ibi.vii.hide geld̅.In dn̅io funt.iiii.car̅.7 x.uitti cu̅.vi.car̅
7 molin̅ de vii.fot 7 vi.den̅.Valuit.viii.lib̅.modo.vii.lib̅.

.XLVI. **R**ᴏᴛʙᴇʀᴛ de Todeni ten RISENDONE. Vlf tenuit

TERRA ROBERTI DE TODENI.IN SALEMANESBERIE HD̅.

Ibi.xiii.hidæ geld̅.In dn̅io funt.iii.car̅.7 xxiii.uitti
7 vi.bord̅ cu̅.x.car̅.Ibi.viii.int feruos 7 ancillas.
7 molin̅ de.x.fot.7 un burg̅fis in Glouuecest̅ de.iii.den̅.

Valuit.xii.lib̅.M.x.lib̅. IN GRIBOLDESTOV HD̅.

Ist Rob̅t ten HOREDONE.Ibi.x.hidæ geld̅.Vlf tenuit.

In dn̅io funt.iii.car̅.7 xi.uitti 7 viii.bord̅.cu̅.viii.car̅.
Ibi.vii.ferui.7 molin̅ de.vi.folid̅.7 xx.ac̅ ꝑti.Silua.ii.leuu
lg̅.7 una lat̅.Valuit xii.lib̅.modo.vii.lib̅. IN BISELEGE HD̅.

Ist Rob̅t ten SAPLETORNE.7 FRANTONE.In uno.v.hide.
7 in alio.v.hidæ.Vlf tenuit.In dn̅io funt.vii.car̅.7 xvii.
uitti 7 ix.bord̅.cu̅.x.car̅.Ibi.xiii.ferui.7 ii.molini
de.vi.folid̅.Silua dimid̅ leuua lg̅.7 ii.ꝗᴣ lat̅.

H̅.ii.ꞔ T.R.E.ualb̅.xiiii.lib̅.fimul.Modo.xvi.lib̅.

.XLVII. **R**ᴏᴛʙᴇʀᴛ difpenfator ten WICVENE.Ibi.x.hidæ geld̅.

TERRA ROBERTI DISPENSAT̅ IN GRETESTANE HD̅.

1 slave; woodland 2 leagues long and 1 wide.
The value was £8; now 100s.

in GARSDON Hundred

HARNHILL. Roger holds from him. 5 hides. Alric, Alwin and
Wulfric held it as three manors.

'AMPNEY' and (South) CERNEY. Roger holds from him. 4 hides.
Four thanes held them as four manors and could go where they
would. In lordship 10 ploughs;
    1 villager and 1 smallholder.
    21 slaves; a mill at 5s; meadow, 30 acres.
The value was £10; now £6.

in SALMONSBURY Hundred

(Lower) SWELL. Drogo holds from him. Erneis held it. 7 hides
which pay tax. In lordship 4 ploughs;
    10 villagers with 6 ploughs.
    A mill at 7s 6d.
The value was £8; now £7.

LAND OF ROBERT OF TOSNY

In SALMONSBURY Hundred

Robert of Tosny holds (Great) RISSINGTON. Ulf held it. 13 hides
which pay tax. In lordship 3 ploughs;
    23 villagers and 6 smallholders with 10 ploughs.
    8 slaves, male and female; a mill at 10s.
    1 burgess in Gloucester at 3d.
The value was £12; now £10.

In GRUMBALDS ASH Hundred

Robert also holds HORTON. 10 hides which pay tax. Ulf held it.
In lordship 3 ploughs;
    11 villagers and 8 smallholders with 8 ploughs.
    7 slaves; a mill at 6s; meadow, 20 acres; woodland 2 leagues
        long and 1 wide.
The value was £12; now £7.

In BISLEY Hundred

Robert also holds SAPPERTON and FRAMPTON (Mansell). 5 hides in
one, and 5 hides in the other. Ulf held them. In lordship 7 ploughs;
    17 villagers and 9 smallholders with 10 ploughs.
    13 slaves; 2 mills at 6s; woodland ½ league long and 2 furlongs
        wide.
Value of these two manors together before 1066 £14; now £16.

LAND OF ROBERT THE BURSAR

In GRESTON Hundred

Robert the Bursar holds CHILDSWICKHAM. 10 hides which pay tax.

Balduin̊ tenuit. In dn̄io ſunt. iii. car̄.7 xxxii. uiłłi 7 x. borð

cū. xii. car̄. Ibi. i. ſeru̇.7 ii. molini de. x. ſoł.7 x. ac̄ p̃ti.

In Wincelcūbe. i. burḡſis de. xvi. den̊. Valuit. xii. liɓ. m̊. xvi. liɓ.

XLVIII. 168 c TERRA ROBERTI DE OILGI. *IN SALEMANESBERIE* ᵀHD·

ROTBERT de Olgi ten̊ *RISENDVNE*. Ibi. x. hidæ gelð.

Siuuard ̇tenuit. In dn̄io. iiii. car̄.7 xii. uiłłi 7 ii. borð cū. v.

car̄. Ibi. viii. ſerui.7 ii. molini de. xx. ſolið.

Valuit. x. liɓ. Modo.⸝viii. liɓ. *IN BRADELEG HD.*

Iſð Rotɓt ten̊ *TVRCHEDENE*. Ibi. v. hidæ.7 ii. uirg̊ 7 dimið

gelð. Siuuard tenuit. In dn̄io ſunt. iiii. car̄.7 xii. uiłłi

cū. vi. car̄. Ibi. viii. int̊ ſeruos 7 Anciłł. Valuit. vi. liɓ. M̊.⸝c. ſoł.

Roger de Olgi ten̊ *NIWETONE*. *IN SALEMANESBERIE HD.*

de osɓno. f. Ricardi. Ibi. v. hidæ gelð. Turſtan tenuit. In

dn̄io. ii. car̄.7 viii. uiłłi cū. iiii. car̄ 7 dimið. Vał. iii. liɓ.

.XLIX. TERRA RICARDI LEGATI. *IN HEDREDESTAN HD.*

RICARD Legat̊ ten̊ de rege *TORMENTONE*. Ibi. viii.

hidæ. Alric̊ tenuit de rege. E. In dn̄io ſunt. vi. car̄.

7 xx. uiłłi 7 iiii. borð 7 pɓr 7 un̊ radchen̊. Int̊ om̄s. xii.

car̄ hn̄t. Ibi. xii. ſerui. Valuit. xii. liɓ. m̊. xv. liɓ.

.L. TERRA OSBERNI GIFARD. *IN LANGELEI HD.*

OSBERN ̊Gifard ten̊ de rege *ROCHEMTVNE*. Ibi. iii. hidæ

gelð. Dunne tenuit. T.R.E. In dn̄io ſunt. ii. car̄.7 vi. uiłłi

7 vii. borð cū. iii. car̄. Ibi. v. ſerui.7 xx. ac̄ p̃ti.7 ſalina

ad Wich. de. iiii. ſūmis ſalis. Silua. i. leuua lḡ.7 dim̊ lat̊. Vł. vi. liɓ.

Iſð Osɓn̊ ten̊ *STQCHE*. Ibi. v. hidæ gelð *IN LETBERG HD.*

Dunne tenuit. In dn̄io ſunt. iiii. car̄.7 viii. uiłłi 7 iii. borð

7 pɓr cū. viii. car̄. Ibi. iiii. ſerui. Valuit. vi. liɓ. m̊. viii. liɓ.

Baldwin held it. In lordship 3 ploughs;
32 villagers and 10 smallholders with 12 ploughs.
1 slave; 2 mills at 10s; meadow, 10 acres.
In Winchcombe 1 burgess at 16d.
The value was £12; now £16.

LAND OF ROBERT D'OILLY

168 c

In SALMONSBURY Hundred

1 Robert d'Oilly holds (Little) RISSINGTON. 10 hides which pay tax. Siward held it. In lordship 4 ploughs;
12 villagers and 2 smallholders with 5 ploughs.
8 slaves; 2 mills at 20s.
The value was £10; now £8.

In BRADLEY Hundred

2 Robert also holds (Upper) TURKDEAN. 5 hides and 2½ virgates which pay tax. Siward held it. In lordship 4 ploughs;
12 villagers with 6 ploughs. 8 slaves, male and female.
The value was £6; now 100s.

In SALMONSBURY Hundred

3 Roger d'Oilly holds NAUNTON from Osbern son of Richard.
5 hides which pay tax. Thurstan held it. In lordship 2 ploughs;
8 villagers with 4½ ploughs.
Value £3.

LAND OF RICHARD THE COMMISSIONER

In EDDERSTONE Hundred

1 Richard the Commissioner holds TORMARTON from the King. 8 hides....
Alric held it from King Edward. In lordship 6 ploughs;
20 villagers, 4 smallholders, a priest and 1 riding man;
between them they have 12 ploughs. 12 slaves.
The value was £12; now £15.

LAND OF OSBERN GIFFARD

In LANGLEY Hundred

1 Osbern Giffard holds ROCKHAMPTON from the King. 3 hides which pay tax. Dunn held it before 1066. In lordship 2 ploughs;
6 villagers and 7 smallholders with 3 ploughs.
5 slaves; meadow, 20 acres; a salt-house at Droitwich at 4 packloads of salt; woodland 1 league long and ½ wide.
Value £6.

In LEDBURY Hundred

2 Osbern also holds STOKE (Gifford). 5 hides which pay tax. Dunn held it. In lordship 4 ploughs;
8 villagers, 3 smallholders and a priest with 8 ploughs. 4 slaves.
The value was £6; now £8.

168 b, c

Iſd Osbñ teñ *BRIMESFELDE*.Ibi.ix.hidæ geld. *IN RESPIGET HD.*

Duns tenuit de Heraldo. In dñio ſunt.iii.cař.7 xvi.uiłłi

7 vi.borđ 7 pbr.cū.xii.cař.Ibi.viii.ſerui.7 iiii.ancille.

7 ii.molini de.lxiiii.deñ.In Glouuec.v.burgſes de.ii.ſoł.

Vał 7 ualuit.xii.lib.

Iſd Osbñ teñ *ALDEBERIE*.ſed ñ ptinuit ad Duns trā

quā osbñ teñ.ut ſcira dicit.   Eilricus tenuit 7 potuit

ire quó uoluit.Ibi.i.hida 7 i.cař.Vał 7 ualuit.x.ſoł.

.LI. GTERRA GOISFRIDI ORLETEILE

Goisfriđ orleteile teñ de rege in *BAVDINTVNE*.

ii.hiđ 7 unā,v.geld.Bolli tenuit.Non.ē in dñio qd.

Ibi.ii.uiłłi 7 viii.borđ.cū.iii.cař.Vał 7 ualuit.xl.ſoł.

Ibi.viii.ač pti.

.LII. GTERRA GISLEBTI FILIJ TVROLD. *IN CIRECESTRE HD.*

Gislebertvs fili Turoldi teñ in *ACHELIE*.i.hiđ de rege.

7 Oſulf de eo.Keneuuard tenuit.T.R.E.In dñio ſunt.ii.

eař.7 iii.borđ 7 vi.ſerui.Valuit.xl.ſoliđ.m̄.xxx.ſoliđ.

Iſd Giſlebt teñ in *TVRSBERIE* dim hidā 7 Oſuuard de eo.

Aluuard tenuit.In dñio.ē.i.cař.Valuit.x.ſoł.m̄.xv.ſoł.

Iſd Giſlebt teñ *CERNEI*.Ibi.vii.hidæ.   *IN RESPIGET HD.*

Duo teini tenuer̄ .p.ii.Ɯ.7 poteraɴ ire quo uoleb.

In dñio ſuɴ.iiii.cař.7 vii.uiłłi 7 vi.borđ.cū.v.cař.Ibi

vi.ſeru.7 moliñ de.viii.ſoliđ.7 vi.ač pti.Silua.ii.q̃ɀ lg.

7 una lat.Ibi.iiii.milites Giſlebti hñt cū ſuis hōibɀ

vii.cař.7 moliñ de viii.ſoł.

Tot T.R.E.ualb.xiiii.lib.modo.xii.lib.

Iſd Giſł.teñ *RINDECOME*.Ibi.v.hidæ geld.Aluric tenuit.

In dñio.ē.i.cař.7 iii.uiłłi 7 vii.borđ cū.iii.cař.Ibi.vii.

ſerui.7 uñ franciġ teñ trā đuoɀ uiłłoɀ.7 moliñ de.viii.

ſoliđ.7 iiii.ač pti.   Valuit.vii.lib.M̄.c.ſoliđ.

In RAPSGATE Hundred

3   Osbern also holds BRIMPSFIELD. 9 hides which pay tax. Dunn held
it from Earl Harold. In lordship 3 ploughs;
> 16 villagers, 6 smallholders and a priest with 12 ploughs.
> 8 male and 4 female slaves; 2 mills at 64d.
> In Gloucester 5 burgesses at 2s.

The value is and was £12.

4   Osbern also holds 'OLDBURY', but it did not belong to the man
Dunn's land which Osbern holds, as the Shire states. Alric held
it and could go where he would. 1 hide and 1 plough.
The value is and was 10s.

51   LAND OF GEOFFREY ORLATEILE

[In CIRENCESTER Hundred]

1   Geoffrey Orlateile holds from the King in BAUNTON 2 hides and
1 virgate which pay tax. Bolle held them. Nothing in lordship.
> 2 villagers and 8 smallholders with 3 ploughs.

The value is and was 40s.
> Meadow, 8 acres.

52   LAND OF GILBERT SON OF THOROLD

In CIRENCESTER Hundred

1   Gilbert son of Thorold holds 1 hide in OAKLEY from the King, and
Oswulf from him. Kenward held it before 1066. In lordship 2
ploughs;
> 3 smallholders and 6 slaves.

The value was 40s; now 30s.

Gilbert also holds

2   in TREWSBURY ½ hide. Osward holds from him. Alfward held it.
In lordship 1 plough.
The value was 10s; now 15s.

in RAPSGATE Hundred

3   (North) CERNEY. 7 hides. Two thanes, Elaf and his brother, held
it as two manors and could go where they would. In lordship 4
ploughs;
> 7 villagers and 6 smallholders with 5 ploughs.
> 6 slaves; a mill at 8s; meadow, 6 acres; woodland 2 furlongs
> long and 1 wide.
> 4 of Gilbert's men-at-arms with their men have 7 ploughs and
> a mill at 8s.

Value of the whole manor before 1066 £14; now £12.

4   RENDCOMB. 5 hides which pay tax. Aelfric held it. In lordship 1
plough;
> 3 villagers and 7 smallholders with 3 ploughs. 7 slaves;
> a Frenchman who holds the land of 2 villagers.
> A mill at 8s; meadow, 4 acres.

The value was £7; now 100s.

Iſd Gisl.ten *RINDECVBE*.7 Walter de eo .Ibi.iii.hidæ
geld In dñio ſunt.ii.caɼ.7 iiii.uiłłi 7 iii.borđ cū.ii.caɼ.
Ibi.vi.ſerui.7 moliñ de.v.ſoliđ.7 iii.ac̄ p̄ti.Val 7 ualuit

Iſd Gisl ten *ELEWRDE*.7 Walter de eo.Aluuin tenuit ꝼ vi.lib
Ibi.iiii.hidæ geld.In dñio.ii.caɼ.7 iii.uiłłi cū.ii.caɼ.7 vi.inɽ
ſeruos 7 ancillas.Val 7 ualuit.xl.ſol.

Iſd Gisl ten *HFRFORD*.Alfer tenuit.Ibi.i.hida geld.In dñio
.ii.caɼ.7 iiii.uiłłi 7 i.borđ cū.ii.caɼ.7 ii.ſerui.7 moliñ de.v.ſol.
Val 7 ualuit.xl.ſoliđ.

168 d

.LIII. DTERRA DVRANDI DE GLOWEC̄. *IN WESTBERIE HĐ.*

DVRAND uicecom ten unū m̄ de iiiɪ.hiđ.
Aluuold tenuit 7 geldab.In dñio.e.i.caɼ.7 iiii.uiłłi 7 iii.borđ
cū.iiii.caɼ.Ibi.ii.ſerui.   Valuit.lx.ſol.m̄.xl.ſol.
Iſd Durand ten in *ESBROC*.i.hiđ 7 miles ej qͩā *IN GERSDONES HĐ.*
de eo.In dñio.i.caɼ.7 i.borđ 7 i.ſeru.Val 7 ualuit.x.ſoliđ.
Iſd Durand ten.ii.hiđ in *DVNTESBORNE*. *IN CIRECESTRE HĐ.*
7 Radulf de eo.Wluuarđ tenuit ꝑ m̄ de rege.E.In dñio
ſunt.ii.caɼ.7 iii.uiłłi 7 un borđ cū.i.caɼ.Ibi.iiii.ſerui.7 ii.
ac̄ p̄ti.   Val 7 ualuit.xl.ſol. *IN LANGETREV HĐ.*
Iſd Durand ten *CVLCORTONE*.7 Rogeri de eo.Ibi.ii.hidæ.
7.ii.v 7 dimiđ.Grim tenuit.In dñio ſunt.ii.caɼ.7 vi.uiłłi
cū.iii.caɼ.   Val 7 ualuit.iiii.lib. *IN GRIBOLDESTOV HĐ.*
Iſd Durand ten *DEDMERTONE*.7 Anſchitil de eo.Ibi.iii.hidæ
geld.Leuuin tenuit de Heraldo.In dñio ſunt.iii.caɼ.7 viii.
borđ cū.i.caɼ.7 iiii.ſerui.7 vi.ac̄ p̄ti.Valuit xxx.ſol.m̄.xl.ſol.

5   RENDCOMB. Walter holds from him. 3 hides which pay tax.
In lordship 2 ploughs;
    4 villagers and 3 smallholders with 2 ploughs.
    6 slaves; a mill at 5s; meadow, 3 acres.
The value is and was £6.

in SALMONSBURY Hundred

6   AYLWORTH. Walter holds from him. Alwin held it. 4 hides which
pay tax. In lordship 2 ploughs;
    3 villagers with 2 ploughs; 6 slaves, male and female.
The value is and was 40s.

7   HARFORD. Alfhere held it. 1 hide which pays tax. In lordship 2
ploughs;
    4 villagers and 1 smallholder with 2 ploughs; 2 slaves.
    A mill at 5s.
The value is and was 40s.

53   LAND OF DURAND OF GLOUCESTER   168 d

In WESTBURY Hundred

1   Durand the Sheriff holds one manor of 3 hides. Alfwold held it;
it paid tax. In lordship 1 plough;
    4 villagers and 3 smallholders with 4 ploughs. 2 slaves.
The value was 60s; now 40s.

Durand also holds

in GARSDON Hundred

2   in ASHBROOK 1 hide. One of his men-at-arms holds from him.
In lordship 1 plough;
    1 smallholder and 1 slave.
The value is and was 10s.

in CIRENCESTER Hundred

3   in DUNTISBOURNE (Rouse) 2 hides. Ralph holds from him. Wulfward
held it as a manor from King Edward. In lordship 2 ploughs;
    3 villagers and 1 smallholder with 1 plough.
    4 slaves; meadow, 2 acres.
The value is and was 40s.

in LONGTREE Hundred

4   CULKERTON. Roger of Ivry holds from him. 2 hides and 2½ virgates.
Grim held it. In lordship 2 ploughs;
    6 villagers with 3 ploughs.
The value is and was £4.

in GRUMBALDS ASH Hundred

5   DIDMARTON. Ansketel holds from him. 3 hides which pay tax.
Leofwin held it from Earl Harold. In lordship 3 ploughs;
    8 smallholders with 1 plough; 4 slaves.
    Meadow, 6 acres.
The value was 30s; now 40s.

Iſd Durand ten WADVNE. Ibi.v.hidæ.　IN DVNESTANE HD.

Quinq̃ frs tenuer̄ ꝑ.v.ꝏ̃.7 poteraꝗ̃ ire quo uoleƀ.7 pares eraꝗ̃.

In dñio funt.v.car̄.7 uñ uilłs 7 vii.borđ.cū.v.car̄.

T.R.E.ualƀ.viii.liƀ.modo:c.foliđ.　IN CELFLEDETORNE HD.

Iſd Durand ten CHIESNECOTE.7 Walter de eo.Ibi.ii.hidæ-7 dim̄

Leuuiñ 7 Leuui tenuer̄ ꝑ.ii.ꝏ̃.In dñio funt.ii.car̄.7 iiii.borđ.

Valƀ.xl.fol:modo:lx.foliđ.　IN SALEMANESBERIE HD.

Iſd Durand ten ICCVBE.7 Walter de eo.Ibi.ii.hidæ gelđ.

Turſtan tenuit.In dñio.ii.car̄.7 ii.uiłłi 7 ii.borđ.cū.i.car̄.

7 vi.int feruos 7 ancillas.　Valuit.xxx.fol.Modo:xl.fol.

Iſd Durand ten SCIPTVNE.7 Radulf de eo.IN WACRESCVBE HD.

Eduui tenuit.Ibi.iii.hidæ 7 dimiđ gelđ.In dñio.funt ii.car̄.7 iii.

uiłłi cū.ii.car̄.7 iiii.ferui.7 x.ac̄ pti.Valuit.iiii.liƀ.m̊.xl.fol.

Iſd Durand ten in HERSEFELD.vii.hiđ gelđ.　IN WITESTAN HD.

Godric 7 Edric.ii.frs tenuer̄ ꝑ.ii.ꝏ̃.7 poterant ire quo uoleƀ.

In dñio funt.iii.car̄.7 ix.uiłłi 7 xi.borđ cū.ix.car̄.Ibi

iiii.ferui.7 v.poters ħguli reddt.xliiii.den.Silua dimiđ leuua łg.

7 iii.q̃ꝝ lat.　Val 7 ualuit.vi.liƀ.

Iſd Durand ten MORTVNE.Ibi.iii.hidæ gelđ.Auti tenuit.

In dñio.ē una car̄.7 iiii.uiłłi 7 vi.borđ cū.iii.car̄ 7 dimiđ.

Ibi.iiii.ferui.7 xx.ac̄ pti.　Valuit.iiii.liƀ.Modo:xl.fol.

Iſd Durand ten LITETVNE.7 Radulf de eo.IN GRETESTAN HD.

Ibi dimiđ hida gelđ.Leuenot tenuit ꝑ uno ꝏ̃.Ibi.ē una car̄.

Val 7 ualuit.x.foliđ.　IN WITELAI HD.

In CONDICOTE ten Osbñ de Durando.i.hiđ 7 dim.Val 7 ualuit.xx.fol.

in DUDSTONE Hundred

6   WHADDON. 5 hides. Five brothers held it as five manors and could
go where they would; they were co-heirs. In lordship 5 ploughs;
1 villager and 7 smallholders with 5 ploughs.
Value before 1066 £8; now 100s.

in CHELTHORN Hundred

7   SEZINCOTE. Walter holds from him. 2½ hides. Leofwin and Leofwy
held it as two manors. In lordship 2 ploughs;
4 smallholders.
The value was 40s; now 60s.

in SALMONSBURY Hundred

8   ICOMB ('Proper'). Walter holds from him. 2 hides which pay tax.
Thurstan held it. In lordship 2 ploughs;
2 villagers and 2 smallholders with 1 plough. 6 slaves, male
and female.
The value was 30s; now 40s.

in WATTLESCOMB Hundred

9   SHIPTON ('Pelye'). Ralph holds from him. Edwy held it. 3½ hides
which pay tax. In lordship 2 ploughs;
3 villagers with 2 ploughs; 4 slaves.
Meadow, 10 acres.
The value was £4; now 40s.

in WHITSTONE Hundred

10   in ('Sheriffs') HARESFIELD. 7 hides which pay tax. Two brothers,
Godric and Edric, held it as two manors and could go where they
would. In lordship 3 ploughs;
9 villagers and 11 smallholders with 9 ploughs. 4 slaves;
5 potters pay 44d.
Woodland ½ league long and 3 furlongs wide.
The value is and was £6.

11   MORETON (Valence). 3 hides which pay tax. Auti held it. In lordship
1 plough;
4 villagers and 6 smallholders with 3½ ploughs.
4 slaves; meadow, 20 acres.
The value was £4; now 40s.

in GRESTON Hundred

12   'LITTLETON'. Ralph holds from him. ½ hide which pays tax.
Leofnoth held it as a manor. 1 plough there.
The value is and was 10s.

In WITLEY Hundred

13   Osbern holds 1½ hides in CONDICOTE from Durand.
The value is and was 20s.

.LII. **D**TERRA DROGONIS FILIJ PONZ. *IN BLACHELEV HD.*

ROGO fili⁹ponz.ten de rege *FRANTONE*.Ibi.x.hidæ geld.

Ernefi tenuit.In dñio funt.III.car̄.7 x.uiłłi 7 VIII.borđ

cū.VI.car̄.Ibi.IX.ferui.7 moliñ de.x.foliđ.7 x.ac̃ p̃ti.

Silua.I.leuua lḡ.7 III.q̃⅟₂ lat̄.In Glouuec̄.I.burḡfis de.VI.den.

Vał 7 ualuit.c.foliđ.De hoc m̃ ten Roḡ de Laci.I.hiđ injufte.

Ifđ Drogo ten *LECE*.łbi.x.hidæ geld *IN BRICSTVOLDES HD.*

Cola tenuit.In dñio funt.IIII.car̄.7 xv.uiłłi 7 IIII.borđ cū IX.

car̄.Ibi.IX.ferui.7 moliñ de.x.foliđ.7 x.ac̃ p̃ti.

Valuit.VIII.lib̄.modo.'x.lib̄.

.LV. **W**TERRA WALTERIJ FILIJ PONZ. *IN BRICSTVOLDES HD.*

ALTERIVS fili⁹ponz ten de rege *LECE*.Ibi.x.hidæ geld.

Tofti com̃ tenuit.In dñio funt.IIIL.car.7 xvi.uiłłi 7 vi.borđ 7 p̃br

cū.VIII.car̄.Ibi.XII.ferui.7 moliñ de.x.foliđ.7 xx.ac̃ p̃ti.

Valuit.XII.lib̄.Modo.'xv.lib̄.

.LVI. **W**TERRA WALTERIJ FILIJ ROGER *IN BERNINTON HD.*

169 a

ALTERI fili⁹ Rogerij⁹ ten de rege *BERNINTONE*.

Ibi.VIII.hidæ.   Turiftan 7 Eduui tenuer̄ p.II.m̃.

In dñio funt.IIII.car̄.7 xIIII.uiłłi 7 p̃br 7 II.borđ cū.IX.

car̄.Ibi.XIIII.ferui.7 moliñ de.x.fol̄.7 xx.ac̃ p̃ti.

Vał 7 ualuit.VIII.lib̄.   *IN GERSDONES HD.*

Ifđ.Walter ten *CERNEI*.łbi.XIIII.hidæ 7 una v̄.

arch⁹

Stigand tenuit.In dñio funt.II.car̄.7 xxv.uiłłi 7 p̃br

7 IX.borđ cū.x.car̄.Ibi.IIII.ferui.7 c.ac̃ p̃ti.7 III.mo

lini fuer̄ de xxx.foliđ. Vałb xvi.lib̄.modo.'xII.lib̄.

Hoc m̃ calūniatū eft ad æcc̄lam Ṣ MARIÆ de abendone.fed om̃ls

comitat⁹ teftificat⁹ eft Stig̃and.x.annis tenuiffe uiuente.E.rege.

Hoc m̃ deđ.W.com̃ Rogerio uicecomiti patri Walterij.

LAND OF DROGO SON OF POYNTZ

In BLACKLOW Hundred

1 Drogo son of Poyntz holds FRAMPTON (on Severn) from the King.
10 hides which pay tax. Erneis held it. In lordship 3 ploughs;
10 villagers and 8 smallholders with 6 ploughs.
9 slaves; a mill at 10s; meadow, 10 acres; woodland 1 league
long and 3 furlongs wide.
In Gloucester 1 burgess at 6d.
The value is and was 100s.
Roger of Lacy wrongfully holds 1 hide of this manor.

In BRIGHTWELLS BARROW Hundred

2 Drogo also holds EASTLEACH (Martin). 10 hides which pay tax.
Cola held it. In lordship 4 ploughs;
15 villagers and 4 smallholders with 9 ploughs.
9 slaves; a mill at 10s; meadow, 10 acres.
The value was £8; now £10.

LAND OF WALTER SON OF POYNTZ

In BRIGHTWELLS BARROW Hundred

1 Walter son Poyntz holds EASTLEACH (Martin) from the King.
10 hides which pay tax. Earl Tosti held it. In lordship 4 ploughs;
16 villagers, 6 smallholders and a priest with 8 ploughs.
12 slaves; a mill at 10s; meadow, 20 acres.
The value was £12; now £15.

LAND OF WALTER SON OF ROGER   169 a

In BARRINGTON Hundred

1 Walter son of Roger holds (Great) BARRINGTON from the King.
8 hides ...... Thurstan and Edwy held it as two manors. In
lordship 4 ploughs;
14 villagers, a priest and 2 smallholders with 9 ploughs.
14 slaves; a mill at 10s; meadow, 20 acres.
The value is and was £8.

In GARSDON Hundred

2 Walter also holds (South) CERNEY. 14 hides and 1 virgate.
Archbishop Stigand held it. In lordship 2 ploughs;
25 villagers, a priest and 9 smallholders with 10 ploughs.
4 slaves; meadow, 100 acres; there were 3 mills at 30s.
The value was £16; now £12.
This manor is claimed for St. Mary's Church at Abingdon, but
all the County testified that Archbishop Stigand had held it for
ten years during King Edward's lifetime. Earl William gave this
manor to Roger the Sheriff, Walter's father.

.LVII. **W**TERRA WALTERIJ DIACONI. *In Witelai* HD.

ALTERI diacon teñ de rege *Chesnecote*. Ibi.IIII.hidæ 7 dlmid.
Goduin tenuit 7 potuit ire quo uoluit. In dñio. II. car. 7 VIII.
uitti cũ. VI. car. 7 x. ferui.   Val 7 ualuit. III. lib.

.LVIII. **W**TERRA WALTERIJ BALISTAR. *In Westeerie* HD.

ALTERIVS baliftari teñ de rege *Bvlelege*. Ibi.IIII.hidæ
geld. Toui tenuit de rege. E. In dñio funt. II. car. 7 IIII. uitti
7 VI. bord cũ. IIII. car. Ibi. IIII. ferui. 7 x. ac pti. In Glouuec
un burgfis redd. XVIII. den.   Valuit. LX. fol. modo. XL. fol.
Ifd Walt teñ *Rodele*. Ibi. I. hida geld. Toui tenuit. In dñio
ē una car. 7 II. uitti 7 IIII. bord cũ. II. car. Valuit. XL. fol. m. x. fol.
Ifd Walt teñ dimid hidã quæ ñ geldat *In Blidelav hvnd*.
Palli tenuit. Ibi. ē moliñ. Val XIX. folid. *In Langelei hvnd*.
Ifd Walt teñ *Frantone*. Ibi. v. hidæ geld. Aleftan tenuit *de bofcube*
In dñio. ē. I. car. 7 x. uitti 7 XI. bord cũ. v. car. Ibi. v. ferui.
7 II. molini de. v. folid. Ibi 7 æccta q̃ ñ fuit. Valuit. VIII. lib. m. III. lib.

.LIX TERRA HENRICI DE FERIERES. *In Brictvoldesberg* HD.

HENRICVS de Ferreres teñ *Lecelade*. Siuuard tenuit.
Ibi. xv. hidæ. T.R.E. geldant. Sed ipfe cceffit. VI. hid detas
á geldo. Hoc teftat oñis comitat. 7 ipfe q̃ figillũ regis detulit.
In dñio funt. IIII. car. 7 XXIX. uitti 7 x. bord 7 un francig
teñ trã uni uitti. Int oñs hñt XVI. car. Ibi. XIII. ferui.
7 III. molini de. xxx. fol. 7 pifcaria de. cc. anguitt. xxv. min.
De pratis. VII. lib 7 VII. fol. pter fenũ boum. In Wicelcũbe
II. burgfes redd. xvi. den. 7 un In Glouuec fine cenfu.
Tot cõ T.R.E. ualb xx. lib. 7 m fimilit.

57 **LAND OF WALTER THE DEACON**

In WITLEY Hundred

1 Walter the Deacon holds SEZINCOTE from the King. 4½ hides.
Godwin held it and could go where he would. In lordship 2
ploughs;
   8 villagers with 6 ploughs; 10 slaves.
The value is and was £3.

58 **LAND OF WALTER THE GUNNER**

In WESTBURY Hundred

1 Walter the Gunner holds BULLEY from the King. 4 hides which
pay tax. Tovi held it from King Edward. In lordship 2 ploughs;
   4 villagers and 6 smallholders with 4 ploughs.
   4 slaves; meadow, 10 acres.
   In Gloucester 1 burgess who pays 18d.
The value was 60s; now 40s.

2 Walter also holds RUDDLE. 1 hide which pays tax. Tovi held it.
In lordship 1 plough;
   2 villagers and 4 smallholders with 2 ploughs.
The value was 40s; now 10s.

In BLEDISLOE Hundred

3 Walter also holds ½ hide which does not pay tax. Palli held it.
   A mill.
Value 19s.

In LANGLEY Hundred

4 Walter also holds FRAMPTON (Cotterell). 5 hides which pay tax.
Alstan of Boscombe held it. In lordship 1 plough;
   10 villagers and 11 smallholders with 5 ploughs.
   5 slaves; 2 mills at 5s. A church which was not there [before 1066].
The value was £8; now £3.

59 **LAND OF HENRY OF FERRERS**

In BRIGHTWELLS BARROW Hundred

1 Henry of Ferrers holds LECHLADE. Siward Bairn held it. 15 hides
which paid tax before 1066, but the King himself assigned 6 hides
exempt from tax. All the County testifies to this and so did he,
and showed the King's seal. In lordship 4 ploughs.
   29 villagers, 10 smallholders and 1 Frenchman hold 1 villager's
      land; between them they have 16 ploughs.
   13 slaves; 3 mills at 30s; a fishery at 200 eels, less 25; from the
      meadows £7 7s besides hay for the oxen.
   In Winchcombe 2 burgesses who pay 16d, and 1 in Gloucester
      without dues.
Value of the whole manor before 1066 £20; now the same.

TERRA ERNVLFI DE HESDING. *IN BRICTVOLDESBERG HD.*

Hᴇʀɴvʟғvs de Hefding teñ *CHENEMERESFORDE.*

Ibi . xxɪ . hida geld . Ofgod tenuit de Heraldo . In dñio fuɴ̃

vɪ . caɾ. 7 xxxvɪɪɪ. uiłłi 7 ɪx . borđ 7 ɪ. radchen cũ . xvɪɪɪ . car.

Ibi . xɪɪɪɪ . ferui . 7 ɪɪɪɪ. molini de . xʟ fol . 7 xʟ . den . 7 de pratis

ɪx . liƀ p̃t paftura boũ . 7 de ouili. cxx . penfas cafeoꝛ.

In Glouuec . vɪɪ . burḡſes . redđ . ɪɪ.folid.

Toĩ T.R.E. ualƀ xxx . liƀ . Modo . ʟxvɪ. liƀ . 7 vɪ.fol 7 vɪɪɪ. deñ.

Iſđ Hernulf teñ *ETHEROPE* . Ibi . vɪɪ . hidæ. Vluuard tenuit.

In dñio funt . vɪ . caɾ. 7 xxɪɪɪ. uiłłi cũ . x . caɾ. Ibi xɪɪ . ferui.

7 moliñ de . xv . folid. Valuit . vɪɪɪ . liƀ . modo. xɪɪ. liƀ.

Iſđ Hernulf teñ in *OMENIE* . ɪɪɪɪ . hid *IN GERSDONES HD.*

7 iĩ . virḡ 7 dim̃ . Elric 7 Godric tenueɾ ꝑ. ɪɪ. ꟽ.

In dñio funt . ɪɪɪ . caɾ. 7 vɪɪ. uiłłi 7 ɪɪ. borđ. cũ. ɪɪ . caɾ. Ibi . ɪɪɪɪ . ferui.

Toĩ ualuit 7 ual . vɪ . liƀ.

169 b

Iſđ Hernulf teñ *ALDEBERIE* . Ibi . v . hidæ geld. *IN GRIBOLDESTOV HVND*

Edric tenuit . In dñio funt . ɪɪɪ . caɾ. 7 ɪɪɪɪ . uiłłi cũ . ɪɪɪɪ. car.

7 ibi . ɪx. ferui. 7 uñ francig hñs. ɪ. caɾ. Ibi . vɪ. ac p̃ti.

Val 7 ualuit . x . liƀ.

Iſđ Hernulf teñ *MADMINTVNE* . Ibi . ɪɪɪɪ . hidæ geld . Edric

tenuit . In dñio. funt . ɪɪ. caɾ. 7 vɪ . uiłłi 7 vɪɪɪ. borđ cũ p̃bro

hñt xɪɪɪ. caɾ. Ibi . ɪx. ferui. 7 vɪɪɪ. ac p̃ti . Val 7 ualuit . x . liƀ.

Iſđ Hernulf teñ *ACHETONE* . Ibi . v . hidæ geld . Edric tenuit.

In dñio funt . ɪɪɪ . caɾ. 7 ɪɪɪɪ . uiłłi 7 ɪɪɪ . borđ cũ . ɪɪɪɪ . caɾ.

Ibi xv . ac p̃ti . Val 7 ualuit . c . fol. *IN SINESHOVEDES HD.*

Iſđ Hernulf teñ *HANVN* . 7 Hubald de eo . Edric tenuit.

Ibi dimiđ hida   In dñio funt . ɪɪ. caɾ. cũ . vɪɪɪ . borđ.

7 ɪɪɪɪ . feruis.   Val 7 ualuit . xʟ . folid.

LAND OF ARNULF OF HESDIN

In BRIGHTWELLS BARROW Hundred

1 Arnulf of Hesdin holds KEMPSFORD. 21 hides which pay tax. Osgot held it from Earl Harold. In lordship 6 ploughs;
38 villagers, 9 smallholders and 1 riding man with 18 ploughs.
14 slaves; 4 mills at 40s 40d; from the meadows £9 besides pasture for the oxen; from the sheepfold 120 weys of cheese.
In Gloucester 7 burgesses who pay 2s.
The value of the whole before 1066 £30; now £66 6s 8d.

Arnulf also holds

2 HATHEROP. 7 hides. Wulfward White held it. In lordship 6 ploughs;
23 villagers with 10 ploughs.
12 slaves; a mill at 15s.
The value was £8; now £12.

in GARSDON Hundred

3 in AMPNEY ('St. Nicholas'). 4 hides and 2½ virgates. Alric and Godric held them as two manors. In lordship 3 ploughs;
7 villagers and 2 smallholders with 2 ploughs. 4 slaves.
The value of the whole was and is £6.

in GRUMBALDS ASH Hundred   169 b

4 OLDBURY (on the Hill). 5 hides which pay tax. Edric held it.
In lordship 3 ploughs;
4 villagers with 4 ploughs; 9 slaves there; 1 Frenchman who has 1 plough.
Meadow, 6 acres.
The value is and was £10.

5 BADMINTON. 4 hides which pay tax. Edric held it. In lordship 2 ploughs.
6 villagers and 8 smallholders with a priest have 13 ploughs.
9 slaves; meadow, 8 acres.
The value is and was £10.

6 ACTON (Turville). 5 hides which pay tax. Edric held it.
In lordship 3 ploughs;
4 villagers and 3 smallholders with 4 ploughs.
Meadow, 15 acres.
The value is and was 100s.

in SWINEHEAD Hundred

7 HANHAM. Hunbald holds from him. Edric held it. ½ hide....
In lordship 2 ploughs with
8 smallholders and 4 slaves.
The value is and was 40s.

.LXI. **H**ERRA HERALDI FILIJ COMITIS.

HERALD fili Radulfi ten de rege *SVDLEGE*.Radulf tenuit.
Ibi. x . hidæ geld . In dñio funt . IIII . car . 7 XVIII . uilli 7 VIII .
bord cu . XIII . car . Ibi . XIIII . int feruos 7 ancill . 7 . VI . molini
de . LII . fol . Silua . III . leuu lg . 7 II . lat.
Ifd Herald ten *TODINTVN* . Pat ej tenuit . Ibi . x . hidæ geld .
In dñio funt . III . car . 7 XVII . uilli 7 VII . bord 7 II . libi hoes
int oms hnt . VIII . car . Ibi . x . int feruos 7 ancill . 7 II . molini
de . xx . folid . De una falina . L . mittas fal .
H duo M ual 7 ualuer . XL . lib .

.LXII. **H**ERRA HVGON DE GRENTEM *IN CEOLFLEDE HD*.

HVGO de Grentemaifnil ten *PEBEWORDE* . Ibi . II . hidæ
7 una v Duo teini tenuer p . II . M . Ibi . III . car . 7 I . uills
7 un bord 7 VII . ferui.
Ifd Hugo ten *MERESTVNE* . Ibi . II . hidæ
Ifd Hugo ten *QVENINTVNE* . Ibi . II . hidæ . Vn tein tenuit .
In dñio . II . car . 7 v . uilli 7 I . bord cu . III . car . Ibi . IIII . ferui
7 una ancilla.   Valuer . VII . lib . m . IIII . lib .
Ifd Hugo ten *QVENINTVNE* . 7 Roger de eo . Ibi . XII . hidæ .
Balduin tenuit T.R.E . In dñio . III . car . 7 XVII . uilli 7 II .
bord . cu . IX . car . Ibi . VI . ferui . Valuit . VII . lib . m . VI . lib .
Ifd Hugo ten *WESTONE* . 7 Roger de eo . Ibi . IIII . hidæ .
Balduin tenuit . In dñio . II . car . 7 VI . uilli 7 cu . III . car .
Ibi . IIII . ferui . 7 v . ancillæ . 7 molin de . x . fol . Valuit . VII . lib .
Ifd Hugo ten *WILCOTE* . 7 cleric ej de eo.   modo . VI . lib .
Ibi . II . hidæ 7 dimid . In dñio . II . car . 7 II . uilli 7 I . bord cu . I .
car . Ibi . IIII . ferui 7 una ancilla . Valuit . XL . fol . m . XXX .
Leuric tenuit .

1   # LAND OF HAROLD SON OF EARL RALPH

[In GRESTON Hundred]
1   Harold son of Earl Ralph holds SUDELEY from the King. His father,
Ralph, held it. 10 hides which pay tax. In lordship 4 ploughs;
18 villagers and 8 smallholders with 13 ploughs.
14 slaves, male and female; 6 mills at 52s; woodland 3 leagues
long and 2 wide.
2   Harold also holds TODDINGTON. His father held it. 10 hides which
pay tax. In lordship 3 ploughs.
17 villagers, 7 smallholders and 2 free men between them have
8 ploughs.
10 slaves, male and female; 2 mills at 20s; from a salt-house
50 measures of salt.
The value of these two manors is and was £40.

2   # LAND OF HUGH OF GRANDMESNIL

In CHELTHORN Hundred
1   Hugh of Grandmesnil holds PEBWORTH. 2 hides and 1 virgate.
Two thanes held it as two manors. 3 ploughs there.
1 villager, 1 smallholder and 7 slaves.
Hugh also holds
2   (Broad) MARSTON. 2 hides ...
3   (Upper) QUINTON. 2 hides. A thane held it. In lordship 2 ploughs;
5 villagers and 1 smallholder with 3 ploughs. 4 male slaves,
1 female.
The value of these was £7; now £4.
4   (Lower) QUINTON. Roger holds from him. 12 hides. Baldwin held
it before 1066. In lordship 3 ploughs;
17 villagers and 2 smallholders with 9 ploughs. 6 slaves.
The value was £7; now £6.
5   WESTON ('Maudit'). Roger holds from him. 4 hides. Baldwin
held it. In lordship 2 ploughs;
6 villagers with 3 ploughs.
4 male and 5 female slaves; a mill at 10s.
The value was £7; now £6.
6   WILLICOTE. His clerk holds from him. 2½ hides. In lordship 2
ploughs;
2 villagers and 1 smallholder with 1 plough. 4 male slaves,
1 female.
The value was 40s; now 30 [s].
Leofric held it.

.LXIII. **H**VGO Lasne ten̄ de rege *BROCOWARDINGE*. Ibi. v.
TERRA HVGONIS LASNE. *IN DVDESTAN HD*.
hidæ. Turchil tenuit de rege. E. In dn̄io sunt. II. car̄.
7 VIII. uilli 7 VI. bord. 7 pbr 7 II. libi hões 7 p̄posit. Int̄ oms
hn̄t. xv. car̄. Ibi. IIII. serui. 7 moliñ de. II. solid. Silua
una leuua l̄g. 7 dim lat. Valuit. VI. lib. m̄. c. solid.
Isd Hugo ten̄ *SCIPTVNE*. Ibi. v. hidæ. geld. Wluard   *IN WACRES*
tenuit. In dn̄io sunt. II. car̄. 7 IIII. uilli 7 I. bord cū. II.   *CVBE HD*.
car̄. Ibi. v. serui. 7 moliñ de. x. solid. Valuit. IIII. lib. M̄. III. lib.
Isd Hugo ten̄ *SALPRETVNE*. Ibi. x. *IN BRADELEGE HD*.
hidæ geld. Wluuard tenuit. In dn̄io sunt. III. car̄. 7 x.
uilli 7 pbr cū. VII. car̄. 7 XI. int̄ seruos 7 ancill. 7 v. ac
p̄ti.   Valuit. IX. lib. modo. VII. lib. *IN CIRECESTRE HD*.
Isd Hugo ten̄ *BENWEDENE*. 7 Gislebt de eo. Ibi. III. hidæ
geld. Wluuard tenuit. In dn̄io sunt. III. car̄. 7 v. uilli cū. III.
car̄. 7 VI. serui. 7 moliñ de. x. sol. 7 VIII. ac p̄ti.
Val 7 ualuit. IIII. lib

.LXI. **M**ILO Crispin ten̄ in *BRVVRNE*. III. uirg terræ.
169 c
TERRA MILONIS CRISPIN. *IN DVDESTAN HD*.
Wigot tenuit.   In dn̄io. I. car̄. 7 VII. bord cū
II. car̄. 7 dimid piscaria. Valuit. xl. sol. modo. xxx. sol.
Isd Milo ten̄ *CERINTONE*. 7 Goisfrid de eo. *IN LANGETREV*
Haminc tenuit de rege. E. Ibi. II. hidæ geldant.   *HD*.
In dn̄io sunt. III. car̄. 7 III. uilli 7 VIII. bord cū. III. car̄
7 dimid. Ibi. XII. serui. 7 moliñ de. xxx. den̄. 7 IIII. ac p̄ti.
Val 7 ualuit. IIII. lib.   *IN GRIBOLDESTOV HD*.
Isd Milo ten̄ *ALRELIE*. Wigot tenuit. Ibi una hida.

LAND OF HUGH DONKEY

In DUDSTONE Hundred

Hugh Donkey holds BROCKWORTH from the King. 5 hides.
Thorkell held it from King Edward. In lordship 2 ploughs;
    8 villagers, 6 smallholders, a priest, 2 free men and a reeve;
        between them they have 15 ploughs.
    4 slaves; a mill at 2s; woodland 1 league long and ½ wide.
The value was £6; now 100s.

In WATTLESCOMB Hundred

Hugh also holds SHIPTON ('Chamflurs'). 5 hides which pay tax.
Wulfward held it. In lordship 2 ploughs;
    4 villagers and 1 smallholder with 2 ploughs.
    5 slaves; a mill at 10s.
The value was £4; now £3.

In BRADLEY Hundred

Hugh also holds SALPERTON. 10 hides which pay tax. Wulfward
held it. In lordship 3 ploughs;
    10 villagers and a priest with 7 ploughs; 11 slaves, male and female.
    Meadow, 5 acres.
The value was £9; now £7.

In CIRENCESTER Hundred

Hugh also holds BAGENDON, and Gilbert from him. 3 hides which
pay tax. Wulfward held it. In lordship 3 ploughs;
    5 villagers with 3 ploughs; 6 slaves.
    A mill at 10s; meadow, 8 acres.
The value is and was £4.

LAND OF MILES CRISPIN

In DUDSTONE Hundred

Miles Crispin holds 3 virgates of land in BRAWN. Wigot held it ...
In lordship 1 plough;
    7 smallholders with 2 ploughs.
    ½ fishery.
The value was 40s; now 30s.

In LONGTREE Hundred

Miles also holds CHERINGTON, and Geoffrey from him. Hemming
held it from King Edward. 2 hides which pay tax. In lordship
3 ploughs;
    3 villagers and 8 smallholders with 3½ ploughs.
    12 slaves; a mill at 30d; meadow, 4 acres.
The value is and was £4.

In GRUMBALDS ASH Hundred

Miles also holds ALDERLEY. Wigot held it. 1 hide.

In dñio ſunt.ii.caſ.7 vii.uitti 7 v.borđ cũ.vii.caſ.

Ibi.iiii.ſerui.7 moliñ de.x.ſot.7 xii.ac̄ p̃ti.Vat 7 ua

luit.c.ſoliđ.

V **TERRA VRSONIS DE ABETOT.** *IN WITELAI HD̃.*

Rso de Wireceſtre teñ in *CHEISNECOTE*.unã hiđ.

Eluuiñ tenuit ⍴ c̃).7 getđ.In dñio.i.caſ 7 iiii.ſerui.

Valuit.xl.ſot.modo.x.ſoliđ.

H **TERRA HASCOIT MVSARD.** *IN WITELAI HD̃.*

Ascoit muſard teñ de rege *SVINEBERIE*.Che

nuicelle tenuit.Ibi.x.hidæ.In dñio.iii.caſ.7 xviii.

uitti 7 iii.borđ cũ.ix.caſ.7 x.int ſeruos 7 ancitt.

7 moliñ de.vi.den. Valuit.xii.lib.m̃.x.lib.

I ſđ Haſcoit teñ.i.hidã in *CHEISNECOTE*.7 getđ.Vluuiñ

tenuit ⍴ c̃).Ibi.i.caſ 7 i.borđ.Vat 7 ualuit.x.ſot.

I ſđ Haſcoit teñ *AIFORDE*.Ibi.v.hidæ getđ *IN SALEMANES*

Erneſi tenuit.In dñio ſunt.ii.caſ.7 xii ſBERIE HD̃.

uitti 7 i.borđ cũ.v.caſ.Ibi.viii.int ſeruos 7 ancitt.

Vat.iiii.lib. *IN GRETESTAN HD̃*

I ſđ Haſc.teñ *ESTVNE*.Ibi.vi.hidæ getđ.Erneſi te

nuit.In dñio ſunt.iii.caſ.7 xii.uitti cũ.iiii.caſ.

7 ix.int ſeruos 7 ancitt.Ibi moliñ de.viii.ſoliđ.

7 xx.ac̄ p̃ti.Vat 7 ualuit.vi.lib. *IN CIRECESTRE HD̃.*

I ſđ Haſcoit teñ *SVDINTONE*.Ibi x.hidæ getđ.p̃ter

dñiũ.Erneſi tenuit.In dñio ſunt.iii.caſ.7 viii.uitti

7 x.borđ cũ p̃bro hñtes.v.caſ 7 dimiđ.Ibi.vii.ſerui.

7 xx.ac̄ p̃ti. Valuit.x.lib.m̃.viii.lib.

In lordship 2 ploughs;
   7 villagers and 5 smallholders with 7 ploughs.
   4 slaves; a mill at 10s; meadow, 12 acres.
The value is and was 100s.

LAND OF URSO OF ABETOT

In WITLEY Hundred
   Urso of Worcester holds 1 hide in SEZINCOTE. Alwin held it as
a manor; it pays tax. In lordship 1 plough; 4 slaves.
The value was 40s; now 10s.

LAND OF HASCOIT MUSARD

In WITLEY Hundred
   Hascoit Musard holds SAINTBURY from the King. Cynwy Chelle
held it. 10 hides. In lordship 3 ploughs;
     18 villagers and 3 smallholders with 9 ploughs; 10 slaves,
       male and female.
     A mill at 6d.
The value was £12; now £10.

Hascoit also holds
   in SEZINCOTE 1 hide. It pays tax. Wulfwin held it as a manor.
1 plough there.
     1 smallholder.
The value is and was 10s.

in SALMONSBURY Hundred
   EYFORD. 5 hides which pay tax. Erneis held it. In lordship 2 ploughs;
     12 villagers and 1 smallholder with 5 ploughs.
       8 slaves, male and female.
Value £4.

in GRESTON Hundred
   ASTON (Somerville). 6 hides which pay tax. Erneis held it.
In lordship 3 ploughs;
     12 villagers with 4 ploughs; 9 slaves, male and female.
     A mill at 8s; meadow, 20 acres.
The value is and was £6.

in CIRENCESTER Hundred
   SIDDINGTON. 10 hides which pay tax besides the lordship (land).
Erneis held it. In lordship 3 ploughs;
     8 villagers and 10 smallholders with a priest who have 5½ ploughs.
     7 slaves; meadow, 20 acres.
The value was £10; now £8.

Isd Hafcoit ten GRENHASTEDE.Ibi.I.hida IN BISELEGE HD.

geld. Ernefi tenuit. In dñio funt. III. car̄.7 VIII. uitti

7 v. bord 7 pbr 7 un radchen. Int oms hñt. IX. car̄.

Ibi. x. ferui.7 VIII. ac̄ p̄ti. Silua. I. leuua lḡ.7 dim lat̄.

Valuit. c. fot. Modo: VII. lib.

.LXII. TERRA TVRSTINI FILIJ ROLF. IN GERSDONES HD.

TVRSTINVS filius Rolf ten de rege OMENIE.

Ibi. VII. hidæ. Toui tenuit de rege. E. In dñio fu̅. III.

car̄.7 VIII. uitti 7 pbr cū. VIII. car̄. Ibi. VIII. ferui.

De hac tra ten Toui. II. uitto₃ tra.7 q̄dā miles tra

IIII. uitto₃. Ad æcclam ptin dim. hida.7 IIII. ac̄ p̄ti.

Valuit. VIII. lib. Modo. VI. lib.

Ibid ten ipfe Turften. I. hid. Vluui tenuit p CO.7 po

terat ire quo uoleb. In dñio. II. car̄. cū. I. bord. Valuit

Isd Turften ten in ACHELIE. unā hid. IN CIRECEST℟ XL. fot.

Brictric tenuit de rege. E. In dñio. ē una car̄.7 III. uitti

cū. III. car̄. Ibi. VI. ferui.7 IIII. ac̄ p̄ti. Val 7 ualuit. L. fot.

Giruius ten de Turftino. IN GRIBOLDESTOV HD.

Isd Turft ten HILDESLEI.7 Bernard de eo. Ibi. I. hida.

Aluric tenuit. In dñio funt. II. car̄.7 v. dimidij uitti.

7 VII. bord cū. II. car̄. Ibi. VIII. ferui.7 III. molini

de XVIII. fot.7 VIII. ac̄ p̄ti. Valuit. XL. fot. m̄. LX. fot.

Isd Turft ten TORTEWORD: Ibi IN BACHESTANES HD.

una hida. Aluuold tenuit. In dñio funt. II. car̄.7 VI. uitti

169 d

7 VII. bord cū. VII. car̄. Ibi. VI. ferui.7 III. molini de. XV. folid.

7 x. ac̄ p̄ti. Silua. I. leuua lḡ.7 dimid lat̄. redd. v. folid.

Valuit. VII. lib. Modo: c. folid. IN BLACHELAVE HD.

Isd Turft ten STANTONE. Ibi. v. hidæ. Toui tenuit de rege. E.

in BISLEY Hundred
MISERDEN. 1 hide which pays tax. Erneis held it. In lordship 3
ploughs;
    8 villagers, 5 smallholders, a priest and 1 riding man;
      between them they have 9 ploughs.
    10 slaves; meadow, 8 acres; woodland 1 league long and ½ wide.
The value was 100s; now £7.

LAND OF THURSTAN SON OF ROLF

In GARSDON Hundred
    Thurstan son of Rolf holds AMPNEY (Crucis) from the King. 7 hides.
Tovi held it from King Edward. In lordship 3 ploughs;
    8 villagers and a priest with 8 ploughs. 8 slaves.
    Of this land Tovi holds the land of 2 villagers, and a man-at-arms
    the land of 4 villagers. ½ hide belongs to the church.
    Meadow, 4 acres.
The value was £8; now £6.

Thurstan holds 1 hide there himself. Wulfwy held it as a manor and
could go where he would. In lordship 2 ploughs, with
    1 smallholder.
The value was 40s.

Thurstan also holds

in CIRENCESTER Hundred
    in OAKLEY 1 hide. Brictric held it from King Edward as a manor.
In lordship 1 plough;
    3 villagers with 3 ploughs.
    6 slaves; meadow, 4 acres.
The value is and was 50s.
    Gerwy holds it from Thurstan.

in GRUMBALDS ASH Hundred
    HILLESLEY. Bernard holds from him. 1 hide. Aelfric held it.
In lordship 2 ploughs;
    5 half-villagers and 7 smallholders with 2 ploughs.
    8 slaves; 3 mills at 18s; meadow, 8 acres.
The value was 40s; now 60s.

in BAGSTONE Hundred
    TORTWORTH. 1 hide. Alfwold held it. In lordship 2 ploughs;
    6 villagers and 7 smallholders with 7 ploughs.   169 d
    6 slaves; 3 mills at 15s; meadow, 10 acres; woodland
      1 league long and ½ wide, which pays 5s.
The value was £7; now 100s.

in BLACKLOW Hundred
    (Kings) STANLEY. 5 hides. Tovi held it from King Edward.

In dñio ſunt . ii . caŕ .7 viii . uiłłi 7 vi . borđ cū . x . caŕ . Ibi . iiii.

ſerui .7 ii . molini de . xxxv ꞈſoliđ .7 x . aͨ p̃ti . Silua .i . leuua

lḡ .7 dimiđ lat́ . Vał 7 ualuit . c . ſoł . De hac t́ra ten̓

Toui . ii . hiđ . elemoſina regis . W.

Iſđ Turſt́ ten̓ *FRIDORNE* . Auti tenuit . Ibi . iii . hidæ gelđ.

In dñio . e̅ una caŕ .7 iii . üiłłi 7 iii . borđ cū . ii . caŕ .7 un̓ ſeru̓.

Valuit . lx . ſoliđ . modo . xxx . ſoł.

.LXV. ATERRA ANSFRIDI DE CORMELIJS. *IN BISELEGE HĐ.*

ANSFRID de Cormelies ten̓ *WINESTANE* . Ibi . v . hidæ

Vluuard tenuit . In dñio ſunt . iii . caŕ .7 x . uiłłi 7 iiii . borđ

7 un̓ francig cū . viii . caŕ . Ibi . viii . ſerui .7 molin̄ de . xx . den̓.

Vał 7 ualuit . vii . łib. *IN CELFLEDETORN HĐ.*

Iſđ Ansfŕ ten̓ *WESTONE* . Duo teini tenueŕ . vn̓ ho̅ Heraldi.

alter Leurici . Ibi . x . hidæ ꝑ . ii . ꝏ .7 poterant ire quo uoleƀ.

In dñio . iiii . caŕ .7 xviii . uiłłi 7 i . borđ cū . ix . caŕ .7 xii . ſerui.

Valueŕ . c . ſoł . Modo . vii . łiƀ.

Iſđ Ansfŕ ten̓ in *NORTVNE* . v . hiđ . Duo teini tenueŕ ꝑ . ii . ꝏ.

7 poteraꞃ ire quo uoleƀ . In dñio . iiii . caŕ .7 ix . uiłłi 7 ii.

borđ cū . iiii . caŕ .7 x . ſerui . Valueŕ . iiii . łiƀ . m̊ . vi . łiƀ.

Iſđ . A . ten̓ *BECESHORE* . Briſmer tenuit . *IN WITELAI HĐ.*

Ibi . iii . hide . In dñio . iii . caŕ .7 x . uiłłi cū . vi . caŕ .7 xvi . ſerui.

7 un̓ ho̅ redđ . vi . ſochs. Valuit . viii . łiƀ . Modo . vi . łiƀ.

Iſđ . A . ten̓ *POTESLEPE* . Godric tenuit . Ibi . iii . *IN GRETESTAN HĐ.*

hidæ gelđ . In dñio ſunt . ii . caŕ .7 iii . uiłłi 7 v . borđ cū . ii . caŕ . Ibi

xi . ſerui .7 ii . molini de . xv . ſoł . Silua . i . leuua lḡ .7 una lat́.

Valuit . c . ſoł . modo . iiii . łiƀ. *IN WACRESCVBE HĐ.*

Iſđ . A . ten̓ in *SCIPTVNE* . iii . Virg t́ræ . Bil tenuit ꝑ ꝏ .7 gelđ.

In dñio . e̅ . i . caŕ . Vał 7 ualuit . x . ſoł . Hic Bil potuit ire q̓ uoluit.

In lordship 2 ploughs;
    8 villagers and 6 smallholders with 10 ploughs.
    4 slaves; 2 mills at 35s; meadow, 10 acres; woodland 1 league
        long and ½ wide.
The value is and was 100s.
    Tovi holds 2 hides of this land in alms from King William.

FRETHERNE. Auti held it. 3 hides which pay tax. In lordship 1 plough;
    3 villagers and 3 smallholders with 2 ploughs; 1 slave.
The value was 60s; now 30s.

LAND OF ANSFRID OF CORMEILLES

In BISLEY Hundred
    Ansfrid of Cormeilles holds WINSTONE. 5 hides. Wulfward held it.
    In lordship 3 ploughs;
        10 villagers, 4 smallholders and 1 Frenchman with 8 ploughs.
        8 slaves; a mill at 20d.
    The value is and was £7.

Ansfrid also holds

in CHELTHORN Hundred
    WESTON (sub Edge). Two thanes, one a man of Earl Harold's, the
    other of Leofric's, held it. 10 hides there as two manors; they
    could go where they would. In lordship 4 ploughs;
        18 villagers and 1 smallholder with 9 ploughs; 12 slaves.
    The value was 100s; now £7.

in (Burnt) NORTON 5 hides. Two thanes held it as two manors;
    they could go where they would. In lordship 4 ploughs;
        9 villagers and 2 smallholders with 4 ploughs; 10 slaves.
    The value was £4; now £6.

in WITLEY Hundred
    BATSFORD. Brictmer held it. 3 hides. In lordship 3 ploughs;
        10 villagers with 6 ploughs; 16 slaves; 1 man who pays
            6 ploughshares.
    The value was £8; now £6.

in GRESTON Hundred
    POSTLIP. Godric held it. 3 hides which pay tax. In lordship 2
    ploughs;
        3 villagers and 5 smallholders with 2 ploughs.
        11 slaves; 2 mills at 15s; woodland 1 league long and 1 wide.
    The value was 100s; now £4.

in WATTLESCOMB Hundred
    in SHIPTON (Oliffe) 3 virgates of land. Bil held it as a manor;
    it pays tax. In lordship 1 plough.
    The value is and was 10s.
        This Bil could go where he would.

Iſdem.A.ten̄ *WINESTVNE*.Edric̄ 7 Leuric *IN BRADELEGE* HD̄
7 Elric̄ tenuer̄ p.III. ꝏ̃.7 poteraɴ̃ ire q̄ uoleƀ.Ibi.v.hidæ
geld.In dn̄io ſunt.IIII.car̄.7 IX.uiłłi 7 IIII.bord̄ cū.v.car̄.
Ibi.x.int ſeruos 7 anciłł.7 molī de.VII.ſoł 7 VI.den̄.7 XV.
acræ p̄ti.Valƀ.VIII.liƀ.modo.VII.łiƀ. *IN CIRECESTRE* HD̄.
Iſd̄.A.ten̄.I.hid̄ in *TANTESBORNE*.Elmer tenuit|7 potuit
ire q̄ uoluit.In dn̄io.ē.I.car̄.7 un̄ uiłłs 7 II.bord̄.7 v.ancillæ.
Valuit.XL.ſoł.m̊.XX.ſoł. *IN RESPIGETE* HD̄.
Iſd̄.A.ten̄ *ELCHESTANE*.Duo Leuuini tenuer̄ p.II.ꝏ̃.Ibi.IIII.
hidæ 7 dimid̄.7 In *COLESBORNE*.I.hid̄ 7 dim̄.Eluuin̄ tenuit p ꝏ̃.
7 poterant ire q̄ uoleƀ iſti.III.teini.
In dn̄io ſunt.II.car̄.7 v.uiłłi 7 II.bord̄.cū.III.car̄ 7 dim̄.Ibi.IIII.
ſerui.7 x.ac̄ p̄ti.Silua dimid̄ leuua łḡ.7 II.q̄ꝫ lat̄
Medietate huꝭ ꝏ̃ ten̄.I.miles de Ansfrido.7 ibi hē.II.car̄.
7 v.uiłł 7 II.bord̄ cū.III.car̄.
7 Alter miles ten̄ coleſburne de eo.7 hē ibi dimid̄ car̄.7 II.uiłłi
7 II.bord̄ cū.I.car̄.7 molī de;L.denar̄.
H̄ ualƀ.VIII.łiƀ.Modo.VII.liƀ 7 x.ſolid̄.
Iſd̄.A.ten̄ *SIDE*.7 Turſtin̄ de eo.Leuuin̄ tenuit de rege.E.
Ibi.III.hidæ geld.In dn̄io ſunt.II.car̄.7 I.uiłł cū pƀro 7 III.
bord̄ cū.I.car̄.7 VI.ſerui.7 IIII.ac̄ p̄ti.Valuit.IIII.liƀ.M̄.XL.ſoł.
Iſd̄.A.ten̄.II.v̄ 7 dimid̄ in *DANTESBORNE*.7 Bernard̄ de eo.
Elmer tenuit p ꝏ̃.7 poterat ire quo uolƀ.Ibi.ē.I.bord̄.
Val 7 ualuit.IIII.ſolid̄.

170 a

Iſd̄ Ansfrid̄ ten̄ *PANTELIE* 7 *CHILFCOT*.7 *CHITIFORD* 7 *HEGE*.
Int tot̄.IIII.hid̄ 7 dimid̄.Vlfel 7 Eluuard 7 Wiga tenuer̄.
p.IIII.ꝏ̃.Vna hida 7 dim̄ liƀa a geldo.
In dn̄io ſunt.II.car̄.7 VII.uiłłi 7 III.bord̄ cū.VII.car̄.
Ibi.II.ſerui.7 molī de.VII.ſoł 7 VI.den̄.
Valƀ.III.liƀ 7 x.ſoł.Modo.IIII.liƀ.Qui has tras teneƀ.
poterant ire quó uoleƀ.

in BRADLEY Hundred
WINSON. Edric, Leofric and Alric held it as three manors and could
go where they would. 5 hides which pay tax. In lordship 4 ploughs;
    9 villagers and 4 smallholders with 5 ploughs.
    10 slaves, male and female; a mill at 7s 6d; meadow, 15 acres.
The value was £8; now £7.

in CIRENCESTER Hundred
in DUNTISBOURNE ('Hotat') 1 hide. Aelmer held it as a manor and
could go where he would. In lordship 1 plough;
    1 villager, 2 smallholders and 5 female slaves.
The value was 40s; now 20s.

in RAPSGATE Hundred
ELKSTONE. Two Leofwins held it as two manors. 4½ hides.
In (Great) COLESBOURNE 1½ hides. Alwin held it as a manor. These
three thanes could go where they would. In lordship 2 ploughs;
    5 villagers and 2 smallholders with 3½ ploughs.
    4 slaves; meadow, 10 acres; woodland ½ league long and
    2 furlongs wide.
A man-at-arms holds half this manor from Ansfrid and has 2 ploughs;
    5 villagers and 2 smallholders with 3 ploughs.
Another man-at-arms holds (Great) COLESBOURNE from him and has
½ plough.
    2 villagers and 2 smallholders with 1 plough.
    A mill at 50d.
The value was £8; now £7 10s.

SYDE. Thurstan holds from him. Leofwin held it from King Edward.
3 hides which pay tax. In lordship 2 ploughs;
    1 villager with a priest and 3 smallholders with 1 plough; 6 slaves.
    Meadow, 4 acres.
The value was £4; now 40s.

in DUNTISBOURNE ('Hotat') 2½ virgates. Bernard holds from him.
Aelmer held it as a manor and could go where he would.
    1 smallholder.
The value is and was 4s.

[in BOTLOE Hundred]   170 a
PAUNTLEY, 1½ hides; KILCOT, 1 hide; KETFORD, 1 hide; HAYES, 1 hide;
total 4½ hides. Wulfhelm, Alfward and Wiga held them as four manors.
1½ hides are free from tax. In lordship 2 ploughs;
    7 villagers and 3 smallholders with 7 ploughs.
    2 slaves; a mill at 7s 6d.
The value was £3 10s; now £4.
    The holders of these lands could go where they would.

Has tras 7 *WINESTAN* 7 *TANTESBORNE* . ſupius ſcriptas.'
habuit Ansfrid de Walterio de Laci cū ej neptē accepit.
Alias û terras. ten de rege.

.LXIX. ## H TERRA HVNFRIDI CAMERARIJ. *IN WITELAI HVND*.
VNFRID camerari ten de rege *LANGEBERGE* . Ibi . IIII.

hidæ geld. Elſtan 7 Blacheman 7 Edric 7 Alric tenueī ⱷ . IIII . Ꝏ.
7 poterant ire quo uoleƀ . In dñio eraɴ . IIII . caī . 7 III . uiłłi
7 v . borđ cū . III . caī . Ibi . IX . ſerui.

Valeƀ . XVI . liƀ . modo. c . ſoliđ.   *IN GERSDONES HĐ.*
Iſđ Hunfrid ten in *OMENIE* . I . hidā . Æluui tenuit ⱷ Ꝏ . de
rege . E . In dñio . II . caī . 7 IIII . ſerui . 7 I . borđ . 7 moliñ de . v . ſoł.

Vał 7 ualuit . XXV . ſoł.   *IN CIRECESTRE HĐ.*
Iſđ . H . ten . I . hiđ in *PRESTITVNE* . Æluuin tenuit ⱷ Ꝏ.
In dñio . ē . I . caī . 7 II . ſerui . 7 III . borđ cū . I . caī . Vał 7 ualuit
XXX . ſoł . hic q̇ teneƀ . Poterat ire quo uoleƀ.

Iſđ . H . ten . I . hiđ in *NORCOTE* . Eluuard tenuit ⱷ Ꝏ
In dñio ſunt . II . caī . 7 II . borđ cū dim caī . Vał 7 ualuit . XL . ſoł.
Has . II . tras ten Wiłłs de hunfrido . Q̇ teneƀ . poteraɴ ire q̇ uoleƀ.

Iſđ . H . ten . II . hiđ in *SVDINTONE* . 7 Anſchitil de eo . Aluuard
tenuit ⱷ Ꝏ . In dñio . ē . I . caī . 7 II . borđ cū dim caī . 7 moliñ
de . v . ſoliđ . Vał 7 ualuit . XL . ſoł . q̇ teneƀ . poterat ire q̇ uoleƀ.

Iſđ . H . ten *ACTVNE* . Herold tenuit   *IN BACHESTANES HĐ.*
hō Eluui hiles . q̇ poterat ire q̇ uoleƀ . Ibi . :I . hidæ 7 dimidia.
In dñio . ē . I . caī . 7 III . uiłłi 7 III . borđ cū dimiđ caī . Ibi . II.
ſerui . 7 moliñ 7 dimiđ de . LXIIII . deñ . 7 v . aē p̄ti.
Vał 7 ualuit XL . ſoł.

Ansfrid had the above-mentioned lands of WINSTONE and
DUNTISBOURNE ('Hotat') from Walter of Lacy when he married
his niece, but he holds the other lands from the King.

LAND OF HUMPHREY THE CHAMBERLAIN

In WITLEY Hundred
Humphrey the Chamberlain holds LONGBOROUGH from the King.
4 hides which pay tax. Alstan, Blackman, Edric and Alric held
it as four manors and could go where they would. In lordship
there were 4 ploughs;
   3 villagers and 5 smallholders with 3 ploughs. 9 slaves.
The value was £16; now 100s.

Humphrey also holds
in GARSDON Hundred
   in AMPNEY (Crucis) 1 hide. Alfwy held it from King Edward as
   a manor. In lordship 2 ploughs; 4 slaves;
      1 smallholder.
   A mill at 5s.
   The value is and was 25s.

in CIRENCESTER Hundred
   in PRESTON 1 hide. Alwin held it as a manor. In lordship 1 plough;
   2 slaves;
      3 smallholders with 1 plough.
   The value is and was 30s.
      The holder could go where he would.

   in NORCOTE 1 hide. Alfward held it as a manor. In lordship 2
   ploughs;
      2 smallholders with ½ plough.
   The value is and was 40s.
William holds these two lands from Humphrey. The holders could
go where they would.

   in SIDDINGTON 2 hides. Ansketel holds from him. Alfward held
   it as a manor. In lordship 1 plough;
      2 smallholders with ½ plough.
   A mill at 5s.
   The value is and was 40s.
      The holder could go where he would.

in BAGSTONE Hundred
   (Iron) ACTON. Harold, a man of Alfwy Hiles', held it and could go
   where he would. 2½ hides. In lordship 1 plough;
      3 villagers and 3 smallholders with ½ plough.
      2 slaves; 1½ mills at 64d; meadow, 5 acres.
   The value is and was 40s.

Iſd.H.ten *WICHEN*.Ibi.IIII.hidæ.Tres hões Brictrici ^{f.Algar}

ᵱ trib tenueꝛ T.R.E.7 poteraɴ ire q̃ uoleƀ.In dñio eraɴ.III.caꝛ.

Maner. 7 IX.uiłłi 7 XIIII.borđ.cū.IX.caꝛ.Ibi.v.ſerui.7 xx.aͫc

p̊ti.7 VI.q̃ꝫ de ſilua.Valƀ 7 uał.XII.liƀ.

Has.II.uiłłas deđ Regina hunfrido.Aꜩune 7 Wichen.

Iſd.H.ten.I.uirg træ in *ESTBROCE*. *IN GERSDONES HD̄*.

7 Wiłłs de eo.Aluuine tenuit ᵱ ꝏ̃.Ibi.ē.I.uiłłs.Vał.II.ſoł.

7 ualuit.

.LXX **H**TERRA HVNFRIDI DE MEDEHAL *IN DVNESTAN HD̄*.

VNFRID de Medehalle ten *VTONE*.Pagen tenuit.Ibi.I.

hida.In dñio.I.caꝛ.7 III.ſerui.7 IIII.borđ cū.II.caꝛ.Valuit

xxx.ſoliđ.modo.xx.ſoł. *IN WITELAI HVND̄*.

Iſd Hunf ten.I.hiđ in *CHEISNECOT*.Aluui tenuit ᵱ ꝏ̃.7 gelđ.

In dñio eraɴ.II.caꝛ.7 VI.ſerui.7 I.borđ.7 ualƀ.L.ſoliđ.

Modo.XII.den tant ᵱpt p̃ta.

.LXX **H** HVNFRIDI COCI *IN SALESMANESBERIE HD̄*.

VNFRID coqus.ten| *LECHETONE*.I.hiđ.7 ibi hꝛ̄.I.caꝛ.cū.IIII.

borđ.7 uał.xv.ſoł.7 gelđ.Osƀn de Kereſburg tenuit.

Ordric tenuit ᵱ ꝏ̃.T.R.E.

.LXXII **S**TERRA SIGARI DE CIOCHES. *IN HOLIFORDE HD̄*.

170 b

IGAR de Cioches ten de rege *HALLINGE*.Goda tenuit ᶜᵒᵐⁱᵗⁱſſᵃ

Ibi.x.hidæ gelđ.In dñio ſuɴ.III.caꝛ.7 xx.uiłłi 7 v.borđ

cū.IX.borđ.Ibi.VI.ſerui 7 III.ancillæ.Silua.ē ibi

Valuit.VII.liƀ.modo.VIII.liƀ. *IN BRADELEGE HD̄*.

Iſd Sigar ten *HASEDENE*.Goda tenuit.Ibi.x.hidæ.

Wiłłs rex c̄ceſſit.III.hiđ ex his đetas á gelđo.In dñio ſuɴ.

III.caꝛ.7 XIIII.uiłłi 7 pƀr cū.x.caꝛ.Ibi.VI.ſerui.

Valuit.VIII.liƀ.modo.VII.liƀ.ſ ut teſtaꞇ comitatus.

WICKWAR. 4 hides. Three men of Brictric son of Algar's held
it as three manors before 1066 and could go where they would.
In lordship there were 3 ploughs;
9 villagers and 14 smallholders with 9 ploughs.
5 slaves; meadow, 20 acres; woodland, 6 furlongs.
The value was and is £12.
The Queen gave these two villages of (Iron) Acton and Wickwar
to Humphrey.

in GARSDON Hundred
in ASHBROOK 1 virgate of land. William holds from him. Alwin
held it as a manor.
1 villager.
The value is and was 2s.

LAND OF HUMPHREY OF MAIDENHILL

In DUDSTONE Hundred
Humphrey of Maidenhill holds UPTON (St. Leonards). Payne held
it. 1 hide. In lordship 1 plough; 3 slaves;
4 smallholders with 2 ploughs.
The value was 30s; now 20s.

In WITLEY Hundred
Humphrey also holds 1 hide in SEZINCOTE. Alfwy held it as a
manor; it pays tax. In lordship there were 2 ploughs; 6 slaves;
1 smallholder.
The value was 50s; now 12d only, for the meadows.

[LAND] OF HUMPHREY COOK

In SALMONSBURY Hundred
Humphrey Cook holds 1 hide in LATTON. He has 1 plough, with
4 smallholders.
Value 15s. It pays tax.
Osbern of Cherbourg held it. Ordric held it as a manor before 1066.

LAND OF SIGAR OF CHOCQUES   170 b

In HOLFORD Hundred
Sigar of Chocques holds HAWLING from the King. Countess Goda
held it. 10 hides which pay tax. In lordship 3 ploughs;
20 villagers and 5 smallholders with 9 smallholders.
6 male and 3 female slaves. Woodland there.
The value was £7; now £8.

In BRADLEY Hundred
Sigar also holds HAZLETON. Goda held it. 10 hides. King William
assigned 3 hides of these exempt from tax, as the County testifies.
In lordship 3 ploughs;
14 villagers and a priest with 10 ploughs. 6 slaves.
The value was £8; now £7.

Iſd Sigar ten *TENEVRDE*.Goda tenuit.Ibi.v.hidæ
ex his.iii.ſt q̇etæ á geldo p.W.regē.ut dicit hō Sigardi.
In dñio ſunt.iii.caŕ.7 xiiii.uiłłi 7 ii.borđ cū.vii.caŕ.
Ibi.vii.ſerui.7 moliñ de.xl.deñ.Silua.iii.q̇ʒ łḡ.
7 ii.laŧ.Valuit.vii.liƀ.modo.́vi.liƀ.

.LXXIII. TERRA MATHIV DE MORETANIE *IN LANGETREWES H*

Maci de Mauritania teñ de rege *SCIPETONE*.Strang^(danus)
tenuit.Ibi.x.hidæ gelđ.In dñio ſunt.ii.caŕ.7 iiii.uiłłi
7 ii.borđ cū.iiii.caŕ.Ibi.iiii.ſerui.7 moliñ de.x.ſoliđ.
De paſtura.ii.ſol.   Valuit.xv.liƀ.modo.́viii.liƀ.

Iſd Maci teñ *SCIPETONE*.7 Rūbald de eo.x.hide
gelđ.Joħs tenuit T.R.E.In dñio ſunt.iii.caŕ.7 iiii.uiłłi
7 viii.borđ cū.iiii.caŕ.Ibi.iiii.ſerui.7 moliñ de.xii.ſoł.
De paſtura.ii.ſoł.   Vaſuit xv.liƀ.modo.́viii.liƀ.

Iſd Maci teñ ibi.i.hiđ 7 Rūbald de eo.Aluuiñ tenuiŧ.
7 poŧuit ire quo uoluit.7 Rainbŧ flandrenſis pea habuit.
In dñio.ē.i.caŕ.7 i.uiłł 7 i.borđ cū dim caŕ.Valuit.xx.
ſoliđ.Modo.́xiiii.ſoliđ.

.LXXIIII. TERRA GOZELINI BRITONIS. *IN BACHESTANES HD.*

Gozeliñ brito teñ de rege *CIRVELDE*.Elfelt tenuit
de rege.E.Ibi.iii.hidæ.In dñio ſuɲ.ii.caŕ.7 iiii.uiłłi
7 vii.borđ cū.iiii.caŕ.Ibi.iiii.ſerui.7 moliñ de.x.ſoliđ.
7 viii.ac̈ p̃ti.Silua dimiđ leuua łḡ 7 laŧ.
Valuit.iiii.liƀ.modo.xl.ſoł.

.LXXV. TERRA ROGERIJ FILIJ RAD.

Rogervs filius Rađ ten uñ Maneriū ^(nōe Cliſtone) *IN SINESHOVED HD.*
qđ tenuit Seuuiñ p̃poſit de Briſtou de rege.E.7 poterat
ire cū hac ŧra quo uoleƀ.nec aliquā firmā inde dabaŧ.
Ibi.iii.hidæ.In dñio ſunt.iii.caŕ.7 vi uiłłi 7 vi.borđ
cū.ii.caŕ.Ibi.iii.ſerui.7 viii.ac̈ p̃ti.
Valƀ.c.ſoliđ.Modo.lx.ſoliđ.

Sigar also holds YANWORTH. Goda held it. 5 hides; 3 of them are exempt from tax by King William, as Sigar's man states.
In lordship 3 ploughs;
    14 villagers and 2 smallholders with 7 ploughs.
    7 slaves; a mill at 40d; woodland 3 furlongs long and 2 wide.
The value was £7; now £6.

LAND OF MATTHEW OF MORTAGNE

In LONGTREE Hundred
Matthew of Mortagne holds SHIPTON (Moyne) from the King. Strang the Dane held it. 10 hides which pay tax. In lordship 2 ploughs;
    4 villagers and 2 smallholders with 4 ploughs.
    4 slaves; a mill at 10s; from the pasture 2s.
The value was £15; now £8.

Matthew also holds SHIPTON (Moyne) and Rumbald from him.
10 hides which pay tax. John held it before 1066. In lordship
3 ploughs;
    4 villagers and 8 smallholders with 4 ploughs.
    4 slaves; a mill at 12s; from the pasture 2s.
The value was £15; now £8.

Matthew also holds 1 hide there, and Rumbald from him.
Alwin held it and could go where he would, and Reinbert the Fleming had it later. In lordship 1 plough;
    1 villager and 1 smallholder with ½ plough.
The value was 20s; now 14s.

LAND OF JOCELYN THE BRETON

In BAGSTONE Hundred
Jocelyn the Breton holds CHARFIELD from the King. Alfhild held it from King Edward. 3 hides. In lordship 2 ploughs;
    4 villagers and 7 smallholders with 4 ploughs.
    4 slaves; a mill at 10s; meadow, 8 acres; woodland ½ league long
    and wide.
The value was £4; now 40s.

LAND OF ROGER SON OF RALPH

In SWINEHEAD Hundred
Roger son of Ralph holds a manor named CLIFTON which Saewin, the reeve of Bristol, held from King Edward; he could go with this land where he would, and gave no revenue whatever for it. 3 hides.
In lordship 3 ploughs;
    6 villagers and 6 smallholders with 2 ploughs.
    3 slaves; meadow, 8 acres.
The value was 100s; now 60s.

Rogeri hr.i.Maneriu de.i.hida træ.7 ibi hr.ii.feruos.
hoc appciat.x.folid.Non fuit qui de hac tra refpondet.
Walter hr.un ꝏ de.i.uirg træ.Valuit.xx.den.m.ii.folid.

.LXXVI. TERRA VXORIS GERI. *IN HOLIFORDE HD.*
Uxor Geri de Loges ten de rege.iiii.hid In *GETINGE.*
Tres taini tenuer p.iii.ꝏ 7 geldab.Guluert Toui 7 Turbern.
In dnio.e.i.car.7 i.uill cu dim car.Valb.xl.fol.m.xx.folid.
.LXXVII.Baldvin ten de rege.iii.virg træ *IN GERSDONES HD.*
In *OMENIE*.Aluuin tenuit T.R.E. Ibi.e.i.car cu.ii.bord.
Val 7 ualuit.x.folid.

.LXVIII. 170 c
Elsi de ferendone ten de rege in *WENRIC*.iii.hid
7 dimid.Wluric 7 Toui 7 Leuuin tenuer p.iii.Maner.
7 poteraȵ ire quo uoleb.In dnio fuȵ.v.car.7 i.uills
7 vii.bord cu.i.car.Ibi.x.ferui.7 molin 7 dimid de
xii.folid.7 vi.den.   Valb.iiit.lib.Modo.viii.lib.
                        IN GERSDONES HD
Chetel ten de rege.i.hid 7 una V in *WENRIC*.Ipfe tenuit T.R.E.
Ibi.i.car 7 iiii.ferui.Val 7 ualuit xx.fol. *IN RESPIGET HD.*
Ifd Chetel ten.iii.virg 7 dimid in *DANTESBORNE*.Ipfe
tenuit.T.R.E.Ibi.i.car 7 ii.bord 7 ii.ferui.Valuit.x.fol.m.xv.

TERRÆ TAINOꝫ REGIS. *IN BERNINTONE HD.*

In SWINEHEAD Hundred

2   Roger has a manor of 1 hide of land. He has 2 slaves there.
It is assessed at 10s.
    There was no one to make a return for this land.

3   Walter has a manor of 1 virgate of land.
The value was 20d; now 2s.

76   LAND OF GERWY'S WIFE

In HOLFORD Hundred

1   Gerwy of Loges' wife holds 4 hides in (Temple) GUITING from the
King. Three thanes, Wulfrith, Tovi and Thorbern, held it as three
manors; it paid tax. In lordship 1 plough;
    1 villager with ½ plough.
The value was 40s; now 20s.

77   [LAND OF BALDWIN]

In GARSDON Hundred

1   Baldwin holds 3 virgates of land in AMPNEY (Crucis) from the King.
Alwin held them before 1066. 1 plough there, with
    2 smallholders.
The value is and was 10s.

78   LAND OF THE KING'S THANES   170 c

In BARRINGTON Hundred

1   Alfsi of Faringdon holds 3½ hides in WINDRUSH from the King.
Wulfric, Tovi and Leofwin held them as three manors and could
go where they would. In lordship 5 ploughs;
    1 villager and 7 smallholders with 1 plough.
    10 slaves; 1½ mills at 12s 6d.
The value was £3; now £8.

In GARSDON Hundred

2   Ketel holds 1 hide and 1 virgate in WINDRUSH from the King. He
held them himself before 1066. 1 plough and 4 slaves there.
The value is and was 20s.

In RAPSGATE Hundred

3   Ketel also holds 3½ virgates in 'DUNTISBOURNE'. He held them
himself before 1066. 1 plough there.
    2 smallholders and 2 slaves.
The value was 10s; now 15[s].

Osward teñ de rege REDMERTÒNE . IN LANGETREV HD.

Ibi . III . virg geld . Ipfe tenuit . T.R.E . Ibi . ē . I . car.

Valuit . xx . fot . modo . x . fot.   IN CIRECESTRE HVND.

EDRIC . f . Ketel teñ BAꝲDINTONE . de rege . Pat ej tenuit . T.R.E.

Ibi . III . hidæ 7 III . virg geld . In dñio funt . II . car . 7 III . uilti cū . I.
car . 7 IIII . ferui . 7 xv . ac pti . Val 7 ualuit . LX . folid.

EDWARD teñ de rege dimid hid ꝓ cõ . IN DVNESTAN HD.

7 ibi ht in dñio . I . car . 7 VI . bord cū . II . car . Val . xxx . fot.

EDDIET teñ de rege BICHEMERSE . IN CEOLFLEDE HVND.

Ipfa tenuit T.R.E . Ibi . I . hida . 7 in dñio . II . car . 7 I . uilt 7 I . bord
7 IIII . ferui . Valet 7 ualuit . xx . folid.   IN SALEMANESBERIE HD.

CVENILD moniat teñ de rege . IX . hid iñ NIꝲETONE . Ex his
IIII . hidæ geldb . Eilmer tenuit ꝓ cõ . In dñio fuꝳ . IIII . car.
7 VII . uilti cū . v . car . 7 m̃ habet . I . car . 7 moliñ de . v . folid.
7 XIII . int feruos 7 ancillas . Valuit . VIII . lib . m̃ . v . lib.

BRICTRIC teñ de rege . IIII . hid In   IN CILTENHA HD.

LECHAMETONE . 7 geld . Ipfe . II . hid . T.R.E . 7 Ordric tenuit
alias . II . Rex . W . utranq̃ eid Brictric ccefit . pgeꝳ in Norman.
In dñio ht . I . car . 7 IX . bord cū . III . car . 7 II . feruos 7 I . ancilt.
Silua . II . q̃ꝗ lg . 7 II . lat . Val . xxx . folid . IN HOLEFORD HD.

ALWOLD teñ de rege PIGNOCSIRE . Ipfe tenuit T.R.E.

Ibi . IIII . hidæ . Vna ex his ñ geldb . In dñio fuꝳ . IIII . car.
7 XI . uilti 7 v . bord . cū . IIII . car . Ibi . VIII . ferui . 7 moliñ
de . xxx . denar . In Wicelcūbe . I . burgfis redd . VIII . denar.
Silua dimid leuua lg . 7 una q̃ꝗ lat . Val 7 ualuit . IIII . lib.

In LONGTREE Hundred

4   Osward holds RODMARTON from the King. 3 virgates which pay tax. He held it himself before 1066. 1 plough there. The value was 20s; now 10s.

In CIRENCESTER Hundred

5   Edric son of Ketel holds BAUNTON from the King. His father held it before 1066. 3 hides and 3 virgates which pay tax. In lordship 2 ploughs;
       3 villagers with 1 plough; 4 slaves.
       Meadow, 15 acres.
The value is and was 60s.

In DUDSTONE Hundred

6   Edward holds ½ hide from the King as a manor. He has in lordship 1 plough;
       6 smallholders with 2 ploughs.
Value 30s.

In CHELTHORN Hundred

7   Edith holds BICKMARSH from the King. She held it herself before 1066. 1 hide. In lordship 2 ploughs;
       1 villager, 1 smallholder and 4 slaves.
The value is and was 20s.

In SALMONSBURY Hundred

8   Cwenhild the nun holds 9 hides in NAUNTON from the King; of these 4 hides paid tax. Aelmer held them as a manor. In lordship 4 ploughs;
       7 villagers with 5 ploughs; now 1 plough is recorded.
       A mill at 5s; 13 slaves, male and female.
The value was £8; now £5.

In CHELTENHAM Hundred

9   Brictric holds 4 hides in LECKHAMPTON from the King and pays tax. He (held) 2 hides himself before 1066 and Ordric held the other 2. King William when he went into Normandy assigned both (holdings) to this Brictric. He has in lordship 1 plough and
       9 smallholders with 3 ploughs; 2 male slaves, 1 female.
       Woodland 2 furlongs long and 2 wide.
Value 30s.

In HOLFORD Hundred

10   Alfwold holds PINNOCK from the King. He held it himself before 1066. 4 hides; 1 of them did not pay tax. In lordship 4 ploughs;
       11 villagers and 5 smallholders with 4 ploughs.
       8 slaves; a mill at 30d; in Winchcombe 1 burgess who pays 8d;
         woodland ½ league long and 1 furlong wide.
The value is and was £4.

Elwad .f. Reinbaldi ten ALDESWRDE. IN BECHEBERIE HD.

Balchi tenuit. Ibi . 11. hidæ geld. In dnio. ē . 1. car .7 1111.

uitti 7 11 . bord cū . 11 . car .7 un seruus. Valuit. xl . solid.

Elsi ten. de rege   IN WITESTAN HD.   Modo. xxx. sot.

LANGENEI. Ibi. v. hidæ. geld. Ipse tenuit T.R.E.

In dnio sunt . 11. car .7 vi . uitti 7 x11. bord cū . 1x. car.

Ibi. 1111. serui .7 x . ac pti .7 piscaria.

Valuit. c . solid. modo. lx. solid. IN SINESHOVEDES HD.

Dons ten de rege BETONE. Ipse tenuit T.R.E. Ibi

.11. hidæ. Vna ex his geldb. alia ad æcclam ptinebat.

In dnio suŋ . 11 . car .7 v . uitti 7 11 . bord. cū . v . car. Ibi

.1111 . serui .7 x . ac pti . Valuit. vi . lib . Modo. 111 . lib.

Brictric ten de rege WIDECESTRE. IN BLACHELEV HD.

Ipse tenuit T.R.E. Ibi . 1 . hida geld. Ibi suŋ . xvi . uitti 7 x11.

bord cū . xvi . car. In dnio nichil . In Glouuec. 1 . burgsis

redd . xx . ferra. Ibi molin de . x . sot. Val 7 ualuit . c . solid.

Hardinc ten in uadimonio de Brictric WITENHERT.

Ipse Brictric tenuit T.R.E. Ibi . v . hidæ geld. In dnio. ē.1.car.

7 pbr 7 11 . uitti 7 vi . bord cū . v . car. Ibi . 111 . serui .7 molin

de . x . sot .7 x . ac pti . Valuit. c . solid. Modo. xxx . solid.

Edric .f. Chetel ten ALCRINTONE. Pat ej tenuit. T.R.E.

Ibi. 1111 . hidæ 7 dimid geld. In dnio. ē . 1. car .7 vi . uitti 7 1111.

bord. cū . viii . car. Ibi . 111 . serui .7 molin de . x . solid .7 x. ac pti.

170 d

Silua . 1 . leuua lg .7 dim lat. Val 7 ualuit. 111 . lib. IN BOTELAV

Madoch ten de rege RVDEFORD. Ipse tenuit T.R.E.   HVND.

Ibi. 11 . hidæ.   In dnio. 11. car .7 111. uitti 7 1111. bord cū. 111. car.

7 molendin redd annonā qtū potest lucrari. Val 7 ualuit. xl. sot.

In BIBURY Hundred

11 Alfward son of Reinbald holds ALDSWORTH. Balki held it.
2 hides which pay tax. In lordship 1 plough;
4 villagers and 2 smallholders with 2 ploughs; 1 slave.
The value was 40s; now 30s.

In WHITSTONE Hundred

12 Alfsi holds LONGLEY from the King. 5 hides which pay tax. He
held it himself before 1066. In lordship 2 ploughs;
6 villagers and 12 smallholders with 9 ploughs.
4 slaves; meadow, 10 acres; a fishery.
The value was 100s; now 60s.

In SWINEHEAD Hundred

13 Dunn holds BITTON from the King. He held it himself before 1066.
2 hides; 1 of them paid tax, the other belonged to the Church.
In lordship 2 ploughs;
5 villagers and 2 smallholders with 5 ploughs.
4 slaves; meadow, 10 acres.
The value was £6; now £3.

In BLACKLOW Hundred

14 Brictric holds WOODCHESTER from the King. He held it himself
before 1066. 1 hide which pays tax.
16 villagers and 12 smallholders with 16 ploughs. Nothing
in lordship.
In Gloucester 1 burgess who pays 20 horseshoes.
A mill at 10s.
The value is and was 100s.

15 Harding holds WHEATENHURST in pledge from Brictric. Brictric
held it himself before 1066. 5 hides which pay tax. In lordship
1 plough;
a priest, 2 villagers and 6 smallholders with 5 ploughs.
3 slaves; a mill at 10s; meadow, 10 acres.
The value was 100s; now 30s.

16 Edric son of Ketel holds ALKERTON. His father held it before 1066.
4½ hides which pay tax. In lordship 1 plough;
6 villagers and 4 smallholders with 8 ploughs.
3 slaves; a mill at 10s; meadow, 10 acres;
woodland 1 league long and ½ wide.   170 d
The value is and was £3.

In BOTLOE Hundred

17 Madog holds RUDFORD from the King. He held it himself before
1066. 2 hides ... In lordship 2 ploughs;
3 villagers and 4 smallholders with 3 ploughs.
A mill which pays corn in so far as it can be sold.
The value is and was 40s.

GLOUCESTERSHIRE HOLDINGS
ENTERED ELSEWHERE IN THE SURVEY
The Latin text of these entries and fuller notes are given in the county volumes concerned

In HEREFORDSHIRE

| 1 | LAND OF THE KING | 179c |

In GLOUCESTERSHIRE

E1 43 The King holds FORTHAMPTON. Brictric held it. 9 hides which   180 d
paid tax for 4 hides. In lordship 3 ploughs;
7 villagers with 5 ploughs. 4 pigmen with 1 plough pay 35 pigs.
The woodland has 3 leagues in both length and width; it is in the
enclosure of the King's woodland; a hawk's eyrie and 2½
hides there.
Ansgot holds 3 virgates of land.
St. Mary's holds this manor's tithes, with 1 villager and 1 virgate
of land.

In BROOMS ASH Hundred

E2 72 In 'NEWARNE' 2½ hides which came to (Hundred) meetings and did   181 b
service there, but in Earl William's time Roger of Pîtres transferred
them to Gloucestershire.

E3 73 In (Lower) REDBROOK 2½ hides. Aelfric, Alfward and Brictsi held
them as two manors. They were waste and are still in the King's wood.

E4 74 There also Brictric held a manor of 1 hide and Earl Godwin held
STAUNTON, a manor of 1 hide. They were waste and are still in the
King's wood.

| 2 | LAND OF THE CHURCH OF HEREFORD | 181 c |

THESE LANDS WRITTEN BELOW BELONG TO THE CANONS OF HEREFORD . . .

In STRETFORD Hundred...

E5 8 In EATON (Bishop) 5 hides...... In lordship 2 ploughs;
12 villagers and 6 smallholders with 7 ploughs. 2 slaves.
A mill at 5s; meadow, 12 acres; woodland 1 league long and
2 furlongs wide.
Value £4.
Earl Harold held this manor. Earl William gave it to Bishop
Walter for land in which the market is now and for 3 hides of Lydney.

In BROOMS ASH Hundred

E6 22 In 'WHIPPINGTON' 3 hides which rightly belong to the Bishopric.   182 a
They are waste and were waste. A fishery there.

| 15 | LAND OF WILLIAM SON OF BADERON | 185 c |

In BROOMS ASH Hundred...

E7 2 William also holds RUARDEAN, and Solomon from him. Hadwig held it.
4 hides which pay tax. In lordship 3 ploughs would be possible.
1 smallholder, 2 villagers and 1 Welshman with 3 ploughs.
The value was and is 30s.

17   LAND OF THURSTAN SON OF ROLF   185 d

In BROOMS ASH Hundred

E8   1   Thurstan son of Rolf holds ALVINGTON. Brictric held it before 1066.
6 hides...... In lordship 2 ploughs;
    12 villagers with 9 ploughs; they pay 20 blooms of iron and
        8 sesters of honey.
    5 slaves, a mill at 40d.
Value before 1066, 20s; now £4.

In SOMERSET
[5]   LAND OF THE BISHOP OF COUTANCES   87 d
                                                        88 b

E9   20   Herlwin holds BISHOPSWORTH from the Bishop. Algar held it
before 1066; it paid tax for 2 hides. Land for 2 ploughs. In lordship
1 plough; 3 slaves;   141 b 2
    2 smallholders.
    Meadow, 12 acres; woodland 6 furlongs long and 1 furlong wide;
        in Bristol 10 houses; in Bath 2 houses which pay 10d.
The value was 20s; now 40s.

In WILTSHIRE
6   LAND OF THE BISHOP OF LISIEUX   66 b

E10   2   The Bishop also holds SOMERFORD (Keynes). Alfward held it before
1066; it paid tax for 10 hides. Land for 7 ploughs, of which 5 hides
are in lordship; 3 ploughs there; 5 slaves;
    14 villagers and 8 smallholders with 4 ploughs.
    A mill which pays 10s; meadow, 100 acres; woodland 3 furlongs
        long and 2 furlongs wide.
Value £7.

8   LAND OF THE CHURCH OF MALMESBURY   66 d

E11   7   The Church itself holds KEMBLE. Before 1066 it paid tax for 30   67 a
hides. Land for 30 ploughs. Of this land 12 hides in lordship; 2 ploughs
there; 6 slaves.
    30 villagers and 15 Cottagers with 18 ploughs.
    2 mills which pay 15s; meadow, 40 acres; woodland 1 league long
        and 3 furlongs wide.
    Of this land Tovi holds 2 hides and 1 virgate of land, William 4 hides,
in CHELWORTH. The holders before 1066 could not be separated
from the church. 2 ploughs there; 6 slaves.
    6 smallholders.
    A mill at 10s; meadow, 8 acres.
    Of the villagers' land Ansketel holds 1 hide.
Value of the Abbot's lordship, £13; value when acquired, £10; value
of what the men hold, £8.

E12   8   The Church itself holds (Long) NEWNTON. Before 1066 it paid tax for
30 hides. Land for 23 ploughs. Of this land 15 hides in lordship; 4
ploughs there; 4 slaves.
    19 villagers, 5 cottagers and 2 Cottagers with 9 ploughs.
    2 mills which pay 30s; meadow, 18 acres; pasture, 80 acres.
    Of this land Osbern holds 3 hides, William 2 hides; they have
    6 ploughs.
    Of the villagers' land the Abbot gave 1 hide to a man-at-arms of his.
Value when the Abbot acquired it, £10; value now of his lordship, £12;
value of what the men hold, £6.

21   **LAND OF EARL ROGER**   68 d

E13   3   The Earl also holds POULTON. Siward held it before 1066; it paid tax for 5 hides. Land for 8 ploughs. Of this land 3½ hides in lordship; 4 ploughs there; 8 slaves;
         8 villagers and 7 Cottagers with 4 ploughs.
     Meadow, 15 acres; pasture 3 furlongs long and 1 furlong wide.
     The value was £12; now £16.

24   **LAND OF EDWARD OF SALISBURY**   69 b

E14   27   Azelin holds POOLE (Keynes) from Edward. Wulfwen held it before   69 c
     1066; it paid tax for 5 hides. Land for 5 ploughs, of which 3 hides are in lordship; 3 ploughs there; 6 slaves;
         6 villagers and 2 smallholders with 2 ploughs.
     A mill which pays 10s; meadow, 60 acres; pasture 3 furlongs
         long and 2 furlongs wide; woodland 1 league in length and
         width.
     The value was 100s; now £6.

30   **LAND OF DURAND OF GLOUCESTER**   71 c

E15   5   Durand holds ASHLEY himself. Aldred held it before 1066; it paid tax for 5 hides, less 1 virgate. Land for 4 ploughs, of which 3 hides are in lordship; 2 ploughs there; 3 slaves;
         5 villagers and 3 smallholders with 2 ploughs; 2 cottagers.
     Meadow, 5 acres; woodland, 5 acres.
     The value was and is £4.
     A man-at-arms of Miles Crispin's claims 1 virgate of land in this village.

45   **[LAND] OF ROGER OF BERKELEY**   72 c

E16   2   Roger also holds 1 hide, less ½ virgate, of the lordship revenue of CHIPPENHAM. Ceolwin held it before 1066 on lease from Edric the Sheriff.

52   **[LAND] OF HUMPHREY THE CHAMBERLAIN**   73 a

E17   1   Humphrey the Chamberlain holds SHORNCOTE from the King. Alfward held it before 1066; it paid tax for 5 hides. Land for 4 ploughs, of which 2½ hides are in lordship; 2 ploughs there; 3 slaves;
         8 villagers with 2 ploughs.
     Meadow, 50 acres; pasture 2 furlongs long and 1 furlong wide.
     The value was 40s; now 60s.

In WORCESTERSHIRE

1   **LAND OF THE KING**   172 b

     In CLENT Hundred...

E18   7   In DROITWICH ½ hide, which belongs to the hall of Gloucester.   172 c

2   **LAND OF THE CHURCH OF WORCESTER**

     [In OSWALDSLOW Hundred]

E19   22   In the same Hundred the Bishop also holds BREDON...   173 a

     23   In (the lands of) this manor lie 3 hides at TEDDINGTON and 1 hide at MITTON. They are for the monks' supplies. In lordship 5 ploughs;
         12 villagers and 6 smallholders with 9 ploughs. 10 male and
             3 female slaves.   A 104
     Meadow, 40 acres; woodland, 2 furlongs.
     The value was and is £4.

E20   24   Archdeacon Alric holds 2 hides of this manor at CUTSDEAN. He has
2 ploughs and
     a priest, 4 villagers and 7 smallholders with 3 ploughs.
The value was and is 30s.
     Bishop Brictheah had leased this land to Doda, but Archbishop
Aldred proved his right to it against his son after 1066.

E21   25   Urso holds 7 hides of this manor at REDMARLEY (d'Abitot), and
William 2 hides of them from him. In lordship 4 ploughs;
     23 villagers and 9 smallholders with 10 ploughs. 6 male
         and 2 female slaves.   A 105
     A mill at 5s 8d; woodland 1 league long and ½ wide.
The value was £8; now 10s less.
     Azor and Godwin held from the Bishop and gave service.

E22   27   Urso also holds 3 hides at (Little) WASHBOURNE. He has 2 ploughs;
     5 villagers and 4 smallholders with 2 ploughs.   A 107
     Meadow, 5 acres.
The value was and is 40s.
     Aelmer held it, and later became a monk; so the Bishop
acquired his land.

E23   38   In the same Hundred the Bishop also holds BLOCKLEY. 38 hides   173 b
which pay tax. Of these, 25½ hides are in lordship; 7 ploughs there;
     A priest who has 1 hide; 4 riders who have 6 hides;
         63 villagers and 25 smallholders; between them they have
         51 ploughs. 14 slaves.   A 117;
         12 mills at 52s, less 3d; meadow, 24 acres; woodland ½   120
         league long and wide.
The value was £16; now £20.

E24   39   Richard holds 2 hides of this manor at DITCHFORD. He has 1 plough;
     2 villagers, 1 smallholder and 2 slaves with 1 plough.
     Meadow, 4 acres.   A 118
The value was and is 30s.
     Alfward held it and rendered service.

E25   40   Ansgot holds 1½ hides of the villagers' own land. He has 1 plough,
with
     1 smallholder.   A 119
     Meadow, 3 acres.
The value is and was 15s.

E26   41   At (Church) ICOMB 1 hide lies in (the lands of) the above manor;
it belongs to the monks' supplies. 2 ploughs there.
     4 villagers, 2 smallholders and 4 slaves with 2 ploughs.
It is assessed with the head of the manor.
     Meadow, 12 acres.

E27   42   Stephen son of Fulcred holds 3 hides at DAYLESFORD. He has
2 ploughs and   A 121
     a priest; 6 villagers with 5 ploughs; 4 male slaves, 1 female.
     Meadow, 20 acres.
The value is and was £3.

E28   43   Hereward held 5 hides at EVENLODE. 2 ploughs.
     9 villagers with 3 ploughs; 1 slave.
     There was a mill at 32d.   A 122
The value is and was £3.

E29 44 The Abbey of Evesham held these two lands, DAYLESFORD and
EVENLODE, from the Bishop of Worcester until the Bishop of
Bayeux received them from the Abbey. These lands were for the
monks' supplies.

7 **LAND OF THE CHURCH OF GLOUCESTER** 174 b

In CLENT Hundred

E30 1 St. Peter's Church of Gloucester holds ½ hide in DROITWICH, with
the same customary dues as the King's ½ hide which is in Droitwich
and which belongs to Gloucester.

8 **LAND OF ST. PETER'S, WESTMINSTER** 174 c

[In PERSHORE Hundred]

E31 9a In LONGDON there are 30 hides...
9b Before 1066 nine free men held 18 hides of this land; they reaped
for 1 day in their lord's meadows and performed service as they
were asked: Alric, Reinbald, Alfward, Brictric, Aelfric, Godric
Clock and Godric, Alfwy and Alfwy Black.
The value, in total, of what they held was £11 11s.

E32 9e Urso holds 5 hides also of this land. Four of the above held them: 174 d
Alfward, Brictric, Alfwy and Godric. In lordship 5 ploughs;
3 villagers and 9 smallholders with 3 ploughs. 8 male and
3 female slaves. A 55–56
Meadow, 28 acres; woodland 3 furlongs long and 2 furlongs wide.
Value 70s.

E33 9g Roger of Lacy holds 5 hides also of this land. Alric held them.
He has nothing in lordship. A 53
Woodland 1 league long and ½ wide.
A rider, Leofric, holds 1 hide and 1 virgate from him.
He has 1 plough;
3 villagers and 8 smallholders with 4 ploughs. 1 male and
3 female slaves.
A mill at 8s; meadow, 12 acres.
Value 20s.

10 **LAND OF THE CHURCH OF EVESHAM** 175 c

In OSWALDSLOW Hundred... 175 d

E34 12 The Church itself holds at BENGEWORTH 4 hides, and Urso holds
a fifth hide. Abbot Walter proved his right to these 5 hides at
Ildeberga in four Shires in the presence of the Bishop of Bayeux
and other barons of the King. 2 ploughs there.
5 villagers and 2 smallholders with 2 ploughs. 6 slaves.
Value before 1066, 60s; later 50s; now 60s.

(WALES)
In HEREFORDSHIRE

1	**LAND OF THE KING**	179 c

E35 48 In MONMOUTH CASTLE the King has 4 ploughs in lordship.   180 d
William son of Baderon has charge of them.
Value of what the King has in this castle, 100s.
   William has 8 ploughs in lordship; more possible. There are
Welshmen there who have 24 ploughs; they pay 33 sesters of honey
and 2s.
   15 slaves, male and female. 3 mills at 20s.
William's men-at-arms have 7 ploughs.
Value of what William holds, £30.
   St. Florent of Saumur holds the church of this castle and all the
tithes with 2 carucates of land.

14	**LAND OF WILLIAM OF ÉCOUIS**	185 c

E36 1 William of Écouis holds 8 carucates of land in the castlery of
CAERLEON. Thurstan holds from him. He has 1 plough in lordship and
   3 Welshmen who live under Welsh law, with 3 ploughs;
      2 smallholders with ½ plough; they pay 4 sesters of honey.
      2 male slaves, 1 female.
This land was waste before 1066 and when William acquired it.
Value now 40s.

APPENDIX

Introduction

In addition to the final version of the survey preserved in DB, several ancillary texts or 'satellites' survive; the latter are copies, included in monastic cartularies, of returns made at earlier stages in the compilation of DB, sometimes revised after 1086. These 'satellites' often contain information additional to that in DB, and also throw light on the process by which DB was compiled. For further discussion see Apps. IV and V of the Worcestershire volume in this series. Notes to the entries printed in this Appendix appear at the end of the main notes.

The Evesham MSS

Three of the Evesham Abbey 'satellites' cover the Domesday county of Gloucestershire: Evesham 'F', 'K' and 'M'. Three other Evesham 'satellites', or ancillaries, Evesham 'A', 'C' and 'P', similarly cover the Domesday county of Worcestershire, including those places now in Gloucestershire. Other Evesham 'surveys', though not strictly related to DB, nevertheless throw light on contemporary conditions. These comprise two lists of manors in dispute between Evesham Abbey and other landholders (Evesham 'D' and 'N'); a county hidage summary for the Evesham Abbey estates (Evesham 'H'); two lists of Abbey manors subinfeudated by 1130 (Evesham 'E' and 'O'); two detailed surveys of two Gloucestershire manors and of Droitwich c.1126 (Evesham 'L' and 'Q'); and a hidage schedule of two secular fiefs in Worcestershire c.1136 (Evesham 'B'). Evesham 'G'. a list of Abbey manors subinfeudated c.1192, is too late to be included, whilst Evesham 'J', another detailed survey of some Abbey manors c.1104, does not include any manors now in Gloucestershire. All the above 'satellites' and 'surveys' are found in two Evesham Abbey cartularies (B. L. Cotton MS. Vespasian B xxiv and B. L. Harleian MS. 3763), the text of which are edited by Dr. H. B. Clarke of University College, Dublin, in his University of Birmingham Ph.D. thesis, 'The Early Surveys of Evesham Abbey' (1977). Dr. Clarke is now preparing these texts for publication in the *Worcestershire Historical Society* series: his generosity in making his text available as the basis for the present translation is very gratefully acknowledged. The details of the relevant 'satellites' and 'surveys' are as follows:

(a) B. L. Cotton MS. Vespasian B xxiv:

A (fols. 6r–7v) A fragmentary list of Worcestershire manors, arranged by Hundreds and with assessments and values, derived from the 'circuit returns' made during the compilation of DB, 1086. See DB Worcs. App. IV for the full translation.

B (fol. 8r) A hidage schedule of the Worcestershire manors of William de Beauchamp and Roger de Tony, 1136.

C (fols. 8v–10v) A Worcestershire hidage schedule probably derived from DB and revised to 1108.

D (fols. 10v–11r) A list of Worcestershire manors obtained by Urso of Abetot and his men-at-arms from Evesham Church, compiled c.1108.

E (fols. 11r,11v) A list of manors subinfeudated by the Abbots of Evesham, compiled c.1130.

F (fol. 11r) A hidage schedule of Evesham Abbey's holdings in Gloucestershire probably derived from pre-DB 'circuit returns', 1086. The order of entries corresponds to the following sections of DB Ch. 12: 3–4;1;5–9;2.

G (fol. 12r,v) A list of Evesham manors subinfeudated, compiled c.1192.

H (fol. 12v) A summary of county assessment totals for Evesham Abbey manors, c.1088.

K (fols. 57r–62r) A hidage schedule of all Gloucestershire holdings in 1086, derived from pre-DB 'circuit returns', but incorporating two surveys of the Boroughs of Gloucester and Winchcombe which have been partly updated to c.1100 (see Notes). The order of entries corresponds to the DB chapters as follows (where the order of the sections differs from that in DB, this is given in brackets): G 1–4. Ch.1 (15–19;21; 7–8;11;2;13;12;1;9–10;6;20;14;22–23;3–5;51–60;63–65;61–62; 24–25;34–37;26–31;33;32;47–50;39–45); Ch.2 (1–3;5–7;9;11–13). Ch.3 (1–5;7;6). Ch.4. Ch.6. Ch.5. Chs.7–9. Ch.10 (1;7). Ch.2 (4;8; 10). Ch.10 (2;6;8–13). B 1. Ch.11 (1–10;14;11–12). Ch.12 (3–4;1; 5–9;2). Chs.13–15. Ch.18. Chs.16–17. Chs.21–22. Ch.24. Ch.23 (2;1). Chs.19–20. Ch.25. Ch.28. Ch.27. Ch.29. Ch.26. Ch.30. Ch.31 (1–7;12;8–11). Ch.35. Ch.33. Ch.32 (2;1;3–4;13;5–6;8;10;9; 7;11–12). Ch.37. Ch.34 (1–11;13;12). Ch.38. Ch.36. Ch.57. Ch.56. Ch.58. Ch.55. Ch.2 (8). Ch.54 (2;1). Ch.53 (3;2;1;4–13). Ch.42. Ch.39 (8–11;1–7;12–21). Ch.41. Ch.40. Ch.48 (3;1;2). Ch.47. Ch.46. Ch.45 (1–3;6;4–5). Ch.44. Ch.43 (2;1). Ch.49. Chs.59–65. Ch.50. Ch.67. Ch.66. Ch.68 (1–8;11;9;12;10). Ch.69 (1–2;4;3;5–8). Chs.70–74. Ch.52. Ch.51. Chs.75–77. Ch.78 (1;12;2–11;13–17). W 9–10; 12–15;18–19.

L (fol. 57v) A detailed survey of the manors of Beckford and Ashton under Hill, c.1126.

M (fols. 62r–63v) An incomplete hidage schedule for Gloucestershire in 1086, derived from DB, excluding the holdings of the King (DB Ch.1) and of all holders after Osbern Giffard (DB Chs.51–78). The order of the entries corresponds to the DB chapters as follows (where the order of the sections within each chapter differs from that in DB, this is given in brackets): Ch.2 (4;8;10;4;8;10;4;8;10). Ch.3 (1–5;7;6). Chs.4–24. Ch.26. Ch.25. Ch.2 (1–13). Ch.27. Ch.28 (1;5;2–4). Chs.29–49. Ch.50 (1 only).

(b) B. L. Harleian MS. 3763:

N (fols. 60v–61r) A list of Worcestershire manors removed from Evesham Church c.1078 by Odo of Bayeux, probably compiled c.1097.

O (fols. 61r,v) A list of manors subinfeudated by the Abbots of Evesham, c.1130.

P (fol. 71v) A hidage schedule of the Worcestershire manors of Evesham Abbey and the Bishop of Bayeux, 1086–1104.

Q (fol. 82r) An incomplete Worcestershire hidage schedule of c.1086, but incorporating a survey of Droitwich, c.1126.

Only those entries which significantly differ from or augment the text of DB are printed below, using Dr. Clarke's numeration. Minor variants are included in the Notes to the DB text. The corresponding Chapter and section references and place-names of DB are given in the left-hand columns.

B.L. Cotton Vespasian B xxiv

Evesham A

DB ref.	Place-name			
PERSHORE HUNDRED		In *Persor'* Hundred ...		folio 6v
E 31	Longdon	(41)	*Langentona*, 11 hides. Value £9.	
E 33	Longdon	(53)	In *Stantona* (Staunton), 5 hides. Value 20s.	
E 32	Longdon	(55)	*Chaddeslege* (Chaceley), 2 hides. Value 20s.	
OSWALDSLOW HUNDRED		In *Oswaldeslawe* Hundred ...		folio 7r
E 19	Bredon	(103)	*Bridona*, 35 hides. Value £9 10s.	
E 19	Teddington and Mitton	(104)	*Tetintona* and *Muttona*, 4 hides. Value £4.	
E 21	Redmarley (d'Abitot)	(105)	*Rudmerlege*, 2 hides. Value of these two, £7. In *Rudmelege Willelmi*, 3 hides.	
E 22	(Little) Washbourne	(107)	*Wasseburna*, 3 hides. Value 40s.	
E 23	Blockley	(117)	*Blocchelai*, 33 hides. Value £20.	
E 24	Ditchford	(118)	Richard holds 2 hides. Value 30s.	
E 25	———	(119)	Asgot (*Astgot*) holds 1½ hides. Value £15.	
E 23 (see note)	Blockley	(120)	Hereward [holds] 5 hides. Value 40s.	
E 27	Daylesford	(121)	*Dailesford*, 3 hides. Value 60s.	
E 28	Evenlode	(122)	*Eunelate*, 5 hides. Value 60s.	

Evesham C

DB ref.	Place-name			
				folio 8v
E 19	Bredon	(22)	In the same Hundred (Oswaldslow) the Bishop holds *Bredona*. 35 hides which pay tax. In lordship 10 hides.	
E 19	Teddington and Mitton	(23)	3 hides at *Tedintona* and 1 hide at *Muttona* are attached to this manor.	
E 20	Cutsdean	(24)	Archdeacon Alric holds 2 hides of this manor at *Codestun*.	
E 21	Redmarley (d'Abitot)	(25)	Of this manor Urso holds 7 hides at *Rudm(er)lege*, and William (holds) 2 of these hides from him.	
E 22	(Little) Washbourne;	(27)	He also (Urso) holds 3 hides at *Wasseburna*.	
E 23	Blockley	(38)	Also in the same Hundred the Bishop holds *Blockelai*. 38 hides which pay tax. In lordship 25½ hides.	
E 24	Ditchford	(39)	Of this manor Richard holds 2 hides in *Dichford*.	
E 25–26	——— and (Church) Icomb	(40)	Ansgot [holds] 1½ hides. 1 hide (at) *Iacumbe* for the monks' supplies belongs to the above manor.	
E 27–29	Daylesford and Evenlode	(41)	Stephen son of Wulfwy [holds] 3 hides in *Dailesford*. Hereward [holds] 5 hides in *Eunelade*. The Abbot of Evesham held these two lands, *Dailesford* and *Eunelade*, from the Bishop of Worcester, until the Bishop of Bayeux received them from the Abbey. These lands were for the monks' supplies.	

Evesham C cont'd...

DB ref.	Place-name		
E 23 (see note)	Blockley and members	(42)	Of this manor Urso holds 5 hides in *Dorna* (Dorn). folio 10r
E 31	Longdon	(102)	In *Langedona*, 30 hides. Of these, 11 hides in lordship.
E 32	(Chaceley and Longdon)	(106)	Also of this land Urso holds 5 hides.
E 33	(Staunton)	(108)	Also of this land Roger of Lacy [holds] 5 hides.

Evesham E

folio 11r

12,7   Weston (Cantilupe)   (10)   William of Seacourt holds *Westune* by gift of Abbot Robert without the chapter ('s consent) (*siñe capitulo*).

folio 11v

12,3   part of Bourton (on the Water)   (25)   William of Donnington has 5½ virgates of lordship (land) in *Dunitona* (Donnington) and he resides in the Abbot's manor-house (*dominica mansione*) by gift of Abbot Walter despite the chapter's opposition (*contradicente capitulo*).

Evesham K

folio 57r

G 1–4   Gloucester   (1)   Before 1066 300 burgesses in lordship in the city of Gloucester who paid £18 10s of tribute (*de gablo*) a year. Of these, 100 less 3 are residing in their own inherited (property) (*hereditate*), and 100 less 3, French and English, are living in purchased residences which are worth £10 a year, and they have held them for 12 years, that is £120. 24 out of these 300 lived within the castle and 82 residences are waste.

The Archbishop of York has in this city 60 burgesses, Bishop Samson 6, the Abbot of this city 52, and apart from these *Stanborc* has 1 residence, Deerhurst 36, the Abbot of Evesham 4, the Abbot of Pershore 1, Earl Hugh of Chester 13, Robert son of Hamo 22, Hugh of Lacy 28, 24 belong to 'Kings Barton', (Roger of) Berkeley 4, Walter of Gloucester 15, Hugh Donkey 2, Walter son of Richard 2, Ralph Blewitt 6, Horsley 1, Wulfmer 1, Azelin of Tetbury 1, W(illiam) of Say 1, William son of Baderon 17, Hamelin 1, Earl Henry 1, William de

Mandeville 6, Patrick of Chaworth 6, Gilbert of Maine 1. The King has full jurisdiction over all these, and 10 churches are in the King's own jurisdiction. In Roger the Sheriff's time they paid £28 4s of revenue. Now they pay £46. Walter the Sheriff had 64s on request and the reeve 40(s). The city has depreciated (in value) by £60.

King Edward had in lordship these lands in Gloucestershire:...   folio 57v

1,21	'Barton (Regis)', Bristol	(7)	(At) *Bristou* or *Bertone* were 6 hides. The church has 3 hides and a man 1 hide of this land.
1,11	Westbury (on Severn), Kyre, Clifton (on Teme), Newent, Kingstone, Edvin (Loach)	(10)	*Westbyrie*, 30 hides. Of this manor 25 hides have been taken away: in *Chire* 6 hides, in *Clistone* 10 hides, in *Noeunt* and *Cligest'* 8 hides, in *ladeuent* 1 hide. The Abbot of Cormeilles, Osbern and William sons of Richard hold these (lands).

(Land) of the Bishop of Worcester:...   folio 58v

3,3–4	Eycot and Bibury	(80)	In *Becheberie* (Bibury) Hundred: *Becheberie* and *Aicote*, 22 hides.

(Land) of St. Peter's, Gloucester:...   folio 59r

2,8	Northleach, (Upper) Coberley	(103)	In *Bradelege* (Bradley) Hundred: *Leche* and *Cumberlee*, 13 hides.
B 1	Winchcombe	(116)	In *Wincelcumbe* Borough. In King Edward's lordship were 60 burgesses who paid 41s of tribute a year. Of these, 52 are living in their inherited (property) (*hereditate*) and 8 other burgesses have (residences) which are worth 30s a year, that is £22 10s over 15 years. Besides, the Abbot has in it 40 burgesses and the Abbot of Evesham 2, the Bishop of Hereford [...], Deerhurst 2, Hugh Donkey 1, Longborough 3, Robert son of Hamo 5, Thurstan of Cormeilles 2 and 1 mill, Harold 10 and 2 mills, Robert of Bellême 3, Walter of St. Valéry and Hugh of Lacy 1, Robert of Ferrers 2, Hugh of Ham 1, Richard of Sollers 1, Ralph of Sacey 3, William Goizenboded 3, Robert of Lacy 1, William Breakwolf 1. The King has his tax from all of them.

In Roger the Sheriff's time it paid £10; now £21 at face value. The Sheriff had 12s on request.

Evesham K cont'd...

DB ref.	*Place-name*		
	(Land) of St. Mary's of Evesham:...		folio 59v
12,5–6	(Upper) Swell, Wickhamford	(133)	In *Widelai* (Witley) Hundred: *Swelle*, 3 hides and 1 hide at *Wicquennam*.
12,6	Willersey	(134)	*Willeresei*, 8 hides.
12,7	Weston (Cantilupe)	(135)	*Westone*, 3 hides, 1 free.
	(Land) of St. Denis' of Paris:		
20,1	Deerhurst	(153)	In *Derherst* (Deerhurst) Hundred 50 hides.
20,1	Deerhurst	(154)	10 hides beyond the Severn belong there.
	(Land) of Earl Hugh:...		
28,5–7	Westonbirt	(159)	In *Langetreu* (Longtree) Hundred: *Westone*, 4 hides.
	(Land) of Walter son of Poyntz:...		folio 60v
2,8	Northleach	(230)	In *Lecche*, 12 hides. St. Peter's of Gloucester claims them.
			folio 62r
W 18	———	(400)	Thurstan son of Rolf [holds] 11½ carucates between the Usk and the Wye, 6 carucates of land beyond the Usk.

Evesham L

folio 57v

1,59–60	Beckford, Ashton (under Hill)	(1)	In *Becchafort* there are 16 hides of land and 2 churches which have 3½ virgates. *Estona* is attached to it. At the said time there were 10 ploughs, and now; then and now 9 cobs; then 6 cows, but there can be 10 more; then 4 sows with their piglets, but there can be 100 more pigs; then 500 sheep, but there can be 200 more; 20 beehives; then 5 male and female slaves; then 32 villagers, now 14 more; then 9 smallholders, now 6 more; then 3 riding men, now 1; 2 fowlers; 1 forester; 1 beadle; 1 porter; 1 smith; all these together had 32 ploughs; now 3 more; then 25 horses, now 1 more. Then this manor rendered £30 of revenue, and now, and in addition to this paid 27s 8d in customary dues. Walter the Sheriff had 40s. The building and lordship of the King and the minster have increased (in value) by £10.

Evesham M

folio 62r

2,8	Northleach, (Upper) Coberley	(3)	*Lecche* and *Cumb(er)lege*, 13 hides. Thomas holds them. Besides these 13 hides, Walter son of Poyntz has 12 hides there, which Archbishop Thomas claims for St. Peter's use.

Evesham M cont'd...

DB ref.	Place-name		
2,10	Standish	(4)	*Stanedis*, 15 hides. Thomas holds it. Of *Stanedis* Earl Humphrey wrongfully holds

folio 62v

1 hide and Durand the Sheriff 3 hides wrongfully, which Archbishop Thomas claims for St. Peter's use.

2,8	Northleach	(6)	Archbishop Aldred holds 24 hides in
		(99)	*Leccha*.
3,1	Westbury (on Trym)	(8)	In *Westberia* 50 hides belong to St. Mary of Worcester.
9,1	Littleton (on Severn)	(32)	The Church of Malmesbury held 5 hides in *Letletona*. Of these, 2½ are exempt.

The Church of Evesham holds:...

12,5	(Upper) Swell	(65)	In *Swella*, 3 hides.
12,6	Willersey	(66)	In *Wilderesheia*, 8 hides.
12,7	Weston (Cantilupe)	(67)	In *Westona*, 3 hides and 1 free.

folio 63r

19,2	Deerhurst, Kemerton, Boddington	(79)	The Church of Westminster holds 70 hides. Of these Gerard the Chamberlain has 11, exempt.
20,1	(Deerhurst)	(80)	The Church of St. Denis holds 60 hides.
2,9	Compton (Abdale)	(100)	Archbishop Stigand holds 10 hides in *Cumtona*.

Earl Hugh holds:...

28,5	Westonbirt	(108)	In *Westona*, 3 hides.
28,7	Westonbirt	(112)	He also holds 4 hides in *Langetreu* (Longtree) Hundred; 2 men, Alnoth and Alwin, held from him.

Evesham N

folio 60v

—	———	(1)	Here are noted the lands which Odo, Bishop of Bayeux, violently took away from the Church of St. Mary, holy mother of God, at Evesham in Abbot Walter's time.

In Worcestershire: ......

E 27–28	Evenlode, Daylesford	(5)	*Eunelad'*, 7 hides of lordship (land); now a man-at-arms called Brian has them. *Deilesford*, 3 hides of lordship (land); William Hastings has them.
62,4	(Lower) Quinton,	(11)	In Gloucestershire: *Quenton'*, 10 hides;
39,20	(Upper) Slaughter		in *Parva Sloutra*, 5 hides. folio 61r
			Hugh of Lacy has them.
45,6	(Lower) Swell	(12)	*Swella*, 7 hides; Ralph of Tosny (*de Tounei*) holds them.
47,1	Childswickham	(13)	Robert the Bursar holds *Childeswicwon*. 10 hides.

Evesham N cont'd...

DB ref.	Place-name		
34,1 62,1	Pebworth	(14)	William Goizenboded holds *Pebewrth*. 2 hides.

Evesham O

folio 61r

12,8	(Lark) Stoke	(1)	Ranulf, Abbot Walter's brother, has ...
12,8	(Lark) Stoke	(3)	in *Stokes* 2½ hides of lordship (land) ...
12,8	(Lark) Stoke	(5)	by Abbot Walter's gift despite the chapter's opposition (*contradicente capitulo*).
12,3	part of Bourton (on the Water)	(6)	William of Donnington has in *Duniton'* (Donnington) 5½ virgates of lordship (land) by Abbot Walter's gift.
12,4	Broadwell	(7)	In *Bradewelle* Walter holds ½ hide and 21 acres of cotland by Walter's gift.
12,2	Adlestrop	(8)	In *Tatlestroppe* Jocelyn's son [has] 4 hides by Walter's gift.
12,1	Maugersbury, Stow (on the Wold)	(9)	In *Melgarebur'* Alfred [has] ½ hide, and the Church of *Stowe* 1 hide of lordship (land) by Walter's gift.
12,3	Bourton (on the Water)	(10)	In *Burchton'* Robert son of Alfred [has] 1 hide of lordship (land) by Walter's gift.

folio 61v

| 12,7 | Weston (Cantilupe) | (25) | William of Seacourt holds *Weston'* ... |
| 12,7 | Weston (Cantilupe) | (26) | ... by Abbot Robert's gift without the chapter ('s consent) (*sine capitulo*). |

Evesham Q

folio 82r

| E 18;30 | Droitwich | (29) | These are the 10 hides in *Wich'* ... Of *la Berton'* ('Kings Barton') in Gloucester Ranulf son of Ringulf holds ½ hide. Of the monks of (St. Peter's) Gloucester Baldwin and Lithwulf [hold] ½ hide. Of the Earl of Warwick Ranulf and Essulf sons of Ringulf hold 3 virgates. Of Walter of 'Burgh' Ranulf and Essulf [hold] ½ hide... Of the monks (of Eynsham) the sons of Grim hold 1 virgate... |

The Worcester MSS

The late 11th–early 12th century Worcester cartulary known as 'Hemming's Cartulary' (B.L. Cotton MS. Tiberius A xiii printed in T. Hearne (ed.) *Hemingi Chartularium Ecclesiae Wigornensis*, Oxford, 2 vols., 1723) contains four texts related to Glos. DB, whilst another text often considered to relate to DB is printed in RBW. For a full critical discussion of Hemming, see Ker pp. 49–75. Hearne did not include in his edition 3 smaller pieces of parchment, now numbered 110, 143 and 153, so the most recent foliation is as much as 3 numbers different from that given by him in the margin. This most recent figure is given after Hearne's foliation where it differs. The letter allotted to each of the texts below is due to the present editor. The same system is adopted and extended in the Worcestershire volume of this series, where further discussions will be found. The texts related to DB are:

A (folio 39r; Hearne pp. 83-4): An incomplete hidage schedule of the Worcester Church lands in Gloucestershire only, antedating DB (see Notes).

B (folios 136v-140v (= 137v-141v); Hearne pp. 298-313): A hidage schedule for the lands of the Worcester Church in both Gloucestershire and Worcestershire, which contains some differences from and additions to DB. It is possibly based on a Worcester 'satellite', but is heavily influenced by DB and may have been compiled or revised after 1086 but certainly before 1095 (see Notes).

C (folios 141r,v (= 142r,v); Hearne pp. 313-6): A revised hidage schedule for the Worcester Church lands in Worcestershire only, dateable to c.1115 (see Notes).

D (folio 174v (= 177v); Hearne pp. 393-5): A summary of taxable hides by major landholders for the county of Worcestershire only, v.1086. This does not contain any additional information for those parts of Worcestershire now in Gloucestershire, and has not been printed in this volume.

E (Hollings ed. pp. 442-3): A hidage schedule for the Worcester Church lands in lordship in Gloucestershire only, which has previously been thought to antedate DB, but is probably mid-12th century in date and is therefore not printed below (see Notes).

Only the sections relating to manors now in Gloucestershire have been printed below.

Worcester A folio 39r
Hearne pp. 83-4

DB ref.	Place-name		
3,3-4	Eycot, Bibury, Barnsley	(1)	To *Begabiria* belong 21 hides; in *Begabiria* and *Abolingatune* (Ablington) 15 hides; in *Beorudeslea* 5 hides and in *Eugkote* 1 hide.
3,5	Withington, (Cassey) Compton, Foxcote, (Little) Colesbourne, Hilcot, Dowdeswell, Pegglesworth, Notgrove, Aston (Blank)	(2)	To *Widiadune* belong 30 hides; in *Eastuna* 10 hides; in *Nategraphe* 5 hides; in *Dotheswella* and *Petleswirthe* 3½ hides; in *Aldeswella* (Owdeswell) 2 hides; in *Foxkota* 3 hides; in *Wlkota* 1 hide; in *Kolesburna* 1 hide; in *Upkota* (Upcote) 1 hide and 1 virgate; in *Comtuna* 1 hide, and to the church belongs ½ hide.
3,7	(Bishops) Cleeve	(3)	To *Cliua* belong 30 hides.

Worcester A cont'd...

DB ref.	Place-name
3,1	Westbury (on Trym), Stoke (Bishop), Compton (Greenfield), Itchington

(4) To *Westbiria* belong 50 hides; the Bishop has 35 hides in lordship and his men-at-arms have 15 hides; in *Icenatune* 5 hides; in *Comtuna* 5 hides; in *Biscopes Stoke* 5 hides.

Worcester B

E 19–22	Bredon, Teddington, Mitton, Cutsdean, Redmarley (d'Abitot), (Little) Washbourne

folio 137v (= 138v)

BREODVN Hearne p. 302

(5) In the same Hundred (Oswaldslow) the Bishop also holds *Breodun*. 35 hides which pay tax. In lordship 10 hides. To this manor are attached 3 hides at *Teotintune* and 1 hide at *Muttune*; they are for the monks' supplies.

Of this manor Archdeacon Alric holds 2 hides at *Codestone*. Bishop Brictheah (*Bricstec*) had leased this land to Doda, but Archbishop Aldred proved his right to it against his son in King William's time. Of this manor Urso holds 7 hides at *Ridmerlege*, and William 2 hides of these from him. Azor and Godwin held from the Bishop and rendered service to him.... Urso also holds 3 hides at *Wasseburne*. Aelmer held them and afterwards became a monk, so the Bishop acquired his land...

folio 138r (= 139r)

BLOKELAI Hearne pp. 303–4

E 23–29	Blockley, Ditchford, (Church) Icomb, Daylesford, Evenlode

(7) In the same Hundred the Bishop also holds *Blokelai*. 38 hides which pay tax. In lordship 25½ hides.

Of this manor Richard holds 2 hides at *Dicford*. Alfward held them and rendered service.

Ansgot holds 1½ hides of the villagers' own land.

To the above manor is attached 1 hide at *Ieacumbe*, which belongs to the monks' supplies.

Stephen son of Fulcred holds 3 hides at *Eilesford*.

Hereward held 5 hides at *Eunilade*.

Of this manor Urso holds 5 hides in *Dorne* (Dorn).

The Abbot of Evesham held these two lands, *Eilesford* and *Eunalade*, from the Bishop of Worcester until the Bishop of Bayeux received them from the Abbey. These lands were for the monks' supplies.

GLOECESTRE SCIRE folio 139v (= 140v)
Hearne pp. 309–10

3,1	Westbury (on Trym)	(15)

Henbury, Redwick,
Stoke (Bishop),
Yate, Aust,
Compton (Greenfield),
Itchington

In Gloucestershire St. Mary of Worcester held and holds *Huesberie* in *Bernintreu* (Brentry) Hundred. There   140r (= 141r) were and are 50 hides. To this manor belong these members: *Henberie, Redewike, Stoke, Giete.* To this manor belong 6 riding men who have 8 hides.

Of this manor's land Thurstan son of Rolf holds 5 hides in *Austrecliue* and Gilbert son of Thorold 3½ hides in *Comtona* and Constantine 5 hides in *Icetona.*

Of this manor's land Osbern Giffard holds 5 hides and does no service.

COLESBVRNE   folio 140r (= 141r)
Hearne pp. 310–11

3,2–3	(Great) Colesbourne, Eycot, Bibury,	(16)

In *Respegete* (Rapsgate) Hundred. The church holds *Colesburne* itself, and Swein from it; he could not withdraw. 8 hides which pay tax. Walter son of Roger holds it from the church. The church holds *Aicocte* itself, and Alric from it. It lies in *Begeberi.* 1 hide. Ordric holds it from the Bishop.

BEGESBERI

3,4	Bibury, Barnsley	(17)

In *Begesberi* (Bibury) Hundred. The church holds *Bercheberi* itself. 21 hides. Of this manor's land Durand holds from the Bishop a manor of 3 hides and 1 virgate of land in *Berneleis,* and Eudo 7 virgates there also as a manor.

WIDINDONA

3,5	Withington, Foxcote, (Little) Colesbourne, Hilcot, Dowdeswell, Pegglesworth, Notgrove, Aston (Blank)	(18)

In *Wacrescymbe* (Wattlescomb) Hundred. The church holds *Widindona* itself. 30 hides. 3 of these have never paid tax. In this manor are 4 riding men who have 2 hides and 3 virgates of land, and priests who have ½ hide. Of this manor's land Morin holds from the Bishop 3 hides in *Fuscote,* Ansketel 2 hides in *Colesb(ur)ne* and *Heldicote,* Robert 4½ hides in *Doddeswelle* and *Peclewrde,* Azelin 5 hides in *Nategraue,* Drogo 10 hides in *Estone.*

Worcester B cont'd...
DB ref.   *Place-name*

CLIVE   folio 140v (= 141v)
                                              Hearne p. 311

3,7   (Bishops) Cleeve,   (19) In *Teodboldestan* (Tibblestone) Hundred.
           Southam,   The church holds *Cliue* itself. 30 hides. Of
           'Sapperton',   this manor's land Durand the Sheriff holds
           Gotherington,   from the church 6 hides in *Sudham*, Ralph
           Stoke (Orchard)   4 hides in *Sapertone*,   140v (= 141v)
                                          Thurstan son of Rolf 6 hides in *Godrintone*.
                                          Of the same land Bernard and Reginald
                                          [hold] 7 hides in *Stokes* and refuse to do
                                          service to St. Mary's.

                                    CONDICOTE
3,6   Condicote   (20) In *Witelai* (Witley) Hundred. The church
                                          holds 2 hides in *Condicote* itself, and Osbern
                                          from the Bishop.

Worcester C   folio 141r (= 142r), Hearne pp. 313–4
E 19;   Bredon   (4)   In *Bredvn* 35 hides. Of these, the monks of
21–22   Worcester have 4 hides and Walter of
                                          Beauchamp 16 hides, the King 1 hide,
                                          Giles 1 hide and the Bishop 13 with his
                                          lordship.

E 23   Blockley,   (6)   In *Bloccelea* 38 hides. Of these, Walter of
(see note) Daylesford, Evenlode,   Beauchamp has 5 [....], (there are) at
E 24–28   Ditchford   *Daeilesford* 3, at *Eunilade* 5, the monks
                                          (have) 1 and the Bishop 24 with his lord-
                                          ships and *Dicford*.

NOTES ON THE TEXT AND TRANSLATION

NOTES ON THE TEXT AND TRANSLATION

BIBLIOGRAPHY and ABBREVIATIONS used in the Notes

Anglo-Norman Families ... L. C. Loyd *The Origins of Some Anglo-Norman Families*, Leeds 1951.
ASC ... *The Anglo-Saxon Chronicle* (translated by G. N. Garmonsway), London 1960.
BCS ... W. de Gray Birch (ed.) *Cartularium Saxonicum* 3 vols. and index, London 1885–1899 (reprinted 1964).
Book of Llan Dâv ... J. G. Evans (ed.) *The Text of the Book of Llan Dâv reproduced from the Gwysaney Manuscript*, Old Welsh Texts iv, Oxford 1893, reprinted Aberystwyth 1980.
Cal CR ... *Calendar of Charter Rolls*, HMSO State Papers.
Charles ... B. G. Charles *Non-Celtic Place-Names in Wales*, London 1938.
Clarke ... H. B. Clarke *The Early Surveys of Evesham Abbey, Worcestershire*, Birmingham University Ph.D. thesis, 1977.
Complete Peerage ... G. E. Cokayne *The Complete Peerage of England, Scotland...* (revised edition 13 vols. by V. Gibbs, H. A. Doubleday, G. H. White, R. S. Lea, London 1910–1959).
DB ... Domesday Book, vols. 1–4 Domesday Book, introduction, indices and associated texts, Record Commission, London 1783–1816.
DBH ... V. H. Galbraith and J. Tait (eds.) *Herefordshire Domesday*, Pipe Roll Society lxiii (new series xxv), London 1950.
DEPN ... E. Ekwall *The Concise Oxford Dictionary of English Place-Names*, 4th edition, Oxford 1960.
DG ... H. C. Darby and G. R. Versey *Domesday Gazetteer*, Cambridge 1975.
DGM ... H. C. Darby and I. B. Terrett *The Domesday Geography of Midland England*, 2nd edition, Cambridge 1971.
DMLBS ... R. E. Latham (ed.) *Dictionary of Medieval Latin from British Sources*, London 1975 on.
Douglas ... D. C. Douglas *William the Conqueror*, London 1964.
Ducange ... G. A. L. Henschel (ed.) *Glossarium Mediae et Infimae Latinitatis*, Niort and London 1884–1887.
EcHR ... Economic History Review.
ECWM ... H. P. R. Finberg (ed.) *Early Charters of the West Midlands*, Leicester 1957.
EHR ... English Historical Review.
Ellis ... Sir H. Ellis *A General Introduction to Domesday Book*, 2 vols. 1833 (reprinted 1971).
Ellis DTG ... A. S. Ellis *Domesday Tenants of Gloucestershire* in TBGAS vol. iv (1879–80) pp. 86–198.
EPNS ... English Place-Name Society. References are to *Gloucestershire* vols. xxxviii–xli (4 parts) ed. A. H. Smith, Cambridge 1964, unless otherwise stated.
EPNS Wilts. ... English Place-Name Society vol. xvi *Wiltshire* eds. J. E. B. Gover, A. Mawer, F. M. Stenton, Cambridge 1939.
EvA-Q ... See Appendix.
Exon. ... *Liber Exoniensis* in DB 4; see above.
Eyton ... R. W. Eyton *Domesday Studies: An Analysis and Digest of the Somerset Survey* 2 vols., London and Bristol 1880.
Farley ... Abraham Farley (ed.) *Liber Censualis seu Domesday Book*, London 1783 (see Introduction).
Farrer ... W. Farrer *An Outline Itinerary of King Henry I* in EHR xxxiv (1919) pp. 505–579.
Fees ... *Book of Fees (Testa de Nevill)* 3 vols., HMSO 1920–31.
Fleta ... H. G. Richardson and G. O. Sayles (eds.) *Fleta* vol. 2, Selden Society no. lxxii, 1953.
Forrsner ... T. Forrsner *Continental-Germanic Personal Names in England in Old and Middle English Times*, Uppsala 1916.
Förstemann ... E. Förstemann *Altdeutsches Namenbuch*, Band 1, *Personennamen* 2nd edition, Bonn 1900.
Freeman ... E. A. Freeman *The History of the Norman Conquest of England* 6 vols., Oxford 1867–79.
GR ... Grid Reference.
GS ... H. P. R. Finberg (ed.) *Gloucestershire Studies*, Leicester 1957.
Habington ... Thomas Habington (ed. J. Amphlett) *A Survey of Worcestershire* 2 vols., Worcestershire Historical Society 1898.

Harmer ... F. E. Harmer *Anglo-Saxon Writs*, Manchester 1952.

Hearne ... see Hemming.

Hemming ... Thomas Hearne (ed.) *Hemingi Chartularium Ecclesiae Wigorniensis* 2 vols., Oxford 1723.

History of Abingdon ... J. Stevenson (ed.) *Chronicon Monasterii de Abingdon* 2 vols., Rolls Series no. 2, London 1858.

History of St. Peter's, Gloucester ... W. H. Hart (ed.) *Historia et Cartularium Monasterii Sancti Petri Gloucestriae* 3 vols., Rolls Series no. 33, London 1863–67.

KCD ... J. M. Kemble *Codex Diplomaticus Aevi Saxonici* 6 vols., London 1839–48.

Ker ... N. R. Ker *Hemming's Cartulary: A Description of Two Worcester Cartularies in Cotton Tiberius A xiii*, in R. W. Hunt, W. A. Pantin and R. W. Southern (eds.) *Studies in Medieval History presented to Frederick Maurice Powicke* pp. 49–75, Oxford 1948.

Leland ... John Leland (ed. L. Toulmin Smith) *Itinerary* 5 vols., London 1906–10.

Lloyd ... J. E. Lloyd *A History of Wales* 2 vols., 2nd edition, London 1912.

Maitland DBB ... F. W. Maitland *Domesday Book and Beyond*, Cambridge 1897.

ML ... Medieval Latin

Mod.E ... Modern English.

Mod.Fr ... Modern French.

Mod.G ... Modern German.

Mon. Ang. ... W. Dugdale *Monasticon Anglicanum* (eds. J. Caley, H. Ellis and B. Bandinel), 6 vols. in 8, London 1817–1830.

MS ... Manuscript.

MW ... Middle Welsh.

Nelson ... L. H. Nelson *The Normans in South Wales 1070–1171*, Austin and London 1966.

OE ... Old English.

OEB ... G. Tengvik *Old English Bynames*, Uppsala 1938 (Nomina Germanica 4).

OED ... Oxford English Dictionary.

OFr ... Old French.

OG ... Old German.

Orderic Vitalis ... A. Le Prévost (ed.) *Historia Ecclesiastica* 5 vols., Paris 1838–1855.

OW ... Old Welsh.

OWScand ... Old West Scandinavian.

Place-Name Elements ... A. H. Smith *English Place-Name Elements* parts 1 and 11 (EPNS vols. 25–26), Cambridge 1956.

PNDB ... O. von Feilitzen *Pre-Conquest Personal Names of Domesday Book*, Uppsala 1937 (Nomina Germanica 3).

Reaney ... P. H. Reaney *Dictionary of British Surnames* 2nd edition, London 1976.

RBW ... M. Hollings (ed.) *The Red Book of Worcester*, Worcestershire Historical Society 4 vols. 1934–1950.

Regesta ... H. W. C. Davis, C. Johnson and H. A. Cronne (eds.) *Regesta Regum Anglo-Normannorum*, vol. i Oxford 1913; vol. ii Oxford 1956.

RMLWL ... R. E. Latham *Revised Medieval Latin Wordlist*, London 1965.

Round FE ... J. H. Round *Feudal England*, London 1909.

Sanders ... I. J. Sanders *English Baronies: a study of their origin and descent 1066–1327*, Oxford 1960.

Sawyer ... P. H. Sawyer *Anglo-Saxon Charters: An Annotated List and Bibliography*, Royal Historical Society 1968.

Taylor ... C. S. Taylor *Analysis of the Domesday Survey of Gloucestershire*, Bristol 1889.

TBGAS ... Transactions of the Bristol and Gloucester Archaeological Society.

TRHS ... Transactions of the Royal Historical Society.

VCH ... The Victoria History of the Counties of England. References are to the Gloucestershire volumes, unless otherwise stated. Glos. vol. vii appeared too late to be considered in the preparation of this edition.

Vinogradoff ... P. Vinogradoff *English Society in the Eleventh Century*, Oxford 1908.

Wightman ... W. E. Wightman *The Lacy Family in England and Normandy 1066–1194*, Oxford 1966.

WoA-E ... See Appendix.

NOTES

This volume has been sub-edited by Caroline Thorn and supplementary notes provided by Caroline and Frank Thorn, and John McNeal Dodgson. John Moore hopes to provide more detailed commentaries on the identification and location of DB manors in a separate publication.

The manuscript is written on leaves, or folios, of parchment (sheepskin), measuring about 15 by 11 inches (38 by 28 cms.), on both sides. On each side, or page, are two columns, making four to each folio. The folios were numbered in the 17th century, and the four columns of each are here lettered a, b, c, d. The manuscript emphasises words and usually distinguishes chapters and sections by the use of red ink. Underlining in the MS indicates deletion.

A study of the MS shows that Gloucestershire is a badly executed county; it would seem that not all the information was available when the scribe began writing up the returns and he encountered difficulties when planning how much space a chapter would occupy and how many entries could be fitted on to a folio. There are numerous gaps (some large as after Ch. 26, col. 166d), misplaced entries, continuation and addition of information in the margins and much compression. There are a number of marginal figures or marks (f, ii, n, ·7 etc.) from cols. 166c,d to 170a,b inclusive; these were written later than DB (though probably not much later, being in a very similar ink) perhaps by some Exchequer clerk as part of a check. They almost all occur beside the first entry in the chapters; Farley omits them. Similar marginal marks occur in some other DB counties, e.g. Northants., Hants., Cambs., Warwicks., and Yorks., possibly by the same scribe, though probably not as part of the same check.

These notes follow the correct order of the text, ignoring displacements; thus the notes for Chs. 25 and 26 follow those for Ch. 24 rather than those for Ch. 29.

References to other DB counties are to the Chapters and Sections of the volume in the present series.

GLOUCESTERSHIRE. *Glowecestscire* is written in red capitals above cols. 162a,b; *Glowecscire* above cols. 162c,d to 169c,d inclusive and cols. 170c,d; *Glowegestscire* above cols. 170a,b. *Glowecscire* is the form used at the head of the List of Landholders on 162c.

G 1-4   FOR THESE SECTIONS see EvK 1 in the Appendix for a more detailed survey of Gloucester, updated to c.1100.

G 1   FACE VALUE. The opposite of payment by weight or in blanched or assayed money. See notes to 1,14 and 1,56 below.

SESTERS. The sester is a measure, sometimes of liquid, as here, sometimes dry, as in 1,48; of uncertain and probably variable size (see next note), reckoned at 32 oz. for honey.

BOROUGH'S MEASURE. A local measure; cf. 'King's measure' for sesters of honey in 19,2, and DB Warwicks. B 5 col. 238a.

36 DICKERS OF IRON. *Dicras ferri*; in the MS *dicras* has probably been altered from *dacras*, the first part of the *a* having been scratched out; *dacra vel dacrum* is the form given in Ducange. A dicker is a measure by ten or multiples of it, a customary unit of exchange. See *Fleta* Bk. II Ch. 12 referring to dickers of skins, pairs of gloves and horseshoes (a dicker of the last mentioned being 20 shoes). Three hundred and sixty lumps of iron could be the meaning here, or *ferri* could be short for *ferri equorum* 'horseshoes', the amount of them being sufficient for 180 horses. Cf. 20 horseshoes (*ferra*) as a render in 78,14, and 120 horseshoes (*ferra*) under the customary dues of the City of Hereford (DB Herefords. C 8 col. 179a). The iron was probably mined in the Forest of Dean.

DRAWN IRON RODS. *uirgas ferreas ductiles*; molten iron was drawn out into rods which were cut and hammered to produce nails.

HALL. *Aula*; the house in which the owner or lord of an estate lived. This royal hall is also mentioned in DB Worcs. 1,7 (= E 18 below).

ORA. An *ora* was literally an ounce; a unit of currency still in use in Scandinavia. It was reckoned at either 16d or 20d. 16d was the normal rate. The 20d rate was primarily a unit of account, found on estates in the King's hands, and was payment 'at face value'. For every 16d due in revenue, 20d was collected, the result being equivalent to a payment in 'blanched' or assayed money (see 1,58). See S. Harvey *Royal Revenue and Domesday Terminology* in EcHR (2nd series) xx (1967) pp. 221–228. On blanching, see 1,56 note below.

THE KING HAS ... MINT. In the MS *ū* (*vero*, not usually translated in this series, but see E 22 note below) is interlined above and between *moneta* and *ħt*.

3 BISHOP OSBERN. Of Exeter; see Ch. 5 note below.

4 GEOFFREY DE MANDEVILLE. Perhaps Mandeville in the département of Eure, France; see OEB p. 96. He was lord of Pleshey and ancestor of the Earls of Essex.

PAID 6s 8d. DB uses the old English currency system which lasted for a thousand years until 1971. The pound contained 20 shillings, each of 12 pence, abbreviated as £(ibrae), s(olidi) and d(enarii). DB often expresses sums above a shilling in pence (as 30d here) and above a pound in shillings (e.g. 40s in S 1).

WILLIAM (SON OF) BADERON. As Ch. 32; *filius* ('son') was no doubt omitted in error (as also in DB Herefords. 1,8), such details often being later interlineations.

WILLIAM THE SCRIBE. *Scriba*. Probably the same man as the William *scriptor* who, with Humphrey and Osbern, was given half of Monmouth Castle by Earl William; *Book of Llan Dâv* pp. 277–278 (see E 35 note below).

DURAND THE SHERIFF. Sheriff of Gloucestershire in 1086; see Ch. 53 note below.

ROBERT HIS OFFICER. Probably the same man as Robert the Bursar; Taylor p. 127. On the duties of *ministri regis* see W. A. Morris, *The Office of Sheriff in the Early Norman Period* pp. 157–8 in EHR xxxiii (1918).

ON THE DAY HE WAS ALIVE AND DEAD. January 5th 1066. This is the only occurrence in DB Glos. of this phrase; it is a standard formula in Exon. Domesday, usually translated 'in 1066', corresponding to the Exchequer DB's *Tempore Regis Edwardi* 'before 1066'.

EARL WILLIAM. William son of Osbern (William Fitz Osbern), brother of Bishop Osbern of Exeter, palatine earl of Hereford from 1067 to his death in battle abroad in 1071. He was most probably also palatine earl of Glos. and perhaps wielded extra powers in Worcs.; see W. E. Wightman *The Palatine Earldom of William Fitz Osbern in Gloucestershire and Worcestershire (1066-1071)* in EHR lxxvii (1962). He was responsible, with Walter of Lacy and others, for defending the border against the South Welsh and was joint 'regent' with Odo, Bishop of Bayeux, during King William's absence in 1067. He was married to Adeline, sister of Ralph of Tosny (see Ch. 45). See DB Herefordshire Introductory note 2 for further details of Earl William.

THE CASTLE. Gloucester Castle; the site is now built over, but Castle Meads (GR SO 825185) preserves the name.

S 1 CASTLE OF CHEPSTOW. GR ST 533940. Chepstow, from OE *ćeap-stow*, 'market place', replaced Strigoil as the name of the town in the early 14th century (Charles p. 243; DEPN s.n. Chepstow). Strigoil, probably from Welsh *istrad-gwy*, 'valley of the Wye', continued as the name of the lordship and manor (see W 16) into the early modern period.

SHIPS GOING INTO THE WOODLAND. Into the steeply wooded valley of the Wye past the Castle.

EARL ROGER. Also called Roger of Breteuil; son of William son of Osbern, and Earl of Hereford from 1071. In 1075 he conspired with his brother-in-law Ralph, Earl of Norfolk, against the King, was imprisoned and his lands forfeited in 1076.

RALPH OF LIMESY. Limésy in the département of Seine-Maritime, France.

S 2 THE PAYMENTS OF CAERLEON. Cf. 'the castlery of Caerleon' in DB Herefords. 14,1 (= E 36 below). It was the later demesne of Caerleon in Caerleon and the land at Pwllpan in Christchurch later granted to Llantarnam Abbey.

7 FISHERIES IN THE WYE AND THE USK. They can be identified from later records: 5 were in the Usk, 2 in the Wye.

W 1 DAIRY FARMS. DB *Harduices* from OE *heord(e)wic* = 'herdsman's farm'. It is glossed 'sheep farm' in DEPN s.n. Hardwick, although *wic* in English place-names often indicates a dairy farm (DEPN s.v. *wic*).

LLANVAIR (DISCOED). *Lamecare* is almost certainly Llanvair Discoed; all three properties were later part of Strigoil lordship.

HALF-VILLAGERS. *Villani dimidii*. 38 half-villagers occur in 4 manors in DB Glos. (here, W 15, 41,5 and 67,4). They were probably men who held half the normal holding of the average villager in the locality (cf. 67,1 note). However, it is possible that their land and services were divided between two lords. In DB Shrops. 2,2 half-villagers are contrasted with 'whole' villagers: *iiii uill'i integri ⁊ vi dimidii*.

ROGER OF IVRY. Styled *pincerna* 'Butler' by 1068 (*Regesta* i no. 23); by 1069 (*Regesta* i p. xxvii). He may also have been Sheriff of Gloucestershire some time after 1066; Taylor p. 130. See Ch. 41 note below.

W 2   UNDER ... REEVE ... VILLAGES. According to DGM p. 54 this was the old Welsh land system, whereby land was divided on the basis of villages; each group is here recorded under its reeve. The four groups of villages under four Welsh reeves were the four commotes of Brynbuga (*alias* Usk, including the later separate lordship of Trelleck), Edlogan (including the later separate lordship of Tregrug), Is Coed (*alias* Caldicot) and Libennith, together constituting the Welsh cantref of Gwent Is Coed and the Norman lordship of Netherwent. Brynbuga commote comprised the later parishes of Cwmcarvan, Kemeys Commander, Kilgwrrwg, Llanbadoc, Llandenny, Llandogo, Llangeview, Llangovan, Llangwm, Llanishen, Llanlowell (*alias* Llanllywel), Llansoy, Llantrisant, Llanvihangel Pontymoel, Llanvihangel Tormynydd, Mitchel Troy, Penallt, Pen-y-clawdd, Raglan, Trelleck, Trostrey, Usk and Wolvesnewton. Edlogan commote comprised the later parishes of Llanddewi Fach, Llanfrechfa, Llangattock (including Caerleon), Llangybi, Llanhennock, Llantarnam, Panteg and Tredunnock. Is Coed commote comprised the later parishes of Caerwent, Caldicot, Chepstow, Dinham, Itton, Llanmartin, Llanvair Discoed, Mathern, Penhow, Penterry, Portskewett, St. Arvans, St. Brides Netherwent, Shirenewton and Tintern. Libennith commote comprised the later parishes of Bishton, Christchurch, Goldcliff, Ifton, Kemeys Inferior, Langstone, Llandevenny, Llanfihangel Rogiet, Llanwern, Magor, Nash, Redwick, Rogiet, Undy, Whitson and Wilcrick. In all, the four commotes contained 62 parishes (M. Richards *Welsh Administrative and Territorial Units, Medieval and Modern* (Cardiff, 1969), pp. 63, 95, 144, 216, 218, 229, 277, 297), equivalent to the 54 inhabited villages of W 2 and the 7 Welsh villages of W 19. Three out of the four reeves — Elmwy, Iudhael and Waswic — appear as witnesses to a charter of 1071–5 (*Book of Llan Dâv* p. 274), Elmwy and Iudhael to a charter of Caradoc ap Gruffyd (*ibid.* p. 273) and Iudhael alone appears in a charter of Gruffyd ap Llywelyn (d.1063) (*ibid.* p. 270); hence at least one of these three had been in office before the Norman Conquest.

KING CARADOC. Caradoc ap Gryffydd of Glamorgan and Wentloog (Gwynllwg), d.1081, who in 1065 led an expedition into Gwent and destroyed a royal hunting-lodge being built by Earl Harold at Portskewett (ASC MSS. C,D,*s.a.* 1065). The villages were perhaps destroyed at the same time, Freeman ii pp. 485–6, but see Ellis i p. 321.

41 COWS. *Uaccās*; the scribe appears to have been unsure whether to use the singular (*uaccā = uaccam*) or the plural (*uaccas*); the line over the *a* may have been written later. For the use of the singular with *xxi, xxxi* etc., see 1,7 note below.

W 3   WALTER THE GUNNER. See Ch. 58 note below.

PAYS ... FOR ONE WASTE LAND. An example of waste land having a value, albeit small; cf. DB Herefords. 6,1 note.

ONE WASTE LAND. Whitson, held with Langstone (see W 9 note) by the Blewitts who had succeeded Walter the Gunner at Ruddle (58, 2–3) by 1096.

W 4   ABRAHAM THE PRIEST. Archdeacon of Gwent (Lloyd ii p. 367); his two villages were probably Llanddewi Fach and Llandogo, later held by the Bishop and chapter of Llandaff.

KING GRUFFYDD. The two possible identifications are (1) Gruffydd ap Maredudd, son of the ruler of Deheubarth who died in 1071. His father's Welsh lands were held first by Rhys ab Owain (until 1078), then passed to Rhys ap Tewdwr. Gruffydd succeeded, however, to his father's English estates, appearing as a landholder in DB Herefords. (29,1. 31,1–7. He may be the same as the Gruffydd found there in 10,50 and the Gruffydd *puer* 'Boy' in 1,34–35). He was killed in 1091 trying to secure his father's throne. Nelson strongly supports the first identification. That this is the Gruffydd intended is given some support by the fact that in Herefordshire the Braose family succeeded to Gruffydd's lands, hence Gruffydd's villages, apart from those held by Abraham the priest, probably comprised the commote of Teirtref (the later lordship of Three Castles), confirmed to William de Braose in 1205. All the other Braose lordships in Wales originated in conquests from the Welsh after 1086, but Teirtref was certainly in Norman hands by 1074, when Llangua Priory was founded. The commote of Teirtref contained four later parishes: Grosmont, Llangua, Llantilio Crossenny and Skenfrith. On the other hand, there is no evidence that Gruffydd was ever a king, whereas DB clearly styles this man *Grifin regis*. Moreover, the arrangement is attributed to Earl William, but Gruffydd could not have succeeded to his father's lands before 1071, by which date Earl William was already abroad fighting (see G 4 note). (2) Gruffydd ap Llywelyn, King of Gwynedd and Powys, then of Deheubarth and much of south Wales. He seems to have come to terms with the Norman conquerors about 1058 (see DB Herefords. Introductory note 2) and the customary dues here mentioned may have been part of the arrangements. Although he died in 1063 it is not impossible that this payment, now in other hands, continued to be known as 'King Gruffydd's customary dues'. Lloyd ii p. 367 appears to support this identification.

W 5   1 VILLAGE. Taylor pp. 102, 214, 216, identified this place as Llanmartin, 'St. Martin's church', and though most of this parish was later recorded as a lay holding of Strigoil lordship (W 16), part was included in the neighbouring episcopal manor of Bishton.
ALE. Cf. DB Cheshire FT 3,7, col. 269b, and also DB Cornwall 2,12 where barrels of ale are mentioned as a payment.

W 6   CARUCATE. *Carucata* here and below is probably not the carucate of the former Danish areas which is the same as the hide (see 1,1 note below), but the equivalent of 'land for *x* ploughs' (see DB Dorset 2,1 note). On many occasions in the south-west counties the term *carucatae terrae* in the Exon. Domesday corresponds to *terra est ... car* in the Exchequer DB (see DB Somerset 1,8 note). This area of Wales was a new acquisition of the Normans and had not yet been assessed in hides, hence the unusual measure. In DB Herefords. there is a distinction between the newly conquered lands assessed still in carucates, and the older acquisitions measured in hides.
1 CARUCATE ... 1 CARUCATE. Taylor pp. 102, 214, 216, identified these places as Llanfihangel Rogiet, 'St. Michael's church', and Llandevaud. Since the latter name means 'St. Tavauc's church', not 'St. David's church', this identification must be changed to Dewstow, 'St. Dewy's holy place' (Charles p. 242), which remained an episcopal manor until 1650. The former place must be Llanfihangel Rogiet, the only place in Lower Gwent with a church dedicated to St. Michael, though this was later part of the manor of Caldicot (W 15) and did not remain in ecclesiastical possession.
SAINTS. That is, the churches of St. Michael and St. Dewy.

W 7   ½ CARUCATE. This probably represents Maesgwenith, which was later absorbed into the main manor of Caerwent (W 12).

W 7-8   THERE IS A GAP of about a line between these two sections. There are similar gaps in the first pages of several counties and it would seem that information was added here as it came to hand.

W 8   FROM PASTURAGE COME 66 PIGS. This is a due for the right of pasturing; sometimes paid in kind, sometimes commuted to money. Both methods of payment seem to be mentioned here. *Exire* is here used in the sense of its derivative noun *exitus* 'payment', 'revenue'; cf. 1,12.
ALL THESE PAY ... £55. The total payments, past and present, presumably refer to W 1-8 inclusive. The sum of itemized payments is £16 14s 4d, together with 1 pig and 1 sester of honey not otherwise valued, if Roger of Ivry's valuation in W 1 is accepted. Perhaps £40 (*xl lib'*) and £55 (*lv lib'*) both result from earlier miscopying of £15 (*xv lib'*); otherwise the high totals must include the lands in W 4-7 later exempted from payment.

W 9   2 CARUCATES. This holding can be identified as Langstone, the main Welsh manor of the Blewitts who had succeeded Walter the Gunner by 1096 (see W 3 note).
SLAVES. The percentage of slaves to other categories of population is higher in Glos. than in any other single DB county, though Cornwall comes a close second.
VALUE. *Valet* (*valebat, valuit*, past tenses) normally means the sums due to lords from their lands (e.g. see DB Herefords. 24,13). *reddit, reddidit*, has a similar meaning and the two verbs are often interchangeable (see the introduction to the Exon. Notes on p. 310 of the Somerset edition).

W 10   GERARD. Perhaps Gerard the Chamberlain, as elsewhere in DB; if so, the land was at Nash and Magor, parts of which were later held by the Chamberlain family.

W 11   OWS THE KING'S REEVE. Perhaps the previous Welsh ruler of Gwent, Owen *Wan* ('the Weak'), who was conquered by Earl William. His land was probably Porton, 'the portreeve's farm' (Charles p. 256) which later was absorbed into the manor of Redwick.
DAGOBERT'S LAND may well be the rest of Redwick manor.

W 12   THIS MANOR later absorbed Maesgwenith (W 7).

W 13   5 CARUCATES. Quite possibly the manors of Bishton and Mathern, episcopal properties both before and after 1086.

W 14   2 CARUCATES. Rogerstone, 'Roger's farm', in St. Arvans (Charles p. 255). Roger's son, Roger (II) of Berkeley, founded Kingswood Abbey, a daughter house of Tintern Abbey, to which Rogerstone belonged.
CHEPSTOW. See S 1 note below.

W 15   CALDICOT included Shirenewton, 'the Sheriff's new farm' (Charles p. 255), named after Durand the Sheriff.
THEY ALL HAVE 12 PLOUGHS. That is, 12 ploughs between them, not 12 ploughs each. Cf. the common DB phrase *inter omnes* (7,2. 12,5 etc.).

W 16 WILLIAM OF EU. He was the current holder of the Holding of Chepstow, which had been held previously by Ralph of Limesy from Earl William and his son Roger (cf. S 1 and later in this entry); Complete Peerage v p. 153 note e.

50 CARUCATES ... 32 CARUCATES. The difference between the 50 carucates transferred to Ralph of Limesy and the 32 carucates held by William of Eu may be accounted for by the 17 carucates 'between the Usk and the Wye' held in 1086 by Thurstan son of Rolf (see W 18 note). William of Eu's land in lordship probably comprised the later demesnes of Strigoil manor at Hardwick (in Chepstow), Llandogo, Llanvaches, Mounton, Penterry and Porthcasseg (in St. Arvans), whilst the 2 mills were probably at Pwllmeyric (in Mathern), and the lands of his men were at Crick, Itton, Llanvaches, Moynes Court (in Mathern), St. Arvans, St. Wormets (? in Howick) and Sudbrook (in Portskewett).

AS IS DONE IN NORMANDY. Whatever the origin of the carucate (see Ellis i p. 150), the Latin *sicut fit in Normannia* cannot explain *carucatas* (i.e. 'carucates measured as in Normandy'), but must refer to the manner of the grant, either that grants of this size were common in Normandy or that one baron could grant to another there. See note above and G 4 note on Earl William's powers. [Mr. Moore noted also the possibility that MS *fit* may be a mistake for *sīt* = *sint*, whence "such as they (the carucates) are in Normandy". Gen. Ed.]

OTHERS WHO TRANSFERRED (THE LAND). *alii liberatores*; *liberator* from Latin *libero* (Mod.Fr *livrer*) in the sense of 'hand over', 'transfer', 'deliver'. The men will have given Ralph formal seizin of the land. Cf. DB Hunts. D1; 25 (cols. 208a,b).

W 17 CHEPSTOW. See S 1 note above.

LAND. Wallstone, 'Walter's farm', in Mathern and St. Pierre (Charles p. 250), named after Roger of Lacy's father Walter, d.1085.

W 18 17 PLOUGHS. *carucas*; undoubtedly a mistake for *carucatas* 'carucates'; the scribe may have wrongly extended *caṝ* in the original return, which would also explain the omission of *terrae* 'of land', which usually succeeds *carucatae* (as in W 16 etc.). It is unusual for the men's ploughs to be stated here, rather than in the second paragraph after the number of 'villagers' has been given (as, e.g. in 1,9). See EvK 400 where Thurstan has '11½ carucates between the Usk and the Wye' (i.e. 17 carucates less the 5½ claimed and presumably acquired by the King's reeves). It is probable that one of the figures for carucates in W 16; 18 is wrong; e.g. the initial assessment of Thurstan's lands at 17 carucates could be corrected to 18 carucates since this is the exact amount by which Ralph of Limesy's original holding of 1066–1070 had been reduced to the 32 carucates held by William of Eu in 1086 (W 16). A further adjustment would then be needed in the figures for the lordship or men's carucates. A simpler correction is to amend the assessment of William of Eu's holding to 33 carucates.

4½ ARE IN LORDSHIP. Probably Magor, the second most valuable of the Marshal family Welsh manors in the mid-13th century, and part of the adjacent manors of Rogiet and Undy. HIS MEN'S LANDS certainly included Castell Coch (in Magor), Ifton, Kemeys Inferior, Llandevenny, Milton (in Christchurch), part of Rogiet, Salisbury (in Magor), St. Brides Netherwent, part of Undy, and Wilcrick, probably also Hendrew (in Kemeys Inferior), Llanmartin, Llanwern and Penhow.

THURSTAN ... 6 CARUCATES ... BEYOND THE USK. These, together with his '8 carucates of land in the castlery of Caerleon' (E 36), comprised Llangattock, Llanhennock, Llantarnam, Malpas and Tredunnock.

4 PLOUGHS. *caṝ*; perhaps 'carucates'.

W 19 ALFRED OF 'SPAIN'. *Hispan(iensis)* here; the byname also occurs as *de (H)ispania* elsewhere in DB. Épaignes in the département of Eure, France; OEB pp. 92, 134. The Latin *Hispaniensis* is a kind of word-play. He held land also in Dorset, Devon, Somerset, Wiltshire and Herefordshire.

2 CARUCATES. Probably at Goldcliff and Nash.

7 VILLAGES. In addition to Goldcliff and Nash; they included Christchurch and its hamlets of Coldra, Liswerry, Pwllpan and Traston, most of which were granted by Alfred's daughter Isabel and her husband Robert de Chandos to their new foundation of Goldcliff Priory.

THESE PAY. In the MS *Hę* is correctly reproduced by Farley as *Hae*; the diphthong mark under the *e* is not visible in the facsimile, however.

B 1 BOROUGH OF WINCHCOMBE. There is an updated and considerably fuller survey of Winchcombe Borough in EvK 116, in the Appendix.

EARL HAROLD. Son of Earl Godwin and brother of Queen Edith; King of England Jan. 6th–Oct. 14th 1066; William the Conqueror did not recognise his title to the crown, hence the use in DB of 'Earl' instead of 'King'. He was Earl of East Anglia (1045), received half of Swein's earldom (1046), was Earl of the West Saxons on his father's death in 1053 and Earl of Hereford (1058).

EARL HAROLD HAD THE THIRD PENNY. A third of the Borough's total revenues, the remaining two-thirds going to the King. See DB Staffs. B 12 (col. 246a) and Cheshire C 2;22 (cols. 262c,d) for examples of this division of a Borough's revenues between the King and the Earl. The third penny sometimes went to the Sheriff instead of to the Earl (e.g. in Shrops. C 12 col. 252a and Devon B 1 col. 100a) and sometimes to an Abbey (Wilts. 9,1). This third penny of the Borough is not to be confused with the third penny of the pleas of a county (as in DB Warwicks. 1,6 and note) or of a Hundred (see Herefords. 19,2 and note). See J. H. Round *Geoffrey de Mandeville* pp. 287–296 and in EHR xxxiv (1919) pp. 62–64.
HUNDRED OF THIS TOWN. The reference to this is early and important. The Hundred may well have been co-extensive with the county of Winchcombe, mentioned in Hemming (folio 130r (= new 131r), Hearne p. 280); see Taylor pp. 43–45 and 12,10 below.
THE THREE ADJOINING HUNDREDS. Chelthorn, Kiftsgate and Witley, possibly fragments of a larger pre-Conquest unit, which by the 13th century had been reunited in one large Hundred of Kiftsgate.

L   NOTES concerning major landholders are to be found at the head of their individual chapters. Notes referring to other individuals are under their first occurrence in the text.

L 49 RICHARD THE COMMISSIONER. *Legatus*; see 1,63 *legatis regis* 'to the King's Commissioners', that is of the DB survey. Richard's name is not given in the list of DB Commissioners in Worcs. F (Hemming; see DB Worcs. App. V), though this may only be because, if he was a Commissioner, it was of a different area.

CH. 1 LAND OF THE KING. The rubricator has omitted the *1* beside the chapter heading; in a great many counties in DB the initial chapter numbers are omitted, probably in error.
1,1 THE INSERTION of the hundredal rubric is justified by the mention of the Hundred, which was attached to the Cheltenham manor, in other entries.
THE TOTAL ASSESSMENT of Cheltenham was 10 hides (8½ + 1½). Reinbald's 1½ hides were the glebe land of St. Mary's, the original parish church of Cheltenham. Reinbald was Reinbald the priest whose lands, including the Cheltenham glebe, were granted to Cirencester Abbey in 1133; See Ch. 26 note.
8½ HIDES. The hide is a unit of land measurement, either of productivity, of extent or of tax liability, and contained 4 virgates. Administrators attempted to standardize the hide at 120 acres, but incomplete revision and special local reductions left hides of widely differing extents in different areas. See Dr. J. Morris in DB Sussex Appendix. See also 6,3 and note.
REINBALD HOLDS THEM. The 1½ hides; Latin uses the singular (*eam*) with 1½.
16s FOR BREAD. For the dogs; an example of a food rent being commuted by 1086. A clear example of commutation is to be found in DB Herefords. 1,49: '(the men) ... give ... 20s for the sheep which they used to give'.
1,1-2 THERE IS A GAP of about 2 lines between these entries; see W 7–8 note above.
1,2 THE INSERTION of the hundredal rubric is justified by the location of '(Abbots) Barton' and 'Morwents (End)' within this Hundred in 10,1.
'(KINGS) BARTON'. See EPNS ii p. 136.
2 FREE MEN HOLD 2 HIDES. These can be identified from later evidence as 2 carucates forming the lordship of Matson.
THEY CANNOT SEPARATE ... MANOR. See 1,16 note below.
ARCHBISHOP ALDRED. Bishop of Worcester 1047–62. He held that See with Hereford 1056–1060 and with the Archbishopric of York from 1061–1062. He held York alone from 1062 until his death in 1069. He crowned William the Conqueror and Queen Matilda.
BRAWN. In Sandhurst; it is partly duplicated by another entry (64,1).
ALWIN THE SHERIFF. *Aluui* here and in 1,13; *Aluuinus* in 34,8;12. The oblique inflexions indicate *Alwin*. The nominative form *Aluui* must therefore be regarded as misinterpretation or miscopying of an abbreviation (from which a nunnation mark has been omitted) e.g. *Aluuĩ, Aluui, Alwin*'. See DB Somerset Exon. Notes 35,24 on Alfwy/Alwin son of Banna, for a similar case.
UPTON (ST. LEONARDS). Humphrey's hide here was represented in the early 13th century by a carucate held in sergeantry by the Grave family, after whom it was later named 'Grove Court'; see EPNS ii p. 171. Humphrey was probably Humphrey of Maidenhill; cf. 70,1.
MURRELLS (END) in Hartpury was known down to the 18th century as Morwents Place.
NIGEL THE DOCTOR. One of King William's doctors, and possibly also doctor to Earl Roger of Shrewsbury (Mon. Ang. vi p. 750), but see VCH Shrops. i p. 290.
1,3 THE ROYAL MANOR OF HARESFIELD formed the later tithing of Harescombe, the eastern part of Haresfield parish; VCH x p. 190.

THIS LAND ANSWERED FOR 2 HIDES. *Se defendebat pro* is a common phrase in other DB counties (e.g. Sussex, Bucks., Beds., Herts.), meaning the same as *geldebat pro* 'it paid tax for'. It also occurs in Glos. in 11,13.

MEADOW SUFFICIENT FOR THE PLOUGHS. Sufficient meadow for the grazing of the oxen in the plough-teams (see 'meadow for the oxen' in DB Worcs. 2,16, and Herefords. 7,3 note). Normally there were 8 oxen to a plough-team, but see notes to DB Wilts. 28,10 and Herefords. 1,50. In several DB counties (e.g. Bucks., Beds., Middx.) meadow was frequently measured in terms of the plough-teams it would support.

1,4 MEADOWS FOR THE PLOUGHS. See 1,3 note.

1,6 ½ HIDE ... EXEMPT. *Quietam*, commonly in DB meaning 'immune from dues or service' (see Herefords. 1,44), 'free from tax' (see 1,24 and 11,4). See DB Worcs. 2,74 note for a slightly different meaning.

COOK OF HIS. Earl William's cook is named as Avenel the cook in a confirmation charter of 1171; D. Walker 'Charters of the Earldom of Hereford 1095–1201' in Camden Soc. 4th ser. vol. i (1964) p. 54. His property was in Quedgeley, probably Netheridge which his descendants held until the 13th century, and which, unlike the rest of Quedgeley, remained in Dudstone Hundred; VCH x pp. 119, 216, 218–9.

1,7 5 HIDES. These formed the main manor of Cirencester, centred on Barton Farm, and are located in Cirencester itself in EvK 8.

31 VILLAGERS. *xxxi vill(an)um*. The singular occurs regularly in DB with 21, 31 etc.; but see 1,24 and 4,1 and the note to W 2 ('41 cows') above.

THE QUEEN HAD THE SHEEP'S WOOL. Cf. DB Surrey 1,8 (Kingston), where Humphrey the Chamberlain had a villager who was in charge of collecting the Queen's wool. According to Taylor (pp. 69–70) this was a payment similar to the mark of gold the Queen was entitled to receive from royal manors worth more than £100 a year.

1,8 2 HIDES. Identifiable from later evidence as Perry Moor; not Wiggold (Taylor p. 163), which was divided between the neighbouring manors of Siddington St. Mary (66,5) and Stratton (39,17).

1,9 36 HIDES. These were probably divided as follows: Bitton 16 hides, Wapley 8 hides, Winterbourne 12 hides. The Wapley member was centred on Codrington Court in Wapley and Codrington, and absorbed another hide at Codrington (43,1) in 1230.

ONE NIGHT'S REVENUE. Many royal manors, especially in the south-west, had to pay this revenue which took the place of the normal tax payment. Originally this meant the amount of food needed to support the King and his household for one night, though by the 11th century these food rents were generally commuted. £80 is a probable figure before 1066, and £100 a night's revenue; see R. L. Poole *The Exchequer in the Twelfth Century* p. 29. From this entry and 1,11;13 it would seem that, as in Dorset, these rents were not commuted in the case of Gloucestershire (but see last note under 1,21). Sometimes a manor combined with one or more others to provide this rent, as would seem to be the case in 1,13. Latin *firma* here = OE *feorm* 'a food rent'; see OED *farm* s.b.i.

1,10 (LOWER) SLAUGHTER. Identified as such in VCH vi pp. 45, 129, 145–6.

1 MARK OF SILVER. 13s 4d.

5s FOR DOGS. Probably instead of loaves of bread for the dogs (as 1,7 etc.; see 1,1 note).

SHERIFF PAID ... WISHED. Or possibly, reading *uicecom* as abbreviating the dative *uicecomiti* and the verbs as plural, 'they paid the Sheriff what they wished from this manor'. An almost identical phrase, equally ambiguous, occurs in 1,53.

1,11 THE INSERTION of the hundredal rubric is justified by the mention of the Hundred, which was attached to Westbury manor, in other entries. In 1086 Clifton on Teme, Edvin Loach and Kyre Parva and Kyre Wyard were in Worcestershire; Kingstone in Weston under Penyard was in Herefordshire.

6 HIDES IN KYRE. These were held by the Bishop of Hereford (2 hides in DB Worcs. 3,2) and Osbern son of Richard (4 hides in Worcs. 19,4;7).

IN CLIFTON (ON TEME) 10 HIDES. Osbern son of Richard held 3 hides in Clifton on Teme, 1½ hides in Stanford on Teme, 1 hide in Shelsley, 1 hide in Homme Castle and 3 hides in Lower Sapey, recorded in DB Worcs. 19,3;5–6;8–9 respectively. The remaining ½ hide of the 10 was held by the Abbey of Cormeilles at Tenbury Wells (DB Worcs. 6,1).

IN NEWENT AND KINGSTONE 8 HIDES. The Abbey of Cormeilles' 6 hides at Newent are recorded in detail in 16,1, and its 2 hides at Kingstone in DB Herefords. 3,1.

IN EDVIN (LOACH) 1 HIDE. *ladeuent*; the MS has initial *1*; Farley misprints *L*. EvK 10 also has *1*. Osbern son of Richard's hide here is recorded in DB Worcs. 19,11.

ABBOT OF CORMEILLES. Or 'Abbey', as *abb'* can abbreviate both *abbas* 'Abbot' and *abbatia* 'Abbey' (as well as, occasionally, *abbatissa* 'Abbess'). The same form *abb'* occurs in EvK 10.

OSBERN AND WILLIAM SONS OF RICHARD. Or perhaps, taking *f* as abbreviating singular *filius*, 'Osbern, and William son of Richard', although Osbern was also the son of Richard Scrope (see 48,3 note). EvK 10 also has the abbreviation *f*? Cf. EvQ 29 and note. William son of Richard is not recorded in the Herefordshire or Worcestershire sections of DB as holding any of these lands taken from Westbury on Severn manor.

FIR-WOOD. *Sapina* is usually translated, as here, 'fir-wood'; it may well, however, refer in this context to the whole Forest of Dean which is also mentioned in a pre-Domesday context in 37,3. However, *sapina* may result from an earlier mistranscription of *Sapian* (Lower Sapey, Worcs.); see BCS 240 and EPNS (Worcs.) p. 75.

1,12 (UPPER) CLOPTON. As Finberg and Smith have pointed out, this holding is not Longborough (GS p. 49; EPNS i pp. 250-1,254-5).

THERE WERE 8 HIDES IN EACH. *Uterque* can mean 'each' or 'both', either translation being as unclear as the Latin, which appears to mean that together the two places total 8 hides. Cf. EvK 17: '*Landeb(er)ge* (Upper Clopton) with *Mene* (Meon), 8 hides'.

WHAT CAME FROM THIS MANOR. That is, in revenue; see first note under W 8 above.

TWO HUNDREDS. Chelthorn and Witley; see note to B 1.

1,13 SALT-HOUSE. *Salina* comprehends all kinds of salt workings from coastal pans to the boilers of Worcestershire and Cheshire, with their associated sheds and buildings. 'Salt-house' is the most comprehensive term. See DB Worcs. 1,3a note on salt extraction.

PACKLOADS OF SALT. *Summis salis*. The size of the packload is unknown, but in the case of salt in Cheshire (S 1,4 col. 268b) it contained 15 *bulliones* 'boilings'. It is used of corn several times in DB Worcs.

HALF A NIGHT'S REVENUE. See 1,9 note. No other manor in Gloucestershire is mentioned as combining with Awre to pay one night's revenue.

1,14 BY WEIGHT. Payment in this manner avoided losses from the clipping of coins or wear, and was therefore carefully noted, as the opposite of money 'at face value' (see notes to G 1 and 1,56).

1,15 THE INSERTION of the hundredal rubric is based on the appearance in the 12th century of Berkeley 'Harness' and Hundred, which was attached to Berkeley manor.

KING EDWARD HAD 5 HIDES. Over the *v* in the MS the scribe mistakenly wrote an abbreviation mark, which usually denotes *virgata(s)*; Farley correctly omits it.

RIDING MEN. *Radchenistres*, similar to *radmans* ('riders' E 33); see DB Herefords. 1,4 note for an example of the two terms being interchangeable. *Radchenistres* are found mainly in the south-western Welsh marches and in Hampshire (in Hants. they are found on the estates of large landholders, chiefly royal and ecclesiastical), whereas *radmans* are common in north-west Mercia up to the river Ribble. Of higher standing than villagers, *radchenistres* are glossed twice in Glos. (here and at 19,2) as *liberi homines* and in Worcs. 8,9b *liberi homines* perform similar services to *radmans* in 8,10a. However, they were apparently not allowed to leave the manor (see 3,1; cf. Herefords. 1,4). Originally they were men who rode as messengers or as escorts for the King or their lord (see Worcs. 2,29 and note), but they also worked their own holdings and those of their lords (see 1,24 and Worcs. 8,10a). They did not owe full military service and were equivalent to the later tenants in sergeantry. Discussion in Maitland DBB pp. 57, 66, 305-8; Vinogradoff pp. 69-71; Nelson pp. 44-51.

17 MEN. Burgesses; GS p. 64.

CAM. The 6 hides constuted the later manors of Billow, Lorring and Stinchcombe in Stinchcombe, which was until the 17th century a chapelry of Cam; the 11 hides formed the main manor of Cam.

CROMHALL ('ABBOTS'). Later given to St. Augustine's Abbey, Bristol. See EPNS iii p. 3.

IN TOTAL. There is a large erasure in the MS after *Int'ⁱ totū*, extending two-thirds of the way along the line. It is not possible to tell what has been erased, or whether the scribe intended to fill in more details at a later stage.

FREEDMEN. *Coliberti*; former slaves. A continental term, not otherwise found in England; used in DB to render a native term, stated on three occasions to be *(ge)bur* (Worcs. 8,10a and Hants. 1,10;23). The *coliberti* are found mainly in the counties in Wessex and western Mercia, particularly in Wiltshire and Somerset. In DB they are generally listed between the slaves and villagers; in Glos., however, they occur in several places, though mostly with slaves after other classes of population. Some of them at least seem to have held land and ploughs (especially the latter in Glos.) and paid various dues (see DB Herefords. 1,6) and in 8,1 two paid 34d. In Glos. they appear only on royal and ecclesiastical holdings. See Vinogradoff pp. 468-9; Maitland DBB pp. 36-7, 328-330; DB Oxon. 1,6 note on boors.

1,16 CROMHALL ('LYGON') remained a lay manor. See EPNS iii p. 3.

COULD TURN ... WHERE THEY WOULD. They were free to choose any lord as their patron and protector of their lands. Many holdings were 'tied' to a particular manor, as occurs in 1,2;52; 3,2 etc.

ASSAYED. *Arsas* = tested by fire; coin was tested for the presence of alloy; similar to blanching (see notes to 1,14 and 1,56).

1,17 2 HIDES. In the MS *.ii. hid'*; Farley misprints *.i. hid'*.

1,18 BERNARD'S prebend can be identified from later evidence as comprising a hide in Hinton (which also contained Oldminster, the site of Berkeley nunnery) and 4 hides at 'Hinworthy' (a lost place in Slimbridge; see EPNS ii p. 248). Both Hinton and 'Hinworthy' contain the OE *hiwan*, 'religious community', referring to Berkeley nunnery, secularised by Earl Godwin (cf. 1,63), of which Bernard may have been the last chaplain.

1,19 A SMALL CASTLE. *Castellum*, possibly the beginning of the present Berkeley Castle (GR ST 6898); see C. S. Taylor *Berkeley Minster* in TBGAS xix (1894–5) p. 82.

1,20 QUEEN EDITH. Wife of King Edward the Confessor, daughter of Earl Godwin (see 1,63 note). She died in 1075.
MARSHFIELD. 14 HIDES. Because of the prevalence of the 5-hide unit of assessment, it might at first sight look as if the scribe had mistakenly included the priest's hide among the 14 hides, when in fact there were 14 hides and the priest's hide. However, another explanation is possible. Throughout the Middle Ages there is evidence of a small manor, variously called 'West', 'Little' or 'Old' Marshfield, held from the Earls of Gloucester, which was completely independent of the main manor given by the Earl of Gloucester to Keynsham Abbey c.1168. This small manor could be a one hide holding, omitted accidentally in DB, which would bring the total assessment of Marshfield up to the normal 15 hides.
PRIEST HAS ONE OF THESE HIDES. Later the rectory manor held by Tewkesbury Abbey.

1,21 THE INSERTION of the hundredal rubric is justified by the inclusion within this Hundred of Clifton to the west (75,1–2) and Bitton (1,9. 78,13), Hanham (60,7) and Oldland (5,1) to the east.
'BARTON (REGIS)'. See EPNS iii p. 94.
6 HIDES. See EvK 7.
AT 27s. *xx* with *vii* interlined to correct the number to *xxvii*.
WHEN ROGER ACQUIRED THIS MANOR. That is, when Roger of Berkeley acquired the collection of the manor's revenue. (See DB Worcs. 11,2.) *Recepit* has here a slightly different meaning from when a landholder acquired a grant of land.
4 SLAVES AND 13 FREEDMEN. In the accusative in error.
BRISTOL CHURCH. St. Peter's, stated in the 12th century to be the oldest church in Bristol, and the mother-church of Mangotsfield chapelry. The church 'with all belonging to it inside and outside the Borough' (i.e. including the 3 hides) 'and the tithe of all the lordship revenues (*dominicorum reddituum*) of Bristol' was given to Tewkesbury Abbey before 1107 (Cal CR ii p. 490). After the foundation of St. James Priory as a cell of Tewkesbury c.1140 it was incorporated, along with later local gifts to the Abbey and Priory, in the 'manor of St. James'. The 3 hides comprised the major part of this manor in the Gloucestershire parishes of Mangotsfield and Stapleton (excluding Ashley which was a later gift) and the Bristol out-parishes of St. James and St. Philip and St. Jacob.
RIDING MAN HOLDS 1 HIDE. This was probably Ridgeway manor in Stapleton.
BISHOP G(EOFFREY). Almost certainly Geoffrey Mowbray, Bishop of Coutances and St. Lô (see Ch. 6 note), who held in the area.
1 MARK OF GOLD. £6, making £28 for the Bishop's share. The total payment of Bristol was thus £101 6s 8d which looks rather like a commuted food rent (see 1,9 note).

1,22 10 HIDES. These formed the manor of Coln Rogers given to St. Peter's Abbey, Gloucester, by Roger of Gloucester in 1105; *History of St. Peter's, Gloucester* i pp. 69, 123, 235–6.
BISHOP OF BAYEUX. Odo, half-brother of King William and elder brother of Count Robert of Mortain. Earl of Kent 1066/7 to 1082, then 1087 to 1088. He was 'regent' during some of King William's absences abroad, notably in 1067 with Earl William of Hereford. At the time when DB was written he was in prison in Rouen and many of his lands (including here and in Worcs.) were forfeited to the King. He was released by King William on his deathbed in 1087 and returned to England, but rebelled against William Rufus, was defeated in 1088 and all his lands in England taken away. He fled to Normandy and died in 1097. Bayeux is in the département of Calvados, France.

1,23 THIS HOLDING was combined with 44,1 as the manor of Hullasey; VCH xi pp. 236–40.

1,24 THE INSERTION of the hundredal rubric is justified by the appearance of Tewkesbury Hundred from 1148 onwards, comprising the lands attached to the DB manor of Tewkesbury.
45 ... IN LORDSHIP. The details given amount to 46½ hides; probably the figure for Natton (3½ hides) was overstated by 1½ hides.
APART FROM THE SERVICE OF THE LORD HIMSELF. Service to the King owed by the lord of the manor.

IN THE HEAD OF THE MANOR. That is, in Tewkesbury itself, rather than in any of the members mentioned below (1,24–37).

HALL. See G 1 note above.

SALT-HOUSE ... WHICH BELONGS. Or 'which belonged', *pertin'* abbreviating *pertinens* which, though the present participle, could refer to the past in view of the *erant* at the beginning of the sentence; (cf. *habentes* 4 lines below and *reddentes* 7 lines below). Although it is not absolutely clear from the Latin whether the details of mills, fishery and salt-house refer to the past, as well as the ploughs, slaves and smallholders, they probably do because of the appearance of the fishery and salt-house in the 'present' details of Tewkesbury 14 lines below.

FIDDINGTON. The King's 6 hides represent the later manor of Fiddington and Natton centred on Fiddington Farm; Bernard's 2 hides became the later Hall Court manor centred on Fiddington Manor (VCH viii pp. 175–9).

WALTON ... 3 HIDES; IN ASTON ... 6 HIDES. The gap of about 7 letters between these two items is caused by an erasure in the MS; Farley does not always print gaps caused by erasures (e.g. in 19,2 the erasure between *Brictric* and *.i. hidā*).

ASTON (ON CARRANT) ...... ASTON (ON CARRANT). The two holdings cannot now be distinguished from each other; VCH viii pp. 175–9. Gerard is almost certainly Gerard the Chamberlain; see 1,40 note.

COURT. *Curia* here means the same as *aula* 'hall'; that is, the lord's house.

QUEEN. Queen Matilda, wife of King William; died 1083.

RALPH here and in 1,38 was probably Ralph of Cardiff, whose descendants were certainly stewards of the Honour of Gloucester from the mid-12th century.

1,26 THIS ENTRY is lined through in red for emphasis.

1,27-33 THESE ENTRIES are marked with a red marginal cross in the MS, the cross beside 1,27 being larger than the others, but of the same shape, not + and X as in Farley. Such crosses, indicating land held by a church, occur in several counties and are undoubtedly contemporary with the text of DB.

1,28 2 PLOUGHS. This is a very low total for 11 villagers and 1 riding man, since most villagers in this area had an average of at least half a plough; perhaps *vii* (7) was miscopied as *ii* (2) during the compilation of DB.

1,29 (LOWER) LEMINGTON, near Moreton in Marsh; VCH vi pp. 217, 252–3.

1,31 IN FIDDINGTON 2 HIDES. Now Rectory Farm in Ashchurch; VCH viii pp. 175–9.

1,33 20 HIDES. This total is the sum of the hidages in 1,27–32; it is thus likely that the 4½ hides of Stanley Pontlarge, which are additional to the 20, were exempt before 1066. The 1086 taxable hides of 1,27–32 total 18, so the exemption of 2 out of the 3 hides of Fiddington and Natton (1,31–2) must have taken place between 1066 and 1086.

1,34 HANLEY (CASTLE). Geographically within Worcs. and seemingly included in the 1200 hides of that county (DB Worcs. App. I), but regarded as a part of Glos. both in DB Glos. and Herefords., Brictric son of Algar having withdrawn it from Worcs. and attached it to his great manor of Tewkesbury. It is duplicated in Herefords. 1,42 because Earl William had withdrawn its revenues there and they remained there after his son Roger had forfeited his lands. The Glos. and Herefords. entries originate from different returns and there are many differences, see Worcs. EG 1 note.

40 VILLAGERS AND SMALLHOLDERS. The total of both classes is 40. Similarly in the next entry.

HEDGED ENCLOSURE. *Haia*, Latinized from OE *(ge)haeg* (cf. Mod. Fr *haie*); a three-sided enclosure, generally hedged, into which game were driven for capture; see DB Worcs. 18,4 *i haia in qua capiebantur ferae*. In Shrops. (4,8,10 and 6,15) 'hays' are 'for capturing roe-deer (*capreolis capiendis*)'. See Ellis i p. 114; Ducange s.v. *haga*; Place-Name Elements s.vv. *(ge)haeg, haga*. Such 'hays' are found frequently in the west midland shires; see DB Herefords. 2,23 note.

1,36 ROBERT ... AT A REVENUE. Probably *ad firmam* here means 'at farm', that is, 'for a fixed sum', but it could, as with other occurrences of the phrase, mean he holds the land and it is part of the King's revenue (cf. 1,34 *firma regis*).

1,36-37 BELONGED. *ptin'*, probably abbreviating the past *pertinebant* as in 1,34–35, rather than the present *pertinent*.

1,37 THE REDUCTION in hidage and value resulted from the separation of Wincot (1,42).

QUEEN. Queen Matilda; cf. DB Devon 27,1, another manor of Brictric's given by the Queen to Roger of Bully.

ROGER OF BULLY. Perhaps Bully-en-Brai in the département of Seine-Maritime, France; see OEB p. 78.

1,38   THE FIRST TWO LINES of this entry are written into the left margin of the MS and the second line is written below the marginal rulings and several lines above it are compressed, probably indicating that they were filled in slightly later by the scribe.

        THE ABOVE MENTIONED 50 (EXEMPT) HIDES. These are the 20 hides of church land (1,27–32; see 1,33 note) and the 30 hides of 1,34–37. The implication is that the 30 hides of 1,34–37 were exempt before 1066; but between 1066 and 1086 all are recorded as paying some tax.

        THE ABOVE MENTIONED ... SERVICE. This means that all of Tewkesbury's 95 hides (the 45 in lordship and the other 50) did not pay tax before 1066.

        RALPH. See note to 1,24.

1,39   BRICTRIC SON OF ALGAR. A great English thane who held much land in the west. See 1,42 note.

1,40   ASHTON (UNDER HILL). The north-eastern part of the parish, later part of the upper division of Tewkesbury Hundred; VCH vi pp. 185–6, 188; viii pp. 243, 246.

        GERARD. Almost certainly Gerard the Chamberlain, as Gerard's land in Ashton (under Hill) was later part of Tewkesbury manor, as were the other lands held by Gerard the Chamberlain; VCH viii pp. 210, 246.

1,41   KEMERTON. BODDINGTON. The entry is duplicated in 19,2 where Gerard is Gerard the Chamberlain.

        KEMERTON. Gerard's 8 hides represented the later manors of Upper and Nether Court; VCH viii pp. 210–3, 217. Kemerton was transferred to Worcs. in 1931.

        LET. Old Norse *Liotr*; PNDB p. 320.

        6 PLOUGHS. The scribe wrote *iiii cā* originally, then wrote a *v* to cover the first three minim strokes, correcting the number to *vi*; Farley misprints *ivi* which is not a Roman numeral.

        BODDINGTON. Gerard's 3 hides were later united with his 3 hides held from Westminster Abbey (19,2) as Boddington manor, comprising the western part of Boddington parish which was later in Tewkesbury Hundred; VCH vi pp. 186, 238; viii pp. 170–1, 188, 190–2.

1,42   WINCOT. Almost certainly a life-grant to Reginald the chaplain out of the Queen's manor of Clifford Chambers (1,37), to which it was later reunited.

        THE QUEEN GAVE. Queen Matilda, here and in 1,44: many of Brictric's lands passed to her, especially in the west country. A romantic tale told by the Continuator of Wace and others (Freeman iv App. Note 0) alleges that Matilda seized his lands because in youth he had spurned her hand. On Matilda's death in 1083 the lands passed to King William.

1,43   'HENTAGE'. A lost site just east of Alderton village; EPNS ii p. 50.

        HUMPHREY'S THREE LANDS were combined as the later manor of Dixton (EPNS ii pp. xi, 50; VCH vi pp. 191–2).

        8 SMALLHOLDERS. In the MS *iiii* corrected to *viii*.

1,44   IN TWYNING ... This part of Twyning was separated from the Abbot of Winchcombe's manor of Twyning (11,3) and became the sub-manor of Mythe in Tewkesbury manor and Hundred.

        4 VILLAGERS is partly obscured by an ink-blot in the MS.

1,45   IN STOKE (ORCHARD) ... This holding was the later manor of Downing in the north-west of Stoke Orchard; VCH viii p. 12.

        ALWIN. It is possible, though unprovable, that Alwin, who is also recorded in 32,6. 73,3 and 77,1, is identical with Alwin the Sheriff (1,2;13. 34,8;12).

        LESS 1 VIRGATE. This may be erroneous, since the other manor in Stoke Orchard (3,7) contained 7 hides, but EvK 67 gives the same assessment in a different form: '2 hides and 3 virgates'.

1,47   LEAGUE. DB *leuga, leuua, leuuede*. A measure of length, usually of woodland, traditionally reckoned at a mile and a half. If so, some woodland will have been or enormous length (see DB Northants. 1,6 note). A sub-division of the league was the furlong, reckoned at 220 yards, an eighth of a mile; see DB Worcs. 1,1c note. Both the league and the furlong are used as square measures as well as linear ones. See 6,1 note.

1,48   CHIPPING SODBURY was formed out of Old Sodbury in the 13th century; GS pp. 66, 86.

        A PARK. Not for leisure, but for hunting (cf. *parcus ferarum* in DB Herefords. 1,41 and *parcus bestiarum* in DB Devon 1,64). It was usually an area of woodland within the manor, contrasting with *foresta* (see 31,4 note), land outside; but see Herefords. 1,41.

1,49   VALUE £27. Entered in the right margin level with the last line of the entry and no doubt written later, though probably by the same scribe; it is cramped.

1,50-51 THE HOLDINGS of John the Chamberlain and Baldwin were located in Eastleach Turville and still owed suit of court to Fairford in the 13th century (*ex inf.* Dr. N. M. Herbert).

1,53   SHERIFF ... MANOR. See 1,10 note.

LATER EARL WILLIAM ... HAD IT. Earl William could have had it only for a few months as he died in 1071.

1,55 THE INSERTION of the hundredal rubric is justified by the location of another holding at Lydney in this Hundred (32,11) and the later attachment of the Hundred to the manor. Earl William's amalgamation remained as the later manor of Lydney.
4 LANDS. It would seem that *terrae* is not being used here as the equivalent of *manerium* (see DB Somerset 2,8 general note), but as a small amorphous unit, land not classified as a manor (see DB Surrey 19,22 note). Cf. 1,60 below 'Earl William made one manor out of these two villages'.
FROM THE BISHOP OF HEREFORD'S LORDSHIP 3 HIDES. In exchange for Eaton Bishop; see DB Herefords. 2,8 (= E 5 below, to which see note).
6 VILLAGERS. In the MS *ii* corrected to *vi*.

1,56 BISHOP OSBERN. 'Bishop' is an anachronism as he did not obtain the bishopric of Exeter until a year or so after Earl William's death.
WALTER OF LACY. Died 1085. Father of Roger of Lacy (see Ch. 39 note).
EXCEPT FOR THE MONKS' SUPPLIES. That is, the only dues the manor paid were to supply the monks with a certain amount of provisions.
ARCHBISHOP STIGAND. Bishop of Elmham (East Anglia) in 1043, then 1044–47, before becoming Bishop of Winchester in 1047, which see he held with the Archbishopric of Canterbury from 1052 until he was deposed in 1070. Died 1072. See R. R. Darlington in EHR li (1936) p. 420 on Stigand's status as Archbishop of Canterbury.
BLANCHED. Or 'white'; *albas, candidas* or *blancas* in DB. A sample of coin was melted as a test for the presence of alloy or baser metal. Money could also be said to be blanched when, without a test by fire, a standard deduction was made to compensate for alloying or clipping, as the rate of 20d to the *ora* here and in 1,58;61. See *Dialogus de Scaccario* (ed. C. Johnson 1950) p. 125, and also G 1 note above on *ora*.

1,57 BOTH WOODLAND AND OPEN LAND AND MEADOW. Similar phrases are found elsewhere in DB (e.g. Worcs. 8,6 and 10,10; Herefords. 1,4; Herts. 10,9). Also occurs here in 10,11. The inclusion of meadow and woodland within the hidated area is noteworthy.

1,58 CYNWY CHELLE. *Chenvichelle* here; *Chenuicelle* in 66,1. OE *Cynewig* with byname *Chelle*; see PNDB p. 221 and OEB p. 299.

1,59 BECKFORD ... 11 HIDES. The royal 8 hides became the later manor of Beckford comprising the tithings of Beckford, Bengrove and Grafton which remained in Tibblestone Hundred; Ansfrid's 3 hides became the later manor of Didcot in Tewkesbury Hundred (VCH viii pp. 243, 253–5).

1,60 ASHTON (UNDER HILL). This manor, which remained amalgamated with the royal manor of Beckford (1,59), comprised the remainder of the parish not included in Gerard's manor (1,40).
3 FEMALE SLAVES. In the MS *iiii*, but an attempt seems to have been made to erase the first *i*; it is difficult to judge the success of the attempt because the tail of the 7 in the line above runs into the first *i*.
NEVER SEEN THEIR WRIT. Cf. DB Surrey 21,3.

1,62 NOT IN THE REVENUE ... It did not pay tax before the Sheriff took it over.

1,63 THIS ENTRY is cramped and in a different colour ink, so may have been entered later when the details of Woodchester were known; the scribe is the same, however.
WOODCHESTER. See note to 78,14. Charter evidence suggests that Woodchester contained 3 hides (ECWM p. 50, no. 85 = Sawyer 1441 = BCS no. 574). The entry refers to a notorious (and perhaps fictitious) historical episode in which Earl Godwin procured the dissolution of Berkeley minster and acquired its lands by arranging for the seduction of its inmates; see Freeman ii pp. 556–558, and C. S. Taylor *Berkeley Minster* in TBGAS xix pp. 80–81. Gytha evidently disapproved of Godwin's conduct, hence her refusal to live off the lands of Berkeley.
EARL GODWIN. Earl of the West Saxons; father of Earl (King) Harold and Edith (wife of King Edward). Died in 1053.
TO CONSUME. *comedere* 'to eat', 'use up'. Cf. DB Worcs. 2,33 *pasceret* 'maintain'.
EDWARD. Edward of Salisbury, Sheriff of Wiltshire in 1086.
AS THE COUNTY STATES. The County Court, as on several other occasions in Glos. (e.g. 1,65. 28,3. 32,9 etc.).
NOBODY ... SURVEY. Cf. 28,7 and 75,2.

1,64 MADGETT. Malmesbury Abbey's ½ hide was at Sheepcot in Madgett; William of Eu's 2 hides and Roger of Lacy's ½ hide (39,10) were added to William's manor of Woolaston (31,5); VCH x p. 107.
ABBOT. Or 'Abbey' (see 1,11 note), which perhaps fits better with the plural *dicunt*.

1,65   REMITTED 5 HIDES OF THESE FOR EDNOTH. Made them exempt from tax; in EvK 39 above the *Omenie xv h'* and the Hundred head is interlined *Ex iss vq; st' lib'e.*

1,66   WIDENESCI. See OEB p. 136.

1,66-67 (GREAT) BARRINGTON. Amalgamated with 56,1 as the manor of Great Barrington; VCH vi pp. 19–20. Cf. EvK 40: 'In *Bernitone* 8 hides' with '2 manors' interlined above the Barrington Hundred head.

CH. 2   ARCHBISHOP THOMAS. Thomas of Bayeux, Archbishop of York 1070 to 1100. Brother of Samson, Bishop of Worcester.

2,1   THE INSERTION of the hundredal rubric is justified by the inclusion within this Hundred of all the surrounding manors.
ARCHBISHOP STIGAND. See 1,56 note.

2,3   BISHOP OF WINCHESTER. Also called Walkelin, bishop from 1070 to 1098.

2,4   ARCHBISHOP ALDRED. See 1,2 note.
ODDINGTON. The 10 hides comprised only Oddington; the outlier at Condicote was joined to another ½ hide there (36,2); it was assessed in 12th century charters at 1½ hides (VCH vi pp. 63–7, 191–2).
THE VALUE WAS. In the MS there is an erasure under *TRE Valb' vi lib'*, which is therefore slightly cramped.
ST. PETER'S OF GLOUCESTER. Aldred had rebuilt Gloucester Abbey Church when he was Bishop of Worcester, and he continued to hold this manor, together with Northleach and Standish (12,8;10), after he had become Archbishop of York in 1061. According to the *History of St. Peter's, Gloucester* i p. 93, they were returned to St. Peter's by Archbishop Thomas in 1095; but a writ (possibly spurious?) dated 1070 appears in *Regesta* i no. 36 stating that, following a lawsuit, King William has confirmed to St. Peter's the lands Archbishop Thomas held unjustly, naming these three manors.

2,5   ST. OSWALD'S (CHURCH). Of Gloucester; see 2,11.

2,6   MANOR OF 1 HIDE IN SHIPTON (SOLERS). Probably absorbed into Lower Hampen manor (32,13).

2,8   NORTHLEACH included Eastington; the total hidage was 25 (12 + 1 + 12) hides. See note to EvK 103.
WALTER SON OF POYNTZ. The MS has the genitive *pontii*; Farley misprints *pontu*.
ARCHBISHOP THOMAS CLAIMS IT. That is, Walter's 12 hides at Farmington, see EvM 3.

2,9   ARCHBISHOP THOMAS' CLAIM to the 3 hides held by Roger of Ivry's man evidently succeeded, since there is no evidence of a holding in Compton Abdale held from the St. Valerys or the Earls of Cornwall as successors of the Ivrys. The hidage figure for the whole manor is uncertain: this entry and EvK 74 give it as 9 hides, but EvM 100 states it to be 10 hides, a rather more probable total.

2,10   STANDISH. The Abbot of Gloucester's hide was at Farley in Hardwicke (1 carucate in 1291); Durand's 3 hides were at Rudge in Hardwicke (3 carucates in 1291); Earl Hugh of Chester's hide was at Field Court in Hardwicke (1 carucate in 1309); VCH x pp. 183, 185, 233. Cf. EvM 4;7.
ABBOT OF GLOUCESTER. Or 'Abbey', see 1,11 note. See Ch. 10 note. on St. Peter's, Gloucester.
RIGHTLY OUGHT TO HOLD IT. See 2,4 note.
EARL HUGH. Of Chester; see Ch. 28 note.
ROGER. Roger of Gloucester (*alias* Roger of Pîtres), brother of Durand, not of Earl William; see 56,2 note.
ARCHBISHOP THOMAS CLAIMS THESE LANDS. That is, Earl Hugh's hide and Durand's 3 hides (see EvM 4) and perhaps also the Abbot of Gloucester's hide.

2,12   NORTH CERNEY. This manor comprised the village itself and the land east of the River Churn (*ex. inf.* Dr. N. M. Herbert).

2,13   ROGER. Roger of Gloucester, probably the son of Durand the Sheriff, who gave 'the land of Ulfketel' (among others) to St. Peter's Abbey, Gloucester, in 1100, in exchange for 'all that Abbot (Serlo) had in Westbury except the tithes of water and wood'; *History of St. Peter's, Gloucester* i pp. 112, 352; ii p. 128; see also G. H. White in *Notes and Queries* 12th ser. vol. v p. 233.

3,1   ST. MARY'S OF WORCESTER. Founded by Oswald Bishop of Worcester (961–992) and Archbishop of York (from 972), and completed in 983. Gloucestershire east of the rivers Leadon and Severn was included in the diocese of Worcester.
WESTBURY (ON TRYM). The original hidage was 76½ (50 + 8 + 5 + 3½ + 5 + 5) hides, but all the 'satellites' (EvK 78; EvM 8; WoA 4; WoB 15) agree with DB in assessing the land

at 50 hides. Later surveys (RBW pp. 380-1, 405-6, 413-7, 429-30, 433, 437; cf. Fees i p. 38) place the 8 hides held by the riding men at Charlton, Henbury and Redland; Osbern Giffard's 5 hides were his manor of 5 hides at Stoke Gifford (50,2), of which the overlordship was in dispute between the Crown and the Bishops of Worcester until the end of the 13th century.

6 SMALLHOLDERS. So MS and Farley; the facsimile does not reproduce the *i* after the *v*.

3,2 HE COULD NOT WITHDRAW. See 1,16 note.

WALTER SON OF ROGER. Roger of Pîtres, Sheriff of Gloucestershire; see Ch. 56 note.

3,3 EYCOT. Cf. WoA 1; WoB 16.

IT LIES IN BIBURY occurs in precisely the same position as the normal Hundred head, though not in capitals or rubricated, and signifies that this holding was in Bibury Hundred, not Rapsgate Hundred, which EvK 80 confirms. Later evidence shows that another 4 hides of Eycot (making a 5-hide manor, see 3,4 note) were included within the 21 hides of Bibury manor in Bibury Hundred.

3,4 BIBURY. Cf. EvK 80; WoA 1; WoB 17. Later surveys locate the 4 hides held by 3 riding men at Eycot in Rendcombe (RBW pp. 412, 414, 417, 439); the priest's 3 hides as the later rectory manor of Bibury and Aldsworth (H. E. Salter *The Cartulary of Oseney Abbey*, Oxford Hist. Soc. 1934-6, vol. i p. 97; vol. ii pp. 1-8, 11, 30-7; vol. iii pp. 193-5, 232, 262-3). The 3¼ hides and 1¾ hides in Barnsley were later united as the manor of Barnsley.

BISHOP WULFSTAN. Bishop of Worcester 1062-1095.

3,5 WITHINGTON. See WoB 18. The priest's ½ hide remained as the later glebe of Withington church. The 2¾ hides held by 4 riding men can be identified from later surveys as 1½ hides in Owdeswell and 1½ hides in Upcote, both hamlets in Withington parish; these surveys and the total hidage for Wattlescomb Hundred both suggest that 2¾ hides should be corrected to 3 hides (RBW pp. 359-60, 367). EvK 81 wrongly gives the number of hides not paying tax as 4. These locations are confirmed in WoA 2, which enables the assessments to be corrected (see note to WoA 2).

AZELIN. *Schelinus*: the same name as *Azelinus*; see Forssner 38 and Förstemann 221.

DROGO. Drogo son of Poyntz, whose collateral descendants, the Cliffords, held Aston Blank from the Bishop in the 12th and 13th centuries.

MEADOW AND WOODLAND ... NOT MUCH. An unclear phrase; the meaning could be 'meadow in certain places; woodland, but not much'; grammatically *multa* agrees with *silva*, not *pratum*, but could refer to both.

3,6 THIS ENTRY was added slightly later in a paler ink at the top of col. 165a on a level with the county heading. See WoB 20.

2 HIDES IN CONDICOTE. This holding is later represented by Hinchwick.

3,7 (BISHOPS) CLEEVE. Cf. WoA 3; WoB 19. Later surveys (RBW pp. 344-5, 348, 351) locate the riding man's hide at Wontley in Southam; the priest's hide was taken into the demesne at Bishops Cleeve.

DRAUGHT ANIMAL. *afrus*. See DMLBS s.v. *Averus*. According to Ducange s.v. *afferi* and also *affrus*: *iumenta vel caballi colonici ... equi, agriculturae idonei* ('beasts of burden or plough horses ... horses suitable for agriculture'). It is probable that these notices of draught animals were included by mistake from the original returns (e.g. Exon.) which listed animals and gave other material additional to DB.

'SAPPERTON'. A lost settlement in Bishops Cleeve (VCH viii pp. 2, 9, 250), not Saberton in Dumbleton or Beckford as previously thought (ECWM pp. 59, 69; EPNS ii pp. 43-4).

VALUE ... £36. *xxx* with *vi* interlined to correct the number to xxxvi.

4,1 BISHOP OF HEREFORD. Walter of Lorraine, chaplain to Queen Edith and Bishop of Hereford from 1061 to 1079; see E 5 note below.

OUTSIDE THAT HUNDRED. That is, in Wattlescomb Hundred, as are other adjacent villages.

DURAND'S 3 HIDES were later represented by the manors of Hampen (in Sevenhampton and Shipton Solers) and Oakley Wood (in Charlton Kings, Prestbury and Sevenhampton).

BISHOP OF THIS TOWN. That is, Hereford. Robert Losinga was Bishop from 1079 to 1095.

CH. 5 BISHOP OSBERN. Bishop of Exeter 1072-1103, brother of Earl William of Hereford. He came over to England from Normandy in King Edward's time and probably became that king's chaplain.

5,1-2 ALFWY may well be Alfwy 'Hiles', whose man Harold in 1066 held Iron Acton (69,6), east of Tytherington.

5,2 IN LORDSHIP 2 PLOUGHS. The villagers' ploughs may have been omitted in error from the MS; see also 6,8 note.

WOODLAND ½ LEAGUE IN LENGTH AND WIDTH. That is, ½ league by ½ league. There are several occurrences of this formula in DB Somerset where the corresponding Exon. entry gives the same measurements for both length and width.

CH. 6 BISHOP OF COUTANCES. Geoffrey of Mowbray, one of King William's chief justices. He held a great deal of land in the south-west, especially in Somerset and Devon. St. Lô is near Coutances in the département of Manche, France.

6,1 'ACTON (ILGER)' was named after the DB tenant; its centre was not Algar's Manor, an antiquarian creation of c.1900 (EPNS iii pp. 1-2), which was the site of the ½ mill, but Church House next to Iron Acton church.
2½ HIDES. 7 dimid' is interlined after ũ hidẹ.
½ MILL. The other half of the mill is probably to be found in 69,6.
WOODLAND, 1 FURLONG. The furlong is probably being used here as a square measure, each side being 1 furlong long; see 1,47 note. See also in E 19.

6,2 THE BISHOP ALSO HOLDS. Repeated at the beginning of 6,2-9.
LAND FOR 5 PLOUGHS. A unique occurrence in Gloucestershire of the 'teamland' formula found in many other DB counties; see note to E 9-16 below. See also note to 11,5.

6,3 A MANOR OF 1 HIDE. Identified from later evidence as Sturden.
GOSMER. Goismerus; OG Gosmer; see Forrsner 127 s.n. Gosmer, Goismer.
WHEN IT IS PLOUGHED, THERE ARE ONLY 64 ACRES OF LAND IN THAT HIDE. Another unique piece of information, presumably indicating the existence of a two-field system. Why this should have been thought worthy of special mention is unknown, though later evidence shows that three-field systems were the norm in the southern Vale region of the country. Later evidence also shows that the area of this manor's lordship land was still about 65 acres in the 13th and 14th centuries.

6,5 ROBERT in this entry and in 6,7-8 is Robert of Doynton, whose descendants held Doynton until the 13th century, and from whom 'Lee' and Gaunts Earthcott were held by St. Mark's Hospital, Bristol, and its founders; C. D. Ross Cartulary of St. Mark's Hospital, Bristol, Bristol Record Society vol. 21 (1959) pp. 180-1, 183-6, 189, 217-9, 243, 247-87.

6,6-9 THESE ENTRIES are written in a cramped style, probably added slightly later by the scribe.

6,6 WAPLEY ('RECTORY'). The later manor of Wapley 'Rectory' in Wapley and Codrington.

6,7-8 ROBERT. See note to 6,5.

6,7 'LEE'. Lee manor was centred on St. Swithun's Farm in Almondsbury and included Over in Almondsbury as well as the St. Swithun's estate. See EPNS iii p. 132.

6,8 CUTHWULF. Cuulf; see PNDB p. 220.
IN LORDSHIP 2 PLOUGHS. It is probable that villagers' ploughs have been accidentally omitted from this entry, as also perhaps in 5,2.
4 VILLAGERS. 7 iiii vill'i was originally omitted in the MS, so written mostly in the margin, hence its unusual position in the list of population (villagers normally precede smallholders).
WOODLAND ... A gap of about 8 letters follows silua, no doubt for the extent of the woodland to be added later, when available.

6,9 ROGER is clearly Roger of Berkeley who held the remainder of Dodington (42,2) from the King: the two holdings undoubtedly formed one agrarian unit in and after 1086, though the overlordship remained in dispute for centuries. The two fractional hidages combine neatly into one 5 hides vill; 'the third part of ½ hide' = one-sixth of a hide.

7,1 ST. PETER'S OF BATH. Bath Abbey.
3 OF THEM PAY TAX AND 2 DO NOT. In the MS tres geldant is added in the right margin and the 7 is squashed in, both written later in paler ink, the original reading having been 'Of these 2 do not pay tax'.
MEADOWS AND WOODLAND TO MAINTAIN THE MANOR. Hens and hay for oxen are two of the items coming from and in woodland and meadows (39,6 and 59,1), apart from pasturage and food for pigs. Hunting, honey, firewood and timber are also mentioned as coming from woodland in DB Worcs. 2,15;31. Cf. 10,8 below.

8,1 PUCKLECHURCH manor included Westerleigh and Wick and Abson.
LUMPS OF IRON. Massas ferri; the quantity of iron represented by a massa, if in fact it was a standard measure, is unknown.

9,1 THIS ENTRY is compressed at the bottom of the column; the scribe is the same, however.

CH. 10 ST. PETER'S OF GLOUCESTER. Serlo, a Norman monk from Mont St. Michel, became its Abbot on the death of Wulfstan in 1072 until 1104.

10,1 '(ABBOTS) BARTON'. See EPNS ii p. 136.
'MORWENTS (END)'. See EPNS iii p. 156. Now represented by Coopey's, Drew's and Laughton's Farms in Hartpury. Later records suggest that its assessment may have been 1¼ hides: Gloucestershire Record Office D. 199/1, a survey of Hartpury manor in 1700, mentions 5 copyhold yardlands 'in Morwents End'.

10,3 THE CHURCH ITSELF HOLDS. Repeated at the beginning of 10,3–11.

10,8 HIGHNAM. The tithings of Highnam, Linton and Over in Churcham parish; VCH x pp. 1, 11, 17.
r. The abbreviation for *require* 'enquire'; it is written in the margin usually when the scribe has left space for some information not then available to remind him to insert it later. In this case it is not certain for what information he was waiting as no space has been left in the text.
WOODLAND SUFFICIENT FOR THE MANOR. Cf. 7,1. Presumably wood for building and repair work, and as firewood and land for pigs to feed on. See DB Worcs. 2,31; Shrops. 4,4,20 and Wilts. 13,10;18.

10,9 PRESTON. Next to Dymock.

10,11 CHURCHAM AND 'MORTON'. The later manor and tithing of Churcham in Churcham parish; VCH x pp. 1, 11, 17. EvM 43, however, just calls this manor 'Morton' (*Mortune*). See EPNS iii p. 197.
WOODLAND AND OPEN LAND. See 1,57 note.
HUNTING ... ENCLOSURES. See 1,34 note.

10,12 AMPNEY ST. PETER manor, named after St. Peter's Abbey, was enlarged in the 12th century by gifts of land in Ampney St. Nicholas (60,3) and Ampney Crucis (67,1). It was centred on the present Can Court (EPNS i 53).
REINBALD'S BROTHER. Reinbald the priest; see Ellis DTG p. 120.

10,13 WALTER OF LACY'S WIFE. Ermelina (Emma). Her grant of Duntisbourne to St. Peter's is recorded in the *History of St. Peter's Gloucester* i p. 73.
DUNTISBOURNE (ABBOTS), named after the Abbot of St. Peter's, was enlarged in 1100 by the gift of Gilbert de Eskecot's 2 hides (39,7; see note).

11,1 10 ... FREE; THEY BELONG TO THE COURT. Free of tax; they were lordship land (cf. 39,6).

11,2 THE CHURCH ITSELF HOLDS. Repeated at the beginning of 11,2–12.

11,3 TWYNING. The main manor of Twyning.

11,4 FRAMPTON. 'Frampton Court'. Now Holt Farm in Winchcombe.

11,5 ALDERTON. Absorbed into Naunton manor (11,6) in the 14th century; VCH vi pp. 191-2. This can be identified as Frampton, now in Winchcombe, but down to 1600 still known as 'Frampton in Alderton'.
A FURTHER 3 POSSIBLE. 3 ploughs; in several DB counties (e.g. Worcs.) it is stated how many more ploughs could be employed on a manor. This formula seems to be used as a substitute for the phrase 'land for *x* ploughs' which is common in a number of DB counties (see 6,2 note).

11,6 A FURTHER 6 WOULD BE POSSIBLE. *possent esse*, subjunctive, perhaps with a different nuance from *possunt esse* (translated as 'possible', see 11,5). Both forms occur also in DB Worcs. See notes to Worcs. 1,1c and 1,5.

11,7 LORDSHIP. SLAVES. An ink blot covers most of both *dnio* and *serui*, but the meaning is clear.

11,10 8 LIABLE FOR SERVICE. Presumably signifying villagers' land, on which service was done; usually in DB the villagers' land, if mentioned at all, is given after their ploughs.

11,12 HIDCOTE (BOYCE), not, as asserted by most historians, Hidcote Bartrim (12,9).

11,13 ANSWERED FOR 60 HIDES. Paid tax for 60 hides (see 1,3 note above). The 1086 total of taxable hides in 11,1–12 appears to be 57½ hides, if the hide at Frampton (11,4) is still exempt.

11,14 THIS ENTRY was no doubt added later because of the compression of the first three lines and the continuation at the foot of the folio below the marginal rulings, in the middle of 12,3. Both lines at the bottom extend into the left margin; the beginning of each is here exdented in the Latin text.
THE INSERTION of the hundredal rubric is justified by both the last line of the entry and the location of all but one of the Windrush manors in this Hundred. This entry is duplicated in 78,1.

12,1 STOW (ON THE WOLD). Previously 'Edwards Stow' after St. Edward's Church. The ninth hide near the church can be identified as Hide Farm and The Hyde in Maugersbury, the parent settlement of Stow; EPNS i p. 223.
KING AETHELRED GAVE IT, EXEMPT. The ninth hide; see ECWM no. 150 p. 67 (= KCD no. 723 = Sawyer 935) for details of the exemption. Aethelred II (the 'Unready') ruled from 978/9 to 1013 and from 1014 to 1016.

12,2 ADLESTROP. By 1104 at the latest, the lordship and the man-at-arms' land had become a sub-manor of 4 hides (EvO 8).

12,3 2 FREE MEN. Their land was probably the hide in Bourton and 5½ virgates in Donnington later recorded as subinfeudated by Abbot Walter before 1104 (EvE 25; EvO 6, 10).

12,4 THE CHURCH ITSELF HOLDS. Repeated at the beginning of 12,4-9.
13 SLAVES. Added later in the left-hand margin and ringed in black ink, but with no sign to indicate its correct position in the entry.

12,5 (UPPER) SWELL. 3 HIDES. Originally held by the Erneis who in 1066 held several other lands in Glos. (see Index); Harleian MS 3763 fol. 64r (= KCD iv no. 801; *Erusio* there being a misprint for *Ernsio*).

12,6 WICKHAMFORD. Philologically, *Wiquennam* could represent either Childswickham (EPNS ii p. 6) or Wickhamford (EPNS (Worcs.) p. 273), and Dr. Clarke favoured the former identification (Clarke pp. 121, 421-2). But Childswickham is entered elsewhere as a manor of 10 hides (47,1), whilst Wickhamford and the associated manor of Bretforton Upper End contained 9 hides (DB Worcs. 10,6; EvA 25-6): with the hide at *Wiquennam*, an original unit of 10 hides can be reconstituted. The identification of *Wiquennam* as Wickhamford is further confirmed by 12,10, in which the total assessment of Evesham Abbey's Gloucester-shire holdings is given as 56 hides, a total also given in EvH 2 and EvM 70. The sum of the assessments in 12,1-9, including the 2 free hides at Maugersbury (12,1) and Weston 'Cantilupe' (12,7) as well as the hide at *Wiquennam*, is 57 hides, as Clarke himself noted (Clarke p. 232), hence the hide at *Wiquennam* must be excluded to conform with the stated Gloucestershire total of 56 hides. Consequently, this hide was not in Gloucestershire and was therefore at Wickhamford, not Childswickham. EvF 5-6 and EvK 133-4 list the hide at *Wiquennam* separately from the 8 hides at Willersey. However, only 8 hides at Willersey and none at *Wiquennam* are mentioned in EvM 66 and in c.1190 Evesham Church had 28 virgates (7 hides) at Willersey (B. L. Cotton MS Vespasian B xxiv, folio 64v; Harley MS 3763 folio 80r).

12,7 WESTON ('CANTILUPE'). In Weston on Avon; EPNS i p. 260. The total assessment was 4 hides; see note to EvE 10.

12,8 (LARK) STOKE. The assessment is given at 2½ hides in EvO 3. The manor had been subinfeudated before Abbot Walter's death in 1104 to his brother Ranulf (EvO 1, 3, 5).

12,9 HIDCOTE (BARTRIM) has been generally confused with Hidcote (Boyce) (11,12); the suffix is derived from Bertram of Hidcote (EPNS i pp. 244-5), a 12th century subtenant of Evesham Abbey.
THE ABBOT. Walter, Abbot of Evesham 1077-1104.

12,10 THE QUARTER OF WINCHCOMBE. *Ferding* = a part, quarter, often used in DB of the ward of a Borough (see Sussex 9,107 note) and as a measurement of land (as in some south-west counties, a quarter of a virgate). Here it refers to the shire of Winchcombe, absorbed into Gloucestershire in the early 11th century, which was roughly a quarter of the size of Glos. (c.2400 hides; DBB p. 456). See ECWM pp. 228-235; Taylor pp. 218-221.
56 HIDES. The sum of the hidages in 12,1-9, excluding the hide at Wickhamford (see 12,6 note).

13,1 6 SLAVES. £12. A large smudge from the ink blot mentioned in 11,7 note obscures part of *Ibi vi* and *xii lib'*.

14,2 [HUNDRED]. *Hd'* or *Hund'* omitted by the scribe, either in error or through lack of space.

CH. 16 ST. MARY'S OF CORMEILLES. A Benedictine Abbey, founded c.1060 by William son of Osbern (see G 4 note above). He died in 1071 and was buried there.

16,1 NEWENT. See 1,11 note.
EARL ROGER ... FATHER'S SOUL. Earl Roger of Hereford; his father Earl William died in 1071.
A REEVE WHO HAS. Farley omits the *Ibi* before *p̄posit' hn̄s* in error.
A MILL AT 20d. There is no indication as to the case of *molin*: it need not be in the accusative after *habent*. See also in 52,3.

DURAND'S HIDE maintained its separate existence as the later manor of Boulsdon in Frampton on Severn and Newent (Taylor p. 202; VCH x p. 147).
HEDGED ENCLOSURES. See 1,34 note.

CH. 17 ST. MARY'S OF LYRE. Founded in 1046 by William son of Osbern (see G 4 note above). La Vieille-Lyre is in the département of Eure, France.

17,1 DUNTISBOURNE (LEER). Named from its possession by Lyre Abbey. Its assessment should probably have been 1½ hides, not 1¼ hides; the section of Duntisbourne in Rapsgate Hundred then becomes a normal 5 hides vill: 1½ hides (17,1) + 2 hides (39,7) + 2½ virgates (68,11) + 3½ virgates (78,3) = 5 hides. Later amalgamated with 78,3.
ROGER OF LACY. Son of Walter of Lacy who died in 1085.

18,1 CHURCH OF EYNSHAM. EvK 143 describes Eynsham Abbey as '[the Church] of All Saints, Eynsham', omnium sanctorum being interlined above Eglesham.
MEASURES OF SALT. Mensurae salis; of uncertain size; used once of corn in DB Shrops. 4,3,45.

19,1 DEERHURST. See Regesta i no. 32 for a notification (1066-69) by King William that St. Peter's, Westminster, should have Pershore (see DB Worcs. 8,1) and Deerhurst as given by King Edward, with all the customs which pertained to them when in Edward's hands. See also Regesta i no. 234. A grant by King William, dated April 13th 1069, of the Church of Deerhurst to St. Denis, previously held by Abbot Baldwin (see 19,2 note), appears in Regesta i no. 26. See Harmer nos. 99-102 for King Edward's grants and also p. 329 ff.

19,2 WATER-MEADOWS. DB Brocę, a first declension Latinization of OE broc; see DB Herefords. 24,2 note. OE broc came to mean 'a brook', but originally the word (like its cognates Middle Dutch and Dutch brock, Low German brok, Old High German and Mod.G bruch) meant 'marsh', 'bog' etc., a sense retained by brook 'water-meadow' in the Mod.E dialects of Kent, Sussex, Surrey and in medieval field names in Cambridgeshire and Essex, and in some place-names; see DEPN s.v. broc. Of these outliers Hardwicke lies on the River Swilgate, and Todenham and Sutton under Brailes lie on tributaries of the River Stour.
REINBALD. Perhaps Reinbald the priest who is mentioned as Reinbald cancellarius in a grant (perhaps spurious; Harmer pp. 289-90) by King Edward of Deerhurst among other manors to St. Peter's, Westminster (KCD iv no 824 = Sawyer 1043).
'ELLINGS'. DB Telinge; it comprised Ellings in Tirley, Nellings in Deerhurst and Yellings in Chaceley. See EPNS ii p. 171.
WALTER PONTHER. Pontherius; perhaps from ML pontarius 'bridge builder' or puntarius 'sword-fighter'; OEB p. 265. The same man apparently occurs with the surname Puchier (occasionally miswritten Pubier) in WoB (folios 136v (= 137v) and 137v (= 138v), Hearne p. 229, 305); Wallterius Pubier and Walterus Puchier = Walter Ponther of Worcs. 2,5;58. This man obviously bore two surnames, he was Walter Ponther but presumably he or his family came from Picardy (whence Le Poher, Puhier), see Reaney p. 278 s.v. Ponter and Poor. Walter Ponther's hide at Todenham was probably reabsorbed into the main manor of Todenham; VCH vi pp. 252-253.
AT HAYDEN 2 HIDES. They were in Boddington and formed the manor of Hayden in the tithing of Hayden and Withybridge within Westminster Hundred; VCH vi pp. 186, 238; viii pp. 170-71, 188, 190-92.
AT BOURTON (ON THE HILL) 2 HIDES. Gerard's 2 hides here became the Bourton House estate; VCH vi pp. 199-200.
KEMERTON ... KEMERTON. The two ½ hides of Gerard and Abbot Baldwin probably became the carucate of glebe at Kemerton recorded at the end of the 13th century; VCH viii pp. 210-213, 217.
THERE ALSO ABBOT BALDWIN ... ½ HIDE. This italicised phrase is lined through in black in the MS indicating deletion; the scribe wrote the line after the wrong Kemerton entry.
ABBOT BALDWIN. A monk of St. Denis, Paris, then prior of Deerhurst before the division of its lands between the Abbeys of Westminster and St. Denis (cf. EvM 79); finally Abbot of Bury St. Edmunds 1065 to 1097/98. He was also King Edward's doctor. See Harmer p. 539; Regesta i no. 26.
('UPPER') LEMINGTON. Now Lemington Manor; EPNS i p. 246.
ALFRITH. Elfridus; see PNDB p. 144 s.n. Alfrith.
GERARD ... 3 HIDES IN BODDINGTON. These were united with his other 3 hides (1,41) as the later manor of Boddington.
THEY RENDERED NEITHER TAX NOR SERVICE. They were exempt (EvM 79), rather than that Gerard failed to pay the tax and service.
KING'S MEASURE. Cf. 'Borough's measure', also for sesters of honey, in G 1 above.

CH. 20 ST. DENIS', PARIS. The Abbey of St. Dionysius in Paris. See *Regesta* i no. 26 for the grant in 1069 by King William of the Church of Deerhurst to St. Denis (it was originally given by King Edward to Baldwin, a monk there and later Abbot of Bury St. Edmunds; see 19,2 note above).

20,1 CHURCH OF ST. DENIS. The total assessment of the Gloucestershire lands of St. Denis' Abbey was similarly 60 hides in EvM 80; cf. EvK 153–4.
2½ HIDES BEYOND THE SEVERN. These have been identified as Haw in Tirley; VCH viii pp. 26–7, 98–100.
KEMERTON, ½ HIDE. This possibly became the 2 yardlands owned by Brasenose College, Oxford, from the early 16th century; VCH viii p. 213.

21,1 COUNTESS GODA. Sister of King Edward (24,1); wife of Count Drogo of Mantes, then the first wife of Count Eustace of Boulogne; died c.1056.

CH. 22 ST. EVROUL'S. St. Evroult-Notre-Dame-du-Bois in the département of Orne, France. See *Regesta* i no. 140 for the grant of Roel by King William 'from his lordship' in 1081 to St. Evroul. It was founded in 1050 by Hugh of Grandmesnil (later Sheriff of Leicestershire) and his brother Robert. For details of the monastery, see Orderic Vitalis who was a deacon, then priest there.

CH. 23 CHURCH OF CAEN. In the département of Calvados, France. *S. Trinit* was no doubt interlined in 23,1 because a need was felt to differentiate this church from St. Stephen's of Caen which held land in Dorset, Devon, etc.

23,1-2 PINBURY. MINCHINHAMPTON. See *Regesta* i no. 149 for William and Matilda's charter of 1082 granting these manors (and others) to the Abbey of Holy Trinity, Caen, 'with their appurtenances, as quit as they were' in 1066. This nunnery was founded c.1066 by Queen Matilda.

CHS. THE THREE TRANSPOSITION signs beside Chs. 24, 25 and 26 are written completely in
24-27 red ink, those beside 27,1 and its continuation at the foot of the col. are only rubricated. Farley prints 'hands' for all 5 signs; in the MS they are all *psi* (ψ) signs.

CH. 24 CHURCH OF TROARN. A Benedictine Abbey founded in 1050 by Roger of Montgomery (later Earl of Shrewsbury). It is in the département of Calvados, France.

24,1 HORSLEY ... 10 HIDES. Only 7 hides paid tax; see *Regesta* i no. 411 for a writ by William II dated 1094–98, addressed to Walter Sheriff of Glos., stating that Horsley was to be 'rated and quit at 7 hides for all claims' as in the time of William I.
5 SMALLHOLDERS. The scribe originally wrote *ii bord'* and corrected the figure first to *vi*, then to *v*.

CH. 25 CHURCH OF CIRENCESTER. A college of secular canons of which Reinbald (see Ch. 26 note) was said by Leland (*Itinerary* v 62) to have been the dean or provost. This land here and the villager and part of the woodland in Painswick (39,8) are the total of this Church's holdings in 1086. In 1133 Henry I founded a new church of St. Mary at Cirencester, granting it all the lands held formerly by Reinbald the priest (Mon. Ang. vi p. 177).

25,1 2 HIDES. These formed the original glebe of the parish church of St. John, Cirencester, that is, Cirencester Rectory.

CH. 26 REINBALD THE PRIEST. Reinbald, or Regenbald, was the first chancellor of England; also called Reinbald of Cirencester (DB Berks. Ch. 61), see Ch. 25 note above. He held lands also in Berks., Dorset, Herefords., Bucks., Somerset and Wilts. A copy of the declaration by King Edward, dated 1042–1066, that Reinbald was to have judicial and financial rights over his land and men 'as fully and completely as any of his predecessors in the days of King Canute', and a copy of King William's confirmation of this, appear in the Cirencester Cartulary (printed in *Archaeologia* xxvi p. 256) and in *Regesta* i no. 19 and Harmer no. 44. For Reinbald, see also Round FE p. 421 ff; *Regesta* i pp. xiii, xv; W. H. Stevenson in EHR xi (1896) p. 731 note.

26,1 AMPNEY (ST. MARY) included part of Ampney Crucis to the north and Harnhill to the west.

26,2 EARL TOSTI. Brother of Earl Harold; Earl of Northumbria after Siward's death in 1055 until his expulsion in 1065; killed in the battle of Stamford Bridge on 25th Sept. 1066.
8 VILLAGERS. *vi* with *ii* interlined to correct the number to *viii*.

26,3 REINBALD'S HIDE IN NORCOTE, a hamlet of Preston, was amalgamated with his main manor of Preston (26,4).

26,4 BESIDES THE LORDSHIP (LAND). The implication is that there are also lordship hides in Preston, number unspecified, which as usual do not pay tax (see 39,6). Also occurs in 39,17 and 66,5.

CHS. THE NUMBERS of these chapters were originally written *xxv* and *xxvi* and corrected to 27,28 *xxvii* and *xxviii*, presumably when the rubricator realised that the scribe had written the holdings of Cirencester Church and Reinbald the priest out of place.

CH. 27 EARL ROGER. Roger of Montgomery, Earl of Shrewsbury from 1074 (or perhaps as early as 1071 when he received lands there on the death of Earl Edwin) until his death in 1094; he also received lands at Arundel and Chichester (Orderic Vitalis ii pp. 178, 220). See J. F. A. Mason *Roger de Montgomery and his Sons (1067–1102)* in TRHS 5th ser. vol. 13 (1963).

27,1 THOROLD, WIGOT'S NEPHEW. Wigot of Wallingford; see Freeman iv App. Note C p. 734. THE LAST LINE OF THIS ENTRY is added later in paler ink below the marginal rulings, extending some seven letters into the left margin.

CH. 28 EARL HUGH. Hugh of Avranches, nephew of King William; Earl of Chester 1071/77 to 1101. His daughter Matilda married Count Robert of Mortain and his sister Count William of Eu.

28,1 ROBERT. Probably Robert of Tilleul, Earl Hugh's cousin; VCH xi p. 12.

28,2-3 THERE ALSO. That is, in Bisley Hundred, the list of manors in this Hundred having been interrupted by the marginal entries for Longtree Hundred.
THROUGHAM, EDGEWORTH. EvM 109–110 repeat the hidages of DB, but EvK 157 has 'At *Troham* 1½ hides', with no mention of Edgeworth, apparently including the ½ hide in Edgeworth with the hide at Througham.

28,3 AT EDGEWORTH ½ HIDE. Probably at Westwood. Roger of Lacy's claim succeeded, since in 1130 the Lacy manor of Painswick, including Edgeworth, by then in the King's hands, was rated at 3 hides, i.e. 1 (39,8) + ½ (28,3) + 1½ (39,9); P.R. 31 Hen. 1 p. 80; Wightman pp. 148, 248–9.

28,5-7 IT IS PROBABLE that 28,5-6, added later in the margin, are an explanation of 28,7 which does not place the 4 hides nor give the size of Alnoth's and Leofwin's holdings. (EvK 159 supports this view with just one entry for Earl Hugh in Longtree Hundred: the 4 hides in Westonbirt.) The scribe of EvM 108;112 appears to have misunderstood DB, giving the 3 hides in Westonbirt (28,5) as separate from the 4 hides in Longtree Hundred (28,7) and ignoring altogether Leofwin's hide in 28,6. Alnoth's 3 hides became the main manor of Westonbirt, and Leofwin's hide became Minchin's Farm in Westonbirt; VCH xi pp. 285–7, 291. By 1285 'Weston Dovel' in Westonbirt (32,4) had been amalgamated with Westonbirt.

28,5;7 ALNOTH. Probably Alnoth/Ednoth the Constable, Earl Hugh's predecessor in many other counties, who was killed in battle against Earl Harold's sons in 1067; see DB Somerset 18,1 and 39,1 General notes.

28,7 THERE WAS NO ONE TO MAKE ... Cf. 1,63 and 75,2.

CH. 29 COUNT OF MORTAIN. Robert, half brother of King William and younger brother of Bishop Odo of Bayeux. He held more land in England than any other follower of King William (see Freeman iv p. 762), especially in Cornwall and other south-west counties. See DB Somerset 19,1 General note. Mortain (not mentioned in OEB) is in the département of Manche, France.

29,1 LONGBOROUGH. The land was Banks Fee.

CH. 30 GILBERT BISHOP OF LISIEUX. Gilbert Maminot, King William's doctor and chaplain, Bishop of Lisieux 1077–1101; Orderic Vitalis ii pp. 311–312. Lisieux is in the département of Calvados, France.

30,1 RODMARTON. The main manor of Rodmarton; VCH xi pp. 236–40. Hugh Maminot was Bishop Gilbert's son; Sanders p. 97.

CH. 31 WILLIAM OF EU. William, Count of Eu, second son of Count Robert of Eu, which is in the département of Seine-Maritime, France. See W 16 note above. His second wife was the sister of Earl Hugh of Chester. He rebelled against William Rufus in 1088 and in 1094 and was charged with treason in 1096, was blinded and castrated and probably died soon after; Orderic Vitalis iii p. 411.

31,1 VINEYARD. 2 *ARPENTS*. An *arpent* was a French measure of uncertain and probably variable size, usually applied in DB to vineyards, but occasionally to meadow and woodland; see DB Wilts. 12,4 note. This is the only reference to vineyards in Glos.

31,2 'ALVERSTON' was a site at Brookend and Plusterwine in Woolaston (VCH x pp. 103, 107-8), not, as usually identified, Allaston in Lydney, which is to be identified as 37,5.
HENRY ... BONDI. Probably Bondi the Constable (on whom see DB Beds. 57,4 note); Freeman v p. 771; PNDB p. 206 note 2. Bondi was the TRE holder of some of Henry of Ferrers' lands in Northants., Berks. and Oxfordshire.

31,4 ALSTAN here and in 31,7;10-11 is clearly the great Anglo-Saxon thane Alstan of Boscombe (cf. 58,4) whose lands in Gloucestershire and elsewhere in England were first granted to Ralph of Limesy and then to William of Eu.
FOREST. ML *foresta* from *foris* 'outside' means land, not necessarily wooded, beyond the bounds of the manor or village. This is the Forest of Dean. In 1086 a large tract of woodland joined Dean to Wyre Forest via Malvern Chase. See VCH (Worcs.) ii p. 197.

31,5 WILLIAM ALSO HOLDS. Repeated at the beginning of 31,5–12.
WOOLASTON. This later absorbed William of Eu's 2 hides (1,64) and Roger of Lacy's ½ hide (39,10) at Madgett.

31,6 IN TIDENHAM 1½ VIRGATES. The land was at Stroat, later reabsorbed in the main manor of Tidenham (1,56).

31,7 'DUNTISBOURNE'. Amalgamated with 32,2 to form the manor of Daglingworth, the church of which was a chapelry of Duntisbourne minster.
RALPH. Most probably Ralph Blewitt who held two manors in Somerset (26,3;5) and one in Hants. (32,4) from William of Eu, which had been held TRE by Alstan of Boscombe (see 31,4 note above). The Blewitts were later lords of both Daglingworth and the Somerset and Hampshire manors mentioned.

31,8 IN TARLTON 1 HIDE. Later combined with 31,10 as the manor of Tarlton; VCH xi pp. 236–40.

31,9 SHIPTON ('DOVEL'). In Shipton Moyne. It is a lost place near Estcourt (EPNS i p. 108): possibly therefore to be identified as Hill Court.
HUGH is probably William of Eu's brother-in-law Earl Hugh of Chester (Sanders pp. 119–20): in the 13th century Shipton Dovel was held of the Earldom of Chester (VCH x p. 252).

31,10 CULKERTON. See note to 31,8.

31,10-11 ALSTAN. See note to 31,4.

31,12 (LOWER) SWELL. Reunited in the 12th century with 45,6 (VCH vi p. 167).
ERNEIS. *Ernesi*. In PNDB 243, the DB form *Ernesi* is taken to represent OE *Earnsige*. PNDB 243, note 2 notes that DB *Ernesi*, Gloucs. fol. 167 is the same man as *Ernsius* (lit. *Erusio*, ablative case) son of *Oca* 1055 KCD 801 (S. 1026), that is, OE *Earnsige*; and that DB *Ernesi*, Gloucs. fol. 168 is the same as *Arnisius* son of *Ealdgy'* c.1070 Evesham Chronicle 94, perhaps a badly Latinized form for OE *Earnsige* since he seems heir to an English-named mother — but the form *Arnisius* could also indicate that she had named her boy with the French name *Erneis* (OG *Ernegis*, Forrsner 82), for von Feilitzen's note observes that the Latinized form *Ernisius* is usually taken to represent OF *Erneis* in sources later than DB; Forrsner 82 also records *Erneisus* DB, and ME *Aernisius, Ernisius, Hernesius*, for OF *Erneis*.

Sir Iain Moncreiffe of that Ilk in correspondence concerning the holdings of Drogo fitz Pons, who was closely associated with Ralf de Todeni (Toesny) in Gloucs. and Herefords. and whose lands became the Clifford estates (see Ellis i 405 note 9) points out that, with one small exception, between them Drogo and Ralf held all Ernesi's TRE lands (for Ralf de Toesny also held Ernesi's former estate in Worcs.); that in view of the rarity of the personal-names *Erneis* and *Pons* in Norman records, Drogo fitz Pons's father — who received lands at the Conquest (he endowed Westminster Abbey, see Berks. 30,1 under Walter son of Poyntz) but died before the Domesday Survey and may reasonably be identified as the Pons who witnessed Ducal charters for Fecamp 1025 and 1066 — was possibly a near relation, perhaps an uncle by marriage, of the only other Pons to appear in the charters of the Dukes of Normandy 911-1066, a monk at St. Wandrille in Normandy c.1049-1066, the brother of Robert fitz Erneis and therefore son of Erneis Taisson, the Norman seigneur of Fontenay, who was the only Erneis to appear in these Ducal charters 911-1066, e.g. that Pons may have married Erneis's sister, since he was apparently not his brother; and that the repeated association of Drogo *fitz Pons* TRW with estates of *Ernesi* TRE therefore suggests that this Ernesi may possibly have been *Erneis*, a Norman, not an Englishman *Earnsige*.

Whether or not this will be proved on genealogical grounds, a question is raised about the name-form. Also, the spelling *Ernesi* DB with persistent medial -e- favours OF *Erneis* (OG *Ernegis*) as von Feilitzen's note hints. It would seem prudent to explain the DB form as either OF *Erneis* (OG *Ernegis*) or OE *Earnsige*, leaving the choice open to definition by contextual or external evidence; and to bear in mind that OF *Erneis* and OE *Earnsige* would both be rather rare personal-names at the time of DB, likely to be confused with each other, especially in their respective Latinized forms *Ernesius* and *Ernsius*.

2,1 2 HIDES IN CIRENCESTER. Chesterton in Cirencester.
HUGH could well be Hugh of Lacy, whose mother and brother held the adjoining manors of Stratton and Siddington Langley (39,17–18). In the 13th century both Chesterton and Siddington Langley were held by the Langley family.
1½ VILLAGERS may well be an error for '1 half-villager'; see W 1 note above.

2,2 WILLIAM ALSO HOLDS. Repeated at the beginning of 32,2–11.
'DUNTISBOURNE'. See note to 31,7.
KETEL AND AELFRIC. In the MS *Chetel 7 Aluric*; Farley omits the 7 in error.

2,3 SIDDINGTON (HOUSE). This estate comprised that part of Siddington east of the R. Churn.

2,4 'WESTON (DOVEL)'. Later amalgamated with the main manor of Westonbirt; see 28,5–7 note. Cf. EvK 187; EvM 135.

2,6 ALWIN. See note to 1,45.

2,7 WULFHEAH. In the MS after *Vlfeg* something had been written, then erased, leaving the line which had been drawn under it.
THESE THANES ... WOULD. The scribe wrote this phrase after, instead of before, '5 hides which pay tax', and put transposition signs to indicate its correct position.

2,9 2½ VIRGATES. Hill House in Newnham; VCH x pp. 36–9. EvK 193 implies that these 2½ virgates were in Newnham, thus confirming this identification.
WIHENOC. Uncle of William son of Baderon; see the foundation charter of Monmouth Priory, founded by Wihenoc c.1075 in Mon. Ang. iv p. 596, which is witnessed by Wihenoc's brother Baderon and, among others, Baderon's son William. See also E 35 note below.

2,10 NEWNHAM. Hyde in Newnham; VCH x pp. 36–9.

2,11 '(LITTLE) LYDNEY', so named to distinguish it from the main manor of Lydney (1,55), was renamed St. Briavels in the 13th century.

2,12 FOREST. Of Dean; see 31,4 note.

2,13 THIS ENTRY is written at the bottom of col. 167a, in the space usually left after the end of a chapter, but not written below the marginal rulings.
(LOWER) HAMPEN. See note to 2,6.
GEOFFREY. Probably the same man who held the adjoining manors of Farmcote (34,7), Shipton Oliffe (38,4) and Lower Turkdean (38,5).

CH. 33 WILLIAM THE CHAMBERLAIN. He also held land in Beds. and Bucks.

CH. 34 WILLIAM GOIZENBODED. Son of Richard; see 34,8 note. Goizenboded is an unexplained byname; OEB p. 390. The ending is -*boded*, past participle of OE *bodian* 'to announce, to foretell'. *Goizen-* is perhaps *Guizen-*, a French form of OE *wiccan* 'witch', where *w* has become *gu* (as in Mod.Fr *guerre* 'war' from OG *werra*), a common feature of Central French, sometimes found in Anglo-Norman, and *z* represents the sounds [ts] or [tʃ], a French rendering of OE -*cc*-. The name may thus be OE *wiccanboded*, 'foretold by a witch' or 'cursed by a witch'. The byname also occurs as *Guezenboeth* in Worcs. D (see DB Worcs. App. V) and as *Cunteboiz'* in EvN 14, and as *Guiz in bod'* in EvK 116.

4,1 PEBWORTH. United c.1100 with the other manor of Pebworth (62,1).

4,2 WILLIAM ALSO HOLDS. Repeated at the beginning of 34,2–13.
EARL ALGAR. Earl of East Anglia 1051–2 and 1053–7, then Earl of Mercia 1057–62. He was outlawed in 1055 and again in 1058, but won back his position on each occasion with the help of Gruffydd ap Llywelyn, King of Gwynedd and Powys. Algar was the son of Earl Leofric and the Lady (Countess) Godiva; father of Earls Edwin and Morcar; he died c.1062.

4,3 HUSCARL. *Huscarle*; OWScand. and late OE *Huscarl* 'bodyguard'; see OEB pp. 255–256 and PNDB pp. 296–297. The word is used in some instances as a personal name, as perhaps here (and in DB Cambs. 14,64; see note), and in others as a descriptive term: 'a member of the King's bodyguard' (see 1,59;66 and DB Middx. 7,2;8 etc.).

4,5 'CALDICOTT'. An earlier name for Westfield in Hawling and Lower Guiting.

4,6 AYLWORTH. Rose Court in Aylworth (VCH vi p. 80).

4,7 GEOFFREY. See note to 32,13.

4,8 LEASED. In the MS the abbreviation line, indicating an omitted *m*, is over the *o* as well as the *c* of *accōmodavit*, not as Farley prints it.
RICHARD, A YOUNG MAN. *Iuvenis*, so also DB Worcs. 25,1, as the predecessor of William Goizenboded, who is later remembered as 'William son of Richard' when land in Moorcroft (prev. Murcott) (*Morcate*) in Minsterworth was given for the sake of his soul to St. Peter's Abbey, Gloucester; *History of St. Peter's, Gloucester* i pp. 99–100, ii p. 32. William himself held Duni in Minsterworth (see 34,12 note). William's mother was probably not Alwin's widow, or William would still have been a minor in 1086.

4,11 (LITTLE) BARRINGTON. So VCH vi pp. 19–20.

34,12 ½ HIDE OF LAND. The mention of a ½ fishery limits the possible site of this land to the riverside in Westbury Hundred. It possibly lay at 'Duni' in Minsterworth, the only part of Minsterworth parish not accounted for separately in DB (see 37,1 and 53,1 notes). There is evidence to associate William son of Richard (who is probably the same man as William Goizenboded styled by DB as Richard's successor; see 34,8 note) with Minsterworth. 'Duni' was a small estate of about 130 acres in the extreme south of Minsterworth, separated by streams from the rest of the chapelry. The ½ fishery may well be the '½ fishery at Duni' given c.1150 to St. Peter's, Glos. (*History of St. Peter's, Glos.* i p. 259 and ii p. 72; see D. Walker 'Charters of the Earldom of Hereford', Camden Miscellany vol. xxii, p. 26).

34,13- THESE THREE ENTRIES are written in a cramped style, suggesting either that the scribe
35,2   had not planned this folio correctly or that more information came to hand after this side of the folio was completed and the other side begun.

34,13 IN DUMBLETON 1 HIDE. 'Littleton' in Dumbleton, a name that survived until the late 19th century, not Littleworth in Winchcombe. See also 36,3. 53,12.

35,1   DYRHAM. The manor of Dyrham in the parish of Dyrham and Hinton. The figure for villagers' ploughs is suspiciously low and should probably be corrected to either 7 or 12, probably either *v* or *x* having been omitted before *ii* during the final compilation of DB.

35,2   3 HIDES. The manor of Hinton, which later records show was approximately half the area of Dyrham manor, in the parish of Dyrham and Hinton.

CH. 36 WILLIAM BREAKWOLF. *Froisseleuu*, from OFr. *froisser* 'to crush, break', and *leuu* 'wolf'; OEB p. 385.

36,1   WOTTON. DB *Vletone* would seem to be from OE $\bar{U}la$-$t\bar{u}ne$ 'owls' village, 'village where there are owls', but no place- or field-name 'Owlton' can be found anywhere in Dudstone Hundred. It seems more likely, therefore, that *Vletone* is a scribal error for *Wotone* (in a badly written or damaged original return a capital *W* could look like *Vl* and a poorly written *o* like an *e*), and that Wotton (St. Mary) is the place. A more precise location in Wotton is probably Paygrove, which was the only major holding in the Wotton area not held by St. Peter's, Glos. in 1086, although it was later given to that Abbey by Richard son of Nigel (*History of St. Peter's, Glos.* i pp. 107, 118, 319; ii p. 89).

36,2   IN WITLEY HUNDRED. Entered in the left margin of the MS. This holding was joined early in the 12th century with the Condicote outlier of Oddington (2,4).

36,3   'LITTLETON'. See note to 34,13.

CH. 37 WILLIAM SON OF NORMAN. He seems to have had some responsibility for supervising the Forest of Dean (see 37,3 and DB Herefords. 1,63). See also Herefords. Ch. 16 note.

37,1   MOORCROFT. Previously Murcott (EPNS, iii p. 163) in the parish of Minsterworth.

37,2   WILLIAM ALSO HOLDS. Repeated at the beginning of 37,2-5.
    MORGANWY. DB *Morganau*, OW *Morcenou*, MW *Morganeu*; PNDB p. 329.

37,3   IN MITCHELDEAN 2 HIDES AND 2½ VIRGATES. Possibly Mitcheldean included Abenhall and Littledean.
    GUARDING THE FOREST. Cf. DB Herefords. 1,44 and DB Berks. 31,3-4.

37,3-4 FOREST. Of Dean; see 31,4 note.

37,5   1 HIDE AND ½ VIRGATE. Identifiable as Allaston in Lydney. See note to 31,2.
    HELD. In the MS the plural *tenue͞r* has been corrected from the singular *tenuit*.

38,1   LECKHAMPTON. Identifiable as Broadwell in Leckhampton.

38,2   WILLIAM ALSO HOLDS. Repeated at the beginning of 38,2-5.

38,4-5 GEOFFREY. See note to 32,13.

38,4   3 HIDES, LESS 1 VIRGATE. EvK 217 gives the same assessment in a different form: '2 hides and 3 virgates'.

38,5   (LOWER) TURKDEAN. Lower and Upper Turkdean (48,2) together total 11 hides; it is possible that the assessment for Lower Turkdean, whose 1086 value was lower than Upper Turkdean's, was 4 hides and 1½ virgates, not 5 hides and 1½ virgates, but the DB assessment is repeated by EvK 218 and EvM 173.

CH. 39 ROGER OF LACY. Son of Walter of Lacy and Ermelina (Emma); see Wightman p. 167 ff. The large number of lands he possessed in Glos., Herefords. and Worcs. (see DB Herefords. Ch. 10 note) made him an important defender of the English frontier against the Welsh. He rebelled in 1088 and in 1094, was banished in 1096 and his lands given to his brother Hugh. He died some time after 1106 in Normandy where he had obtained high office under Duke Robert. Lassy is in the département of Calvados, France.

,2 ROGER ALSO HOLDS. Repeated at the beginning of 39,2-15;17-19.

,4 ICOMB ('PLACE'). Combined with 53,8 as the Icomb 'Place' estate, still held from two different lords as late as 1331. The second manorial site in the Gloucestershire part of Icomb was at Icomb 'Proper', west of Icomb village, where a series of 'Court' field-names survived down to the 19th century.

,5 (WICK) RISSINGTON (VCH vi pp. 100, 108, 115), not Little Rissington (Taylor pp. 257, 261).
HUGH here and in 39,16 is probably Roger's brother and successor Hugh of Lacy; VCH vi p. 115.
VALUE ... £7 10[s]. In the MS *7 x lib'* is written slightly below the line on which *vii lib'* and the rest were written, perhaps indicating that it was added later. The *lib'* is no doubt an error for *sol'*.

,6 PASTURE. One of the few references to pasture in DB Glos.; it would seem that for some reason either no normal record of pasture was made for this county or that it was 'deliberately excluded'; DGM p. 35. DB Herefords. (see 1,5 note) likewise has only two mentions of pasture.

,7 GILBERT. Gilbert de Eskecot who gave this land to St. Peter's Abbey, Gloucester in 1100 (*History of St. Peter's, Gloucester* i p. 73); it was then amalgamated with Duntisbourne Abbots (10,13).
THE VALUE IS AND WAS 40s. Or possibly 'value 40s; the value was [£ x/the same]'. The dot after *ualuit*, however, suggests that *ualuit* was simply omitted after *Val'*, not that the scribe intended to fill in a past value later.

,8 A PRIEST. In the MS and Farley *pbr*; the facsimile fails to reproduce half the *r*.
ST. MARY'S ... HOLDS. The land held by Cirencester Abbey has been identified as Stroudend in the south of Painswick; VCH xi p. 68.

,9 EDGEWORTH. See note to 28,3.
3 SMALLHOLDERS. *ii* corrected to *iii* with *es* (for *tres*) added above to clarify the correction.

,10 THE INSERTION of the hundredal rubric is based on the inclusion of Madgett in this Hundred in 1,64. Amalgamated in the 12th century with William of Eu's manors of Madgett (1,64) and Woolaston (31,5).

,11 IN TIDENHAM ½ HIDE. This holding was at Stroat, later reabsorbed into the main manor of Tidenham (1,56).

,12 1 BURGESS WHO PAYS 4 PLOUGHSHARES. 4 burgesses pay 18 ploughshares (*socos carrucis*) in DB Herefords. 1,7, and a house in Worcester similarly pays 2 ploughshares (*uomeres*) (Herefords. 1,41). See also 68,4 below.

,13-14 WILLIAM has been identified as William Devereux; Wightman pp. 144, 154 note 5.

,14 HATHEROP. This holding is later known as Williamstrip derived from the subtenant, William Devereux, whose family held it until the 14th century.

,15 WINDRUSH. Hungerford in Windrush; VCH vi pp. 179-80.

,16 ALSO ... THERE. Pinchpool in Windrush; VCH vi pp. 179-80.
HUGH. See note to 39,5.

,17 ROGER ALSO HOLDS. See 39,2 note.
BESIDES THE LORDSHIP (LAND). See 26,4 note.

,18 SIDDINGTON. Siddington Langley manor in Siddington St. Peter parish, centred on Home Close at the north end of Lower Siddington village.

,18;20 HIS MOTHER. Ermelina (Emma), wife of Walter of Lacy; Wightman pp. 168-9.

,19 OAKLEY. Coates 'Randulf' in Oakley, still held from the Lacy family in the 1230s.
GERARD. Perhaps Gerard the Chamberlain; or *Girardus* could be a mistake for *Giruius* 'Gerwy' who holds Coates Cockerell in Oakley in 67,3.

,20 (UPPER) SLAUGHTER. The assessment of Upper Slaughter was increased to 5 hides, and that of Lower Quinton (62,4) reduced from 12 hides, c.1097 (EvN 11).
KING'S USE. *ad opus regis*; or perhaps 'for the King's work' as in DB Dorset 30,4. Cf. DB Herefords. 1,2 'Value of what the Sheriff has for his use...'. See DB Som. 6,1 General note and Worcs. H 2 in DB Worcs. App. V. Cf. the example quoted in Ch. 52 note below.

,21 ARCOLD. Ercoldus; see OEB p. 180.

CH. 40 ROGER OF BEAUMONT. Roger, who also held land in Dorset (Ch. 28), appears to have been an old man by the time of DB. About 1094-5 he entered the monastery of St. Pierre at Préaux, which his father Humphrey of Vieilles had founded c.1034. He died some years later; Orderic Vitalis ii p. 14 and iii pp. 426-7. Roger's son Robert inherited the title of the Count of Meulan through his mother Adelina. Another son Henry became Earl of Warwick c.1089. Beaumont is most probably Beaumont-le-Roger in the département of Eure, France; OEB p. 71.

40,1 ROBERT. Probably Robert the Butler, ancestor of the Botelers who appear to have held Dorsington in the 12th century (VCH Warwicks. v p. 199). Or, possibly, Roger's son Robert, Count of Meulan, although one would expect the scribe to have added 'his son' (but see 34,8 where William Goizenboded is not called Richard's son but his successor).

CH. 41 ROGER OF IVRY. He was married to Azelina (Adeline), a daughter of Hugh of Grandmesnil (Orderic Vitalis iii p. 361). See W 1 note above. Ivry la Bataille is in the département of Eure, France; OEB p. 92.

41,3-4 (TETBURY) UPTON. CULKERTON. Later absorbed in Tetbury (41,2); VCH xi pp. 236–40.

41,4 AELFRIC. *Aluric* in the MS and Farley; the facsimile reproduces the name as *Alliric*, or possibly *Allinc*.

41,5 HAZLETON. The main manor of Hazleton; VCH xi pp. 236–40.
HALF-VILLAGERS. See W 1 note above.

CH. 42 ROGER OF BERKELEY. An important man in Gloucestershire; the 'reeve of Berkeley' in 1,16, he also appears to have collected the revenue from Barton Regis (1,21). Died 1093.

42,2 DODINGTON. See note to 6,9. '2 parts of ½ hide' = one-third of a hide.

43,1 WAPLEY. Amalgamated in the 13th century with the main estate in Wapley and Codrington centred on Codrington Court (1,9).

CH. 44 RALPH PAGNELL. Sheriff of Yorkshire in 1088.

44,1-2 THESE TWO ENTRIES are combined in EvK 289 as 'In Longtree Hundred: *Torentone* (Tarlton) 4½ hides and 1½ virgates'.

44,1 TARLTON. Combined with 1,23 as the manor of Hullasey; VCH xi pp. 236–40.
RALPH. Probably Ralph of Reuilly who was Ralph Pagnell's subtenant in 4 out of his 5 Somerset manors (DB Somerset 31,1-4).
MERLESWEIN. No doubt the Merleswein who was Sheriff of Lincolnshire in 1066. Ralph Pagnell inherited almost all his land.

44,2 THIS ENTRY is added in pale brown ink in the right margin in a smaller hand than the main text; there is not the marked diminution in size after *Iurei* that Farley prints. It probably refers not to Little Tarlton (VCH xi pp. 236–40), but to land in Culkerton in Rodmarton. RALPH PAGNELL. In the MS *pagen* (not *page*, as Farley) is interlined above *Rad*' and rubricated. It is written at the extreme edge of the folio and there is no abbreviation sign; however, *pagenel* is obviously intended, the diminutive form of *pagen* ('a villager, heathen', from Latin *paganus* 'member of a *pagus* (village or country district)' whence Mod. Fr *paysan* 'peasant, countryman' and *paien* 'pagan', which is rendered in this series as 'Payne', as in 70,1 below).

CH. 45 RALPH OF TOSNY. Ralph III, also called Ralph of Conches. He was son of Roger I of Tosny and brother-in-law of William son of Osbern (see G 4 note above). He was lord of Clifford Castle in Hereford, his chief seat being at Flamstead in Herts. (DB Herts. 22,1). He died some time before March 1102; see Douglas pp. 85–6. Tosny and Conches-en-Ouche are in the département of Eure, France; place-names with Toney (e.g. Newton Toney in Wilts.) are named after his descendants.

45,1-2; ROGER. The Roger who held 'Combe Baskerville' (45,2) was almost certainly Roger
4-5 Baskerville (VCH vi p. 184), who may also have held Charingworth, Driffield and Harnhill, though none of these manors remained with his descendants.

45,2 RALPH ALSO HOLDS. Repeated at the beginning of 45,2-6.
'COMBE (BASKERVILLE)' comprised the whole parish of Westcote; VCH vi p. 174; see EPNS i p. 221.

45,4 5 HIDES. The *v* has been corrected from another number, possibly *i*.

45,5 'AMPNEY' AND (SOUTH) CERNEY. The Ampney portion of this manor lay in Driffield; the Cerney portion was Cerney Wick in South Cerney. The agricultural details may well refer to Harnhill (45,4) as well as Driffield and Cerney Wick.

45,6 (LOWER) SWELL. See notes to 31,12 and EvN 12–13.
DROGO. Drogo son of Poyntz, whose descendants, the Poyntz family, held Lower Swell until the 13th century.

CH. 47 ROBERT THE BURSAR. Brother of Urso of Abetot who was Sheriff of Worcs. Robert held the castle and honour of Tamworth (Staffs.); see Empress Maud's charter to William of Beauchamp, printed in J. H. Round *Geoffrey de Mandeville* pp. 313–315.

47,1 CHILDSWICKHAM. See notes to 12,6 and EvN 12–13.

H. 48   ROBERT D'OILLY. Sheriff of Warwickshire from the early to the late 1080s, of Oxfordshire and perhaps also Berkshire. He was Castellan of Oxford Castle under King William and is called the Constable of Oxford; *History of Abingdon* ii pp. 7, 12. See G. H. White 'The Household of the Norman Kings' in TRHS 4th ser. vol. xxx (1948) pp. 149-151. He was probably married to one of the daughters of Wigot of Wallingford; see Freeman iv App. Note C, and also 64,1;3 note below. For Oilly, see OEB p. 103.

8,1   (LITTLE) RISSINGTON. So VCH vi pp. 100, 108, 115, not Wyck Rissington (Taylor pp. 257, 261).

8,2   (UPPER) TURKDEAN. See note to 38,5.

8,3   ROGER D'OILLY. In the MS *oger'* and part of the *R* are written over an erasure, probably at once before the rest of the line was written. Though it is impossible to read what was originally written, it would seem that the scribe began, at least, to write *Isd'* as in 48,2, because the ascender of the *R* has a 'tail' like an *I*, rather than an *R*; also there is room for the scribe to have written *Isd' Rotb't'*, the *Roger'* being written larger than usual and with a gap between the *R* and *o*. It would therefore seem likely that the scribe intended to write *Roger'*, not that he made a careless slip, as has been suggested, nor that the DB scribe wrote *Radulf'* or *Ricard'* and a later scribe mistakenly corrected the name to *Roger'* rather than *Rotb(er)t'*. Roger d'Oilly was presumably some relative; see G. H. White 'Constables under the Norman Kings' in the *Genealogist* xxx (1922) p. 117. A Roger d'Oilly was the witness to several notifications of grants from c.1105-1114, appearing in one as constable; see Farrer nos. 114-115, 127, 129, 195, 216, 316 and also the *History of Abingdon* ii p. 126. It is rather unusual that it is not stated that he held the land 'from Robert'; cf. 75,3.
      NAUNTON. Reunited with 78,8 by 1287 to form Naunton manor.
      OSBERN SON OF RICHARD. Son of Richard Scrope, a Norman who settled in Herefords. at the time of the Confessor and continued a landholder after the Conquest (see DB Worcs. 19,1 note). Osbern succeeded him and was lord of Richard's Castle in Herefordshire.

CH. 49   RICHARD THE COMMISSIONER. See L 49 note above.

49,1   8 HIDES ... There is a gap of about 6 letters in the MS after *hidę*, perhaps for the later inclusion of *geld'* (as occurs in many other entries in DB Glos.) or of a fraction; see DB Worcs. Ch. 14 note. Such gaps after the hidage occur very regularly in DB Herefords (see E 5;8 notes below and Herefords. 1,9 note). Farley does not print the gap, though he does in the similar cases of 56,1. 60,7 and 78,17.

50,1   VALUE £6. Written completely in the right margin (not as Farley), obviously later but by the same scribe as the rest.

50,2   STOKE (GIFFORD). See note to 3,1.

50,4   'OLDBURY' in Elkstone, now Slutswell Farm.
      SHIRE STATES. The Shire Court. The gap of about 6 letters after this is caused by an erasure.

CH. 51   GEOFFREY ORLATEILE. See OEB p. 385.

51,1   THE INSERTION of the hundredal rubric is justified by the inclusion of Priors Court in Baunton (78,5) in this Hundred.

CH. 52   GILBERT SON OF THOROLD. Probably the same man as Gilbert of Bouillé (see DB Warwicks. B 2 note). He was a fairly important follower of Earl William of Hereford, holding land in Worcs., Glos., Herefords. and Somerset with a few manors in Warwicks., Cambs. and Essex. In DB Worcs. 11,2 (Sheriffs Lench) he is said to have 'collected the gold for the King's use' (*qui aurum recepit ad opus regis*).

52,1-2   1 HIDE IN OAKLEY. IN TREWSBURY ½ HIDE. These two holdings were later combined as the manor of Trewsbury.

52,2   GILBERT ALSO HOLDS. Repeated at the beginning of 52,2-7.

52,3   (NORTH) CERNEY included Calmsdean, Woodmancote and the area of the parish west of the R. Churn (*ex. inf.* Dr. N. M. Herbert).
      MEN-AT-ARMS ... MILL AT 8s. See 16,1 note above.

52,4-5   RENDCOMB. RENDCOMB. The identification of these two manors with the later manors of Upper and Lower Rendcombe respectively is not absolutely certain; in any case, Upper Rendcombe, later renamed Marsden, included some land in Lower Rendcombe.

52,5-6   WALTER. Fairly certainly Walter Delamare: both manors are later held by the Delamare family (VCH vi p. 80).

52,6-7   THESE TWO ENTRIES are squeezed in at the bottom of the col. (the final line being below the last ruling), though not apparently written later; another example of the scribe's bad planning in this county.

52,6   IN SALMONSBURY HUNDRED. Entered in the left margin of the MS. The manor was reunited with Rose Court (34,6) in 1566; VCH vi p. 80.

CH. 53 DURAND OF GLOUCESTER. Durand of Pîtres, Constable of Gloucester Castle (*History of St. Peter's, Gloucester* i p. lxxvi), and Sheriff of Glos. in 1086 after his brother Roger (on whom see 56,2 note). He seems to have been dead by 1095 as his successor and nephew Walter was holding most of his land by the first half of that year. See D. Walker 'The 'Honours' of the Earls of Hereford in the Twelfth Century' in TBGAS lxxix (1960) pp. 174, 179; D. Walker *Charters of the Earldom of Hereford 1095–1201* in Camden Soc. 4th ser. vol. i (1964) pp. 37–38.

53,1   ONE MANOR. This can be identified from later evidence as the manor of Minsterworth. 3 HIDES. Originally *ii* corrected to *iii*; the addition of the interlined *b*; (= *bus*) does not help clarify the correction (see, e.g. 39,9 note), as it could be read as the ending for both *duabus* and *tribus*.

53,2   DURAND ALSO HOLDS. Repeated at the beginning of 53,2–12.
ASHBROOK. Although by the 18th century it was synonymous with Ampney St. Mary, in the medieval period it also included part of Ampney Crucis.

53,3   RALPH is almost certainly Ralph Blewitt who held Daglingworth (31,7; see note) immediately to the north, and is probably the same man who held Shipton 'Pelye' (53,9) and 'Littleton' (53,12) from Durand of Gloucester.

53,4   CULKERTON The main manor of Culkerton; VCH xi pp. 236–40.

53,5   DIDMARTON in 1086 included the sub-manor of Leighterton to the north, of which Durand's descendants, the Bohun Earls of Hereford, were overlords in the 13th and 14th centuries.

53,6   CO-HEIRS. *Pares erant* with the same meaning as *pariter* 'jointly'; see DB Somerset Exon. Notes Introduction p. 310 on 'parage' as a form of land tenure.

53,7-8 WALTER is probably Walter Cockerell whose descendants held both Icomb and Sezincote in the 12th century.

53,7   SEZINCOTE. The main manor of Sezincote, comprising the part of Sezincote parish east of the main Broadway to Stow on the Wold road (A424) except for Lower and Upper Rye (65,1. 66,2).

53,8   ICOMB ('PROPER'). See note to 39,4.

53,9   SHIPTON ('PELYE'). In Shipton Solers; EPNS i p. 180. The site of Shipton 'Pelye' manor house survived until the late 18th century as 'Pullers Close' or 'Pool House Close' south of Shipton Oliffe church; see note to 63,2.
RALPH. See note to 53,3.

53,10 ('SHERIFFS') HARESFIELD. This manor comprised the tithings of Haresfield and Parkend in Haresfield parish; VCH x pp. 188, 190. See EPNS ii p. 182.
POTTERS. The OE word *poters* has been glossed over the regular Latin word *figuli*.

53,12 'LITTLETON'. See notes to 34,13 and 36,3.
RALPH. See note to 53,3.

53,13 1½ HIDES IN CONDICOTE. The main manor of Condicote; VCH vi pp. 63–7, 191–2.

54,1   ROGER OF LACY'S HIDE became Frampton Manor Farm which remained separate from the 'Frampton Court' estate until reunited by purchase in 1839; VCH x pp. 143–8.

54,2   EASTLEACH (MARTIN). Divided into two halves in 1089, when St. Peter's Abbey, Gloucester, acquired Fyfield ('the land of 5 hides'); the remainder became the manor of 'Boutherop'; EPNS i p. 31.

55,1   EASTLEACH (MARTIN). The manor of Southrop, later held by Walter's descendants, the Poyntz family.

CH. 56 WALTER SON OF ROGER. Nephew of Durand (DB Herefords. 22,5–6), Constable of Gloucester Castle (*History of St. Peter's, Gloucester* i p. lxxvi) and Sheriff of Gloucestershire after Durand, though perhaps not immediately (Round FE p. 313). See notes to Ch. 53 and 24,1. He was Constable under Henry I.

56,1   (GREAT) BARRINGTON. See note to 1,66–67.
8 HIDES ... A gap of about 6 letters follows; see 49,1 note above.

56,2   (SOUTH) CERNEY. The main manor of South Cerney, to which Cerney Wick (45,5) was reunited by 1285.
THIS MANOR ... FATHER. These last three lines are compressed and were no doubt written after the rest of the entry, perhaps as a result of the lawsuit.

ROGER THE SHERIFF. Roger of Pîtres, brother of Durand, was created Constable of Gloucester Castle by King William (*History of St. Peter's, Gloucester* i p. lxxvi) and was Sheriff of Gloucestershire in Earl William's time, though dead by 1086 (see DB Herefords. 1,61).

7,1 SEZINCOTE. Clapley manor formed the part of Sezincote parish west of the A424 road.

CH. 58 WALTER THE GUNNER. *Balistarius*; *ballista* included all missile weapons, from crossbow to large artillery piece. The English word 'gun' was used of such weapons before the introduction of gun-powder.

58,2 RUDDLE in Newnham, not Rodley in Westbury on Severn (VCH x pp. 37, 89, 98).

58,3 BLEDISLOE HUNDRED. The S written above the E in *BLIDELAV* is intended to go after the E, not to replace it (see also the interlined R in *ELWAD*, 78,11).
½ HIDE. The part of Ruddle manor in Awre parish and hence in Bledisloe Hundred.

58,4 A CHURCH WHICH WAS NOT THERE [BEFORE 1066]. The Church of St. Peter, Frampton Cotterell, was presumably founded between 1066 and 1086.

CH. 59 HENRY OF FERRERS. One of the Domesday Commissioners named in Worcs. F (Hemming; see DB Worcs. App. V). His heirs were the Earls of Derby and Nottingham. He held much land in 1086. Ferrières-Saint-Hilaire is in the département of Eure, France; OEB p. 88.

59,1 SIWARD BAIRN. He joined Hereward and Earls Edwin and Morcar in the Ely rebellion of 1071; ASC for 1071. 'Bairn' probably had the same meaning as OE *cilt* 'childe', 'born to an inheritance', 'well born'. He is called Earl Siward in DB Derbys. 4,1.
6 HIDES EXEMPT ... KING'S SEAL. King Edward; see ECWM no. 173 p. 76 and Harmer p. 544 no. 13.
VILLAGERS ... FRENCHMAN HOLD. Reading *ten* as the abbreviation for *tenent*, though it could equally well abbreviate *tenens* 'holding', referring only to the Frenchman.
200 EELS, LESS 25. 25 eels normally made up one 'stick' (*sticha*), hence the amount abstracted.

CH. 60 ARNULF OF HESDIN. A large landholder in Wiltshire. Hesdin is in the département of Pas-de-Calais, France.

60,1 WEYS OF CHEESE. *pensas*; its size is unknown.

60,2 ARNULF ALSO HOLDS. Repeated at the beginning of 60,2–7.
WULFWARD WHITE. *Uuit* here; also *Wit, Wite, albus* elsewhere in DB. He is called a thane of King Edward in DB Middx. 8,5, and was Arnulf's predecessor in several other counties.

60,3 AMPNEY ('ST. NICHOLAS') was named as such in the 12th century when 2 hides were given to St. Peter's Abbey, Gloucester, and incorporated in Ampney St. Peter (10,12); *History of St. Peter's, Gloucester* i pp. 105, 164. Most of the residue formed the 5-hide manor of Ampney 'Bret' in Ampney Crucis parish, probably centred on Eastington House. The assessment should therefore perhaps be corrected to 7½ hides, raising the total hidage for Garsdon Hundred to 75 hides; the DB figure may have arisen from a miscopying of 7 (*vii*) as 4 (*iiii*) and a wrong conflation of variant endings, ½ hide and 2 virgates. But the DB assessment is repeated in EvK 296.

60,7 ½ HIDE ... A gap of about 4 letters follows this; see 49,1 note. The fact that there is no dot after *hida* strengthens the idea that the information intended for the gap concerned the hidage. There may have been doubt as to whether it was separately assessed: if it was not separately assessed, the vill of Bitton probably originally contained 20 hides (Bitton 1,9: ?16 hides; Oldland 5,1: 2 hides; Bitton 'Prebend' 78,13: 2 hides), conforming to the 5 hides assessment system.

CH. 61 HAROLD SON OF EARL RALPH. Ralph the Timid, son of Countess Goda (King Edward's sister) and Count Drogo. He came to England in 1041, and was Earl of Hereford from 1053 or earlier to 1057. He may have inherited part of the earldom of Swein; see Harmer p. 570. In 1066 Harold was presumably a minor because in Middx. 9,1 he is said to have been then in the charge of Queen Edith, his aunt. In 1086 he held land in Worcs. and Warwicks; Ewyas Harold in Herefords. (19,1) is named after him.

61,1 THE INSERTION of the hundredal rubric is based on topographical probability, all the surrounding manors definitely being in Greston Hundred.

61,2 MEASURES OF SALT. Latin *mitta*, English 'mit', a measure of uncertain volume, perhaps containing 6 or 8 bushels. See VCH (Worcs.) i p. 270 and ii p. 257 and Habington ii p. 297. Cf. DB Worcs. 22,1 where the same Harold has 7 salt-houses in Droitwich which pay 50 measures of salt.

CH. 62 HUGH OF GRANDMESNIL. Sheriff of Leicestershire; died 1094. Grandmesnil is in the département of Calvados, France.

62,1 PEBWORTH. See notes to 34,1 and EvN 14.

62,2 HUGH ALSO HOLDS. Repeated at the beginning of 62,2–6.
2 HIDES. The rest of the line is left blank and there is no dot after *hide*; the scribe probably intended to enter details of the manor later when available; see 49,1 and 60,7 notes.

62,3 (UPPER) QUINTON. The agricultural details may well refer to Broad Marston (62,2) as well as Upper Quinton.

62,4-5 ROGER. Since Lower Quinton was held c.1097 by Hugh of Lacy (EvN 11), 'Roger' can be identified as Roger of Lacy, Hugh's brother (see Ch. 39 note).

62,5 WESTON ('MAUDIT'). In Weston on Avon; EPNS i p. 260.
WITH. In the MS *7cū*; the *7* was probably written first and should have been scratched out when the scribe saw his error and wrote in the correct *cū*.

62,6 VALUE ... 30[s]. In the MS the abbreviation *sol'* (shillings) was accidentally omitted after *xxx* (perhaps through lack of space), as happens on several occasions in DB (e.g. 78,3 below).

CH. 63 HUGH DONKEY. *Lasne, asne*, the initial *l* being the definite article, from OFr. *asne* 'ass'. 'donkey'; also the Latin *asinus* in DB Worcs. 27,1. Hugh probably came over to England with William son of Osbern and served under him in defending the English border against the Welsh.

63,1 THORKELL. Perhaps the Thorkell White who was Hugh's predecessor in many of his Herefordshire manors; see DB Herefords. 1,65 note.

63,2 SHIPTON ('CHAMFLURS'). A lost place in Shipton Solers; EPNS i p. 181. United by 1303 with Shipton 'Pelye' (53,9) and Shipton Oliffe (68,6) as the manor of Shipton Solers.

63,4 GILBERT is almost certainly the man of the same name who held part of Duntisbourne Abbots immediately west of Bagendon, and who can be identified as Gilbert de Eskecot (see note to 39,7).

CH. [64] THIS CHAPTER was probably misnumbered *lxi* because the *iii* of the *lxiii* in the preceding chapter is on the right hand side of the large *h* of *Hugo* in 63,1 (which is outlined in red) and therefore easily missed when the rubricator began the next fief and looked over the page to see what number he had reached. The misnumbering continues until Ch. 69.
MILES CRISPIN. He was probably married to one of the daughters of Wigot of Wallingford; see Freeman iv App. Note C, but see G. H. White in the *Genealogist* xxxviii (1922) pp. 116–119. See also 64,1;3 note.

64,1 3 VIRGATES ... IN BRAWN. See 1,2 and note.
WIGOT HELD IT ... A gap of about 7 letters follows this, perhaps because the earlier history was disputed.

64,1;3 WIGOT. Probably Wigot of Wallingford, predecessor of Miles Crispin and Robert d'Oilly in several DB counties. He was kinsman and butler to King Edward and Sheriff of Oxfordshire and made his peace with King William; Freeman iv App. Note C.

64,2 GEOFFREY. Probably Geoffrey Delamare, as the Delamares held the manor certainly from 1201 until 1410; VCH xi p. 168.

CH. 65 URSO OF ABETOT. Brother of Robert the Bursar and Sheriff of Worcestershire. He held much land in Worcs., Herefords., Warwicks. and Glos. He rapaciously acquired much church land, especially from the Churches of Worcester, Pershore and Westminster, and, with the help of Bishop Odo of Bayeux, Evesham church. See Freeman v App. pp. 757–66 and Round in Worcs. VCH i p. 262 ff. He helped to crush Earl Roger of Hereford's revolt in 1075. Abetot is in the département of Seine-Maritime, France.

65,1 IN SEZINCOTE. The 2 hides in Sezincote (65,1. 66,2) are certainly the two farms later known as Lower and Upper Rye, each containing about 150 acres, but it has not yet been possible to allocate the two holdings more precisely.

CH. 66 HASCOIT MUSARD. A Breton and landholder in many counties; he became a monk of Ely. *Musardus* in ML means 'lazy', 'stupid' (Ducange).

66,2 HASCOIT ALSO HOLDS. Repeated at the beginning of 66,2–6.
IN SEZINCOTE. See 65,1 note.

66,3 12 VILLAGERS. There is no gap in the MS after *xii*, as appears in Farley.

66,5 SIDDINGTON. Siddington 'St. Mary' manor, centred on Barton Farm in Upper Siddington village. The assessment should perhaps be corrected to 11 hides, making a round total of 20 hides for all the Siddington manors; the missing hide is the hide in Chesterton later held by the Musards.

BESIDES THE LORDSHIP (LAND). See 26,4 note.

6,6 MISERDEN, named from the Musards, superseded Greenhampstead as a name in 1300; EPNS i pp. 120-30.

H. 67 THURSTAN SON OF ROLF. Perhaps the standard bearer at Hastings (see Ellis DTG pp. 186-7) who was rewarded with land in Glos., Somerset, Dorset, Herefords., and other counties.

7,1 AMPNEY (CRUCIS) was given to Tewkesbury Abbey in 1100 (Mon. Ang. ii p. 65; Cal CR ii p. 490), apart from Tovi's 'land of 2 villagers' previously given to St. Peter's Abbey, Gloucester, in whose cartulary it is described as '½ hide' (*History of St. Peter's, Gloucester* i pp. 61, 77, 164, 334; *Regesta* ii Addenda p. 410). This equation suggests that at least in this part of Gloucestershire the normal holding of a villager in 1086 was already a virgate, as it certainly was in the 13th century. The ½ hide was probably at Charlham, a detached portion of Ampney St. Peter parish. The main manor absorbed 67,2. 69,2;8 and 77,1; it was centred on Ampney Knowle and hence often later known as 'Up Ampney'.

7,2 1 HIDE. Ampney 'Mareys' manor which was in Ampney Crucis and Ampney St. Mary parishes.

7,3 THURSTAN ALSO HOLDS. Repeated at the beginning of 67,3-7.
IN OAKLEY 1 HIDE. The manor of Coates Cockerell.
GERWY. *Giruius*; see 76,1 note.

7,4 BERNARD. Perhaps Bernard Pancevolt who held land from Thurstan in Somerset and probably Dorset too. Pancevolt is 'paunch-face'; OEB pp. 324-5.
HALF-VILLAGERS. See note to W 1 above.

7,6 TOVI'S 2 HIDES became the Stanley Park estate in the east of the parish; VCH x pp. 242, 244-8, 256, 259.

H. 68 ANSFRID OF CORMEILLES. Cormeilles in the département of Eure, France.

8,2 ANSFRID ALSO HOLDS. Repeated at the beginning of 68,2-12.
10 HIDES THERE AS TWO MANORS. Unusual word order; it looks as though the scribe omitted the *Ibi x hidae* after *Westone* (cf. 68,3. 69,7 etc.). An identical misplacement occurs in DB Shrops. 4,7;5.

8,4 PLOUGHSHARES. *Sochs* from *soccus*; RMLWL s.v. *soccus* (2). More exactly, the iron tips for the wooden ploughshares. See 39,12 and note for other renders of ploughshares.

8,6 SHIPTON (OLIFFE). See note to 63,2.

8,8 IN DUNTISBOURNE ('HOTAT') 1 HIDE. This holding was combined with 68,11 as the manor of Duntisbourne 'Hotat', which is a lost manor in Duntisbourne Abbots; EPNS i p. 71.

8,9 ELKSTONE. (GREAT) COLESBOURNE. Cf. EvK 342: '*Elchestane* and *Coleborne* 6 hides'. The 1½ hides in (Great) Colesbourne were at Combend in Elkstone, immediately west of (Great) Colesbourne.
A MAN-AT-ARMS HOLDS HALF THIS MANOR. Of (Great) Colesbourne (i.e. Combend). He can be identified as the Bernard who held Duntisbourne 'Hotat' (68,11): before 1109 William son of Bernard gave to Eynsham Abbey the titles of his demesnes, which are explicitly located in (Great) Colesbourne and Duntisbourne in the 14th century.

8,11 DUNTISBOURNE ('HOTAT'). See 68,8 note. In EvK 341 this Duntisbourne is included with the 68,8 Duntisbourne under a Cirencester Hundred head.

8,12 THE INSERTION of the hundredal rubric is based on topographical probability, all the adjoining manors definitely being in Botloe Hundred.

8,13 NIECE. Presumably a daughter of Walter of Lacy's brother Ilbert.

H. 69 HUMPHREY THE CHAMBERLAIN. Probably of the household of Queen Matilda (see 69,7 and DB Surrey Ch. 31); he held much land in DB. He was the brother of Aiulf Sheriff of Dorset.

9,2 HUMPHREY ALSO HOLDS. Repeated at the beginning of 69,2-8.
IN AMPNEY (CRUCIS) 1 HIDE. Added to 67,1.

9,3-4 IN PRESTON 1 HIDE. IN NORCOTE 1 HIDE. These two holdings were later held as a sub-manor from Humphrey's main manor of Fairford (1,50); *ex. inf.* Dr. N. M. Herbert.

9,5 IN SIDDINGTON 2 HIDES. At 'Bowley' in Siddington St. Mary.

9,6 (IRON) ACTON. The main manor of Iron Acton, centred on Acton Court.
1½ MILLS. See 6,1 note.

9,7 AS THREE MANORS. Entered in the left margin of the MS.
QUEEN GAVE. Wickwar may have come to Queen Matilda at the same time as other of Brictric son of Algar's lands; see 1,42 note.
VILLAGES. In the MS *uill'as* ('female villagers') in error for *villas* ('villages').

69,8 IN ASHBROOK 1 VIRGATE. Absorbed into 67,1.

70,1 MAIDENHILL. The MS *Medehalle* is a miscopying of *Medēhulle*, i.e. Maidenhill in N.E. Longborough, immediately east of Sezincote, which Humphrey himself held (70,2). UPTON (ST. LEONARDS). *Vtone* is a scribal error for *Upetone*, i.e. Upton (St. Leonards), if the Humphrey of 1,2 is this Humphrey, which seems likely as the details given correspond. DG identifies this place as Wotton.

CH. 71 [LAND]. *Terra* omitted in error, as happens quite frequently, e.g. in DB Wilts. This chapter appears to have been added later, probably when the folio was complete; the last line of the entry is written below the bottom marginal ruling.

71,1 LATTON. *Lechetone* cannot be either Leckhampton or Clapton, as Taylor suggested (Taylor pp. 19, 143, 150, 261), since Clapton was part of Bourton on the Water manor (VCH vi pp. 40–1, 59–61), whilst Leckhampton was in Cheltenham Hundred (38,1. 78,9); also, all the medieval versions of Leckhampton have a medial '-ham-' (EPNS ii p. 109). *Lechetone* must represent an OE *leactun*, which is the origin of Latton in the extreme north of Wiltshire (EPNS (Wilts.) p. 45), where with Eysey manor 9 hides are recorded in DB (Wilts. 18,2). With the hide of *Lechetone*, Latton becomes a normal 10-hide vill and the half-hundred of Cricklade in which it was situated then contains exactly 50 hides, although in 1086 this hide seems to have been in Gloucestershire. Humphrey's hide was Latton Manor in the north of Latton parish; the main manor was centred on Latton Court south of Latton village.
OSBERN OF CHERBOURG. Cherbourg in the département of Manche, France; see OEB p. 94.

CH. 72 SIGAR OF CHOCQUES. Chocques in the département of Pas-de-Calais, France.

72,1 9 SMALLHOLDERS. In the MS *bord'* is repeated where *car'* 'ploughs' would normally occur, almost certainly in error.
WOODLAND. The gap after this is only one or two letters wide, though it looks more because *bord'* in the line above extends beyond the side marginal ruling. The scribe may, however, have intended to add the dimensions of the woodland later; there is no dot after *silva ē ibi*.

72,2 AS THE COUNTY TESTIFIES. Entered after the values, but with a mark to denote its correct position.

72,3 3 ... EXEMPT FROM TAX. EvK 358 does not mention the claimed exemption of 3 hides, but this may merely be due to lack of space for an interlineation, the interlined statement about the exempt 3 hides of Hazleton (EvK 357 = DB 72,2), as well as the interlined Bradley Hundred head, occupying almost all the MS line.

CH. 73 MATTHEW OF MORTAGNE. Mortagne in the département of Manche, France.

73,2-3 SHIPTON (MOYNE). 1 HIDE THERE. See VCH xi pp. 249–251. The land may have been at Estcourt in Shipton Moyne.

73,3 ALWIN. See note to 1,45.

74,1 ALFHILD. DB *Elfelt*, OE *Aelfhild*; PNDB p. 175.

75,2-3 THESE TWO ENTRIES may have been added later. A space of about 2 lines was left after 75,1, similar to the space frequently left between chapters. This and the fact that the Swinehead Hundred head is repeated despite there being no change in Hundred between 75,1 and 75,2, the fact that *Rogerius* is written in 75,2 where one would expect *Isdem R.*, and the fact that Walter in 75,3 is not said to hold from Roger (cf. 48,3 note), suggest that 75,2-3 do not form part of Ch. 75 at all, the Roger of 75,2 not being Roger son of Ralph and Walter not being a mere scribal error for Roger (as Ellis DTG p. 193). The scribe appears to have been unsure where the entries of the manors of *Rogerius* and *Walterus* belonged, perhaps believing them to form a separate chapter (the Hundred head is written in the exact position it would occupy when the rubricator has to insert a Ch. heading; cf. 74,1). Cf. DB Wilts. 49,1a, another oddly placed holding. See Chs. 76-77 note below.

75,2 MANOR OF 1 HIDE. Later evidence enables this holding to be identified as the 'smaller manor of Clifton' (St. Lawrence), owned by Westbury College at the Dissolution.

75,3 MANOR OF 1 VIRGATE. Probably Mugland Farm, the nucleus of Blacksworth manor in St. George.

CHS. 76–77 IT WOULD SEEM from the fact that the rubricator had to squeeze in the number and heading for Ch. 76 and had no room at all for the heading for Ch. 77, that the scribe forgot, or did not realise, that he had two different tenants-in-chief to deal with here. It may be that these two entries also were added later, the scribe not being sure where they belonged, perhaps believing them to form with 75,2–3 a chapter of miscellaneous tenants such as the 'King's Servants or Officers' which appears at the end of other DB counties; cf. also the three odd entries at the end of DB Worcs. (X 1–3).
The heading [LAND OF BALDWIN] is added from the list of landholders.

6,1 GERWY OF LOGES. *Geri* is genitive, the nominative being *Gerus* or more correctly *Ger'* for *Geruius* (cf. *Giruius* in 67,3), from OG *Gerwig* (Forrsner 111). Les Loges is in the département of Calvados, France. Edvin Loach in Worcs. is named after one of his heirs. Gerwy's wife was called Gunhilda (*Gunuldus*) according to a record of her grant to St. Peter's, Glos., of 2 hides in Guiting for the soul of her husband *Juricus* in the time of Abbot Serlo (1072–1104), confirmed by King William and later by Henry I; see *History of St. Peter's, Gloucester* i pp. 80–81. The form *Juricus* is probably due to Norman French alternation of initial *G* and *J* (Forrsner 101–2, 103) and a slip of the pen (*Juricus* in error for *Jiruicus, Iiruicus*), but could also be 'of Ivry', there being perhaps some intermarriage between the families of Loges and Ivry.
4 HIDES IN (TEMPLE) GUITING. The land was at 'Beales Place'.

7,1 ALWIN. See note to 1,45.

78,1–2 THE GAP of a couple of lines between these entries is another example of the scribe's bad planning of this county. 78,1 is written rather larger than the rest of the page.

78,1 WINDRUSH. This entry is duplicated in 11,14. The discrepancy in TRE holders could be because Bolle held the 3½ hides after Wulfric, Tovi and Leofwin.

78,2 GARSDON HUNDRED is probably an error for Barrington Hundred as all the other Windrush entries are in the latter Hundred. This holding is identifiable as Le Mary Farm; VCH vi pp. 179–80.

78,3 'DUNTISBOURNE'. See note to 17,1. Identifiable as 'Nutbeam' in Duntisbourne Leer.

78,4 RODMARTON. Identifiable as 'Chamberlains' in Rodmarton; VCH xi pp. 236–40.

78,5 BAUNTON. Identifiable as Priors Court in Baunton.
3 VILLAGERS. Originally written *ii* and corrected to *iii* with *es* (for *tres*) interlined.

78,6 ½ HIDE ... AS A MANOR. Probably Elmore.

78,7 EDITH. An example of a woman being classed among thanes (see also Cwenhild in the next entry); see DB Somerset Exon. Notes 2,6.
BICKMARSH. Partly in Glos. in 1086 and partly in Warwicks. (Warwicks. 43,2). Until recent times it was a hamlet in that part of the Gloucestershire parish of Welford that lay in Warwickshire. In 1931 the major part was joined with Pebworth (transferred into Worcs. at the same time), a part remaining in the Warwickshire parish of Dorsington.

78,8 CWENHILD. DB *Cuenhild*; OE feminine personal name *Cwēnhild*; Reaney s.n. *Quenell*.
NAUNTON. See note to 48,3.

78,9 SLAVES. In the accusative after *habet*.

78,11 ALFWARD SON OF REINBALD. For Alfward see 58,3 note.
ALDSWORTH. The manor was at Wall, a site at the north end of Aldsworth village. BALKI was described as 'the Dane' (*Daci*) in 1133; C. D. Ross *The Cartulary of Cirencester Abbey*, 1964, vol. i p. 22.

78,12 ALFSI. EvK 376–7 (= DB 78,1;12), by bringing together the two holdings of *Elsi*, implies that the Alfsi of 78,12 is the same as the holder of 78,1, i.e. Alfsi of Faringdon.

78,13 DUNN. *Dons*; see PNDB p. 228 s.n. *Duns*. Probably the same man as the Dunn in 50,1–4. The *-s* is the Anglo-Norman nominative singular inflexion (PNDB § 158); cf. *Bruns* in DB Herefords. 14,4 (PNDB p. 210) for which DBH p. 54 has the Latinized *Brunus*.
BITTON. Bitton 'Prebend', granted to Salisbury Cathedral c.1115 (H. T. Ellacombe *History of Bitton* (1881), pp. 42–63).

78,14 WOODCHESTER. It is uncertain whether Edward of Salisbury's possession of Woodchester (1,63) was an illegal intrusion on the whole or only a part of Brictric's manor: later there was a second manorial site in Woodchester at Atcombe Court (VCH x pp. 296–7).

78,17 2 HIDES ... There is an erasure after *hidę*, but the scribe may have intended a gap to be left anyway; see 49,1 note. Erasures were frequently written over (see 2,4 and 48,3 notes).

E 1–8 THE WHOLE AREA west of the rivers Leadon and Severn had been part of Herefordshire until after 1020, and was not totally incorporated into Gloucestershire for secular purposes until the 12th century; it remained, as the Forest Deanery, in Hereford diocese until 1542 (ECWM pp. 225–7).

E 1   FORTHAMPTON. Lying in the extreme north of Gloucestershire, almost completely surrounded by Worcestershire, Forthampton's revenue had been withdrawn to Hereford by Earl William (as 1,35 above makes clear). There are many discrepancies between this entry and 1,35. This entry is more detailed, though only 1,35 gives the values in 1066 and 1086 (because the value of E 1 is included in the value of six manors given in Herefords. 1,47).
BRICTRIC. Brictric son of Algar, lord of Tewkesbury manor in 1066 (1,39).
WOODLAND ... IS IN THE ENCLOSURE OF THE KING'S WOODLAND. *Silua ... in defenso siluae regis est.* Similar phrases in DB Oxon. 1,5 (*silua est in defens' regis*), Warwicks. 27,3 (*silua ... sed in defenso regis est*) and Berks. 1,1 (*silua missa est in defensa*) suggest that the woodland had been put into the King's Forest. Herefordshire entries show the (ablative) forms *defenso, defensu* and *defensione* (2,2;9;24;56).
ANSGOT. Probably the 'Ansgot, Earl William's man' who held part of the nearby manor of Eldersfield (DB Herefords. 1,46).
ST. MARY'S. The Abbey of Lyre (Mon. Ang. vi p. 1092); see Ch. 17 note. In and after the 12th century it leased its tithes and land in Forthampton to Tewkesbury Abbey, the owner of Forthampton manor from 1107 (VCH viii pp. 199, 203).

E 2   'NEWARNE' in East Dean (EPNS iii pp. 218–9), probably the site of the later Speech House, the judicial centre of the Forest of Dean. The derivation is OE *niwe aern* 'new house'.
2½ HIDES ... DID SERVICE. That is, representatives of the men working the 2½ hides formerly attended Hundred meetings and did service in Herefordshire; see notes to DB Herefords. 1,72 and Worcs. 8,25.
ROGER OF PITRES. Brother of Durand the Sheriff and his predecessor as Sheriff of Gloucestershire; see 56,2 note above. Pîtres is in the département of Eure, France.

E 3   (LOWER) REDBROOK in Newland, the nucleus of the later royal manor of Newland, first recorded in 1221 (EPNS iii p. 237).

E 3-4   THE KING'S WOOD. The Forest of Dean.

E 4   BRICTRIC HELD A MANOR. Upper Redbrook, partly in Newland and partly in Staunton. STAUNTON near Coleford, not Staunton in Corse.

E 5   5 HIDES ... There is a gap of about 4 letters' width in the MS after *hide*, which has no dot after it; the scribe probably left the gap deliberately for the later inclusion of some such word as *geld* 'which pay tax', as appears in E 7 below. See 49,1 note above and cf. E 8 note.
EARL WILLIAM'S 3 HIDES at Lydney were amalgamated into his manor of Lydney (1,55).
BISHOP WALTER. Bishop of Hereford 1061–1079, the predecessor of Robert Losinga; see 4,1 note above.
MARKET. Presumably in Hereford; see DGM pp. 104, 107 and VCH (Herefords.) i p. 272.

E 6   'WHIPPINGTON'. Not 'Whittington' in Staunton, which is a mythical name, but 'Whippington', a name still applied to the stream separating the parishes of Staunton and English Bicknor. See EPNS iii p. 213.

E 7   HADWIG. *Hadeuui*; see PNDB p. 282.

E 8   6 HIDES ... There is a gap of about 4 letters' width in the MS after *hide*, which has no dot after it; probably the space was left for *geld'* or another word; see E 5 note.
BLOOMS OF IRON. *Bloma*, or *plumba* (as in DB Somerset 17,3). A dish used as a measure for ore; afterwards the due payable on the measure; see Eyton i p. 41.

E 9-16   THE SOMERSET AND WILTSHIRE SECTIONS of DB usually contain an entry for the teamlands ('land for *x* ploughs'), unlike Gloucestershire, Herefordshire and Worcestershire; see note to 6,2. The significance of such entries is examined in J. S. Moore *The Domesday Teamland: a reconsideration* (TRHS 5th ser. xiv (1964) pp. 109–30).

E 9   THIS ENTRY also appears as the second entry on Exon. 141b. The only additional detail there is the description of Bath as a 'Borough' (*in burgo*). Herlwin is not specifically said to have held the plough in lordship, but the words *in dominio* are frequently omitted in Exon. when given in the corresponding DB entry.

E 10-11   SOMERFORD (KEYNES) AND KEMBLE were transferred from Wiltshire to Gloucestershire in 1897 (GS p. 50).

E 10   BISHOP OF LISIEUX. Gilbert Maminot; see Ch. 30 note above.
OF WHICH. *De ea* (literally 'of it'), referring to *terra* 'land', not *car(ucas)* 'ploughs'.

E 11-13   COTTAGERS. *Coscet*, sing., *coscez, cozets*, plural, represent Anglo-Norman versions of OE *cot-seta*, sing., *cot-setan*, plural, 'a cottage-dweller', 'cottage-holder'. 'Cottagers' are almost entirely confined to the south-west counties in DB, Wiltshire providing about 80% of the total entries. See DB Somerset General Note 8,30.

E 11   CHELWORTH, although in the manor of Kemble, was in the parish of Crudwell and has remained in Wiltshire. The detailed assessments require explanation: in 1065, Malmesbury Abbey was confirmed in possession of 30 hides in Kemble, or which 4 were at Chelworth (ECWM no. 180 p. 78 = Sawyer 1038). Nevertheless, DB accounts for only 19¼ hides and does not specifically mention the 10¾ hides held by the villagers. These 10¾ hides, together with William's 4 hides in Chelworth, probably constituted the bulk of the 15 hides purchased by the Abbey c.1156 and reunited with the main manor of Kemble. Ansketel's hide was probably the hide in Kemble sold to Abbot Eadwulf by Hugh of Kemble between 1106 and 1118. Tovi's 2 hides and 1 virgate can certainly be identified as the 2 hides in Kemble and 1 virgate in Morley (in Crudwell) held from the Abbey from the 12th to the 14th centuries by the Morley family. The corrected hidage figures should therefore be:

In lordship:	Kemble	12 hides
Villagers:	Chelworth & Kemble	10¾ hides
Sub-tenants:	Kemble (Tovi)	2¼ hides
	Kemble (Ansketel)	1 hide
	Chelworth (William)	4 hides
Total (as in DB):		30 hides

12 LONG NEWNTON was transferred from Wiltshire to Gloucestershire in 1930 (GS p. 51). In addition to the 15 hides in lordship, the villagers had 10 hides (of which 1 hide was given to a man-at-arms); together these, with the 5 hides held by Osbern and William, comprise the DB total of 30 hides. Osbern's 3 hides were still intact as a separate sub-manor c.1280, when they were held by Roger le Brech or Bret. William's 2 hides appear to be represented c.1280 by two holdings, each of 5 virgates, held by Robert de la Lee and Walter Husey. It has not proved possible to identify these three properties more precisely within Long Newnton parish.

13 EARL ROGER. Earl of Shrewsbury; see Ch. 27 note above.
POULTON was transferred from Wiltshire to Gloucestershire in 1844; GS pp. 49–50.

14 EDWARD OF SALISBURY. Sheriff of Wiltshire.
POOLE (KEYNES) was transferred from Wiltshire to Gloucestershire in 1897; GS p. 50.

15 ASHLEY was transferred from Wiltshire to Gloucestershire in 1930; GS p. 51.

16 1 HIDE, LESS ½ VIRGATE. Probably Kingswood, a detached outlier of Wiltshire until 1844 (GS pp. 40, 50); it was held by the Berkeleys until they founded Kingswood Abbey c.1140. The addition of the assessments for Kingswood and Wotton under Edge (1,15) produces a total of exactly 16 hides.
ON LEASE FROM. In the MS p $prest\bar{u}$ is compressed into a space at the end of the line below and it is therefore impossible to tell whether the scribe intended the p to be a separate word per (the usual extension of p) making the phrase per $prest(it)um$ 'on lease from', or to represent pur to form, with $prest\bar{u}$, the one word $purprest(ur)um$ 'as a purpresture of'; in both cases an abbreviation mark over the t was omitted. 'Purpresture', an encroachment on, or unauthorized enclosure from, a forest, appears to fit the identification of the land as Kingswood better than the more common DB phrase 'on lease from' (adopted by the editors of DB Wilts. for this entry): Kingswood was in the part of the royal Forest of Horwood disafforested in 1228–9.
EDRIC THE SHERIFF. Sheriff of Wiltshire; Edward of Salisbury's predecessor.

17 SHORNCOTE, later a hamlet in Somerford Keynes, was transferred from Wiltshire to Gloucestershire in 1897; GS p. 50.

18 DROITWICH. See note to E 30 and EvQ 29.
HALL OF GLOUCESTER. That is, the royal hall; see G 1 note above.
A GAP of about 14 lines follows this entry before Worcs. Ch. 2. Some material such as people, value and customs may have been omitted from this entry (see E 30 note) or the whole space left for additional lands of the King in Worcestershire. See W 7–8 note above.

19- THE TRANSFERS OF THESE MANORS from Worcestershire to Gloucestershire were:
2 Teddington, Cutsdean, Redmarley d'Abitot, Blockley, Ditchford in Blockley, Daylesford, Evenlode and Chaceley in 1931; Little Washbourne and Church Icomb in 1844 (GS pp. 49–51).

19- THE REFERENCES in small type beside these entries are to the corresponding sections
4 in EvA.

19 TEDDINGTON. Probably included Alstone manor; VCH (Worcs.) iii p. 471.
MITTON has remained in Worcestershire. Cf. EvA 104; EvC 23; WoB 5.
WOODLAND, 2 FURLONGS. See 6,1 note above.

20 CUTSDEAN. Cf. EvC 24; WoB 5. See note to EvA below.
BISHOP BRICTHEAH. A late 11th century form of Beorhtheah; PNDB p. 194; called Brictric in DB Herefords. 1,45. He was Bishop of Worcester 1033–1038.
ARCHBISHOP ALDRED. Archbishop of York; see 1,2 note above.
HIS SON. Doda's son, Brictric; see DB Worcs. 2,63 and note.

21-22 URSO. Urso of Abetot; see Ch. 65 note above.

21 REDMARLEY (D'ABITOT). Cf. EvA 105; EvC 25; WoB 5. See note to EvA 105. Redmarley d'Abitot took its name not from Urso of Abetot, Sheriff of Worcestershire in 1086, but from a junior branch of his family who were subtenants of the Beauchamps in the 12th and 13th centuries.

WILLIAM 2 HIDES. These can be identified as Innerstone, which was reunited to the main manor in 1230; VCH (Worcs.) iii pp. 484–5. The name Innerstone derived from Inard Parler, a 12th century holder, who was probably descended from William (?Parler).

E 22 (LITTLE) WASHBOURNE. Cf. EvA 107; EvC 27; WoB 5; WoC 4.
SO THE BISHOP. *episcopus vero*: *vero* here probably means as a result of Aelmer becoming a monk. Elsewhere in DB it can have adversative force 'but' (as in Herefords. C 14 and 10,50).

E 23 BLOCKLEY. Cf. EvA 117; EvC 38; WoB 7; WoC 6. This entry omits any reference to the sub-manor of Dorn, whose existence is suggested in EvA 120 and mentioned in EvC 42; WoB 7. See notes to EvA 120; WoB 7; WoC 6.

E 24 DITCHFORD. Cf. EvA 118; EvC 39; WoB 7; WoC 6.

E 25 ANSGOT HOLDS 1½ HIDES. Cf. EvA 119; EvC 40; WoB 7.

E 26 (CHURCH) ICOMB. Cf. EvC 40; WoB 7; WoC 6; see note to EvA below. Church Icomb formed the northern part of the modern parish of Icomb in Gloucestershire, to which it was added in 1844 (GS pp. 49–50).
ASSESSED WITH THE HEAD OF THE MANOR. That is, with Blockley. This sentence replaces a value clause which should fall at the end of the entry, the meadow statement having been originally omitted in error.

E 27-29 DAYLESFORD. EVENLODE. Cf. EvA 121–2; EvC 41; EvD 7; EvN 5; WoB 7; WoC 6.

E 28 HEREWARD HELD. *tenuit* is probably an error for the present *tenet* which seems to be implied in EvC 41 and EvD 7. However, *tenuit* may be an indication that the land had not been returned to Hereward after the Bishop of Bayeux had removed it (E 29); see 1,22 note above on the forfeiture of the Bishop's lands.

E 29 BISHOP OF BAYEUX RECEIVED THEM. 'Seized them'; see EvD 7 (in DB Worcs. App. IV) and EvC 41 note below.
½ HIDE ... ½ HIDE. See note to EvQ 29.

E 30 WITH THE SAME CUSTOMARY DUES. Or perhaps 'right' or 'custom'. The King's ½ hide is E 18 (= Worcs. 1,7) above. No due or right is there mentioned, but it may have been a toll on the conveyance of salt, remitted under King Stephen (VCH (Worcs.) iii p. 73 note 19). For such a toll see 1,57 above.

E 31 REINBALD. Probably Reinbald the priest (see Ch. 26 note) who held the adjacent Eldersfield in 1066 (DB Herefords. 1,46).
GODRIC CLOCK. See OEB p. 304.

E 32 THIS HOLDING comprised the two manors of Chaceley and Chambers Court in Longdon, both held in later centuries from Urso's descendants, the Beauchamp Earls of Warwick, as a ½ knight's fee each (VCH (Worcs.) iv pp. 54–5, 112–5). See note to EvA 55; cf. EvC 106.
URSO. Urso of Abetot; see Ch. 65 note above.
FOUR OF THE ABOVE. Four of the nine free men mentioned in E 31.
8 MALE ... SLAVES. In the MS *vi* with *ii* added above to make *viii*.

E 33 THIS HOLDING has been identified as Staunton in Corse; VCH (Worcs.) iv pp. 198–9. It was transferred from Worcestershire to Gloucestershire in 1931; GS p. 51. See note to EvA 53. Cf. EvC 108.

E 34 URSO. Urso of Abetot; see Ch. 65 note above.
ABBOT WALTER. Abbot of Evesham 1077–1104. See DB Worcs. 10,12 note.
PROVED HIS RIGHT. For a discussion of the rival claims of Evesham Abbey and Worcester Church to Hampton and Bengeworth, see DB Worcs. 10,12 note and App. V.
ILDEBERGA. A lost barrow-site in Evenlode (EPNS i p. 219). It appears in the bounds of Evenlode (ECWM no. 118 p. 58 = BCS no. 1238 = Sawyer 1325) to be on the road between Moreton in Marsh and the four stones which were the predecessors of the Four Shires Stone. The four shires which met at this stone were Gloucestershire, Oxfordshire, Warwickshire and Worcestershire.

E 35 MONMOUTH CASTLE. The Castle no doubt played an important rôle in the consolidation of Anglo-Norman rule in Archenfield (the area between the rivers Wye and Monnow) and in the conquest of Gwent; see DB Herefords. Introductory note 3.
THE LANDS of the King and William son of Baderon comprised the later manor of Monmouth in Monmouth and Dixton. The lands held by William's men-at-arms were in Dingestow, Dixton, Garth (in Dixton), Newcastle (in Llangattock Vibon Avel), Perth Hîr (in Rockfield), Rockfield, St. Maughans and Wyesham (in Dixton). The property of the Abbey of St. Florent in Saumur later became the estates of its daughter-house, Monmouth Priory, and comprised 2 carucates in Monmouth and Dixton (the later Priory Farm), and the churches and tithes of Monmouth, Dixton (including Ganarew (now in Herefordshire), Garth and Wyesham), Llangattock Vibon Avel (including Llanllwydd, Newcastle and St. Maughans), Rockfield and Wonastow in Monmouthshire, Welsh Bicknor (a detached part of Monmouthshire until 1844) and Llanrothal and Tregate in Herefordshire. The original

donation by William's uncle Wihenoc c.1075 (Mon. Ang. iv p. 596 no. 1) had consisted of 5 carucates (3 at Monmouth, 1 at Llangattock Vibon Avel, 1 at Siddington) and two-thirds of the tithes (as well as various churches); this was said shortly before 1086 by William son of Baderon to comprise 2 ploughlands, a hide at Siddington and all the tithes (P. Marchegay *Chartes Anciennes du Prieuré de Monmouth en Angleterre*, Les Roches-Baritaud, 1879, pp. 15–16 nos. i–ii and pp. 18–19 no. iv). Some additional information is preserved in the early twelfth century Welsh chronicle-cartulary, the 'Book of Llandaff': 'In the time of King William, Earl William, Walter of Lacy and Ralph of Bernay, Sheriff of Herefordshire, the castle of Monmouth was built, and Earl William gave half the castle to three of his barons: Humphrey, Osbern and William the Scribe. On his death Earl Roger succeeded him and because of his treason was captured by the King with his traitors. These three with many others were disinherited. After these things the castle was given to Wihenoc, and in his time Bishop Herwald consecrated the church of Monmouth Castle, at which (ceremony) King Caradoc was present. Later he (Wihenoc) became a monk. Ranulf of Colville succeeded him and on his death William son of Baderon succeeded him'; *Book of Llan Dâv* pp. 277–8. Herwald was Bishop of Llandaff from 1056 to 1104; Lloyd ii p. 449.

36 8 CARUCATES. See note to W 18 above.
CASTLERY OF CAERLEON. Subject to the jurisdiction of Caerleon Castle. See S 2 note above and DB Herefords. 14,1 note and Introductory note 3.
THURSTAN. Thurstan son of Rolf, who held other land in the Caerleon area (e.g. 6 carucates beyond the Usk directly from the King; W 18 and see note).
2 MALE SLAVES, 1 FEMALE. There is no full-stop after *ancilla* in the MS, although Farley prints one, and the rest of the line has been left blank, perhaps for details of 'resources' to be added later if and when available.

Notes to the Appendix

EvA   THIS TEXT has been printed with a commentary in P. H. Sawyer, *Evesham A: a Domesday text*, Worcestershire Historical Society, Miscellany I (1960) pp. 3–36. There is also a translation and discussion in DB Worcs. Appendix IV. Both Professor Sawyer and Dr. Clarke agree that it is based on the original 'circuit returns'. As a result of scribal omission, neither Cutsdean nor Church Icomb is mentioned in this text.

EvA 53 THIS ENTRY confirms the location of Roger of Lacy's 5 hides at Staunton in Corse (which E 33 and EvC 108 fail to name) suggested by later evidence; VCH (Worcs.) iv pp. 198–9.

EvA 55 THIS ENTRY confirms the location of two of Urso's 5 hides at Chaceley (which E 32 and EvC 106 fail to name) by Round, based on EvB 6 (VCH (Worcs.) i pp. 327–8), and supported by later evidence (VCH (Worcs.) iv pp. 54–5, 112–5).

EvA   THIS ENTRY, unlike E 19, EvC 23 and WoB 5, does not distribute the 4 hides between
104   Teddington and Mitton.
TETINTONA AND. At the end of the line in the MS, after *et*, the letters *Mu* (probably the beginning of *Muttona*) have been written and then erased (though still visible), presumably through lack of space for the rest of the place-name.

EvA   THE TEXT OF THIS ENTRY is corrupt as a result of faulty transmission. The total
105   assessment of Redmarley d'Abitot was 7 hides, of which William held 2 hides (E 21; EvC 25; WoB 5); probably 7 (*vii*) was miscopied as 2 (*ii*), and William's 2 hides as 3 (*iii*). The intermediate scribe also took the phrase 'Value of these two £7' to refer to his erroneous figure of 2 hides rather than to the 2 holdings together. The stated value of £7 in this entry, presumably submitted by either the Bishop's or Urso's officials, had become £7 10s in E 21, as a result of later revision, possibly in the light of comments by county or hundredal juries.

EvA   THIS ENTRY, unlike E 23, EvC 38, WoB 7 and WoC 6, gives the total assessment of Blockley as 33 hides, in addition to 5 hides at Dorn subinfeudated to Hereward by 1086 (cf. EvA 120) and subsequently acquired by Urso of Abetot (cf. EvC 42; WoB 7) and his Beauchamp descendants (cf. WoC 6), though the total value of Blockley in both E 23 and EvA 117 is £20. As E 24–28 make clear, the remaining sub-holdings (EvA 118–22) were included in the total assessment for Blockley: this comprised 25½ hides in lordship (E 23) and 12½ hides of sub-holdings (E 24–28).

EvA   2 HIDES. At Ditchford, a hamlet in Blockley parish; E 24, EvC 39 and WoB 7.
118

EvA   VALUE £15. An obvious mistake for 15s.
119

EvA HEREWARD'S 5 HIDES are clearly the 5 hides at Dorn later held by Urso of Abetot and
120 the Beauchamps (cf. EvC 42; WoB 7; WoC 6) since, though he also held 5 hides of the
Bishop at Evelode in 1086, the latter are separately mentioned (in EvA 122).

EvA DAYLESFORD. In the MS *Dailesford* is substituted in the margin, with transposition
121 signs beside it, for *Aleford* which is lined through for deletion.

EvC A COMPARISON OF THIS TEXT with DB, EvA and WoB shows that it contains some
information not found in DB. This may have been derived from the original 'circuit returns',
but the document as a whole is heavily influenced by the order and phrasing of DB. It was
probably based on DB and subsequently updated (e.g. Urso of Abetot had replaced Hereward
as the holder of Dorn; see note to EvA 120). The date of revision cannot be later than
1108, when Urso died, since he was clearly still alive when the final version of EvC was
compiled. See DB Worcs. App. IV for further discussion of EvC and translation of various
sections of it.

EvC THIS ENTRY is repeated word-for-word in EvD 7, except that 'took away' (*abstulit*)
41   replaces 'received' (*accepit*) in the penultimate sentence. Until the final downfall of Odo of
Bayeux in England in 1088, it was impossible, or at least very impolitic, to be frank about
his numerous shortcomings (see 1,22 note; cf. EvN 1 and DB Worcs. 11,2).
STEPHEN SON OF WULFWY both here and in EvD 7 replaces 'Stephen son of Fulcred' in
E 27 and WoB 7. If this is the same man, the parental name presents a problem, unless
Fulcred is his father's name and Wulfwy(nn) his mother's name. (But Latin text has *Wlui*,
whereas OE *Wulfwynn* is usually represented *Uluuen*.)

EvC THIS ENTRY is written in the right margin of the MS probably by a different scribe with
42   transposition signs to show its correct position in the text.

EvC 106 SEE NOTE to EvA 55 above.

EvC 106; 108 ALSO OF THIS LAND. Longdon

EvC 108 SEE NOTE to EvA 53 above.

EvE THIS TEXT and EvO were dated by Dr. Clarke as c.1130, the occasion for their compilation
being the vacancy between the death of Abbot Robert of Evesham and the accession of
Abbot Reginald (Clarke pp. 35–6, 235, 289).

Eve THIS ENTRY, paralleled by EvO 25–6, shows that Weston Cantilupe, held by Evesham
10   Abbey in 1086 (12,7; EvK 135), had been subinfeudated in Abbot Robert's time (c.1121–
29). The corresponding section of the list of subinfeudations made c.1192 states 'Robert of
Seacourt holds 4 hides in Weston (Cantilupe) ... ' (EvG 5); this shows that the free hide of
1086 was additional to the 3 taxable hides, as EvM 67 also stated.

EvE THIS ENTRY, paralleled by EvO 6, shows that part of Donnington, included in 1086 and
25   later (VCH vi pp. 51, 53, 151–2) in Evesham Abbey's manor of Bourton on the Water
(12,3), had been subinfeudated between 1086 and Abbot Walter's death in 1104. The
corresponding section of the list of subinfeudations made c.1192 describes the holdings
of a later William of Donnington as '5½ virgates in Donnington, which pay tax ... [and]
1 hide and 1 virgate in Bourton (on the Water) ... ' (EvG 30).

EvF THIS DOCUMENT has not been printed: it contains no information not included in Ch. 12,
apart from showing that the hide at Wickhamford (EvF 5) was additional to the 8 hides at
Willersey (EvF 6; cf. 12,6), and that Weston Cantilupe contained 3 hides (EvF 7; cf. 12,7
and EvM 67: 3 hides and 1 free).

EvK THIS DOCUMENT is basically a Domesday 'satellite' of 1086 but the borough surveys have
been updated to some time between 1096 (consecration of Bishop Samson of Worcester and
the succession of Hugh of Lacy) and 1101 (death of Earl Hugh of Chester). It is probable
that the period of revision can be narrowed down to 1100 or 1101: William de Mandeville (I)
probably succeeded his father Geoffrey de Mandeville (I) in 1100, whilst Hugh Donkey last
occurs in 1100; 'Earl Henry' may be Earl Henry of Warwick, but could be Count Henry of
Eu who first appears as 'Count of Eu' in 1101. Patrick of Chaworth is also first unambiguously
recorded in 1100.

APART FROM folio 57r (EvK 1) and EvK 116 (on Winchcombe) on 59r this document is
written on every other line with much interlining, in a paler ink, of Hundred heads, fuller
descriptions of holders and other information such as exempt land (see 72,3 note); except
in K 135 attention is not drawn in the excerpts printed here to such interlineations.

EvK 1 HAMELIN OF BALLON. *de badelun*; Ballon in the département of Sarthe, France (Anglo-Norman Families p. 12).
PATRICK OF CHAWORTH. *de caworī*; Sourches (anglicized as Chaworth) in the département of Sarthe, France (Anglo-Norman Families p. 27).
CITY HAS DEPRECIATED (IN VALUE) BY £60. *Civitas vero peiorata est de lx l*'; possibly to be translated 'the city has depreciated (in value) from £60, £60 being its previous value. Cf. EvL 1.

EvK 10 HOLD. *tenet*, singular, in the MS, agreeing with only the first of the holders whom it precedes.

EvK 78 NOT PRINTED. No mention is made here or in EvM 8 of the additional 26½ hides held by various military tenants (3,1), though these are recorded in WoA 4 and WoB 15.

EvK 80 THIS ENTRY proves that the hide at Eycot (3,3), though geographically in Rapsgate Hundred, was part of Bibury Hundred for administrative purposes.

EvK 103 THIS ENTRY, together with EvK 230, EvM 3,6,99 and 2,8, clarifies the assessment of the Northleach estate: the total was 25 hides, consisting of Northleach (including Stowell), 12 hides; Farmington, 12 hides; and Upper Coberley, 1 hide. In 2,8 it is not clear whether Walter son of Poyntz's 12 hides at Farmington were part of, or additional to, the Archbishop's 13 hides; they were additional according to EvM 3.

EvK 116 8 OTHER BURGESSES HAVE (RESIDENCES) WHICH ARE WORTH. *viii habent alii burgenses que ualent ...* . Because of the unusual word order of the Latin the meaning could be read 'other burgesses have 8 (residences) which are worth ... ', the assumption being that one burgess has one house (on which see DB Shrops. C 1 col. 252a; cf. A. Ballard, *The Domesday Boroughs* p. 56). With either translation *domus* 'houses' or *mansiones* 'residences', is to be understood before the feminine nominative plural *que*. Cf. EvK 1.
BISHOP OF HEREFORD [...]. No figure has been entered in the MS and no gap left for one to be inserted later.
WALTER OF ST. VALÉRY. *de Walerico*, normally *de Sancto Walerico*; Saint-Valéry-en Caux in the département of Seine-Maritime, France (Anglo-Norman Families p. 92).
RICHARD OF SOLLERS. *de solariis*; Soliers in the département of Calvados, France; see DBH pp. 91, 116 and DEPN s.n. Bridge Sollers.
RALPH OF SACEY. *de Salceto*; see OEB p. 112.

EvK 133-5 A COMPARISON OF Evk 133-5 with EvF 5-7, EvM 65-67 and 12,6-7 makes it clear that Willersey was rated on its own at 8 hides, that the free hide at Weston 'Cantilupe' was additional to the 3 taxable hides there, and that there was an additional hide at Wickhamford, mentioned in EvK 133 (where it follows Upper Swell), in EvF 5, and in 12,6, but not in EvM 65-67 (see note to 12,6).

EvK 135 3 HIDES, 1 FREE. The *.i.libera* is interlined, preceded by a gallows sign (as are many interlineations in this document).

EvK 153 THE TOTAL OF 50 HIDES refers only to the manors listed in the first 4 lines of 20,1.

EvK 154 THIS ENTRY presumably refers to the 2½ hides 'beyond the Severn', which can be located at Haw in Tirley, and the 7½ hides at Woolstone, Leigh in Evington, Deerhurst Walton and Kemerton (20,1), though these 7½ hides were in fact east of the Severn. See note to EvM 80.

EvK 159 SEE NOTE to 28,5-7.

EvK 230 SEE NOTE to EvK 103.

EvL THIS DOCUMENT is written in 6½ lines below the bottom marginal rulings of folio 57v into both margins; the writing is cramped and the hand is different to that of the rest of the folio (which contains part of EvK). There are no interlineations.

EvL 1 ACCORDING to Dr. Clarke this survey was probably made c.1126, before these two manors were given to the priory of St. Barbara, and that 'in the said time' and 'then' refer to a time nearer to 1126 than to 1086 (Clarke pp. 276, 277 note 2). As such, it is the earliest detailed survey of any manor in Gloucestershire, and amongst the earliest surveys for England generally, though some of the Evesham Abbey manors in Worcestershire have detailed surveys from c.1104 (EvJ; see DB Worcs. App. IV).
BEADLE. An under-bailiff, subordinate to a reeve, unpopular, with minor police functions; see Ellis i p. 247.
PAID 27s 8d. Or perhaps 27s 7d, as the last *i* of *viii d'* may have been erased, or was smudged; there is a squiggle ⟩ over the number.
MINSTER. The Minster Church at Beckford; VCH viii p. 259. The 'building' presumably refers to the other church mentioned in Beckford.
INCREASED (IN VALUE) BY £10. *est melioratus de x li*'; cf. EvK 1.

EvM THIS DOCUMENT was considered by Dr. Clarke to be a later abbreviation of DB. There are a number of small divergences and additions to DB, but apart perhaps from *tenet* in EvM 100, they are such as a later abbreviation would naturally make; see notes to EvM 3,4,32,79,108, 112.

EvM 3 SEE NOTE to EvK 103. 2,8 does not state that Archbishop Thomas was claiming Walter's manor on behalf of St. Peter's Abbey, Gloucester.

EvM 4 STANDISH. 2,10 includes 1 hide held by the Abbot of St. Peter's, Gloucester, but does not state that Archbishop Thomas was claiming the 5 hides on behalf of St. Peter's. The statement of hidage for the whole manor and for Durand's holding only is repeated in EvM 7.

EvM 6 99 SEE NOTE to EvK 103.

HOLDS. Or perhaps 'held', as *ten* can abbreviate both *tenet* 'holds' and the past *tenuit*. Archbishop Aldred died in 1069. Cf. EvM 100 and note.

EvM 8 SEE NOTE to EvK 78.

EvM 32 HELD. *tenuit* may well be a scribal error for *tenet* 'holds' (see EvM 100 note), but could indicate that Malmesbury Abbey had lost the land.

EvM 66-67 SEE NOTE to EvK 133–5.

EvM 79 70 HIDES. '59 hides' in 19,1–2 which include Gerard's 11 hides. The abbreviator here no doubt mistakenly added the 11 to the 59 to reach his total of 70.

EvM 100 HOLDS. *tenet* in full here, as also in EvM 96; *tenuit* in full in DB. Archbishop Stigand died in 1072. This could be taken to indicate that EvM preceded DB, but on the other hand a lazy abbreviator, accustomed to the predominance of the abbreviation *ten* in DB, could have failed to notice the change in tense. Cf. EvM 6;99 and note.

10 HIDES. EvK 74, like 2,9, gives the assessment of Compton (Abdale) as 9 hides. 10 hides may be a scribal error, but seems a more probable assessment in terms of the 5 hides unit system.

EvM 108, 112 SEE NOTE to 28,5–7. A comparison of EvM 112 with 28,5–7 also reveals that the pre-Conquest holders of the 4 hides — Alnoth (*Elnod*) and Leofwin (*Leuuin'*) — were after the Conquest initially succeeded by Alnoth (*Elnot*) and Alwin (*Elwine*) holding under Earl Hugh. The terminal alliteration of Al*win* and Leof*win* tends to suggest that Alwin was Leofwin's son. However, it is also possible that *Elwine* is a scribal error for *Lewine* or vice versa, and that Earl Hugh, when he took over the 4 hides, allowed the former holders to remain as his sub-tenants initially.

EvN THIS TEXT is dated to c.1097; Clarke p. 285. For further discussion of it and translation of certain parts, see DB Worcs. App. IV.

EvN 1 IN THE LEFT MARGIN of the MS *Odo Episcopus* is written in red. On Odo, see notes to 1,22 and EvC 41 above.

EvN 5 *EUNELAD'*, 7 HIDES. 7 (*vii*) is probably a mistake for 5 (*v*), which is the assessment given in E 28, EvA 122, EvC 41 and EvD 7.

BRIAN. It is not possible to link Brian with the Poers and their sub-tenants, the Evenlodes *alias* Devylls, who held Evenlode from the 12th to the 15th century (VCH (Worcs.) iii p. 348).

WILLIAM HASTINGS was the founder of the Hastings family who held Daylesford until the 19th century; VCH (Worcs.) iii pp. 336–7.

EvN 11 HUGH OF LACY was the brother of Roger of Lacy, and succeeded to his lands in 1096; see Ch. 39 note above. In 1086 Upper Slaughter was held by Roger of Lacy but assessed at 3 hides (39,20) whilst Lower Quinton was held by 'Roger' (clearly Roger of Lacy) from Hugh of Grandmesnil, but assessed at 12 hides (62,4). Neither entry mentions Evesham Abbey's former tenure or its dispossession by Odo of Bayeux.

EvN 12-13 (LOWER) SWELL. CHILDSWICKHAM. Neither of the corresponding DB entries mentions Evesham Abbey's former tenure or its dispossession by Odo of Bayeux.

EvN 14 PEBWORTH. 2 HIDES. Cf. 34,1, where William Goizenboded holds the larger manor of Pebworth, assessed at 6¼ hides, and 62,1, where Hugh of Grandmesnil holds the smaller manor of Pebworth, assessed at 2¼ hides. Neither of these entries mentions Evesham Abbey's former tenure or its dispossession by Odo of Bayeux. EvN 14 therefore suggests that William Goizenboded was also holding the smaller manor of Pebworth by the time EvN was compiled and he is known from the Abingdon Abbey cartulary (*History of Abingdon* ii pp. 102–3, 110) to have commended himself to Robert of Beaumont (the Count of Meulan, later Earl of Leicester) who succeeded to the lands of Hugh of Grandmesnil after Hugh's death c.1094 and the exile of Hugh's brother Ivo in 1102.

EvO THIS TEXT, which is very similar to EvE, is dated, like EvE, to c.1130; Clarke p. 289.

EvO 1,3,5 2½ HIDES. Lark Stoke is assessed at 2 hides in 12,8.

EvO 7 21 ACRES. Originally *xx acs* was written, but corrected to *xxi ac*.

EvO 10 ALFRED. Probably the Alfred holding ½ hide in Maugersbury in the previous entry.

EvQ THIS DOCUMENT is written in two columns on folio 82r, with no interlining or marginalia. The bulk of it is an incomplete Worcestershire hidage schedule, possibly derived from 'circuit returns' or abstracted from DB itself (though in a different order), but updated to c.1122–47; but it also contains a survey of Droitwich c.1126 (Clarke pp. 299–303). See DB Worcs. App. IV for discussion of it and translation of EvQ 1–28 inclusive.

EvQ 29 RANULF ... ½ HIDE ... BALDWIN AND LITHWULF ... ½ HIDE. These holdings, attached to the manors of 'Kings Barton' and 'Abbots Barton', are not mentioned in 1,2 or 10,1, but the King's ½ hide is mentioned in E 18 and both are mentioned in E 30. By the 13th century both these holdings had been united; VCH (Worcs.) iii p. 74 note 37. It is not possible to be certain about the identification of the remaining Droitwich holdings, but the virgate held by Grim's sons 'of the monks' may well represent the land from which 24 measures of salt were paid to the Eynsham Abbey manor of Mickleton (18,1), since another Gloucestershire entry (1,48) states that a virgate rendered 25 sesters of salt. If, however, we assume that Ringulf's sons Essulf and Ranulf held the Droitwich lands attached to Gloucestershire manors, their 5 virgates could represent the 1 virgate and 3–5 salt-houses attached in 1086 to Rockhampton (50,1), (Old) Sodbury (1,48), Stanway (1,27), Tewkesbury (1,24; see note) and Thornbury (1,47).

RANULF AND ESSULF SONS OF RINGULF. Or perhaps 'son' referring only to Essulf, though it is likely that this Ranulf is the same as the son of Ringulf mentioned a couple of lines above. In the MS *fil'*, which could abbreviate the singular *filius* or plural *filii*: in the case of 'the sons of Grim' below *fil'* is obviously the plural because of the plural verb. Cf. EvK 10 (1,11 note).

WALTER OF 'BURGH', *del Burc* here; *Burch* in EvC 65, probably referring to the same man. DB Worcs. 2,69 *Burh*, from OE *Burg, Burh* 'fort', 'fortified place', 'manor', 'town', 'Borough'. The 'Burgh' here implied is not known, perhaps Eastbury (Worcs. 2,69), or the neighbouring *Burgh* of Worcester.

WoA THE TEXT OF THIS DOCUMENT is incomplete: the entry for Bishops Cleeve (WoA 3) lacks the details of its internal composition, and there are no entries for Great Colesbourne (3,2) and Condicote (3,6). It must, however, antedate DB, since in 1086 (see DB 3,1) and later (a) Aust was certainly subinfeudated out of Westbury on Trym; (b) Stoke Gifford (see 3,1 note) was claimed as a subinfeudation from Westbury; (c) Compton Greenfield was assessed at 3½ hides; (d) Stoke Bishop remained as part of the Bishop of Worcester's demesne in Westbury manor. Dr. Clarke (p. 320) suggested a date of 1066–86, which seems reasonable. It should be noted that though WoA occurs in the early 11th century first part of Hemming's Cartulary, it is a late 11th century addition to the text (see Ker p. 54), written in the top margin. The first line (= WoA 1) is now illegible due to fire damage and Hearne's text has been used here, the rest of WoA being checked against the MS.

WoA 1 THIS ENTRY confirms the location of the 5 hides at Barnsley (held in DB by Durand and Eudo) and the hide at Eycot, but implies the location of the remaining 15 hides as at Bibury and Ablington. However, it includes the hide of Eycot (3,3) within the 21 hides of Bibury itself (3,4).

WoA 2 WITHINGTON. There are some discrepancies between this entry and DB 3,5. Both agree on a stated total assessment of 30 hides, and on the individual assessment of Aston Blank (*alias* Cold Aston) (10 hides), Foxcote (3 hides), Hilcot and Little Colesbourne (2 hides), Notgrove (5 hides) and the parish church (½ hide). WoA 2 also confirms the location of the riding men's lands, deduced from RBW (see note to 3,5), at Owdeswell and Upcote, but gives the assessment as 3¼ hides rather than 2¾ hides; it also locates one of the 3 hides in lordship at Cassey Compton, where 3,5 has only a plough in lordship. But the individual items in both 3,5 and WoA 2 do not add up to the stated total of 30 hides, and these items, together with suggested amendments, are listed below:

	DB 3,5; WoB 18	WoA 2	Suggested Amendments
Cassey Compton	–	1 h.	1 h.
Owdeswell } Upcote }	2¾ h.	{ 2 h. { 1¼ h.	2 h. 1 h.
Priest	½ h.*	½ h.**	½ h.
Foxcote	3 h.	3 h.	3 h.
Little Colesbourne } Hilcot }	2 h.	{ 1 h. { 1 h.	1 h. 1 h.
Dowdeswell } Pegglesworth }	4½ h.	3½ h.	3½ h.
Notgrove	5 h.	5 h.	5 h.
Aston Blank	10 h.	10 h.	10 h.
Lordship	3 h.	[3 – 1 = 2] h.	2 h.
Total	30¾ h.	30¼ h.	30 h.

h. = hide
* priests in WoB 18
** held by the church

PETLESWIRTHE. Or perhaps *Pecleswirthe.*

WoA 3   THIS ENTRY is incomplete presumably as a result of scribal omission.

CLIUA. In the MS *ad cliuā*; Hearne misprints *ad clitiam.*

WOA 4   THIS ENTRY differs in several respects from DB. Aust is not mentioned at all; the assessment of Compton Greenfield is given as 5 hides, where DB has 3½ hides; Stoke Bishop is mentioned as 5 hides held by a man-at-arms, whilst DB includes it amongst the 'members' in lordship; Osbern Giffard's 5 hides at Stoke Gifford are not mentioned at all unless these have been confused with the 5 hides at Stoke Bishop.

WoB   THIS DOCUMENT appears to be an abstract of DB, but it contains some additional information and minor differences: for instance, the order of WoB 15–20 differs from the corresponding entries in DB (3,1–5;7;6). Although its order and phrasing are largely influenced by DB, the differences and additions may derive from other sources, such as the preliminary 'circuit returns'. It is written in the main cartulary hand and is thus no later than the beginning of the 12th century. Although Durand, Sheriff of Gloucestershire, is mentioned as the tenant at Barnsley (WoB 17) and Southam (WoB 19), this does not in itself prove that the abbreviation was completed before his death in 1095, since the document will not necessarily have been updated to take account of the deaths of individual DB landholders. For further discussion and translation of certain parts of it, see DB Worcs. App. V.

WoB 7   THIS ENTRY, like EvC 42, mentions the sub-manor of Dorn in Blockley held by Urso of Abetot, which either was included within the 25½ hides in lordship in E 23 or was subinfeudated after 1086.
IN LORDSHIP 25½ HIDES. Written in the right margin of the MS with transposition signs to show its correct position in the text.
IEACUMBE. In the MS *Ɩ͑acūbe*; Hearne misprints *Leacumbe.*
WHICH BELONGS. Hearne prints dots after *pertinens*, although there is no gap or erasure in the MS and the phrase makes perfect sense.
OF THIS MANOR ... *DORNE.* Written in the right margin of the MS.

WoB 15   *ICETONA.* So MS; Hearne misprints *Laetona.*
OSBERN GIFFARD HOLDS 5 HIDES. In Stoke Gifford; see 3,1 note above.

WoB 16   SWEIN. *Suein* in the MS; Hearne misprints *Suem.*
IN THE RIGHT MARGIN of the MS, level with *Aicocte*, is written *Aicote* in red ink.

WoB 19   *TEODBOLDESTAN.* So MS; Hearne misprints *TEOBOLDESTAN.*
BERNARD. *Bernandus*, probably a scribal error for *Bernardus.*

WoC J. H. ROUND, without stating his grounds, dates this text to 1108–1118, presumably because this was the period during which Robert, Count of Meulan, one of the church's tenants in Worcestershire, held the Earldom of Leicester (VCH (Worcs.) i p. 324). But a closer dating is possible, between 1114–5, when two other tenants, Robert Marmion and Walter of Beauchamp, both succeeded to their estates, and 1118. Dr. Clarke (p. 203) suggested that this document was compiled during the vacancy of the see of Worcester between 1112 and 1115, and if this probability is accepted, the date can be narrowed down to early in 1115.

WoC 4 *BREDVN.* So MS; Hearne misprints *BREDVNE.*
MONKS OF WORCESTER HAVE 4 HIDES. At Teddington and Mitton (E 19).
WALTER OF BEAUCHAMP 16 HIDES. At Redmarley d'Abitot, Little Washbourne, Pendock and Westmancote (E 21–22; DB Worcs. 2,26;28).
THE KING 1 HIDE. At Bushley (DB Worcs. 2,30).

WoC 6 38 HIDES. In the MS $\overset{x}{xxviii}$, the interlined *x* being in darker ink.
OF THESE ... 1. The punctuation of this part of the entry is crucial. The MS reads *De his h't Walt^l de bealcap .v. ad daeilE^{S}FORD .iii. Ad EVNilade .v. m̄ .i.* (with a new line beginning at *FORD*), which, when extended, reads *De his habet Walterus de bealcamp .v. ad daeilesford .iii. Ad Eunilade . v. monachi .i.* Although it is possible that the scribe wrote the first *.v.* in error and forgot to erase it, it is more probable that he omitted a place-name after the first *.v., Dorne* being a likely candidate as it was acquired probably after 1086 by Urso of Abetot whose lands in Worcs. passed to the Beauchamps; see EvA 117 note above and VCH (Worcs.) i p. 293 note 7. Thus punctuated, the hidage corresponds to the division of E 26–28.
THE MONKS (HAVE) 1. At Church Icomb (E 26).
THE BISHOP 24 WITH HIS LORDSHIPS AND *DICFORD.* The lordship total in E 23 is 25½ hides. The Bishop presumably lost the 5 hides at Dorn, which were part of the lordship land (see DB Worcs. 2,38 note), but gained the 2 hides held in 1086 by Richard at Ditchford (E 24) and the 1½ hides of villagers' land held in 1086 by Ansgot (E 25).

WoD THE NAMES of the Worcestershire landholders in this summary of the hidage of each fief
(*not* are identical with those in DB. The text cannot be later than 1096, the latest date at which
prin- Roger of Lacy held land in England, and could be as early as 1088. Since it provides only a
ted) summary by fiefs and contains no information additional to DB or to the other Evesham and Worcester 'satellites', it has not been printed in this volume. Discussion and translation of all of it appear in DB Worcs. App. V.

WoE THIS DOCUMENT was considered by both Miss Hollings (RBW pp. v, 442 note 2, 443 note 1)
(*not* and Dr. Clarke (p. 320) to antedate DB; however, the late Professor Darlington has
prin- conclusively shown that it cannot be earlier than 1089–93 and more probably can be dated
ted) later than 1112 (R. R. Darlington (ed.) *The Cartulary of Worcester Cathedral Priory*, Pipe Roll Soc. Publications lxxvi (new series xxxviii) 1968 pp. xlvi–xlvii). Professor Darlington's arguments for a 12th century date for this document are confirmed by a comparison of the sizes of the Worcester church lordships in DB and in WoE (hides said to be taxpaying and exempt have been added together here for the sake of comparison):
Bibury 9 hides in 3,4 : 2½ hides and 1½ virgates (WoE 15)
Blockley 25½ hides in E 23 : 15 hides and 1 virgate (WoE 8)
Bishops Cleeve 5 hides in 3,7 : 3 hides (WoE 18)
Westbury on Trym 23½ hides in 3,1 : 13 hides and 1 virgate (WoE 16)
Withington 3 hides in 3,5 : 3 hides (WoE 17)
With the exception of Withington, the lands in lordship in WoE are considerably smaller than in DB because of subinfeudations since 1086. Since these post-1086 subinfeudations are listed in RBW under the Bishops who first granted them, it would be possible to establish the date of WoE more exactly. But since WoE is clearly not related to DB, it has not been printed in this volume and its precise dating does not require consideration here.

Familiar modern spellings are given when they exist. Unfamiliar names are usually given in an approximate late 11th century form, avoiding variants that were already obsolescent or pedantic. Spellings that mislead the modern eye are avoided where possible. Two, however, cannot be avoided: they are combined in the name of 'Leofgeat', pronounced 'Leffyet' or 'Levyet'. The definite article is omitted before bynames, except where there is reason to suppose that they described the individual's occupation. The chapter numbers of listed landholders are printed in italics. It should be emphasized that this is essentially an index of personal names, not of persons; it is probable that more than one person bearing the same name has been included in the same entry in some cases, especially in the case of pre-Conquest landholders.

Robert of Bellême	EvK 116
Robert (of Doynton)	6,5;7-8
Robert of Ferrers	EvK 116
Robert of Lacy	EvK 116
Robert d'Oilly	*48.* 1,36
Robert (of Tilleul)	28,1
Robert of Tosny	*46*
Robert son of Alfred	EvO 10
Robert son of Hamo	EvK 1;116
Robert the Bursar	*47.* EvN 13
Robert (the Butler)	40,1
Robert, King William's officer	G 4
Robert	3,5. WoB 18
Earl Roger (of Hereford)	S 1. W 19. 1,53;56;58. 16,1. E 14
Earl Roger's father (Earl William of Hereford)	16,1
Earl Roger (of Shrewsbury)	*27*
Roger (Baskerville)	45,1-2;4-5
Roger of Beaumont	*40*
Roger of Berkeley	*42.* G 2. W 14. 1,13. E 16
Roger (of Berkeley)	1,16-19;21. 6,9. EvK 1
Roger of Bully	1,37
Roger (of Gloucester)	2,13
Roger of Ivry	*41.* W 1. B 1. 1,5;60. 2,9. 44,2. 53,4
Roger of Lacy	*39.* G 4. W 17. 1,64. 17,1. 28,3. 54,1. E 33. EvC 108
Roger of Lacy's mother	39,18;20
Roger (of Lacy)	62,4-5
Roger d'Oilly	48,3 (see note)
Roger son of Ralph	*75*
Roger (of Pîtres), Sheriff (of Gloucestershire), brother of Durand the Sheriff	2,10. 56,2. E 2. EvK 1;116 See Walter
Roger	41,5
Rolf, see Thurstan	
Rotlesc, King Edward's guard	1,59
Rumbald	73,2-3
Saewin, the reeve of Bristol	75,1
Saewin	34,13
Bishop Samson (of Worcester)	EvK 1
Saxi	40,1
Sessibert	W 4
Sheerwold	31,10
Sigar of Chocques	*72*
Siward Bairn	59,1
Siward	37,5. 41,2. 48,1-2. E 14
Solomon	E 8
Stephen son of Fulcred	E 27. WoB 7
Stephen son of Wulfwy	EvC 41
Archbishop Stigard (of Canterbury)	1,56. 2,1-3;5;9. 31,6. 39,11. 56,2. EvM 100
Strang the Dane	73,1
Swein	3,2. WoB 16
Theobald	6,4
Archbishop Thomas (of York)	2. EvM 3-4
Thorbern	76,1
Thorbert	1,60
Thorkell	39,2. 63,1
Thorold, Wigot's nephew	27,1
Thorold, see Gilbert	
Thurstan of Cormeilles	EvK 116
Thurstan son of Rolf	*67.* W 18. 3,1;7. 19,2. 35,2. E 9. EvK 400. WoB 15;19
Thurstan (son of Rolf)	E 36
Thurstan	48,3. 53,8. 56,1. 68,10

Wisnoth	43,2
Wulfgar	1,61. 37,4
Wulfgeat	34,1
Wulfheah	32,7-8;12. 37,1
Wulfhelm	32,5. 39,3. 68,12
Wulfmer	EvK 1
Wulfnoth	6,9. 31,3
Wulfric	11,14. 39,15. 45,4. 78,1
Wulfrith	76,1
Bishop Wulfstan (of Worcester)	3,4-7
Wulfward White	60,2
Wulfward	1,6;57. 22,1. 34,1. 53,3. 63,2-4. 68,1
Wulfwen	E 15
Wulfwin	66,2
Wulfwy	19,2. 31,9. 39,5. 67,2
Wulfwy, see Stephen	
Wynric	33,1

CHURCHES AND CLERGY

Abbeys:	of Abingdon	*13*
	(of Berkeley?)	*1,63*
	of Cormeilles	*16. 1,60*
	of Coventry	*15*
	of Evesham	*12. E 29. EvC 41*
	of Eynsham	*18*
	of Glastonbury	*8*
	of Gloucester	*10*
	of Lyre	*17. 1,56*
	of Malmesbury	*9*
	of Pershore	*14*
	of Westminster	*19*
	of St. Mary, Winchcombe	*11*

Abbots:	of Bath	1,56
	of (St. Mary's), Cormeilles	1,11. 16,1. EvK 10
	of Evesham	EvC 41. EvK 1;116; WoB 7
	(of St. Mary's, Evesham)	12,9
	of Gloucester	2,10. EvK 1
	of Malmesbury	1,64. E 12-13
	of Pershore	EvK 1
	of Winchcombe	EvK 116
	(of St. Mary's, Winchcombe)	11,5-6;14
	see Baldwin, Robert, Walter	

| Archbishop: | of York | 2. EvK 1 |
| | see Aldred, Stigand, Thomas | |

Archdeacon, see Alric

Bishops:	of Bayeux	1,22-23;65. 41,5. E 29;34. EvC 41. WoB 7
	of Coutances/St. Lô	*6.* W 13. E 10
	of Exeter	*5*
	of Hereford	*4.* 1,55. EvK 116
	of Lisieux	*30.* E 11
	of Winchester	2,3
	of Worcester	*3.* E 19;21-23;29. EvC 22;38;41. EvK 80. WoA 4. WoB 5;7;16-18;20. WoC 4;6

see Brictheah, Geoffrey, Gilbert Maminot, Odo, Osbern, Robert, Samson, Walter, Wulfstan

Canons:	of Hereford	E 6

Chaplain, see Reginald

Chapter:	(of Evesham)	EvE 10;25. EvO 5;25

Churches:	of St. Mary, Abingdon	*13*. 56,2
	of St. Peter, Bath	*7*
	of Bristol	1,21. EvK 7
	of the nuns of Holy Trinity, Caen	*23*
	of Cirencester	*25*
	of St. Mary, Cormeilles	*16*
	of St. Mary, Coventry	*15*
	of St. Mary, Evesham	*12*. E 34. EvM 65-67. EvN 1
	of Eynsham	*18*
	of St. Mary, Glastonbury	*8*
	of St. Peter, Gloucester	E 30
	of Hereford	*4*. E 7
	of St. Mary, Lambeth	*21*
	of St. Mary, Lyre	*17*
	of St. Mary, Malmesbury	*9*. E 12-13. EvM 32
	of St. Denis, Paris	*20*. EvM 80
	of St. Mary, Pershore	*14*
	of St. Edward (Stow on the Wold)	12,1. EvO 1
	of Tewkesbury	1,26
	of St. Martin, Troarn	*24*
	of St. Peter, Westminster	*19*. E 31. EvM 79
	of St. Mary, Winchcombe	*11*
	of St. Mary, Worcester	*3*. E 19. WoB 15-20
	of St. Evroul	*22*

Deacon, see Walter

Monks:	of Bath	1,56
	of Eynsham?	EvQ 29
	of St. Peter's, Gloucester	10,14. EvQ 29
	of Pershore	1,55
	of Worcester	WoC 4
	of the Church of Worcester?	E 19;26;29. EvC 40-41. WoB 5;7. WoC 6

see Aelmer

Nun, see Cwenhild

Priests:	1,1;20;50;53;65. 3,4-5;7. 4,1. 7,1. 9,1. 12,1;3-7. 23,2. 26,1-2. 27,1. 28,1. 30,1-2. 34,8. 39,6;8;12;17-19. 41,1-2. 49,1. 50,2-3. 55,1. 56,1-2. 60,5. 63,1;3. 66,5-6. 67,1. 68,10. 72,2. 78,15. E 20;23;27
	see Abraham, Arnulf, Bernard, Reinbald

Saint:	Peter's, Bath	*7*
	Mary's, Cirencester	1,7. 39,8
	Mary's, Evesham	EvK 133-135
	Mary's, Glastonbury	*8*
	Oswald's, Gloucester	2,5(?);11;12(?)
	Peter's, Gloucester	*10*. 2,4;8;10. EvK 103;116;230. EvM 3-4
	Mary's, (Lyre)	E 1
	Mary's, Malmesbury	*9*
	Denis', Paris	EvK 153-154
	Mary's, Pershore	35,2
	Florent's, Saumur	E 35
	Mary's, Worcester	EvM 8. WoB 19

Mary's, (Worcester?)	3,7
Dewy's	W 6
Michael's	W 6

SECULAR TITLES AND OCCUPATIONAL NAMES

Bursar (*dispensator*) ... Robert. Chamberlain (*camerarius*) ... Gerard, Humphrey, John, William. Clerk (*clericus*) ... 62,6. Commissioner (*legatus*) ... Richard. 1,63. Cook (*coquus*) ... Avenel, Humphrey. 1,6. Count (*comes*) ... Henry(?) Robert. Countess (*comitissa*) ... Goda. Doctor (*medicus*) ... Nigel. Earl (*comes*) ... Algar, Godwin, Harold, Henry, Hugh, Ralph, Roger, Tosti, William. Guard (*huscarle*) ... Rotlesc, Tovi Widenesci. Gunner (*balistarius*) ... Walter. Jester (*joculator*) ... Berdic. King (*rex*) ... Aethelred, Caradoc, Edward, Gruffydd, William. Officer (*minister*) ... Robert. Potters (*figuli, poters*) ... 53,10. Queen (*regina*) ... Edith, Matilda. Reeve (*prepositus*) ... Bleio, Elmwy, Iudhael, Ows, Saewin, Waswic. W 18. 1,1-2;14;16;47-49; 54;58;61. 16,1. 39,12. 63,1. Scribe (*scriba*) ... William. Sheriff (*vicecomes*) ... Alwin, Durand, Roger, Urso of Abetot. 1,8;10-13;53;57;62. Smith (*faber*) ... 23,1. 39,12. Thane (*tainus, teignus, teinus*) ... Alfward, Alric, Alwin, Brictric, Dena, Edmer, Edric Lang, Elaf, Ernsy, Ernwy, Forne, Godric, Kenvikel, Kenward, Leofwin, Thorbern, Thorbert, Tovi, Wulfgar, Wulfheah, Wulfrith. 1,40;42-44;55. 34,2. 45,5. 62,1;3. 68,2-3.

INDEX OF PLACES

The name of each place is followed by (i) the number of its Hundred or Commote (numbered west to east working southwards) and its location on the maps in this volume; (ii) its National Grid reference; (iii) chapter and section references in DB. Bracketed figures here denote mention in sections dealing with a different place. The word 'note' or 'n' after a figure indicates that the place does not appear in the text of DB, but is identified in a note.

Unless otherwise stated, the identifications of EPNS and the spellings of the Ordnance Survey are followed for places in England; of OEB for places abroad. Inverted commas mark lost places with known modern spelling; in many cases only an approximate grid reference can be given. Unidentifiable places are given in DB spelling, in italics. Difficulties are discussed in the notes above. The National Grid reference system is explained on all Ordnance Survey maps and in the Automobile Association Handbooks: the figures reading from left to right are given before those reading from bottom to top of the map. Gloucestershire and Wales south of a line from Panteg to Cirencester is in square ST, and Gloucestershire south of a line from Cirencester to Lechlade is in square SU. Gloucestershire and Wales north of that line and west of a line from Cirencester to Beckford is in square SO; Gloucestershire east of that line is in square SP. The initial S has been omitted in Grid References in this index. Places with bracketed Grid References do not appear on modern one-inch or 1:50,000 maps. Bracketed place-names do not appear in the text of DB, but are mentioned in ancillary documents or in the notes. The Gloucestershire Hundreds and Welsh Commotes with the numbers used in the index are listed after the index, immediately before the maps.

The letters a, b, c, etc. following the Hundred number refer to separated portions of the Hundred on the maps. Within each Hundred, or portion of a Hundred, places are numbered west–east working southwards, though listed alphabetically in the map keys. Places in adjacent counties in 1086 but subsequently transferred to Gloucestershire are distinguished by letters in the Hundreds column: H here stands for Herefordshire; WI for Wiltshire and WO for Worcestershire. A name in brackets following a place-name is that of the parish or an adjacent manor settlement, given to distinguish this place from others of the same name. Some places that were in Gloucestershire in 1086 are now in adjacent counties: their modern (pre-1974) county is given after the place-name.

a) Gloucestershire

	Map	Grid	Text
(Ablington)	23b-3	P 1007	WoA 1
'Acton Ilger'	33-6	(T 6783)	6,1
Iron Acton	33-5	T 6784	69,6;(7)
Acton Turville	34a-10	T 8080	60,6
Adlestrop	10a-3	P 2426	12,2. EvO 8
Admington (Warks.)	1a-11	P 2046	11,11
Alderley	34a-2	T 7690	64,3
Alderton	5f-4	P 0033	1,43. 11,5
Aldsworth	23b-2	P 1510	(3,4 note). 10,5. 78,11
Alkerton	21-4	O 7705	78,16
Alkington	27c-12	T 6998	1,15
(Allaston)	20-6	O 6404	(37,5 note)
Almondsbury	27f-1	T 6084	1,15
(Alstone)	WOd-2	O 9832	(E 19 n)
'Alverston'	24-5	(T 5999)	31,2-3
Alveston	32-6	T 6288	1,14
Alvington	Hb-1	O 6000	E 8
'Ampney'	—	— —	45,5
Down Ampney	30-12	U 0996	1,65
Ampney Crucis	30-3	P 0601	67,1-2. 69,2. 77,1.
(Ampney 'Mareys')	30-1	(P 0704)	(67,2 n)
Ampney St. Mary	30-2	P 0802	26,1

	Map	Grid	Text	
Ampney 'St. Nicholas'	30-5	(P 0801)	60,3	
Ampney St. Peter	30-4	P 0701	10,12	
Arlingham	27b-1	O 7010	1,15	1,15
Arlington	23b-4	P 1006	1,58	
Ashbrook	30-3	(P 0902)	53,2. 69,8	
Ashleworth	27a-1	O 8125	1,15	
Ashley	WIb-6	T 9394	E 15	
Cold Ashton	38b-5	T 7572	7,2	
Ashton under Hill (Worcs.)	(3b-1) (5d-1)	O 9937	1,60. EvL 1 1,40	
Aston Blank (*alias* Cold Aston)	14b-2	P 1219	3,5. WoA 2. WoB 18	
Aston on Carrant	5f-1	O 9434	1,24	
Aston Somerville (Worcs.)	6b-1	P 0438	66,4	
Aston Subedge	1a-15	P 1341	21,1	
Aust	35a-1	T 5789	3,1. WoB 15	
Avening	28-4	T 8897	1,49	
Awre	20-3	O 7008	1,13	
Aylworth	10a-11	P 1022	34,6. 52,6	
Badgeworth	12-9	O 9019	31,11	
Badminton	34a-9	T 8082	60,5	
Bagendon	29-2	P 0106	63,4	
(Banks Fee)	4g-7	P 1728	(29,1 n)	
Barnsley	23b-6	P 0705	3,4. WoA 1. WoB 17	
Barnwood	12-13	O 8518	10,1	
Great Barrington	19-2	P 2013	1,66-67. 56,1	
Little Barrington	19-6	P 2012	34,11	
'Abbots Barton'	12-11	(O 8418)	10,1	
'Kings Barton'	12-11	(O 8418)	1,2. (EvQ 29 n)	
'Barton Regis'	39b-9	(T 5973)	1,21. EvK 7	
Bath (Somerset)	–	– –	(E 9)	
Batsford	4f-1	P 1833	68,4	
Baunton	29-8	P 0204	51,1. 78,5	
('Beales Place')	9b-3	(P 0828)	(76,1 n)	
Beckford (Worcs.)	3b-2	O 9735	1,59-60. EvL 1	
Bengeworth (Worcs.)	–	– –	E 34	
Berkeley	27c-9	T 6899	1,15-19;(63)	
Beverstone	27c-20	O 8693	1,15	
Bibury	23b-5	P 1106	3,(3);4. EvK 80. WoA 1. WoB 16-17	
Bickmarsh (Worcs.)	1a-2	P 1049	78,7	
English Bicknor	16a-1	O 5815	37,2	
Bishopsworth (Somerset)	–	– –	E 9	
Bisley	22-5	O 9005	28,1	
Bitton	39b-13	T 6869	1,9. 78,13	
(Bitton Prebend)	39b-14	(T 6869)	(78,13 n)	
(Blacksworth)	39b-10	(T 6273)	(75,3 n)	
Bledington	10a-16	P 2422	11,2	
Bledisloe	20-2	O 6808	1,13	
Blockley	WOa-2	P 1634	E 23. EvA 117;119 n. EvC 38;40. WoB 7. WoC 6	
Boddington	5j-1	O 8925	1,41. 19,2	
(Boulsdon)	7-12	O 7024	(16,1 n)	
Bourton on the Hill	8f-1	P 1732	19,2	
Bourton on the Water	10a-19	P 1620	12,3. EvO 10	
('Bowley')	29-21	(U 0199)	(69,5 n)	
Boxwell	34a-1	T 8192	10,3	
Brawn	12-1	O 8224	1,2. 64,1	
Bredon (Worcs.)	–	– –	E 19. EvA 103. EvC 22. WoB 5. WoC 4	
Brimpsfield	18-4	O 9312	50,3	
Bristol	39b-8	T 5873	1,21. (3,1. 75,1. E 9) EvK 7	

	Map	Grid	Text
(Broadwell) (in Leckhampton)	13-4	(O 9419)	(38,1 n)
Broadwell (near Stow on the Wold)	10a-2	P 2027	12,4. (EvO 7)
Brockworth	12-15	O 8916	63,1
Bromsberrow	7-1	O 7433	45,3
Brookthorpe	12-23	O 8312	1,5
Buckland	4d-1	P 0835	10,6
Bulley	16b-2	O 7619	58,1
Bushley (Worcs.)	—	— —	WoC 4
Calcot	8j-2	P 0910	20,1
'Caldicott'	10a-17	(P 0821)	34,5
Cam	27c-11	T 7599	1,15
Chipping Campden	4e-4	P 1539	28,4
Carswall	7-8	O 7427	39,3
Castlett	9b-5	P 0925	34,9
North Cerney	18-14	P 0107	2,12. 52,3
South Cerney	30-10	U 0497	56,2
Cerney Wick	30-11	U 0796	45,5
(Chaceley)	WOf-1	O 8530	(E 32 n) EvA 55. EvC 106
('Chamberlains')	28-7	(T 9497)	(78,4 n)
Charfield	33-2	T 7291	74,1
Charingworth	4e-5	P 1939	45,1
(Charlham)	30-9	U 0999	(67,1 n)
(Charlton)	35a-4	(T 5880)	(3,1 n)
Charlton Abbots	6b-14	P 0324	11,8
Chedworth	18-7	P 0512	1,57
Cheltenham	13-3	O 9522	1,1
Cherington	28-5	T 9098	64,2
(Chesterton)	29-15	P 0100	(32,1 n)
Childswickham (Worcs.)	6b-2	P 0738	47,1. EvN 13
Chippenham (Wilts.)	—	— —	E 16
Churcham	16b-4	O 7618	10,11
Churchdown	12-8	O 8819	2,1
Cirencester	29-13	P 0201	1,(7);8. 32,1
(Cirencester Rectory)	29-13	(P 0201)	(25,1 n)
(Clapley)	4g-1	(P 1530)	(57,1 n)
Bishops Cleeve	3c-3	O 9627	3,7. (WoA 3. WoB 19)
Clifford Chambers (Warks.)	5a-1	P 1952	1,37
Clifton	39b-7	T 5673	75,1;(2 n)
Clifton on Teme (Worcs.)	—	— —	(1,11. EvK 10)
Clingre	27c-10	T 7299	1,17
Lower Clopton (Warks.)	1a-12	P 1645	34,3
Upper Clopton (Warks.)	2-2	P 1744	1,12
Coaley	27c-7	O 7701	1,15
(Coates 'Cockerell')	29-14	O 9700	(67,3 n)
(Coates 'Randulf')	29-14	O 9700	(39,19 n)
Coberley	18-1	O 9615	42,1
Upper Coberley	15a-1	O 9715	2,8. EvK 103. EvM 3
(Codrington)	38b-1	T 7278	1,9. (43,1 nn)
Great Colesbourne	18-3	P 0013	3,2. 68,9. WoB 16
Little Colesbourne	14a-15	P 0013	3,5. WoA 2. WoB 18
(Coln Rogers)	15c-1	P 0809	(1,22 n)
Coln St. Aldwyns	31-1	P 1405	10,4
Coln St. Dennis	8j-1	P 0810	20,1
'Combe Baskerville'	10a-20	(P 2120)	45,2
(Combend)	18-8	O 9811	(68,9 n)
Compton Abdale	15b-5	P 0616	2,9. EvM 100
Cassey Compton	14a-14	P 0415	3,5. WoA 2
Compton Greenfield	35a-3	T 5782	3,1. WoA 4. WoB 15
Little Compton (Warks.)	8g-1	P 2630	20,1
Condicote	4g-6	P 1528	2,4. 3,6. 36,2. 53,13. WoB 20
Cowley	18-2	O 9614	14,1

	Map	Grid	Text
Cromhall 'Abbots'	27d-1	(T 6890)	1,15
Cromhall 'Lygon'	27d-2	(T 6990)	1,16
Culkerton	28-8	T 9395	31,10. 41,4. (44,2 n) 53,4
Cutsdean	WOg-1	P 0830	E 20. EvC 24. WoB 5
(Daglingworth)	29-6	O 9905	(31,7. 32,2 nn)
Daylesford	WOi-1	P 2425	E 27;29. EvA 121. EvC 41. EvN 5. WoB 7. WoC 6
Deerhurst	8h-2	O 8729	19,1. EvK 153-4
Deerhurst, see Deerhurst Walton			
(Didcot)	3b-3	P 0035	(1,59 n)
Didmarton	34a-5	T 8287	53,5
Ditchford	WOa-1	P 2136	E 24. EvA 118 n. EvC 39. WoB 7. WoC 6
Dixton	5f-12	O 9830	1,43
Dodington	37-2	T 7579	6,9. 42,2
(Donnington)	10a-1	P 1928	EvE 25. EvO 6
(Dorn)	WOa-3	P 2033	EvA 120 n. EvC 42. WoB 7. WoC 6
Dorsington (Warks.)	1a-3	P 1349	40,1
Dowdeswell	14a-3	P 0019	3,5. WoA 2. WoB 18
(Downing)	5f-15	(O 9228)	(1,45 note)
Doynton	38b-4	T 7274	6,5
Driffield	30-7	U 0799	26,2. (45,5 n)
Droitwich (Worcs.)	—	— —	(1,24;27;47-48. 18,1. 50,1. E 18;30. EvQ 29
Dumbleton	6b-5	P 0135	13,1. 34,13. 36,3. 53,12
(Duni)	16b-6	O 7616	(34,12 note)
'Duntisbourne'	—	— —	31,7. 32,2. 78,3
Duntisbourne Abbots	(29-1) (18-11)	O 9707	(10,13 (39,7
Duntisbourne 'Hotat'	(29-4) (18-15)	O 9806	(68,8;13 (68,11;13
Duntisbourne Leer	18-12	O 9707	17,1
Duntisbourne Rouse	29-3	O 9805	53,3
Dursley	27c-15	T 7598	1,15
Dymock	7-2	O 7031	1,53
Dyrham	34b-2	T 7475	35,1
Gaunts Earthcott	32-7	T 6384	6,8
Eastleach Martin	31-5	P 2005	54,2. 55,1
Eastleach Turville	31-4	P 1905	39,13
Eaton Bishop (Herefords.)	—	— —	E 5
Ebrington	4e-1	P 1840	34,4
Edgeworth	22-6	O 9405	28,3. 39,9
Edvin Loach (Herefords.)	—	— —	(1,11. EvK 10)
Elberton	27e-1	T 6088	1,15
Elkstone	18-5	O 9612	68,9
'Ellings'	8h-1	(O 8629)	19,2
(Elmore)	12-17	O 7815	(78,6 note)
Elmstone	8h-12	O 9226	19,2
(Estcourt)	28-12	T 8991	(73,3 note)
Etloe	20-5	O 6705	1,13
Evenlode	WOh-2	P 2229	E 28-29. EvA 122. EvC 41. EvN 5. WoB 7. WoC 6
Evington	8h-11	O 8726	19,2
Eycot	23a-1	P 0010	3,3-4. EvK 80. WoA 1. WoB 16
Eyford	10a-8	P 1424	66,3
Fairford	31-8	P 1501	1,50

	Map	Grid	Text
Farmcote	9b-1	P 0629	34,7
Farmington	15b-7	P 1315	2,8. EvM 3
Fiddington	5f-10	O 9230	1,24;31
Forthampton	5f-5	O 8532	1,35. E 1
Foxcote	14a-7	P 0118	3,5. WoA 2. WoB 18
Frampton	6b-7	P 0133	11,4; (5 note)
Frampton Cotterell	32-8	T 6681	58,4
('Frampton Court')	6b-10	P 0132	(11,4 note)
Frampton Mansell	22-9	O 9202	46,3
Frampton on Severn	21-3	O 7407	54,1
Fretherne	21-1	O 7309	67,7
Frocester	21-6	O 7803	10,2
Gloucester	12-G	O 8318	G 1-4. (1,24;47. 3,5. 8,1) 10,14. (12,4. 20, 1. 24,1. 28,1. 39,2;6; 12. 46,1. 50,3. 54,1. 58,1. 59,1. 60,1. 78, 14. E 18;30) EvK 1
Gossington	27c-6	O 7302	1,15
Gotherington	3c-1	O 9629	3,7. WoB 19
('Grove Court')	12-22	(O 8514)	(1,2 note)
Guiting Power	9b-7	P 0924	34,8
Temple Guiting	9b-4	P 0928	39,6. 76,1
Hailes	6b-11	P 0430	38,2
Hambrook	39b-4	T 6478	6,2
Hampen	14a-5	P 0520	2,7. (4,1 note)
Lower Hampen	14a-4	(P 0519)	(2,6 n) 32,13
Hampnett	15b-6	P 1015	41,1
Meysey Hampton	30-8	U 1199	27,1
Hanham	39b-12	T 6470	60,7
Hanley Castle (Worcs.)	5b-1	O 8341	1,34
Hardwicke	8h-9	O 9127	19,2
Harescombe	12-25	O 8310	1,4
Haresfield	12-24	O 8110	1,3
'Sheriffs' Haresfield	17-2	(O 8110)	53,10
Harford	10a-12	P 1322	52,7
Harnhill	30-6	P 0700	45,4
Hasfield	8h-7	O 8227	19,2
Down Hatherley	12-6	O 8622	1,3
Hatherop	31-2	P 1505	39,14. 60,2
(Haw)	8h-8	O 8427	(20,1 note)
Hawkesbury	34a-6	T 7686	14,2
Hawling	9b-8	P 0622	72,1
Hayden	8h-15	O 9023	19,2
Hayes	7-5	(O 7229)	68,12
Hazleton (near Andoversford)	15b-2	P 0718	72,2
Hazleton (in Rodmarton)	28-6	T 9298	41,5
Hempsted	12-16	O 8116	1,62
Henbury	35a-5	T 5678	3,1. WoB 15
'Hentage'	5f-4	(P 0033)	1,43
Hereford (Herefords.)	—	— —	1,34
Hewelsfield	24-4	O 5602	32,12
Hidcote Bartrim	4b-2	P 1742	12,9
Hidcote Boyce	1a-17	P 1741	11,12
(Hide)	12-12	(O 8418)	(36,1 note)
Highnam	11b-2	O 7919	10,8
Hilcot	14a-11	O 9916	3,5. WoA 2. WoB 18
Hill	27c-18	T 6495	1,15;18
(Hill House)	16b-11	O 6912	(32,9 note)
Hillesley	34a-3	T 7689	67,4
Hinchwick	4g-4	P 1429	3,6
Hinton (in Sharpness)	27c-4	T 6803	1,15; (18 note)
(Hinton (in Dyrham))	34b-1	T 7376	(35,2 note)

	Map	Grid	Text
Hinton on the Green (Worcs.)	3a-1	P 0240	10,7
('Hinworthy')	27c-2	(T 7403)	(1,18 note)
Cow Honeybourne (Worcs.)	1a-13	P 1143	11,10
Horfield	27h-1	T 5976	1,15
Horsley	28-3	O 8397	24,1
Horton	34a-7	T 7685	46,2
Hucclecote	12-14	O 8717	2,2
Hullasey	29-17	T 9699	1,23
('Hungerford')	19-1	(P 1913)	(39,15 note)
Huntley	7-17	O 7219	32,6
Hurst	27c-5	O 7102	1,17
(Hyde)	16b-9	O 6812	(32,10 note)
Church Icomb	WOj-1	P 2122	E 26. EvC 40. WoB 7. WoC 6
Icomb 'Place'	10a-15	(P 2122)	39,4
Icomb 'Proper'	10a-14	(P 2022)	53,8
Ildeberga	WOh-1	(P 2332)	(E 34)
(Innerstone)	WOe-2	(O 7529)	(E 21. EvA 105. EvC 25. WoB 5. WoC 4 nn)
Itchington	35b-1	T 6586	3,1. WoA 4. WoB 15
Kemble	WIb-2	T 9897	E 11
Kemerton (Worcs.)	(5c-1) (8c-1)	O 9437	(1,41 (19,2. 20,1
Kempley	7-4	O 6729	39,1
Kempsford	31-10	U 1696	60,1
Ketford	7-3	O 7230	68,12
Kilcot	7-11	O 6925	68,12
Kingscote	27c-17	T 8196	1,15
Kingstone (Herefords.)	—	— —	(1,11. EvK 10)
Kingsweston	27g-1	T 5578	1,15
(Kingswood)	WIa-1	T 7491	(E 16 note)
Kyre (Herefords.)	—	— —	(1,11. EvK 10)
Lasborough	28-10	T 8294	30,2
Lassington	11b-1	O 7921	2,13
Latton (Wilts.)	10b-1	U 0995	71,1
Lechlade	31-9	U 2199	59,1
Leckhampton	13-5	O 9419	38,1. 78,9
'Lee'	36a-4	(T 5881)	6,7
Leigh	8h-10	O 8726	20,1
(Le Mary)	19-4	(P 1913)	(78,2 note)
Lower Lemington	5i-1	P 2134	1,29
'Upper' Lemington	8d-2	(P 2233)	19,2
'Littleton'	6b-3	(P 0236)	(34,13 n) 36,3. 53,12
Littleton on Severn	32-3	T 5989	9,1. EvM 32
Longborough	4g-5	P 1729	29,1. 69,1
Longdon (Worcs.)	—	— —	E 31. (E 32 n) EvA 41. EvC 102;106 n
Longhope	16b-1	O 6819	32,7
Longney	17-1	O 7612	78,12
Lydney	24-3	O 6303	1,55. (E 5)
'Little Lydney' (*alias* St. Briavels)	24-2	O 5504	32,11
Madgett	26-1	O 5500	1,64. 39,10
Mangotsfield	39b-5	T 6676	1,21
Marshfield	37-4	T 7873	1,20
Broad Marston (Worcs.)	1a-9	P 1446	62,2
Long Marston (Warks.)	1a-5	P 1548	15,1
(Matson)	12-20	O 8415	(1,2 note)
Maugersbury	10a-6	P 2025	12,1. EvO 9
Meon (Warks.)	2-1	P 1845	1,12
Meyseyhampton, see Meysey Hampton			
Mickleton	1a-14	P 1643	18,1
Minchinhampton	28-2	O 8700	23,2
(Minchins)	28-13	(T 8689)	(28,5 note)

	Map	Grid	Text
(Minsterworth)	16b-7	O 7717	(53,1 note)
Miserden	22-2	O 9308	66,6
Mitcheldean	16b-3	O 6618	37,3
Mitton	WOb-1	O 9033	E 19. EvA 104. EvC 23. WoB 5. WoC 4
Moorcroft	11b-3	O 7917	37,1
Moreton in Marsh	8f-2	P 2032	19,2
Moreton Valence	17-3	O 7709	53,11
'Morton'	16b-5	(O 7017)	10,11
'Morwents End'	12-4	(O 7922)	10,1
Murrells End	12-5	O 7822	1,2
(Mythe)	5f-2	O 8934	(1,44 note)
Nass	20-8	O 6402	1,54
Natton	5f-8	O 9232	1,24;32
Naunton (near Bourton on the Water)	10a-9	P 1123	48,3. 78,8
Naunton (in Toddington)	6b-8	P 0133	11,6
(Netheridge)	12-18	(O 8115)	(1,6 note)
'Newarne'	Ha-4	(O 6011)	E 2
Newent	7-10	O 7225	(1,11) 16,1. EvK 10
Newington Bagpath	27c-19	T 8194	1,17
Newnham	16b-11	O 6912	32,10
Long Newnton	WIb-7	T 9191	E 12
Norcote	29-11	P 0402	26,3. 69,4
Northleach	15b-8	P 1114	2,8. EvK 103;230. EvM 3;6;99
Bishops Norton	12-2	O 8424	2,3
Burnt Norton	1a-16	P 1441	68,3
Notgrove	14b-1	P 1120	3,5. WoA 2. WoB 18
('Nutbeam')	18-13	(O 9707)	(78,3 note)
Nympsfield	27c-8	O 8000	1,15
Oakley	29-10	(O 9802)	39,19. 52,1. 67,3
Oddington	10a-7	P 2325	2,4
'Oldbury'	18-6	(O 9812)	50,4
Oldbury on the Hill	34a-4	T 8188	60,4
Oldland	39b-11	T 6671	5,1
Olveston	32-4	T 6087	7,1
Oridge Street	8h-6	O 7827	19,2
(Owdeswell)	14a-8	(P 0218)	(3,5 n. WoA 2)
Oxenhall	7-7	O 7126	39,2
Oxenton	5f-11	O 9531	1,25
Ozleworth	27c-22	T 7993	1,15
Painswick	22-1	O 8609	39,8
Pamington	5f-3	O 9433	1,24
Pauntley	7-6	O 7429	68,12
(Paygrove)	12-7	(O 8520)	(36,1 note)
Pebworth (Worcs.)	1a-8	P 1246	34,1;(2). 62,1. EvN 14
Pegglesworth	14a-6	O 9818	3,5. WoA 2. WoB 18
Pendock (Worcs.)	—	— —	WoC 4
(Perry Moor)	29-12	(O 9901)	(1,8 note)
Pinbury	29-5	O 9504	23,1
(Pinchpool)	19-5	(P 1913)	(39,16 note)
Pinnock	9b-2	P 0728	78,10
Poole Keynes	WIb-4	U 0095	E 14
Postlip	6b-12	O 9926	68,5
Poulton (in Awre)	20-4	O 6906	(1,54)
Poulton (nr. Cirencester)	WIb-1	P 1000	E 13
Prestbury	13-2	O 9723	4,1
Preston (nr. Cirencester)	29-16	P 0400	26,4. 69,3
Preston (in Dymock)	11a-1	O 6734	10,9
Preston on Stour (Warks.)	8b-1	P 2049	20,1
(Priors Court)	29-7	(P 0204)	(78,5 note)
Pucklechurch	38b-2	T 6976	8,1
Purton	20-7	O 6704	1,13;(54)

	Map	Grid	Text
Quenington	31-6	P 1404	39,12
Lower Quinton (Warks.)	1a-7	P 1847	62,4. EvN 11
Upper Quinton (Warks.)	1a-10	P 1746	62,3
Lower Redbrook	Ha-6	O 5309	E 3
(Upper Redbrook)	Ha-5	O 5310	(E 4 note)
(Redland)	35a-8	T 5774	(3,1 note)
Redmarley d'Abitot	WOe-1	O 7531	E 21. EvA 105. EvC 25. WoB 5. WoC 4
Redwick	35a-2	T 5485	3,1. WoB 15
Rendcomb	18-10	P 0109	52,4-5
(Ridgeway)	39b-6	(T 6176)	(1,21 note)
Great Rissington	10a-22	P 1917	46,1
Little Rissington	10a-21	P 1919	48,1
Wick Rissington	10a-18	P 1921	39,5
Rockhampton	32-1	T 6593	50,1
Rodmarton	28-7	T 9497	30,1. 78,4
Roel	9b-6	P 0724	22,1
('Rose Court')	10a-11	(P 1022)	(34,6 note)
Ruardean	Ha-1	O 6117	E 7
Ruddle	(16b-12 (20-1	O 6811) (O 6608))	58,2 (58,3 note)
Rudford	7-16	O 7721	78,17
Rye	8h-3	O 8430	19,2
(Lower Rye)	4g-3	P 1930)	(65,1. 66,2 nn)
(Upper Rye)	4g-2	(P 1831))	
St. Briavels, see 'Little Lydney'			
Saintbury	4e-3	P 1139	66,1
Salperton	15b-1	P 0719	63,3
Sandhurst	12-3	O 8223	1,3
'Sapperton' (in Bishops Cleeve)	3c-4	(O 9626)	3,7. WoB 19
Sapperton (nr. Cirencester)	22-8	O 9403	46,3
Sevenhampton	14a-1	P 0321	4,1
Sezincote	1b-1	P 1730	53,7. 57,1. 65,1. 66,2. 70,2
Sharpness	27c-3	O 6702	1,19
Shenington (Oxon.)	5e-1	P 3742	1,36
Sherborne	10a-23	P 1714	11,1
Shipton 'Chamflurs'	14a-9	(P 0318)	63,2
Shipton 'Dovel'	28-12	(T 8991)	31,9
Shipton Moyne	28-14	T 8989	73,1-3
Shipton Oliffe	14a-10	P 0418	38,4. 68,6
Shipton 'Pelye'	14a-10	(P 0418)	53,9
Shipton Solers	14a-9	P 0318	2,6
Shorncote	WIb-3	U 0296	E 17
Siddington	29-19	U 0299	39,18. 66,5. 69,5
Siddington House	29-20	P 0400	32,3
Siston	38b-3	T 6875	42,3
Lower Slaughter	10a-13	P 1622	1,10
Upper Slaughter	10a-10	P 1523	39,20. EvN 11
Slimbridge	27c-1	T 7303	1,17
Snowshill	9a-1	P 0933	11,9
Little Sodbury	34a-8	T 7583	30,3
Old Sodbury	37-1	T 7581	1,48
Somerford Keynes	WIb-5	U 0195	E 10
Southam	3c-5	O 9725	3,7. (WoB 19)
(Southrop)	31-7	P 2003	(55,1 note)
Southwick	5f-9	O 8830	1,24
Standish	17-4	O 8008	2,10. EvM 4
Kings Stanley	21-8	O 8103	67,6
Leonard Stanley	21-7	O 8003	43,2
Stanley Pontlarge	5f-13	O 9930	1,33
Stanton	6b-6	P 0634	11,7
Stanway	5h-1	P 0632	1,27

	Map	Grid	Text
Staunton	Ha-3	O 5512	E 4
(Staunton (in Corse))	WOe-3	O 7829	(E 33 n. EvA 53. EvC 108)
Staverton	8h-14	O 8923	20,1
Stears	16b-10	O 6812	32,8
(Stinchcombe)	27c-13	T 7298	(1,15 note)
Stoke Bishop	35a-7	T 5675	3,1. WoA 4. WoB 15
Stoke Gifford	(35d-1) (36b-1)	T 6279	((3,1. WoB 15 nn) (50,2
Harry Stoke	39b-3	T 6278	6,4
Lark Stoke (Warks.)	4b-1	P 1943	12,8. (EvO 1 n;3;5 n)
Stoke Orchard	3c-2	O 9228	1,45. 3,7. (WoB 19)
Stonehouse	21-5	O 8005	31,1
Stow on the Wold	10a-5	P 1925	(12,1. EvO 9)
Stowell	15b-10	P 0813	2,8
Stratton	29-9	P 0103	39,17
(Stroat)	26-3	T 5797	(31,6. 39,11 notes)
(Sturden)	39b-2	(T 6480)	(6,3 note)
Sudeley	6b-13	P 0327	61,1
Sutton under Brailes (Warks.)	8e-1	P 2937	19,2
Lower Swell	10a-4	P 1725	31,12. 45,6. EvN 12
Upper Swell	4g-8	P 1726	12,5. EvK 133. EvM 65
Swindon	13-1	O 9324	2,5
Syde	18-9	O 9410	68,10
Symonds Hall	27c-16	T 7996	1,15
Taddington	5h-2	P 0831	1,28
Tarlton	29-17	T 9599	31,8. 44,1
Taynton	7-14	O 7321	34,10
Little Taynton	7-13	(O 7423)	37,4
Teddington	WOc-1	O 9633	E 19. EvA 104. EvC 23. WoB 5. WoC 4
Tetbury	28-11	T 8993	41,2
Tetbury Upton, see Upton			
Tewkesbury	5f-6	O 8932	1,24-6;34-5;37-9
Thornbury	32-2	T 6390	1,47
Througham	22-4	O 9207	28,2
Tibberton	7-15	O 7521	32,5
Tidenham	25-1	T 5595	1,56. 31,6. 39,11
Tockington	32-5	T 6086	1,61
Toddington	6b-9	P 0333	61,2
Todenham	8d-1	P 2436	19,2
Tormarton	37-3	T 7678	49,1
Tortworth	33-1	T 7093	67,5
Tredington	5f-14	O 9029	1,24
Trewsbury	29-18	T 9899	52,(1 note); 2
Tuffley	12-19	O 8115	10,1
Lower Turkdean	15b-3	P 1017	38,5
Upper Turkdean	15b-4	P 1017	48,2
Twyning	6a-1	O 8936	1,44. 11,3
Tytherington	33-3	T 6688	5,2
Uckington	8h-13	O 9124	20,1
Uley	27c-14	T 7998	1,15
Ullington (Worcs.)	1a-6	P 1047	34,2
(Upcote)	14a-12	P 0216	(3,5 note. WoA 2)
Upleadon	7-9	O 7626	10,10
Upton St. Leonards	12-21	O 8514	1,2. 70,1
Tetbury Upton	28-9	T 8895	41,3
(Wall)	23b-1	P 1510	(78,11 note)
Walton Cardiff	5f-7	O 9032	1,24
Deerhurst Walton	8h-5	O 8828	20,1
Wapley	39a-1	T 7179	1,9. 43,1
Wapley 'Rectory'	38a-1	T 7179	6,6
Great Washbourne	5g-1	O 9834	1,30

	Map	Grid	Text
Little Washbourne	WOd-1	O 9933	E 22. EvA 107. EvC 27. WoB 5. WoC 4
Welford on Avon (Warks.)	8a-1	P 1452	20,1
Westbury on Severn	16b-8	O 7114	1,11. (32,9. 34,12) EvK 10
Westbury on Trym	35a-6	T 5777	3,1. EvM 8. WoA 4. WoB 15
Westmancote (Worcs.)	–	– –	(WoC 4)
Kings Weston, see Kingsweston			
Weston 'Cantilupe' (in Weston on Avon, Warks.)	4a-1	(P 1651)	12,7. EvE 10. EvK 135. EvM 67. EvO 25-6
'Weston Dovel'	28-13	(T 8689)	32,4
Weston 'Maudit' (in Weston on Avon, Warks.)	1a-1	(P 1651)	62,5
Weston Subedge	1a-18	P 1240	68,2
Westonbirt	28-13	T 8689	28,5. EvK 159. EvM 108;112
(Westwood)	22-7	(O 9205)	(28,3 note)
Whaddon	12-22	O 8313	53,6
Wheatenhurst	21-2	O 7609	78,15
'Whippington'	Ha-2	(O 5614)	E 6
Whittington	14a-2	P 0120	38,3
Childs Wickham, see Childswickham			
Wickhamford (Worcs.)	4c-1	P 0641	12,6. EvK 133
Wick Rissington, see Rissington			
Wickwar	33-4	T 7288	69,7
Widford (Oxon.)	19-7	P 2712	2,11
Wightfield	8h-4	O 8628	19,2
Willersey	4e-2	P 1039	12,6. EvK 134. EvM 66
(Williamstrip)	31-3	P 1505	(39,14 note)
Willicote (Warks.)	1a-4	P 1849	62,6
Winchcombe	6b-W	P 0228	B 1. (1,25;43. 3,5. 4,1. 12,4;10. 20,1. 34,3;8. 39,6. 41,1. 47,1. 59,1. 78,10) EvK 116
Wincot (Warks.)	(4a-2) (5a-2)	P 1849	(33,1 (1,42
Windrush	19-3	P 1913	11,14. 39,15-16. 78,1-2
Winson	15c-2	P 0908	68,7
Winstone	22-3	O 9609	68,1;13
Winterbourne	39b-1	T 6480	1,9
Withington	14a-13	P 0315	3,5. WoA 2. WoB 18
Woodchester	(21-9) (28-1)	O 8402	(78,14 (1,63
Woolaston	26-2	T 5899	31,5
Woolstone	8i-1	O 9630	20,1
Wormington	6b-4	P 0336	39,21
Wotton St. Mary	12-10	(O 8520)	36,1
Wotton under Edge	27c-21	T 7593	1,15
Wyegate	24-1	O 5506	31,4
Yanworth	15b-9	P 0713	72,3
Yate	35c-1	T 7182	3,1. WoB 15

b) Wales (All places were later in Monmouthshire unless otherwise stated)

	Map	Grid	Text
(Welsh Bicknor) (Herefords.)	41-6	O 5917	(E 35 note)
(Bishton)	44-13	T 3887	(W 2;5;13 notes)
Caerleon	43-10	T 3390	S 2. W 2. E 36
Caerwent	45-18	T 4690	W (2;7);12;15

	Map	Grid	Text
Caldicot	45-26	T 4888	W 2;15
(Castell Coch)	44-7	T 4188	(W 18 n)
Chepstow	45-10	T 5393	S 1. W (2);14;16-17
(Christchurch)	44-5	T 3389	(W 2;19 nn)
(Coldra)	44-3	T 3490	(W 19 n)
(Crick)	45-19	T 4890	(W 16 n)
(Cwmcarvan)	42-5	O 4707	(W 2 n)
(Dewstow)	45-25	T 4688	(W 6 n)
(Dingestow)	41-15	O 4510	(E 35 n)
Dinham	45-14	(T 4792)	W 1;(2)
(Dixton)	41-11	O 5113	(E 35 n)
(Ganarew) (Herefords.)	41-7	O 5216	(E 35 n)
(Garth)	41-12	O 5213	(E 35 n)
(Goldcliff)	44-23	T 3683	(W 2;19 nn)
(Grosmont)	40-2	O 4024	(W 4 n)
(Hardwick)	45-11	(T 5393)	(W 16 n)
(Hendrew)	44-2	T 3991	(W 18 n)
(Ifton)	44-16	T 4688	(W 2;18 nn)
(Itton)	45-6	T 4995	(W 2;16 nn)
(Kemeys Commander)	42-8	O 3404	(W 2 n)
(Kemeys Inferior)	44-1	T 3892	(W 2;18 nn)
(Kilgwrrwg)	42-22	T 4698	(W 2 n)
(Langstone)	44-4	T 3789	(W 2;9 nn)
(Liswerry)	44-9	T 3487	(W 19 n)
(Llanbadoc)	42-18	O 3700	(W 2 n)
(Llandegveth)	43-4	T 3395	(W 2 n)
(Llandenny)	42-10	O 4103	(W 2 n)
(Llandevenny)	44-17	T 4186	(W 2;18 nn)
(Llanddewi Fach)	43-3	T 3395	(W 2;4 nn)
(Llandogo)	42-11	O 5204	(W 2;4;16 nn)
(Llanfihangel Rogiet)	44-14	T 4587	(W 2;6 nn)
(Llanfrechfa)	43-7	T 3193	(W 2 n)
(Llangattock)	43-10	(T 3390)	(W 2;18. E 36 nn)
(Llangattock Vibon Avel)	41-8	O 4515	(E 35 n)
(Llangeview)	42-17	P 3900	(W 2 n)
(Llangybi)	43-2	T 3796	(W 2 n)
(Llangovan)	42-6	O 4505	(W 2 n)
(Llangua)	40-1	O 3925	(W 4 n)
(Llangwm)	42-19	T 4299	(W 2 n)
(Llanhennock)	43-8	T 3592	(W 2;18. E 36 nn)
(Llanishen)	42-13	O 4703	(W 2 n)
(Llanlowell *alias* Llanllywel)	42-21	T 3998	(W 2 n)
(Llanllwydd)	41-2	O 4117	(E 35 n)
(Llanmartin)	45-22	T 3989	(W 2;5;18 nn)
(Llanrothal) (Herefords.)	41-1	O 4618	(E 35 n)
(Llansoy)	42-12	O 4402	(W 2 n)
(Llantarnam)	43-6	T 3093	(W 2;18. E 36 nn)
(Llantilio Crossenny)	40-4	O 3914	(W 4 n)
(Llantrisant)	42-23	T 3996	(W 2 n)
(Llanvaches)	45-16	T 4391	(W 16 n)
Llanvair Discoed	45-13	T 4492	W 1;(2)
(Llanvihangel Pontymoel)	42-15	O 3001	(W 2 n)
(Llanvihangel Tormynydd)	42-14	O 4601	(W 2 n)
(Llanwern)	44-11	T 3787	(W 2;18 nn)
(Maesgwenith)	45-8	(T 4493)	(W 7 n)
(Magor)	44-18	T 4287	(W 2;10;18 nn)
(Malpas)	43-9	T 3090	(W 18. E 37 nn)
(Mathern)	45-21	T 5290	(W 2;13 nn)
(Milton)	44-6	T 3688	(W 18 nn)
(Mitchel Troy)	42-2	O 4910	(W 2 n)
Monmouth	41-13	O 5012	E 35
(Mounton)	45-12	T 5192	(W 16 n)
(Moynes Court)	45-20	T 5190	(W 16 n)

	Map	Grid	Text
(Nash)	44-22	T 3483	(W 2;10;19 nn)
(Newcastle)	41-3	O 4417	(E 35 n)
(Panteg)	43-1	T 3199	(W 2 n)
(Penallt)	42-1	O 5210	(W 2 n)
(Penhow)	45-17	T 4290	(W 2;18 nn)
(Penterry)	45-2	T 5299	(W 2;16 nn)
(Pen-y-Clawdd)	42-4	O 4507	(W 2 n)
(Perth Hîr)	41-9	O 4815	(E 35 n)
(Porthcasseg)	45-3	T 5298	(W 16 n)
(Porton)	44-25	T 3883	(W 11 n)
Portskewett	45-27	T 4988	W 1;(2)
(Pwllmeyric)	45-15	T 5192	(W 16 n)
(Pwllpan)	44-10	T 3587	(S 2. W 19 nn)
(Raglan)	42-3	O 4107	(W 2 n)
(Redwick)	44-21	T 4184	(W 2;11 nn)
(Rockfield)	41-10	O 4814	(E 35 n)
(Rogerstone)	45-4	T 5096	(W 14 n)
(Rogiet)	44-15	T 4587	(W 2;18 nn)
(St. Arvans)	45-5	T 5196	(W 2;16 nn)
(St. Brides Netherwent)	45-23	T 4289	(W 2;18 nn)
(St. Maughans)	41-4	O 4617	(E 35 n)
(St. Wormets)	45-7	(T 5095)	(W 16 n)
(Salisbury)	44-8	T 4288	(W 18 n)
(Shirenewton)	45-9	T 4793	(W 2;15 nn)
(Skenfrith)	40-3	O 4520	(W 4 n)
('Strigoil')	45-10	(T 5393)	(W 14;16-17 nn)
(Sudbrook)	45-28	T 5087	(W 16 n)
(Tintern)	45-1	O 5300	(W 2 n)
(Traston)	44-20	(T 3385)	(W 19 n)
(Tredunnock)	43-5	T 3794	(W 2;18. E 35 nn)
(Tregate) (Herefords.)	41-5	O 4817	(E 35 n)
(Trelleck)	42-7	O 5005	(W 2 n)
(Trostrey)	42-9	O 3604	(W 2 n)
(Undy)	44-19	T 4386	(W 2;18 nn)
(Usk)	42-16	O 3700	(W 2 n)
(Wallstone)	45-24	(T 5189)	(W 17 n)
(Whitson)	44-24	T 3883	(W 2-3 nn)
(Wilcrick)	44-12	T 4088	(W 2;18 nn)
(Wolvesnewton)	42-20	T 4599	(W 2 n)
(Wonastow)	41-16	O 4810	(E 35 n)
(Wyesham)	41-14	O 5112	(E 35 n)

Places in Gloucestershire occurring in Indices of Persons, Churches and Clergy (information in brackets is not found in the text of DB Glos.)

Berkeley ... Ralph, Roger, (Abbey).
Bristol ... Church.
Cirencester ... Church.
(Donnington ... William).
(Doynton) ... Robert.
Gloucester ... Durand, (Roger), (Walter), Abbey, Abbot, Church, Monks.
Maidenhill ... Humphrey.
Stanton ... Godwin.
(Stow on the Wold) ... Church.
(Tetbury ... Azelin).
Tewkesbury ... Church.
Winchcombe ... Abbey, (Abbot), Church.

Places not in Gloucestershire

Names starred are in the Index of Places above; others are in the Indices of Persons or of Churches and Clergy. (Information in brackets is not found in the text of DB Glos.)

Elsewhere in Britain

BERKSHIRE Abingdon ... Abbey, Church; Faringdon ... Alfsi; (Seacourt ... William).

CHESHIRE (Chester) ... Earl Hugh.

DEVON Exeter ... Bishop Osbern.

HAMPSHIRE Winchester ... Bishop; Boscombe ... Alstan.

HEREFORDSHIRE (Welsh Bicknor)*; Eaton Bishop*; Edvin Loach*; (Ganarew)*; Hereford* ... Bishop Robert, (Earls Ralph, Roger), (Bishop Walter), (Earl William), Canons, Church; Kingstone*; Kyre*; (Llanrothal)*; (Tregate)*.

KENT (Canterbury) ... Archbishop Stigand.

MIDDLESEX Lambeth .. Church; Westminster ... Abbey, Church.

OXFORDSHIRE Eynsham ... Abbey, Church, (Monks); Shenington*; Widford*.

SHROPSHIRE (Shrewsbury) ... Earl Roger.

SOMERSETSHIRE Bath* ... Abbot, Church, Monks; Bishopsworth*; Glastonbury ... Abbey, Church.

SUFFOLK (Bury St. Edmunds) ... Abbot Baldwin.

WARWICKSHIRE Admington*; Clifford Chambers*; Lower Clopton*; Upper Clopton*; Little Compton*; Coventry ... Abbey, Church; Dorsington*; Long Marston*; Meon*; Preston on Stour*; Lower Quinton*; Upper Quinton*; Lark Stoke*; Sutton under Brailes*; (Warwick ... Earl Henry); Westbury on Severn*; Weston 'Cantilupe'*; Weston 'Maudit'*; Willicote*; Wincot*.

WILTSHIRE Chippenham*; Latton*; Malmesbury ... Abbey, Abbot, Church; Salisbury ... Edward.

WORCESTERSHIRE Ashton under Hill*; Aston Somerville*; Beckford*; Bengeworth*; Bickmarsh*; Bredon*; Bushley*; Childswickham*; Clifton on Teme*; Droitwich*; Evesham ... Abbey, (Abbots Robert, Walter), (Chapter), Church; Hanley Castle*; Hinton on the Green*; Cow Honeybourne*; Kemerton*; Longdon*; Broad Marston*; Pebworth*; Pendock*; Pershore ... Abbey, (Abbot), Church, Monks; Ullington*; Westmancote*; Wickhamford*; (Worcester) ... Bishops Brictheah, Samson, Wulfstan; Church, (Monks).

YORKSHIRE (York) ... Archbishops Aldred, Thomas.

WALES Caerwent ... Belward; (?Cardiff) ... Ralph.

Outside Britain

Abetot ... Urso. (Ballon ... Hamelin). Bayeux ... Bishop Odo. (Beauchamp ... Walter). Beaumont ... Roger. (Bellême ... Robert). Bully ... Roger. Caen ... Church. (Chaworth, see Sourches). Cherbourg ... Osbern. Chocques ... Sigar. Cormeilles ... Ansfrid, (Thurstan), Abbey, Abbot, Church. Coutances ... Bishop Geoffrey. Écouis ... William. Épaignes, see 'Spain'. (Eskecot) ... Gilbert. Eu ... (?Count Henry), William. Ferrers ... Henry, (Robert). Grandmesnil ... Hugh. Hesdin ... Arnulf. Ivry ... Roger. Lacy ... (Hugh, Robert), Roger, Walter. Limesy ... Ralph. Lisieux ... Bishop Gilbert. Loges ... Gerwy. Lyre ... Abbey, Church. (Maine ... Gilbert). Mandeville ... Geoffrey, (William). Mortagne ... Matthew. Mortain ... Count (Robert). Oilly ... Robert, Roger. Paris ... Church. (Pîtres) ... Roger. (Sacey ... Ralph). (Sai (Say) ... William). Saint Lô ... Bishop. (Saint Valéry ... Walter). Saumur ... St. Florent's. (Soliers (Sollers) ... Richard). (Sourches (Chaworth) ... Patrick). 'Spain' (Épaignes) ... Alfred. (Tilleul) ... Robert. Tosny ... Ralph, Robert. Troarn ... Church.

Unidentified

('Burgh') ... Walter). (Ham ... Hugh).

THE COUNTY BOUNDARY

The 1086 County boundary differed in several important ways from the modern (pre-April 1974) County. On the western edge, the earliest 11th-century boundary of the County seems to have been formed by the rivers Leadon and Severn, the area to the west of these rivers and to the east of the river Wye being at first in Herefordshire (E 1–8 note). By 1086, some places in this area had come into Gloucestershire leaving Alvington as a detached part of Herefordshire. The process continued and by the 12th century, 'Newarne', Redbrook, Ruardean, Staunton and 'Whippington' had been transferred fully into Gloucestershire. Domesday records some transfers as incomplete: 'Newarne' (DB Herefords. 1,72 = E 2 here) had been transferred into Gloucestershire where it has remained, though still recorded only in the Herefordshire folios, while Kingstone (DB Herefords. 3,1; see 1,11 note) is said to pay tax and do service in Gloucestershire, but to come to Hundred meetings in Brooms Ash Hundred in Herefordshire. The village subsequentially remained in Herefordshire.

The land between the Wye and the Usk and some land beyond the Usk is said to be in Wales and has Welsh customs (W 1–19), but is in 1086 mainly under Norman administration and attached for this purpose to Gloucestershire. This area was to form the county of Monmouthshire. North of it, bounded by the river Monnow, lay Archenfield, a Welsh area with Welsh customs, but under Norman rule and attached to Herefordshire (see DB Herefords. Introductory Note 4).

On the southern side of the County the boundary with Somerset was, in 1086 and for centuries following, marked by the river Avon. Since 1832 however, the growth of Bristol has been recognised by a series of Boundary Orders which have transferred into the City the former Gloucestershire parishes of Clifton, Westbury on Trym, Stapleton, Horfield and Henbury (in part), containing several Domesday places. Bristol has similarly expanded south of the Avon and has absorbed the Somersetshire Domesday villages of Bedminster and Knowle.

The changes on the northern, eastern and south-eastern boundaries of the County are listed below. In 1086, the Gloucestershire, Worcestershire, Warwickshire and Oxfordshire boundaries were much interlaced. It seems that the Mercian shires were first mapped out in the early 11th century with the intention of allocating 1200 hides, or multiples of them, to a 'county' town (see DB Worcestershire App. I). The simple arrangement which might have resulted was complicated by an attempt to keep all the scattered holdings of a particular church in its County, as a round 100 hides or multiple thereof. Thus the Gloucestershire churches of Tewkesbury and Deerhurst, like several of the Worcestershire churches, have a number of detached holdings surrounded by other counties. The effect of the 19th- and 20th-century Boundary Orders has been to abolish all such detachments.

Places in **Gloucestershire in 1086,** *later transferred to Oxfordshire*
Shenington in 1844
Widford in 1844

Places in **Gloucestershire in 1086,** *later transferred to Warwickshire*
Admington (including Lark Stoke) in 1935
Clifford Chambers (including Willicote and Wincot) in 1931
Upper and Lower Clopton in 1935
Little Compton in 1844
Dorsington in 1931
Long Marston in 1931
Preston on Stour in 1931
Upper and Lower Quinton (including Meon) in 1935
Sutton under Brailes in 1844
Welford on Avon in 1931
Weston on Avon (including Weston 'Cantilupe' and Weston 'Maudit') in 1931

Places in **Gloucestershire in 1086,** *later transferred to Worcestershire*
    Ashton under Hill in 1931
    Aston Somerville in 1931
    Beckford (a part) in 1931
    Bickmarsh in 1931 (see 78,7 note)
    Childswickham in 1931
    Hinton on the Green in 1931
    Cow Honeybourne in 1931
    Kemerton in 1931
    Pebworth (including Broad Marston and Ullington) in 1931
    [Also transferred in 1931 was a part of Forthampton. For Hanley Castle, geographically in Worcestershire, but counted in Gloucestershire in 1086, see 1,34 note].

Places in Worcestershire in 1086, later transferred to **Gloucestershire**
    Alstone in 1844
    Blockley (including Ditchford and Dorn) in 1931
    Chaceley in 1931
    Cutsdean in 1931
    Daylesford in 1931
    Evenlode (including the site of *Ildeberga*) in 1931
    Church Icomb (a part) in 1844
    Mitton (a part) in 1931
    Redmarley d'Abitot (including Innerstone) in 1931
    Staunton in 1931
    Teddington in 1931
    Little Washbourne in 1844

Places in Wiltshire in 1086, later transferred to **Gloucestershire**
    Ashley in 1930
    Kemble in 1897
    Kingswood in 1844
    Long Newnton in 1930
    Poole Keynes in 1897
    Poulton in 1844
    Somerford Keynes (including Shorncote) in 1897

Frank Thorn

Maps and Map Keys

GLOUCESTERSHIRE HUNDREDS AND WELSH COMMOTES

The figures used for Gloucestershire Hundreds and Welsh Commotes in index and maps are:

1 Chelthorn	16 Westbury	31 Brightwells Barrow
2 Kiftsgate	17 Whitstone	32 Langley
3 Tibblestone	18 Rapsgate	33 Bagstone
4 Witley	19 Barrington	34 Grumbalds Ash
5 Tewkesbury	20 Bledisloe	35 Brentry
6 Greston	21 Blacklow	36 Ledbury
7 Botloe	22 Bisley	37 Edderstone
8 Deerhurst	23 Bibury	38 Pucklechurch
9 Holford	24 Lydney	39 Swinehead
10 Salmonsbury	25 Tidenham	40 Teirtref
11 Longbridge	26 Twyford	41 Monmouth
12 Dudstone	27 Berkeley	42 Usk
13 Cheltenham	28 Longtree	43 Edlogan
14 Wattlescomb	29 Cirencester	44 Libennith
15 Bradley	30 Garsdon	45 Is Coed

Places in other counties in 1086, but later transferred into Gloucestershire (or Monmouthshire) are indicated by

       H   Herefordshire
       WI Wiltshire
       WO Worcestershire

Places are mapped in their 1086 Hundreds as evidenced in the text. On the maps and in the keys, separated parts of Hundreds are distinguished by letters (a, b; c, etc.) after the Hundred figure. Detachments and places within Hundreds are counted West–East, working southwards. A number on the maps sometimes represents more than one place; this is recorded in the map keys. Places in brackets do not appear in the text of DB, but in subsidiary documents or in the notes.

Apart from dots, the following symbols indicate places on the map:
- ■   A borough. (G for Gloucester; W for Winchcombe)
- o   A place not evidenced in the text but in one of the associated documents discussed in the notes.
- ▲   A place in another county in 1086, later transferred to Gloucestershire.
- ‡   Parts of a village divided by a Hundred boundary. Each part is indexed in its respective Hundred and cross referenced in the map keys.

County names in brackets after a place-name in the map keys are those of the modern (pre-April 1974) county to which places in the Domesday county of Gloucester were later transferred. The Domesday county included the later area of Monmouth county and contained a number of isolated detachments of Worcestershire and Herefordshire.

The County Boundary is marked on the maps by thick lines, continuous for 1086, dotted for the modern pre-1974 boundary; the Hundred and Commote boundaries by thin lines, dotted where uncertain.

National Grid 10-kilometre squares are shown on the map borders.

Each four-figure square covers one square kilometre, or 247 acres, approximately 2 fiscal hides at 120 acres to the hide.

NORTH EAST GLOUCESTERSHIRE

1 Chelthorn
1a
11 Admington (Warks.)
15 Aston Subedge
2 Bickmarsh (Worcs.)
12 Lower Clopton (Warks.)
3 Dorsington (Warks.)
17 Hidcote Boyce
13 Cow Honeybourne (Worcs.)
9 Broad Marston (Worcs.)
5 Long Marston (Warks.)
14 Mickleton
16 Burnt Norton
8 Pebworth (Worcs.)
7 Lower Quinton (Warks.)
10 Upper Quinton (Warks.)
6 Ullington (Worcs.)
1 Weston 'Maudit' (Warks.)
18 Weston Subedge
4 Willicote (Warks.)
1b
1 Sezincote

2 Kiftsgate
2 Upper Clopton (Warks.)
1 Meon (Warks.)

3 Tibblestone
3a
1 Hinton on the Green (Worcs.)

4 Witley
4a
1 Weston 'Cantilupe' (Warks.)
2 Wincot (Warks.)(see 5a-2)
4b
2 Hidcote Bartrim
1 Lark Stoke (Warks.)
4c
1 Wickhamford (Worcs.)
4d
1 Buckland
4e
4 Chipping Campden
5 Charingworth
1 Ebrington
3 Saintbury
2 Willersley
4f
1 Batsford
4g
7 (Banks Fee)
1 (Clapley)
6 Condicote
4 Hinchwick
5 Longborough
3 (Lower Rye)
2 (Upper Rye)
8 Upper Swell

5 Tewkesbury
5a
1 Clifford Chambers (Warks.)
2 Wincot (Warks.)(see 4a-2)
5e
1 Shenington (Oxon.)

5h
1 Stanway
2 Taddington
5i
1 Lower Lemington

6 Greston
6b
1 Aston Somerville (Worcs.)
14 Charlton Abbots
2 Childswickham (Worcs.)
5 Dumbleton
7 Frampton
10 ('Frampton Court')
11 Hailes
3 'Littleton'
8 Naunton
12 Postlip
6 Stanton
13 Sudeley
9 Toddington
4 Wormington
W Winchcombe

8 Deerhurst
8a
1 Welford on Avon (Warks.)
8b
1 Preston on Stour (Warks.)
8d
2 'Upper' Lemington
1 Todenham
8e
1 Sutton under Brailes (Warks.)
8f
1 Bourton on the Hill
2 Moreton in Marsh
8g
1 Little Compton (Warks.)

9 Molford
9a
1 Snowshill
9b
3 (Beales Place)
5 Castlett
1 Farmcote
7 Guiting Power
4 Temple Guiting
8 Hawling
2 Pinnock
6 Roel

10 Salmonsbury
10a
3 Adlestrop
11 Aylworth
16 Bledington
19 Bourton on the Water
2 Broadwell
17 'Caldicott'
20 'Combe Baskerville'
1 (Donnington)
8 Eyford
12 Harford
15 Icomb 'Place'
14 Icomb 'Proper'

6 Maugersbury
9 Naunton
7 Oddington
22 Great Rissington
21 Little Rissington
18 Wick Rissington
11 (Rose Court)
23 Sherbourne
13 Lower Slaughter
10 Upper Slaughter
5 Stow on the Wold
4 Lower Swell

14 Wattlescomb
14a
15 Little Colesbourne
14 Cassey Compton
3 Dowdeswell
7 Foxcote
5 Hampen
4 Lower Hampen
11 Hilcot
8 (Owdeswell)
6 Pegglesworth
1 Sevenhampton
9 Shipton 'Chamflurs'
10 Shipton Oliffe
10 Shipton 'Pelye'
9 Shipton Solers
12 (Upcote)
2 Whittington
13 Withington
14b
2 Aston Blank (*alias* Cold Aston)
1 Notgrove

15 Bradley
15b
5 Compton Abdale
7 Farmington
6 Hampnett
2 Hazleton
8 Northleach
1 Salperton
10 Stowell
3 Lower Turkdean
4 Upper Turkdean
9 Yanworth

19 Barrington
7 Widford (Oxon.)

Worcestershire
WOa
2 Blockley
1 Ditchford
3 (Dorn)
WOg
1 Cutsdean
WOh
2 Evenlode
1 *Ildeberga*
WOi
1 Daylesford
WOj
1 Church Icomb

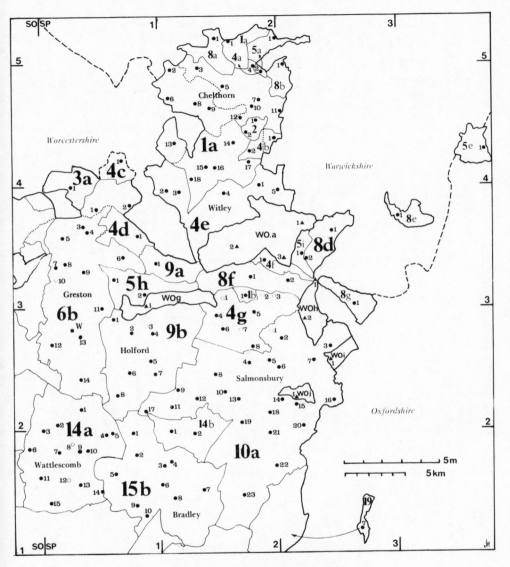

NORTH-EAST GLOUCESTERSHIRE

NORTH WEST GLOUCESTERSHIRE

3 Tibblestone
3b
2 Ashton under Hill (Worcs.)(see 5d-1)
2 Beckford (Worcs.)
3 (Didcot)
3c
3 Bishops Cleeve
1 Gotherington
4 'Sapperton'
5 Southam
2 Stoke Orchard

5 Tewkesbury
5b
1 Hanley Castle (Worcs.)
5c
1 Kemerton (Worcs.)(see 8c-1)
5d
1 Ashton under Hill (Worcs.)(see 3b-1)
5f
4 Alderton
1 Aston on Carrant
12 Dixton
15 (Downing)
10 Fiddington
5 Forthampton
4 'Hentage'
2 (Mythe)
8 Natton
11 Oxenton
3 Pamington
9 Southwick
13 Stanley Pontlarge
6 Tewkesbury
14 Tredington
7 Walton Cardiff
5g
1 Great Washbourne
5j
1 Boddington

6 Greston
6a
1 Twyning

7 Botloe
12 (Boulsdon)
1 Bromsberrow
8 Carswall
2 Dymock
5 Hayes
17 Huntley
4 Kempley
3 Ketford
11 Kilcot
10 Newent
7 Oxenhall
6 Pauntley
16 Rudford
14 Taynton
13 Little Taynton
15 Tibberton
9 Upleadon

8 Deerhurst
8c
1 Kemerton (Worcs.)(see 5c-1)
8h
2 Deerhurst
1 'Ellings'
12 Elmstone
11 Evington
9 Hardwicke
7 Hasfield
8 (Haw)
15 Hayden
10 Leigh
6 Oridge Street
3 Rye
13 Staverton
13 Uckington
5 Deerhurst Walton
4 Wightfield
8i
1 Woolstone

11 Longbridge
11a
1 Preston
11b
2 Highnam
1 Lassington
3 Moorcroft

12 Dudstone
9 Badgeworth
13 Barnwood
11 'Abbots Barton'
11 'Kings Barton'
1 Brawn
15 Brockworth
23 Brookethorpe
8 Churchdown
17 (Elmore)
22 ('Grove Court')
25 Harescombe
24 Haresfield
6 Down Hatherley
16 Hempsted
12 (Hide)
14 Hucclecote
20 (Matson)
4 'Morwents End'
5 Morrells End
18 (Netheridge)
2 Bishops Norton
7 (Paygrove)
3 Sandhurst
19 Tuffley
21 Upton St. Leonards
22 Whaddon
10 Wotton St. Mary
G Gloucester

13 Cheltenham
4 (Broadwell)
3 Cheltenham
5 Leckhampton
2 Prestbury
1 Swindon

16 Westbury
16b
2 Bulley
4 Churcham
6 (Duni)
11 (Hill House)
9 (Hyde)
1 Longhope
7 (Minsterworth)
3 Mitcheldean
5 'Morton'
11 Newnham
12 Ruddle (see 20-1)
10 Stears
8 Westbury on Severn

17 Whitstone
2 'Sheriffs' Haresfield
1 Longney
3 Moreton Valence
4 Standish

27 Berkeley
27a
1 Ashleworth

Herefordshire
Ha (see also W map)
4 'Newarne'
1 Ruardean

Worcestershire
WOb
1 Milton
WOc
1 Teddington
WOd
2 (Alstone)
1 Little Washbourne
WOe
2 (Innerstone)
1 Redmarley d'Abitot
3 (Staunton)
WOf
1 (Chaceley)

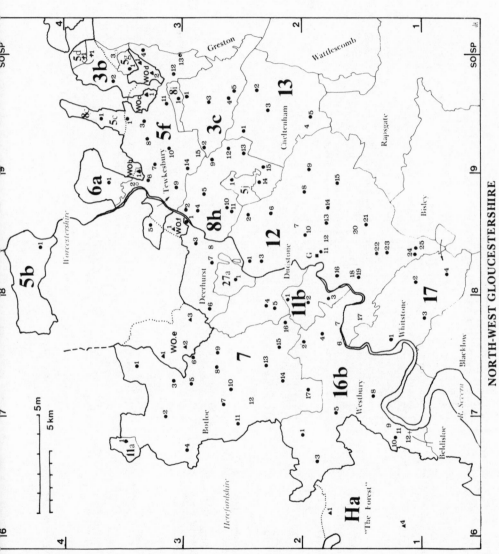

NORTH-WEST GLOUCESTERSHIRE

SOUTH EAST GLOUCESTERSHIRE

8 Deerhurst'
8j
2 Calcot
1 Coln St. Dennis

10 Salmonsbury
10b
1 Latton

15 Bradley
15a
1 Upper Coberley
15c
1 (Coln Rogers)
2 Winson

18 Rapsgate
4 Brimpsfield
14 North Cerney
7 Checkworth
1 Coberley
3 Great Colesbourne
8 (Combend)
2 Cowley
11 Duntisbourne Abbots (see 29-1)
15 Duntisbourne 'Hotat' (see 29-4)
12 Duntisbourne Leer
5 Elkstone
13 (Nutbeam)
6 'Oldbury'
10 Rendcomb
9 Syde

19 Barrington
2 Great Barrington
6 Little Barrington
1 (Hungerford)
4 (Le Mary)
5 (Pinchpool)
[7 Widford (Oxon.) (see NE map)]
3 Windrush

22 Bisley
5 Bisley
6 Edgeworth
9 Frampton Mansell
2 Miserden
1 Painswick
8 Sapperton
4 Througham
7 (Westwood)
3 Winstone

23 Bibury
23a
1 Eycot
23b
3 (Ablington)
2 Aldsworth
4 Arlington
6 Barnsley
5 Bibury
1 (Wall)

28 Longtree
4 Avening
7 (Chamberlains)
5 Cherington
5 Culkerton
12 (Estcourt)
6 Hazleton
10 Horsley
2 Lasborough
2 Minchinhampton
13 (Minchins)
7 Rodmarton
14 Shipton 'Dovel'
14 Shipton Moyne
11 Tetbury
9 Tetbury Upton
13 Westonbirt
13 'Weston Dovel'
1 Woodchester (see 21-9)

29 Cirencester
2 Bagendon
8 Baunton
21 (Bowley)
15 (Chesterton)
13 Cirencester
13 (Cirencester Rectory)
14 (Coates Cockerell)
14 (Coates Randulf)
6 (Daglingworth)
1 Duntisbourne Abbots (see18-11)
15 Duntisbourne 'Hotat' (see 18-15)
3 Duntisbourne Rouse
17 Hullasey
11 Norcote
10 Oakley
12 (Perry Moor)
5 Pinbury
16 Preston
7 (Priors Court)
20 Siddington House
19 Siddington
9 Stratton
17 Tarlton
18 Trewsbury

30 Garsdon
12 Down Ampney
3 Ampney Crucis
1 (Ampney 'Mareys')
2 Ampney St. Mary
5 Ampney 'St. Nicholas'
4 Ampney St. Peter
2 Ashbrook
10 South Cerney
11 Cerney Wick
9 (Charlham)
7 Driffield
6 Harnhill
8 Meysey Hampton

31 Brightwells Barrow
1 Coln St. Aldwyns
5 Eastleach Martin
4 Eastleach Turville
8 Fairford
2 Hatherop
10 Kempsford
9 Lechlade
6 Quenington
7 (Southrop)
3 (Williamstrip)

Wiltshire
WIb
6 Ashley
2 Kemble
7 Long Newnton
4 Poole Keynes
1 Poulton
3 Sharncote
5 Somerford Keynes

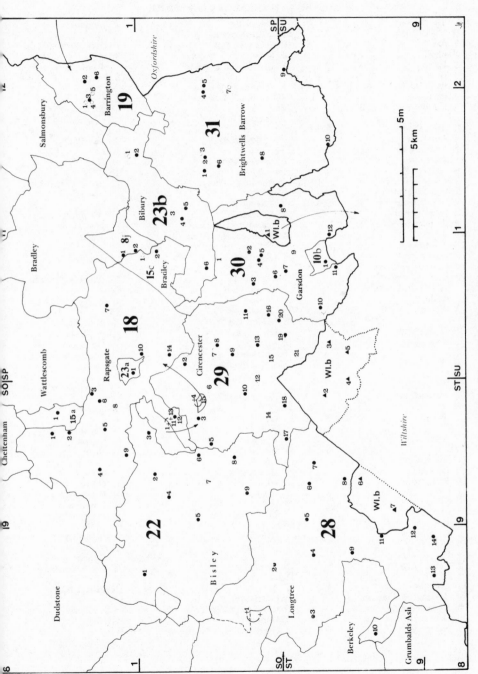

SOUTH-EAST GLOUCESTERSHIRE

SOUTH GLOUCESTERSHIRE

20 Bledisloe
6 (Allaston)
3 Awre
2 Bledisloe
3 Etloe
8 Nass
4 Poulton
7 Purton
1 Ruddle (see 16b-12)

21 Blacklow
4 Alkerton
3 Frampton on Severn
1 Fretherne
6 Frocester
8 Kings Stanley
7 Leonard Stanley
5 Stonehouse
2 Wheatenhurst
9 Woodchester (see 28-1)

24 Lydney
5 'Alverston'
4 Hewelsfield
2 Little Lydney
(*alias* St. Briavels)
3 Lydney
1 Wyegate

25 Tidenham
1 Tidenham

26 Twyford
1 Madgett
3 (Stroat)
2 Woolaston

27 Berkeley
27b
1 Arlingham
27c
12 Alkington
9 Berkeley
20 Beverstone
11 Cam
10 Clingre
7 Coaley
15 Dursley
6 Gossington
18 Hill
4 Hinton
2 ('Hinworthy')
5 Hurst
17 Kingscote
19 Newington Bagpath
8 Nymphsfield
22 Ozleworth
3 Sharpness

1 Slimbridge
13 (Stinchcombe)
16 Symonds Hall
14 Uley
21 Wotton under Edge
27d
1 Cromhall 'Abbots'
2 Cromhall 'Lygon'
27e
1 Ellerton
27f
1 Almondsbury
27g
1 Kingsweston
27h
1 Horfield

32 Langley
6 Alveston
7 Gaunts Earthcott
8 Frampton Cotterell
3 Littleton on Severn
4 Olveston
1 Rockhampton
2 Thornbury
5 Tockington

33 Bagstone
6 'Acton Ilger'
5 Iron Acton
2 Charfield
1 Tortworth
3 Tytherington
4 Wickwar

34 Grumbalds Ash
34a
10 Acton Turville
2 Alderley
9 Badminton
1 Boxwell
5 Didmarton
6 Hawkesbury
3 Hillesley
7 Horton
4 Oldbury on the Hill
8 Little Sodbury
34b
1 (Hinton)
2 Dyrham

35 Brentry
35a
1 Aust
4 (Charlton)
3 Compton Greenfield
5 Henbury
8 (Redland)

2 Redwick
7 Stoke Bishop
6 Westbury on Trym
35b
1 Itchington
35c
1 Yate
35d
1 Stoke Gifford
(see 36b-1)

36 Ledbury
36a
1 'Lee'
36b
1 Stoke Gifford
(see 35d-1)

37 Edderstone
2 Dodington
4 Marshfield
1 Old Sodbury
3 Tormarton

38 Pucklechurch
38a
1 Wapley 'Rectory'
38b
5 Cold Aston
1 (Codrington)
4 Doynton
2 Pucklechurch
3 Siston

39 Swinehead
39a
1 Wapley
39b
9 'Barton Regis'
13 Bitton
14 (Bitton Prebend)
10 (Blacksworth)
8 Bristol
7 Clifton
4 Hambrook
12 Hanham
5 Mangotsfield
11 Oldland
6 (Ridgeway)
3 Harry Stoke
2 (Sturden)
1 Winterbourne

Herefordshire
Hb
1 Alvington
Wiltshire
WIa
1 (Kingswood)

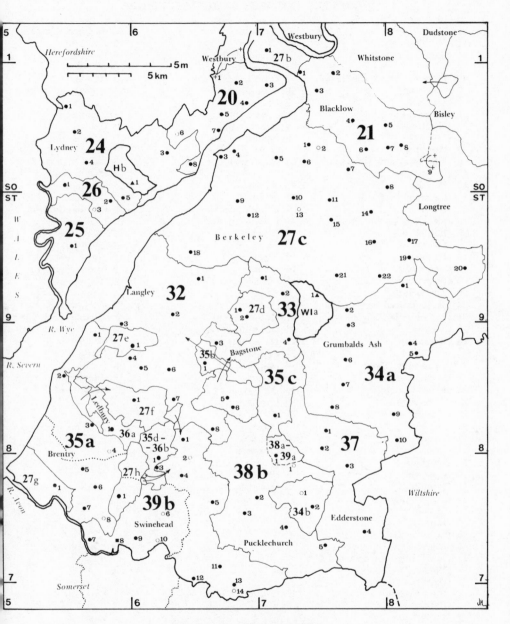

SOUTH GLOUCESTERSHIRE

WALES AND WEST GLOUCESTERSHIRE

16 Westbury
16a
 1 (English Bicknor)

40 Teirtref (Three Castles)
 2 (Grosmont)
 1 (Llangua)
 4 (Llantilio Crossenny)
 3 (Skenfrith)

41 Monmouth
 6 (Welsh Bicknor) (Herefs.)
15 (Dingestow)
11 (Dixton)
 7 (Ganarew) (Herefs.)
12 (Garth)
 8 (Llangattock Vibon Avel)
 2 (Llanllwydd)
 1 (Llanrothal) (Herefs.)
13 Monmouth
 3 (Newcastle)
 9 (PerthHîr)
10 (Rockfield)
 4 (St. Maughans)
 5 (Tregate) (Herefs.)
16 (Wonastow)
14 (Wyesham)

42 Brynbuga (Usk)
 5 (Cwmcarvan)
 8 (Kemeys Commander)
22 (Kilgwrrwg)
18 (Llanbadoc)
10 (Llandenny)
11 (Llandogo)
17 (Langeview)
 6 (Llangovan)
19 (Llangwm)
13 (Llanishen)
21 (Llanlowell) or
     (Llanllywel)
12 (Llansoy)
23 (Llantrisant)
15 (Llanvihangel Pontymoel)
14 (Llanvihangel Tormynydd)
 2 (Mitchel Troy)
 1 (Penallt)
 4 (Pen-y-Clawdd)
 3 (Raglan)
 7 (Trelleck)
 9 (Trostrey)
16 (Usk)
20 (Wolvesnewton)

43 Edlogan
10 Caerleon
 4 (Llandegveth)
 3 (Llanddewi Fach)
 7 (Llanfrechfa)
10 (Llangattock)
 2 (Llangybi)
 8 (Llanhennock)
 6 (Llantarnam)
 9 (Malpas)
 1 (Panteg)
 5 (Tredunnock)

44 Libennith
13 (Bishton)
 7 (Castell Coch)
 5 (Christchurch)
 3 (Coldra)
23 (Goldcliff)
 2 (Hendrew)
16 (Ifton)
 1 (Kemeys Inferior)
 4 (Langstone)
 9 (Lịswerry)
17 (Llandevenny)
14 (Llanfihangel Rogiet)
11 (Llanwern)
18 (Magor)
 6 (Milton)
22 (Nash)
25 (Porton)
10 (Pwyllpan)
21 (Redwick)
15 (Rogiet)
 8 (Salisbury)
20 (Traston)
19 (Undy)
24 (Whitson)
12 (Wilcrick)

45 Is Coed (Caldicot)
18 Caerwent
26 Caldicot
10 Chepstow
19 (Crick)
25 (Dewstow)
14 Dinham
11 (Hardwick)
 6 (Itton)
22 (Llanmartin)
16 (Llanvaches)
13 Llanvair Discoed
 8 (Maesgwenith)
21 (Mathern)
12 (Mounton)
20 (Moynes Court)
17 (Penhow)
 2 (Penterry)
 3 (Porthcasseg)
27 Portskewett
15 (Pwllmeyric)
 4 (Rogerstone)
 5 (St. Arvans)
23 (St. Brides
     Netherwent)
 7 (St. Wormets)
 9 (Shirenewton)
10 ('Strigoil')
28 (Sudbrook)
 1 (Tintern)
24 (Wallstone)

Herefordshire

Ha
 4 'Newarne'
 6 Lower Redbrook
 5 (Upper Redbrook)
 1 Ruardean
 3 Staunton
 2 'Whippington'

Note: in Hundreds 40-45, unless otherwise stated, all places were later in Monmouthshire.
Bracketed place-names do not appear in the text of DB but are mentioned in ancillary documents
or in the Notes.

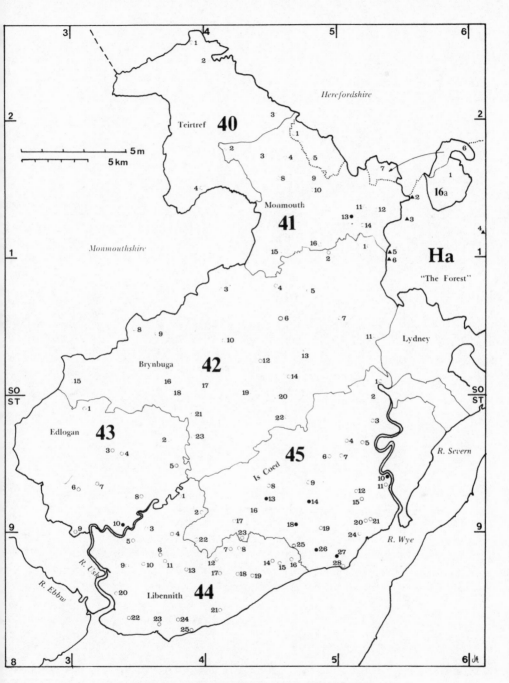

WALES AND WEST GLOUCESTERSHIRE

SYSTEMS OF REFERENCE TO DOMESDAY BOOK

The manuscript is divided into numbered chapters, and the chapters into sections, usually marked by large initials and red ink. Farley did not number the sections and later historians, using his edition, have referred to the text of DB by folio numbers, which cannot be closer than an entire page or column. Moreover, several different ways of referring to the same column have been devised. In 1816 Ellis used three separate systems in his indices: (i) on pages i–cvii, 435–518, 537–570; (ii) on pages 1–144; (iii) on pages 145–433 and 519–535. Other systems have since come into use, notably that used by Vinogradoff, here followed. The present edition numbers the sections, the normal practicable form of close reference; but since all discussions of DB for two hundred years has been obliged to refer to folio or column, a comparative table will help to locate references given. The five columns below give Vinogradoff's notation, Ellis's three systems, and that used by Welldon Finn and others. Maitland, Stenton, Darby, and others have usually followed Ellis (i).

Vinogradoff	Ellis (i)	Ellis (ii)	Ellis (iii)	Finn
152 a	152	152 a	152	152 ai
152 b	152	152 a	152.2	152 a2
152 c	152 b	152 b	152 b	152 bi
152 d	152 b	152 b	152 b2	152 b2

In Gloucestershire, the relation between the Vinogradoff column notation, here followed, and the chapters and sections is

162a	G 1–4. S 1–2. W 1–4		167a	31,9–32,12. 33,1. 32,13
b	W 5 – W 19		b	34,1 – 35,2
c	B. Landholders		c	36,1 – 38,5
d	1,1 – 1,10		d	39,1 – 39,15
163a	1,10 – 1,15		168a	39,16 – 42,3
b	1,16 – 1,24		b	43,1 – 47,1
c	1,24 – 1,38		c	48,1 – 52,7
d	1,38 – 1,50		d	53,1 – 55,1
164a	1,51 – 1,59		169a	56,1 – 60,3
b	1,59 – 1,67		b	60,4 – 63,4
c	2,1 – 2,10		c	64,1 – 67,5
d	2,10 – 3,5		d	67,5 – 68,11
165a	3,5 – 6,2		170a	68,12 – 71,1
b	6,2 – 9,1		b	72,1 – 77,1
c	10,1 – 10,13) 11,14 continues across		c	78,1 – 78,16
d	10,14 – 12,3) foot of 165c,d		d	78,16 – 78,17
166a	12,3 – 17,1		171a	)
b	18,1 – 20,1		b	)
c	21,1-24,1. 27,1-29,1. 25,1) 27,1 continues		c	) blank
d	26,1-26,4. 30,1-31,8) at foot of 166c,d		d	)

TECHNICAL TERMS

Many words meaning measurements have to be transliterated. But translation may not dodge other problems by the use of obsolete or made-up words which do not exist in modern English. The translations here used are given in italics. They cannot be exact; they aim at the nearest modern equivalent.

ARPENT. A French measure of uncertain size, usually applied to vineyards in DB (see 31,1 note). *arpent*

BEREWICA. An outlying place, attached to a manor. *outlier*

BORDARIUS. Cultivator of interior status, usually with a little land. *smallholder*

CARUCA. A plough, with the oxen that pulled it, usually reckoned as 8. *plough*

CARUCATA. Normally the equivalent of a *hide* in former Danish areas, but in Gloucestershire, Herefordshire and the south-west counties it is the equivalent of 'Land for *x* ploughs' (see W 6 note). *carucate*

COLIBERTUS. A former slave, sometimes holding land and ploughs and rendering dues (see 1,15 note). *freedman*

COSCET, COSCEZ. A cultivator who lived in a cottage (see E 11–13 note). *Cottager*

COTARIUS. Inhabitant of a *cote*, cottage, often without land. *cottager*

DOMINICUS. Belonging to a lord or lordship. *lordship* or *household*

DOMINIUM. The mastery or dominion of a lord (*dominus*); including ploughs, land, men, villages, etc., reserved for the lord's use; often concentrated in a *home farm* or *demesne*, a 'Manor Farm' or 'Lordship Farm'. *lordship*

FEUDUM. Continental variant of *feuum*, not used in England before 1066; either a landholder's holding, or land held by special grant. *Holding*

FIRMA. Old English *feorm*, provisions due to the King or lord; a fixed sum paid in place of these and of other miscellaneous dues (see 1,9 note). *revenue*

GELDUM. The principal royal tax, originally levied during the Danish wars, normally at an equal number of pence on each *hide* of land. *tax*

HIDA. A unit of land measurement, reckoned at 120 acres (see 1,1 note). *hide*

HUNDREDUS. A district within a shire, whose assembly of notables and village representatives usually met about once a month. *Hundred*

LEUUA. A measure of length, usually of woodland, generally reckoned at a mile and a half, possibly shorter. *league*

MANERIUM. A territorial and jurisdictional holding. *manor*

MITTA. A measure, usually of salt, perhaps of 6 or 8 bushels (see 61,2 note). *measure*

PREPOSITUS. Old English *gerefa*, a royal officer. *reeve*

QUARENTINA. A furlong, sometimes used as a square measure. *furlong*

r. Marginal abbreviation for *require* 'enquire', occurring generally when the scribe has omitted some information.

RADMAN, RADCHENISTRE. Of higher status than a villager, apparently free (see 1,15 note). Respectively *rider, riding man*

SEXTARIUM. A liquid or dry measure of uncertain size, reckoned at 32 oz for honey (see G 1 note). *sester*

STICHA. A measure, usually of eels, at 25 to the *sticha*. *stick*

SUMMA. A dry measure, mainly of salt, corn and fish (see 1,13 note). *packload*

TAINUS, TEINUS, TEIGNUS. Person holding land from the King by special grant; formerly used of the King's ministers and military companions. *thane*

T.R.E. *tempore regis Edwardi* 'in King Edward's time'. *before 1066*

T.R.W. *tempore regis Willelmi* 'in King William's time'. *after 1066*

VILLA. Translating Old English *tun* 'town'. The later distinction between a small *village* and a large *town* was not yet in use in 1066. *village* or *town*

VILLANUS. Member of a *villa*, usually with more land than a *bordarius*. *villager*

VIRGATA. A fraction of a hide, usually a quarter, notionally 30 acres. *virgate*